WHAT O1.....S ARE SAYING

"I am pleased and honored to offer my highest endorsement for Stephanie Cox's work in support of reducing family violence. Stephanie's perspective is an important one, which seeks to increase understanding among Christians who continue to advocate for administering corporal punishment on children. Stephanie's background in child development supplements her vast historical and biblical knowledge. I look forward to learning from Stephanie for many years to come." Samuel Martin, author of *Thy Rod And Thy Staff They Comfort Me*.

"You're not going to find a more well-researched book on this topic. If you are the type of person to always want to know the truth and care about the effect your parenting will have on your children, you will definitely want to read this book!" Dara Stoltzfus, mother of 8 and author of *Jungle Breezes*.

"*Gentle Firmness* is much more than a 'how to' book on how to properly care and discipline children. With a broader and more discerning brush, it paints a vivid picture of why parents need to choose to grow in compassion and wisdom and learn other ways as parents. Stephanie Cox offers valuable, practical methods for doing so; as a result I will share this warm and glowing book with many of my personal and professional friends." Paola Garcia, Founder/President of Faces Of Child Abuse, Child Abuse Prevention.

"Stephanie gives the issue of spanking a thorough breakdown as she examines the verses used to support spanking, the beliefs that are most often expressed about spanking, and the history of spanking children in Christianity. She challenges how this practice, found nowhere in Scripture, has become a salvific issue in some circles and she questions why something so counter-Gospel is so popular.

Stephanie gives this topic a very thorough examination. By taking the pro-spanking beliefs to their natural conclusion Stephanie shows where they break down. In their place she presents a strong argument for discipline that is kind and firm and rooted in grace.

Those who want to wrestle with this issue will find a wealth of information to challenge the typical pro-spanking information that is out there. Those who need a resource to defend their decision to not spank will not be disappointed." Crystal Lutton, Author of *Biblical Parenting* and *Grace-Based Living*.

GENTLE FIRMNESS

GENTLE FIRMNESS

Conveying the True Love of Jesus
to Your Children Through His Example

STEPHANIE G. COX, M.S.ED.

WINTERS
PUBLISHING GROUP

Published by Winters Publishing, LLC
2448 E. 81st St. Suite #4802 | Tulsa, Oklahoma 74137 USA

Book design copyright © 2014 by Winters Publishing, LLC. All rights reserved.
Cover design by Anne Gatillo
Interior design by Jomar Ouano

Published in the United States of America

ISBN: 978-1-62854-236-3
1. Religion / Christian Life / Family
2. Family & Relationships / Parenting / Child Rearing
13.12.18

Dedication

This book is dedicated to all children and their families.

Acknowledgements

First, I would like to thank God for leading me on this crazy, amazing journey. Thank You, Jesus for choosing me to do Your work.

Second, my heartfelt thanks goes to Mr. Thomas J. Winters, Dr. Richard Tate, and Allison Winters for taking on this project. It has been an absolute pleasure working with you. Thank you, Allison, for always answering my questions no matter how silly they seemed to me. I could not have asked for a better project manager!

Third, my amazing husband deserves so much credit and thanks for all he did to make this book a reality. Thank you, Chip, for spending hours upon hours writing notes that I dictated to you and copying pages of quotations from books and articles, so that I could write each chapter. Thank you for emotionally supporting me through the ups and downs of this journey. Thank you for comforting me as I cried from dealing with sad stories, losing people I loved because they just didn't understand why I was writing this book and my personal story, and helping me keep going. On top of all of this, thank you for caring for me 24/7, taking me to classes and meetings at school, and doing all the day-to-day duties of life. Thank you for spending hours at your computer with me after I finished writing this book editing and formatting it. And thank you for helping me find literary agents and publishers to which I submitted my manuscript. God blessed me with the perfect partner. I could not have asked for a more loving, supportive, caring, wise, and funny man to spend my life with. I'm so glad we didn't listen to the naysayers that didn't think we should be together. God had/has an amazing plan for us. I love you truly madly deeply forever!

In addition, I must thank Dr. Christie McIntyre for spending so much time with me in order to guide me throughout this project. I spent many hours in her office talking with her about each topic in this book, and getting prayer. She made sure I was on track and biblically accurate during the writing process. I must also thank her husband, Dr. John McIntyre, for spending hours editing this book. He also taught me how to go about submitting my manuscript to publishers and literary agents. I will forever be grateful to the both of you for all you did to make this book a reality! Thank you both from the bottom of my heart!

Another person I want to thank is Dr. Susan Pearlman for all she taught me in her early childhood classes. Thank you for helping me to become the early childhood professional that I am today. Thank you for the ongoing support and mentoring that you give me.

Along the same lines, I would like to thank the entire early childhood faculty at Southern Illinois University-Carbondale for teaching and challenging me. Thank you for allowing me to prove to all of you that I could excel in the program.

Thank you to Carla Ahmann, my first early childhood professor at Waubonssee Community College, for introducing me to the Resources for Infant Educarers (RIE) Approach, which further cultivated my passion for treating infants and all children with respect.

I also must say thank you to my family for supporting me throughout this journey. You know who you are. I love all of you so much!

A big thank you to all my friends some of which I met during this journey. I am so grateful that I met you guys and I honestly cannot imagine my life without you! All my friends' support, prayers, and encouragement made this journey possible. This includes my church family at Grand Avenue Christian Church. You all bring joy to my life!

Last but not least, thank you to every single one of you who contributed to this book. Your stories enrich this book so much. Thank you for sharing your pain and wisdom in order to make this world a better, safer place for children.

God bless each and every one of you that helped make my dream come true!

Contents

The Effects of Spanking

Discipline without Harm

Introduction

This book really is a lifetime in the making. Ever since I was a child, I have had a deep love for young children. They, especially infants and toddlers, have always fascinated me. Being severely physically disabled, I would sit in my wheelchair or lie on the floor and observe and interact with infants whenever they were around. I still do. I have been given a gift by God to be able to see children as the beautiful, unique people that they are. While I am very grateful for this gift, as child advocate Magda Gerber once said, this gift can be a blessing and a curse; I can also see the horrible treatment a great deal of these little people get by often well-meaning adults.

As you will read later in this book, my childhood was quite difficult in many ways, but I always knew that I wanted to work with and help children when I grew up, despite the teachers in my life telling me that I wouldn't be able to due to my disability. Thankfully, God has also blessed me with a strong dose of determination. I went on to graduate high school with honors and in 2008 I graduated with my bachelor's degree in science in early childhood education, Magna Cum Laude, from Southern Illinois University in Carbondale. SIUC is recognized as having one of the best early childhood education programs in the United States. As a senior in the program, I received the highest honors award for my program. I am also a member of a number of international honor societies including Kappa Delta Pi, Pi Lambda Theta, Phi Kappa Phi, Golden Key International Honor Society, National Scholars Honor Society, and Wellgates Scholar Program. After graduating, I began teaching the Resources for Infant Educarers (RIE) approach to college courses and parent groups. I have also presented at professional conferences. I worked as an infant teacher at the child development labs at SIUC. I finished my master's degree in early childhood education in December 2013 from SIUC.

I became a born again Christian in 1995 and have been studying the Bible ever since. I have always struggled with the rod verses in the book of Proverbs that seem to advocate spanking children, because seeing how children react to being spanked and knowing what I know about how young children learn, it just never made sense that God would want children to be spanked. What finally led me to this journey of truly understanding the rod verses and ultimately writing this book was seeing some wonderful Christian parents "lovingly" spank their young children. I began to wonder if "lovingly" spanking really was what God wanted. Maybe "spanking in love" was necessary at times. However, something deep down still didn't feel right, and hearing their children cry out in pain haunted me for weeks. I also began observing certain behaviors in some of these children common to children who are spanked. Fear in their eyes and aggression as well as hiding certain things from their parents that they felt safe doing in front of me even though I would verbally correct them. They always accepted my verbal correction.

Out of concern for these children, I began doing intense, prayerful research into these rod verses. I read books and articles from Christian leaders and theologians on both sides of the spanking controversy. I tried to find other verses besides the well-known rod verses to try and back up the belief that spanking was indeed biblical. I also spoke with many people that grew up in good, Christian homes that were "lovingly spanked" as children. (For privacy reasons, the names of the people who shared their stories have been changed or I have only used their first names with permission). The deeper I got into this journey, the more I found that the Holy Bible does not support spanking children in any way. The Holy Bible does teach gentle but firm discipline for children, hence, the title of this book, *Gentle Firmness*. This book has been the best and hardest thing I have ever done in my life. My knowledge of who God is has grown tremendously in writing this book. But this book has been very emotional for me to write. Hearing the stories included in this book have broken my heart and brought me to tears many times. I have also received much criticism from Christians and non-Christians for writing this book. I have lost family and friends due to writing this book. But I have seen many eyes opened to the Truth through this book—all to the glory of God! Please note as you read the following pages that I have taken this journey extremely seriously. Accurately teaching God's Word is of upmost importance to me as James 3:1 states, "Not many of you should become teachers, my fellow believers, because you know that we who teach will be judged more strictly." Also, I intentionally do not capitalize "satan" as a form of blatant disrespect. Because of my disability and its associated physical limitations, the laborious process of typing practically every character, every word, every paragraph, and every page was done with my nose. My motivation and passion allowed me to surpass any perceived human limitations because God gave me the strength and endurance to complete this book. Please understand that this book comes from a pure heart that desires to do God's will and that I would not have gone through the seemingly insurmountable obstacles in writing it without recognizing and acting upon God's will.

What follows in this book is what God has shown me about how He wants His young to be treated. I pray you will read this book with your heart open to Him. Finally, I pray this book will be a blessing to your family and will be used for God's glory!

Blessings,
—Stephanie G. Cox

Part One

Does God Really Want Us to Spank Children?

Chapter 1

How Should We Interpret the Book of Proverbs?

All too often Christians cite the "rod" verses in the book of Proverbs in the Bible to promote the idea that God mandates the use of corporal punishment in the training of children. After reading several books by theologians such as Samuel Martin, William Webb, and Theresa Whitehurst, I believe that we are misinterpreting the rod verses. In this chapter, I would like to take a closer look at these verses, as well as the way in which the book of Proverbs is meant to be read.

The Hebrew Ages and Stages, and the Law Versus Grace

The book of Proverbs was not meant for verses to be taken out of context. Even Jewish scholars believe that spankings are for boys twelve years and up and only as an absolute *last* resort. Proverbs was written under the Law of Moses. Christians are under the Law of Christ. What is the Law of Christ? Grace, peace, mercy, and love. "But the fruit of the Spirit is love, joy, peace, forbearance, kindness, goodness, faithfulness, gentleness and self-control. Against such things there is no law" (Galatians 5:22-23).

Jesus freed us from the Law. "But if you are led by the Spirit, you are not under the law" (Galatians 5:18). When we spank, we are parenting under the Law. We are not accepting the grace, mercy, and forgiveness of Jesus. Jesus died for us. He was beaten to a bloody pulp for us. Why do we feel we must beat, spank, and hit our young children who *do not* understand sin nor physical punishment? "In regard to evil be infants" (1 Corinthians 14:20b).

Even Jewish scholars forbid the use of physical punishment for children under six, which is the very age Christian advocates of spanking say it's best. Every time you hit a child, even "lovingly," you create confusion, anger, fear, and resentment, which breed sin later on.

To impress the importance of children and warning about causing them to sin, the Bible says, "At that time the disciples came to Jesus and asked, 'Who, then, is the greatest in the kingdom of heaven?'"

He called a little child to him and placed the child among them. And he said:

> Truly I tell you, unless you change and become like little children, you will never enter the kingdom of heaven. Therefore, whoever takes the lowly position of this child is the greatest in the kingdom of heaven. And whoever welcomes one such child in my name welcomes me. If anyone causes one of these little ones—those who believe in me—to stumble, it would be better for them to have a large millstone hung around their neck and to be drowned in the depths of the sea. Woe to the world because of the things that cause people to stumble! Such things must come, but woe to the person through whom they come.
>
> Matthew 18:1-6

As some background, we should note that the book of Proverbs is the oldest book in the Holy Bible. While King Solomon and King Hezekiah wrote most of Proverbs, some of it was also written by authors of ancient Egypt hundreds of years prior to King Solomon and King Hezekiah. In the Hebrew Bible, the Wisdom Literature (Job, Psalms, and Proverbs) are arranged in a different order than they appear in our modern day Bibles. Instead of Job, Psalms, and Proverbs, it's Psalms, Proverbs, and Job. These books were written by men inspired by God for men.

The Hebrew language breaks up each stage of childhood in the Bible into specific names from birth to adulthood. There are nine different Hebrew-defined stages of childhood. Each stage is a specific age, and each stage is mentioned throughout the Bible. For example, Yeled is the stage of a newborn to the time of weaning. We see this stage in Genesis 21:8. Usually, children were weaned at three years of age. But, there are many other Hebrew words that are used for young children throughout the Bible. Here is a graph from Samuel Martin's book, *Thy Rod And Thy Staff They Comfort Me*, which shows when each Hebrew stage of development begins:

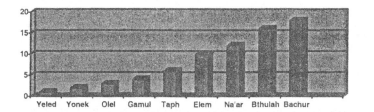

What is key to point out here is that the book of Proverbs was written for young men (Hebrew: Na'ar). Na'ar is the teenage years, twelve years to roughly nineteen. During this stage of life during biblical times, young men were considered ready to learn the Law, looking to marry, and able to understand abstract concepts. This makes sense as renowned psychologist Jean Piaget recognized that people twelve and up were in the formal operational stage of cognitive development. Young children cannot think abstractly. That is why a young child will run to the window if you say it's raining cats and dogs. The young child truly expects to see cats and dogs falling from the sky. The young child takes everything at its literal meaning. For infants and toddlers, everything they learn is through senses. Therefore, if you slap their hands, despite what pro-spanking Christian advocates may say, they do not, cannot, understand exactly why they're being hit. Life is all trial and error for young children. As I've pointed out, Jewish scholars and leaders recognize this fact and absolutely forbid the use of harshness and physical punishment for young children, especially those *under* six years of age. "What the evidence from the Bible shows is that the biblical writers had specific terms that they employed to each phase of life. The catchall phrase 'child' is not sufficient to describe the multiplicity of terms used by the biblical writers" (Martin, 2006, p. 29). Therefore, we cannot take Proverbs to mean all children because it is obvious that the authors of Proverbs meant to address a specific age.

Many Christian prospankers give specific age limits for spanking. However, if God really wanted corporal punishment to be used with children, then why is there no age limits for the use of it? Many prospankers say to stop spanking by the age of twelve, but yet, when we look at the book of Proverbs, we see that beatings are called for adults. There is no specific age at which to stop spanking. "Given this larger biblical context, the idea of primarily spanking preschoolers, tapering off from there, and eliminating all spankings for teenagers, while appearing reasonable to contemporary readers, is simply not biblical at the level of that the Bible explicitly teaches" (Webb, 2011, p. 30). Now, some prospankers, such as Michael Pearl, do spank children throughout the teenage years. However, the point I am making is that Christian prospankers are not biblical by using Proverbs to justify hitting children at any age. We can see how easy it is to create our own rules by picking certain verses out of context without having the rules actually be biblically correct.

Discipline in the New Testament— Where's the Spanking?

The writers of the New Testament were well-versed in the book of Proverbs. And yet, Proverbs is quoted only in a few books of the New Testament. None of the quotes deal with the harsh punishment of children! Jesus doesn't even mention the punishment of children in His Sermon on the Mount where He changed and added to the Law (Matthew 5 and 6). Instead, He held children up in high esteem for that day. Look at this passage:

> People were bringing little children to Jesus for him to place his hands on them, but the disciples rebuked them. When Jesus saw this, he was indignant. He said to them, "Let the little children come to me, and do not hinder them, for the kingdom of God belongs to such as these. Truly I tell you, anyone who will not receive the kingdom of God like a little child will never enter it." And he took the children in his arms, placed his hands on them and blessed them.
>
> Mark 10:13-16

Notice that Jesus was indignant when His disciples rebuked parents for bringing their children to Him. Nowhere does it say Jesus hit children or taught people to spank children. If Jesus wanted to teach about spanking children, this would have been a perfect time for Him to do so. Instead, we see a beautiful picture of Jesus taking each child in His arms and blessing him or her. Other New Testament writers didn't include anything about striking children as a teaching tool. Paul gave many instructions regarding families and children, and yet, they do not quote any of the Proverbs that seem to advocate spanking. Instead, Paul writes: "Fathers, do not embitter your children, or they will become discouraged" (Colossians 3:21). The word "fathers" is also translated into parents. The one passage in the New Testament that Christian prospankers often point to in order to claim that we are to spank is Hebrews 12:5-6, which states:

> And have you completely forgotten this word of encouragement that addresses you as a father addresses his son? It says, "My son, do not make light of the Lord's discipline, and do not lose heart when he rebukes you, because the Lord disciplines the one he loves, and he chastens everyone he accepts as his son."

Notice that the author quoted Proverbs 3:11-12 in this verse. Proverbs 3:11-12 states: "My son, do not despise the Lord's discipline, and do not resent his rebuke, because the Lord disciplines those he loves, as a father the son he delights in."

If this verse was really talking about the use of physical punishment, why didn't the author quote one of the many verses dealing with the rod? And if we look at the whole chapter of Hebrews 12, it doesn't seem to be even discussing actual children but adults who are God's children. Now let's look at the definition of the word chastise. Does it automatically mean physical punishment? No! Here's what Merriam-Webster's Dictionary says:

1: to inflict punishment on (as by whipping);

2: to censure severely: castigate;

3: archaic: chasten 2

Now before we go and say, "See, it does mean physical punishment," look at how it's used in these two sentences from this dictionary: "The waiter was chastised for forgetting the customer's order. The coach is always chastising the players for minor mistakes." Obviously, *chastise* is being use as a verbal correction in these sentences! Now look at some of the synonyms of *chastise:* Rebuke, Lecture, Scold, Reprimand, Bawl Out, Dress Down, and Lecture. Yes, it can mean physical punishment, but it also means many other things! Given the biblical context in which *chastise* is being used here in Hebrews, we are walking on very shaky ground if we choose to interpret it as a command to spank our children. God rebukes us all the time. No, it's not pleasant, but it's not in a harsh tone and He immediately forgives us when we repent. And yes, if we choose to do our own thing against His will, He will *allow, not inflict,* pain into our lives. But even when we do His will, He still allows pain into our lives. Look at these verses:

> The apostles left the Sanhedrin, rejoicing because they had been counted worthy of suffering disgrace for the Name.
>
> Acts 5:41

> Not only so, but we [Or let us] also glory in our sufferings, because we know that suffering produces perseverance.
>
> Romans 5:3

> (See also: Romans 8:17, 2 Thessalonians 1:5, James 1:2-4)

Let me reiterate that the Holy Bible is all divinely inspired by God. The Law of Moses is still holy. But to accurately interpret Scripture, we must look at it in the context of the whole Bible, Old and New Testaments. Jesus fulfilled and thus freed us from the Law! As the Apostle Paul states:

For when we were in the realm of the flesh, the sinful passions aroused by the law were at work in us, so that we bore fruit for death. But now, by dying to what once bound us, we have been released from the law so that we serve in the new way of the Spirit, and not in the old way of the written code.

What shall we say, then? Is the law sinful? Certainly not! Nevertheless, I would not have known what sin was had it not been for the law.

Romans 7:5-7a

The Claim that Physical Punishment Saves Children's Souls from Hell

Many Christian advocates of spanking children quote the following Proverb in order to support their philosophy that spanking children will save their souls from hell. It says: "Withhold not correction from the child: for if thou beatest him with the rod, he shall not die. Thou shalt beat him with the rod, and shalt deliver his soul from hell" (Proverbs 23:13-14, KJV). The Hebrew word for *hell* is *sh'ol*. However, throughout the Hebrew Bible, *sh'ol* doesn't always mean the eternal, firey hell that we immediately conjure up in our minds. Look at Jonah 2:1-2 (NIV) where Jonah is talking about being stuck in the whale's belly:

> From inside the fish Jonah prayed to the LORD his God. He said: "In my distress I called to the LORD, and he answered me. From deep in the realm of the dead I called for help, and you listened to my cry."

Obviously, Jonah wasn't in eternal hell or permanently dead. In Job 17:13-16, Job speaks of his only hope in following his family to the grave. *Sh'ol* is translated as grave and corruption. *Sh'ol* is also translated as pit, as in falling into a pit. It is clear that the Hebrew word *sh'ol* does not always mean the eternal hell and it's not used any place in the book of Proverbs. The new NIV translation shows a bit more accurate translation of Proverbs 23:13-14: "Do not withhold discipline from a child; if you punish them with the rod, they will not die. Punish them with the rod and save them from death."

It is clear, given the historical context in which the book of Proverbs was written, that the more accurate meaning of the word *sh'ol* in this verse is death as in dying a premature death from getting involved in a life of crime as an adult. Young children are not capable of purposely committing sin like adults. Young children do not know what sin is. Even though it may feel to a parent or teacher that they purposely disobey, they in fact do not. Young children cannot control their impulses. A five-year-old does have better impulse control than a two-year-old, but they still are developing it and can't be expected to always be in control. Therefore, young children, who believe in Jesus wholeheartedly, do not go to hell if they die. Look at the following passage from the book of Isaiah about heaven and children:

> The wolf will live with the lamb, the leopard will lie down with the goat, the calf and the lion and the yearling together; and a little child will lead them. The cow will feed with the bear, their young will lie down together, and the lion will eat straw like the ox. The infant will play near the cobra's den, the young child will put its hand into the viper's nest. They will neither harm nor destroy on all my holy mountain, for the earth will be filled with the knowledge of the LORD as the waters cover the sea.
>
> Isaiah 11:6-9

And to prove even more that young children go to heaven, Jesus says, "Truly I tell you, unless you change and become like little children, you will never enter the kingdom of heaven" (Matthew 18:3). Only after a child is able to truly understand sin and purposely reject Jesus Christ as Savior will he or she go to hell if he or she dies.

What About the Fact that the Apostles Were Beaten for Breaking the Jewish Laws?

Some prospankers point to the fact that Paul and other apostles received beatings for crimes they committed to justify the use of physical punishment with children. Here is a passage from the book of Acts that describes the Apostle Paul being beaten:

> Paul looked straight at the Sanhedrin and said, "My brothers, I have fulfilled my duty to God in all good conscience to this day." At this the high priest Ananias ordered those standing near Paul to strike him on the mouth. Then Paul said to him, "God will strike you, you whitewashed wall! You sit there to judge me according to the law, yet you yourself violate the law by commanding that I be struck!" Those who were standing near Paul said, "How dare you insult God's high priest!" Paul replied, "Brothers, I did not realize that he was the high priest; for it is written: 'Do not speak evil about the ruler of your people.'" Then Paul, knowing that some of them were Sadducees and the others Pharisees, called out in the Sanhedrin, "My brothers, I am a Pharisee, descended from Pharisees. I stand on trial because of the hope of the resurrection of the dead." When he said this, a dispute broke out between the Pharisees and the Sadducees, and the assembly was divided. (The Sadducees say that there is no resurrection, and that there are neither angels nor spirits, but the Pharisees believe all these things.)
>
> There was a great uproar, and some of the teachers of the law who were Pharisees stood up and argued vigorously. "We find nothing wrong with this man," they said. "What if a spirit or an angel has spoken to him?"

The dispute became so violent that the commander was afraid Paul would be torn to pieces by them. He ordered the troops to go down and take him away from them by force and bring him into the barracks.

The following night the Lord stood near Paul and said, "Take courage! As you have testified about me in Jerusalem, so you must also testify in Rome."

Acts 23:1-11

"The crowd joined in the attack against Paul and Silas, and the magistrates ordered them to be stripped and beaten with rods. After they had been severely flogged, they were thrown into prison, and the jailer was commanded to guard them carefully" (Acts 16:22-23).

And, of course, Jesus Himself was beaten. What we need to remember is at that time in history society was still under the Law of Moses and beatings and prison time were the punishments called for when adults broke one of the laws. Notice that Paul was an adult at the time of his beating for bringing a non-Jew into the temple. Children were never spanked for breaking the Law, only adults.

Therefore, when a parent spanks a child, he/she is parenting under the Law and acts as a judge. The child commits an offense, the parent tries the child and decides a spanking is necessary, the parent doles out the punishment, then the child is free to go on since he/she paid the price. Only, as Christians, the Law is no longer binding. If we want children to learn the grace, peace, love, and mercy of the Law of Christ, why do we parent under the Law of Moses?

"For the law was given through Moses; grace and truth came through Jesus Christ" (John 1:17).

Not Sparing Children Spankings Because of Their Crying

Many prospankers quote the following Proverb to support their argument that the spanking should cause crying in children. And not just crying but a broken will.

"Chasten thy son while there is hope, and let not thy soul spare for his crying" (Proverbs 19:18, KJV).

One of the most prominent and most followed Christian advocates of spanking children—especially young children—is Dr. James Dobson. In his book, *Dare to Discipline*, Dobson (1970) states:

> Real crying usually lasts two minutes or less, but may continue for five. After that point, the child is merely complaining, and the change can be recognized in the tone and intensity of his voice. I would require him to stop the protest crying, usually by offering him a little more of what caused the original tears (p. 13).

Does this sound like a loving way to "discipline" our children? A parent purposely inflicts pain on a child to break his or her will and then tells the child to quit crying or he or she will purposely inflict more pain on the child. When I'm in pain, I complain a lot. I remember how awful it felt when my dad hit me and then told me to quit crying. It was all I could do to stifle both the emotional and physical pain that I felt. God commands us to live in peace with one another to the best of our ability. "If it is possible, as far as it depends on you, live at peace with everyone" (Romans 12:18). (See also 2 Corinthians 13:11). Does inflicting pain on children and then telling them to stop crying or else you'll inflict more pain on them sound like "living in peace" with them?

There are over twenty Hebrew words that relate to weeping or actual crying with tears in the Bible, but none of them are found in the book of Proverbs. These are used when someone important or a family member dies throughout Scripture or to an infant as seen in Exodus 2:6. Let's take a look at the five Hebrew words that are used in Proverbs and their English translations.

The first Hebrew word in Proverbs that we come across for crying is *rahnan*. Proverbs 1:20 (KJV) states, "Wisdom crieth without; she uttereth her voice in the streets." And Proverbs 8:3 (KJV) says, "She crieth at the gates, at the entry of the city, at the coming in at the doors." These two verses are speaking about "Lady Wisdom," and *rahnan* is being translated as singing, cry out, rejoice, and shouting or shout aloud for joy. It is clear from these verses that "Lady Wisdom" is shouting and shouting aloud for joy. *Rahnan* is used throughout Proverbs in this way. See Proverbs 29:6 as well.

Another Hebrew translation used in Proverbs for crying is *hah-mah*. It means loud, clamorous, or raging. Let's look at a few Proverbs in which *hah-mah* is translated to *crying*.

> She crieth in the chief place of concourse, in the openings of the gates: in the city she uttereth her words.
>
> Proverbs 1:21 (KJV)

> She is loud and stubborn; her feet abide not in her house.
>
> Proverbs 7:11 (KJV)

> A foolish woman is clamorous: she is simple, and knoweth nothing.
>
> Proverbs 9:13 (KJV)

> Wine is a mocker, strong drink is raging: and whosoever is deceived thereby is not wise.
>
> Proverbs 20:1 (KJV)

It is clear from the context of these verses that crying is being used to describe someone being loud and obnoxious, not as in actual crying with tears. The next Hebrew translation for crying does mean crying with tears and is used even when speaking of children. Yet, it is not used in Proverbs 19:18. This Hebrew word is *z-gah-kah*. It, as mentioned before, is used in Exodus 2:6. Even Jesus Himself wept when He came to His friend Lazarus's tomb before He raised him from death.

> Now Jesus had not yet entered the village, but was still at the place where Martha had met him. When the Jews who had been with Mary in the house, comforting her, noticed how quickly she got up and went out, they followed her, supposing she was going to the tomb to mourn there. When Mary reached the place where Jesus was and saw him, she fell at his feet and said, "Lord, if you had been here, my brother would not have died."
> When Jesus saw her weeping, and the Jews who had come along with her also weeping, he was deeply moved in spirit and troubled. "Where have you laid him?" he asked.
> "Come and see, Lord," they replied.
> Jesus wept.
>
> John 11:30-35

Z-gah-kah is also used in Proverbs 21:13 (KJV), which says, "Whoso stoppeth his ears at the cry of the poor, he also shall cry himself, but shall not be heard." It is interesting that this has nothing to do with children. So, what is the Hebrew translation for crying that we see in Proverbs 19:18? It is *mooth* and is used over 500 times in the Hebrew Bible. It has forty different meanings that refer to death. The NIV version of Proverbs 19:18 says it like this: "Discipline your children, for in that there is hope; do not be a willing party to their death."

This means not allowing your child to go down the wrong road that could lead to a premature death. This has absolutely nothing to do with actual crying as Dobson and many other Christian advocates of spanking believe. Children do need limits and discipline. We wouldn't let a toddler run out in the street to be run over by a car, but instead of spanking the toddler we should firmly tell the toddler that the street is dangerous and then show the toddler the safe way to cross the street holding onto Mommy's or Daddy's hands. Does hitting a toddler really teach him or her why the street is dangerous and how to be safe? No. It teaches them that danger makes Mommy and Daddy hurt me; that Jesus wants me to be hurt when I'm in danger. Remember, young children cannot make abstract connections like adults.

Christian advocates of spanking are obviously misinterpreting Scripture and are thereby teaching false doctrine. The Apostle Paul warns about this:

> Since you died with Christ to the elemental spiritual forces of this world, why, as though you still belonged to the world, do you submit to its rules: "Do not handle! Do not taste! Do not touch!"? These rules, which have to do with things that are all destined to perish with use, are based on merely human commands and teachings. Such regulations indeed have an appearance of wisdom, with their self-imposed worship, their false humility, and their harsh treatment of the body, but they lack any value in restraining sensual indulgence.
>
> Colossians 2:20-23

We are not to obey these regulations anymore. We are to obey Jesus Christ.

What Is Discipline?

Older infants and toddlers require boundaries and limits. These help young children to feel safe and secure. For example, securely attached infants and toddlers will often look at their parent or caregiver when they encounter something that they are unsure about. If the adult smiles approvingly, the child will usually continue exploring. If the adult frowns, the child will usually stop exploring. Infants and toddlers need discipline and guidance because they lack self-control. Unfortunately, many people think of discipline and punishment as one-in-the-same. This should not be the case whatsoever. "Webster's Dictionary describes discipline as 'training that corrects, molds, or perfects.' I believe the best and most long-lasting training comes from within. Discipline is first learned externally, based on parental, and then societal expectations" (Gerber & Johnson, 1998, p. 204). Positive guidance strategies such as modeling, redirection, and natural consequences work better to truly teach children more appropriate ways of behaving. For example, if a toddler gets up from the table, then the natural consequence is that he will be finished eating. This is not punishment; it is cause and effect that directly relates to the toddler's behavior.

Christian pediatrician Dr. William Sears implores the importance of understanding the child's perspective in order to appropriately respond and guide the child.

> Authority is vital to discipline, and authority must be based on trust. If an infant can trust his mother to feed him when he's hungry, he will be more likely as a toddler to listen to her for what to do when, for example, he encounters breakable objects on Grandma's coffee table (Sears & Sears, 2001, p. 20).

Again, discipline means to teach and to guide children in appropriate behaviors. Spanking does not do this; it controls. "Physical punishment such as hitting or spanking will mean two things to her: one, that you are bigger than she and you can get away with it, and two, that you believe in aggression" (Brazelton & Sparrow, 2006, p. 146). Spanking children causes them to slowly lose their trust in their parents and caregivers. This makes them less likely to listen to parents without the threat of punishment. Discipline, however, has the opposite effect on children.

> Discipline is the second most important thing you do for a child. Love comes first, and discipline second. Discipline means teaching, not punishment. The goal is for the child to incorporate her own limits. Each opportunity for discipline becomes a chance for teaching. Hence, after a brief disciplinary maneuver, sit down to comfort and hold her, saying, "You can't do that. I'll have to stop you until you can learn to stop yourself" (Brazelton & Sparrow, 2006, p. 147).

Brazelton recommends using time-outs not as punishments but to help the child calm down.

Do we really want children growing up believing that Jesus wants them to be hurt every time they make a mistake or misbehave? Do we really want children to equate hitting and causing pain to love? Numerous studies suggest that children from violent homes are at an increased risk of becoming violent themselves. Yes, someday Jesus will come back to unleash His final wrath on the Earth, but He's giving everyone a chance before He does. He does not want anyone to perish. Shouldn't children be taught God's love, grace, mercy, and forgiveness by us modeling it to them? Or would we rather model:

The acts of the flesh are obvious: sexual immorality, impurity and debauchery; idolatry and witchcraft; hatred, discord, jealousy, fits of rage, selfish ambition, dissensions, factions and envy; drunkenness, orgies, and the like. I warn you, as I did before, that those who live like this will not inherit the kingdom of God.

Galatians 5:19-21

Conclusion

Do not let satan deceive you. Famous Christian theologian Dwight Moody did not let satan deceive him. Despite being spanked as a child, he chose to live by the Law of Christ and did not spank his own children.

As in the words of Christ, "He who has ears, let him hear!"

References

Brazelton, T. B. & Sparrow, J. (2006). *Touchpoints: Birth to Three.* Cambridge, MA: Da Capo Press.

Dobson, J. (1970). *Dare to Discipline.* Carol Stream, IL: Tyndale House Publishers.

Gerber, M. & Johnson, A. (1998). *Your Self-Confident Baby.* New York, NY: John Wiley & Sons Inc.

Martin, S. (2006). *Thy Rod and Thy Staff They Comfort Me.* Jerusalem, Israel: Sorensic.

Webb, W. (2011). *Corporal Punishment in the Bible.* Downers Grove, IL: InterVarsity Press.

Chapter 2

The Blood of the Lamb and Forgiveness Applies to Everyone

In this chapter, we will examine forgiveness. The Old and New Testaments have very different requirements to get forgiveness. Blood was very important in gaining forgiveness. We need to understand why we shouldn't make our children pay for their sins before we offer forgiveness to them. Also in this chapter, we will examine briefly some of the negative feelings that children who are regularly spanked often have, and why teaching children to "fear God" isn't exactly what God wants despite what many Christian prospankers claim.

Forgiveness—Old versus New Testament

Forgiveness. It's the main theme of Christianity. As Christians, we are forgiven because God sent Jesus to Earth to be the atonement for all our sins—past, present, and future. Through the precious blood of Christ, we are made clean. "For God so loved the world that he gave his one and only Son, that whoever believes in him shall not perish but have eternal life" (John 3:16). We no longer have to pay for our sins as the people of the Old Testament did through sacrificial offerings. Blood is a big deal throughout the Holy Bible as we can see in the following Scriptures.

"Moses then took the *blood*, sprinkled it on the people, and said, 'This is the *blood* of the covenant that the LORD has made with you in accordance with all these words'" (Exodus 24:8). (See also Exodus 29:1-14, Exodus 30:10). Next we see that Christ is now the sacrifice for sins.

"God presented *Christ* as a sacrifice of atonement [The Greek for sacrifice of atonement refers to the atonement cover on the ark of the covenant (see Lev. 16:15,16)] through the shedding of his *blood*—to be received by faith. He did this to demonstrate his righteousness, because in his forbearance he had left the sins committed beforehand unpunished" (Romans 3:25).

God knew that we humans could not keep the Law of Moses no matter how hard we tried. He knew that He had set such a high standard of living that there was no way we could ever live up to it. So He provided a way for the Israelites to atone for their sins. Lambs were used regularly for blood sacrifices. Throughout the Hebrew Bible, we also see God's people rebel against Him, God allowing His wrath to come on the people, the people crying out to Him in repentance, and God having compassion on His people, only to have His people rebel against Him again. This cycle repeated itself for thousands and thousands of years. Yet, God had a plan to save His people once and for all because He loves us all so much! God sent His Son, who is actually God Himself, to suffer and die in order to pay for all of humanity's sins. Jesus commands us to forgive just as we have been forgiven. "For if you forgive other people when they sin against you, your heavenly Father will also forgive you. But if you do not forgive others their sins, your Father will not forgive your sins" (Matthew 6:14-15). When we ask Jesus to forgive us when we sin against Him and break His heart every day, He immediately forgives us even though we don't deserve it. He no longer makes us pay for our sins through a sacrifice because He is our sacrifice. He constantly, freely forgives us no matter how sinful we are being or have been.

John 8:3-11 is a perfect example of how Jesus freely forgives. Let's look at it:

> The teachers of the law and the Pharisees brought in a woman caught in adultery. They made her stand before the group and said to Jesus, "Teacher, this woman was caught in the act of adultery. In the Law, Moses commanded us to stone such women. Now what do you say?" They were using this question as a trap, in order to have a basis for accusing him. But Jesus bent down and started to write on the ground with his finger. When they kept on questioning him, he straightened up and said to them, "Let any one of you who is without sin be the first to throw a stone at her." Again he stooped down and wrote on the ground. At this, those who heard began to go away one at a time, the older ones first, until only Jesus was left, with the woman still standing there. Jesus straightened up and asked her, "Woman, where are they? Has no one condemned you?"
>
> "No one, sir," she said.
>
> "Then neither do I condemn you," Jesus declared. "Go now and leave your life of sin." John 8:3-11

The penalty for a woman caught in the act of adultery in biblical times under the Law was stoning. The people were ready to stone this woman to death without even knowing all the details of the situation. But how did Jesus respond? By telling them to let the one without sin be the first to throw a stone at her. None of the people there, except for Jesus, were without sin as Romans 3:23 points out "for all have sinned and fall short of the glory of God." Therefore, the only person who had the right to condemn the woman and make her pay for her sin was Jesus. But instead He *forgave* her and let her go *free!*

So why is it that parents who believe in spanking make our children pay for their sins through a spanking before or in spite of offering their forgiveness? We adults sin much more than young children do and yet the children are the ones who are made to pay. We are called to be patient with one another. "Be completely humble and gentle; be patient, bearing with one another in love. Make every effort to keep the unity of the Spirit through the bond of peace" (Ephesians 4:2-3). Spanking a child for a sin that he/she committed against you is not being humble, gentle, or patient as the Apostle Paul charged us to be. It is the adult telling the child that the adult is bigger, wiser, and in control. This does not teach or make the child want to *repent*. It does not make the child *want* to obey or freely communicate with either the parent or God. It makes children hide their sins in their hearts over repeatedly being punished. People led astray due to spanking and harshness are described in the following verse:

> They are darkened in their understanding and separated from the life of God because of the ignorance that is in them due to the hardening of their hearts. Having lost all sensitivity, they have given themselves over to sensuality so as to indulge in every kind of impurity, and they are full of greed.
>
> Ephesians 4:18-19

They cannot see the truth because their parents gave them an inaccurate view of who God really is, as God never punishes us before He forgives us. As I point out all throughout this book, God does allow natural consequences into our lives but never punishment.

Young children are quite forgiving in nature. If you've ever watched a group of young children playing, one minute they are fighting with each other and the next minute all is well and they are best friends again. Young children do not hold grudges. Even abused children will often forgive their abusive parents and will ask to go back home with them despite the horrible abuse. Perhaps this is one reason Jesus calls us to be like them in Matthew 18:3. When we spank or treat children in other harsh ways, we are not building them up. Even if we "lovingly" spank them, we still are not building them up in the way God commands us to do so with each other.

> Do not let any unwholesome talk come out of your mouths, but only what is helpful for building others up according to their needs, that it may benefit those who listen. And do not grieve the Holy Spirit of God, with whom you were sealed for the day of redemption. Get rid of all bitterness, rage and anger, brawling and slander, along with every form of malice. Be kind and compassionate to one another, forgiving each other, just as in Christ God forgave you.
>
> Ephesians 4:29-32

Sadly, by not showing children true forgiveness without the use of physical punishment, many parents wind up teaching children to be afraid of God and them.

Fearing the Lord Is NOT the Way God Wants Us to Approach Him

Fear and anger are emotions that children who are spanked feel regularly. They will often plead with the parent not to spank them. Toddlers will try to shrink away if they think their hands are about to be spanked. I have felt this way as a child and have often observed this in young children. Many people will say, "But he's perfectly happy after I spank him." Yes, he/she may appear happy, but young children are not going to tell their parents, "You hurt me and I'm angry, sad, and fearful of you." They either don't have the words and/or are afraid of how their parents will react if they say something. As I mentioned above, children are quick to forgive. They are also eager to be back in their parents' good graces, even briefly.

Is being fearful biblical? No! Throughout the Bible we are commanded to fear the Lord. Some prospankers even quote this as a reason why they spank their children. But "fear the Lord" does *not* mean to be *afraid* of God. It means to be *reverent* toward Him. In fact, throughout Scripture we see God and angels of God telling people not to be afraid in their presence. Let's look at some of these scriptures in which God tells people *not* to be afraid of Him:

> After this, the word of the LORD came to Abram in a vision: "Do not be *afraid*, Abram. I am your shield, [Or sovereign] your very great reward. [Or shield; / your reward will be very great]."
>
> Genesis 15:1

> That night the LORD appeared to him and said, "I am the God of your father Abraham. Do not be *afraid*, for I am with you; I will bless you and will increase the number of your descendants for the sake of my servant Abraham."
>
> Genesis 26:24

(See also: Joshua 1:9, Matthew 28:10)

The Apostle John made it very clear that there should be no fear in love and that *God is love!*

> God is love. Whoever lives in love lives in God, and God in them. This is how love is made complete among us so that we will have confidence on the day of judgment: In this world we are like Jesus. There is no fear in love. But perfect love drives out fear, because fear has to do with punishment. The one who fears is not made perfect in love.
>
> 1 John 4:16-18.

Love also covers a multitude of sins. "Above all, *love* each other deeply, because *love covers* over a multitude of sins" (1 Peter 4:8).

Again, I'm not saying that there should never be consequences for children's behavior as there always are consequences—whether positive or negative. What I am saying and what God is saying is that children should be forgiven without having to pay for their sins through punishment; that children should be taught respect and reverence instead of fear. They should be taught love and that God loves them no matter what and is always ready to forgive them when they come to Him and repent. When raising children, we should always "consider how we may spur one another on toward love and good deeds" (Hebrews 10:24). Do spankings really stimulate children onto love and good deeds? From all my research and experiences, which you will see throughout this book, the answer is *no*. Grace, love, mercy, understanding, respect, forgiveness, and discipline do.

Keeping this in mind, the Apostle Paul writes that we must "see to it that no one takes you captive through hollow and deceptive philosophy, which depends on human tradition and the elemental spiritual forces of this world rather than on Christ" (Colossians 2:8).

He also states:

> When you were dead in your sins and in the uncircumcision of your flesh, God made you alive with Christ. He forgave us all our sins, having canceled the charge of our legal indebtedness, which stood against us and condemned us; he has taken it away, nailing it to the cross. And having disarmed the powers and authorities, he made a public spectacle of them, triumphing over them by the cross.
>
> Colossians 2:13-15.

We need to treat our children as God has so graciously treated us.

Spanking, Relationships, and God

Many Christian parents argue that spanking did not hurt them as children and did not ruin their relationships with their parents and that parents need to be "God" to their children. Spanking does not automatically mean you will have a bad relationship with your children. Remember, children are very forgiving and want to be in their parents' good graces.

It is clear from the Hebrew translations that God does *not* want children to be spanked (hit). The verse cited, Hebrews 12:5-6, is often used by Christian prospankers to justify spanking children, but this verse is not talking about physical punishment nor about young children. "Once dislodged from their biblical moorings, this package of Proverbs often is blessed by citing Hebrews 12 about a loving God disciplining his children" (Webb, 2011, p.29). Yes, God disciplines us as His children.

God does not punish us. Jesus rebuked His disciples, but He *never* punished them. Even after Peter denied Jesus, Jesus *forgave* him!

> Then Jesus told them, "This very night you will all fall away on account of me, for it is written: 'I will strike the shepherd, and the sheep of the flock will be scattered.'
>
> But after I have risen, I will go ahead of you into Galilee."
>
> Peter replied, "Even if all fall away on account of you, I never will."
>
> "Truly I tell you," Jesus answered, "this very night, before the rooster crows, you will disown me three times."
>
> But Peter declared, "Even if I have to die with you, I will never disown you." And all the other disciples said the same.
>
> Matthew 26: 31-35

(See Matthew 26:69-75)

—⟋⟍—

When they had finished eating, Jesus said to Simon Peter, "Simon son of John, do you love me more than these?"

"Yes, Lord," he said, "you know that I love you."

Jesus said, "Feed my lambs."

Again Jesus said, "Simon son of John, do you love me?"

He answered, "Yes, Lord, you know that I love you."

Jesus said, "Take care of my sheep."

The third time he said to him, "Simon son of John, do you love me?"

Peter was hurt because Jesus asked him the third time, "Do you love me?" He said, "Lord, you know all things; you know that I love you."

Jesus said, "Feed my sheep. Very truly I tell you, when you were younger you dressed yourself and went where you wanted; but when you are old you will stretch out your hands, and someone else will dress you and lead you where you do not want to go." Jesus said this to indicate the kind of death by which Peter would glorify God. Then he said to him, "Follow me!" John 21:15-19

Jesus could have easily condemned Peter, but He did not!

Punishment such as spanking, isolating time-outs, shaming, grounding, and removal of toys does *not* teach young children proper behavior. It teaches them to fear and resent us. The Bible makes it very clear that there is *no fear* in *love*. "There is no fear in love. But perfect love drives out fear, because fear has to do with punishment. The one who fears is not made perfect in love" (1 John 4:18).

Dear friends, let us love one another, for love comes from God. Everyone who loves has been born of God and knows God. Whoever does not love does not know God, because God is love. This is how God showed his love among us: He sent his one and only Son into the world that we might live through him. This is love: not that we loved God, but that he loved us and sent his Son as an atoning sacrifice for our sins. Dear friends, since God so loved us, we also ought to love one another. No one has ever seen God; but if we love one another, God lives in us and his love is made complete in us.

1 John 4:7-12

As an early childhood professional, I have observed that modeling, redirection, natural and logical consequences, simple choices, and firm guidance work better to teach proper behavior than punishment does (Hammond, 2009; Gerber & Johnson, 1998; Brazelton, 2006). Also, brain research shows that young children cannot control their impulses (Newton & Thompson, 2010). "The expectation that young children will be able to control their impulses or manage their emotions, especially during stressful events (e.g., when children are frustrated or upset) is misplaced" (Newton & Thompson, 2010, p. 14). Prospankers may think it's the spanking that is working, but aside from fear, brain development is one reason that older children need less spanking. That is why I find it so interesting that Jewish rabbis absolutely *forbid* the use of physical punishment for children six and under.

Toddlers do need limits and guidance from the adults in their lives. Children need to know that their caregivers will not allow them to spin out of control as they are learning to become autonomous and independent. For example, letting toddlers know when it is time to get dressed, eat, play, clean up, and sleep offers gentle guidance and firmness as the toddlers struggle to strike a balance between independence and dependence on their caregivers.

Firmness must protect him against the potential anarchy of his as yet untrained sense of discrimination, his inability to hold on and to let go with discretion. As his environment encourages him to 'stand on his own feet,' it must protect him against meaningless and arbitrary experiences of shame and early doubt.

(Erikson, 1963, p. 252)

What this means is that children in this stage need a great deal of support from their parents and caregivers in order to achieve a healthy sense of autonomy and independence otherwise they are at risk of a sense of shame and doubt. This will potentially last a lifetime.

Interestingly, in the book of Matthew we see that Moses and Jesus's lives parallel each other. Moses and Jesus faced death as infants. Both were tempted. Both taught God's Law to the people. Both were taken up to heaven after they finished God's will for their lives. However, there's one *huge* difference between Moses and Jesus! Jesus is God and was (still is) on the move with His people. Speaking of Jesus, "He said to them, 'This is what I told you while I was still with you: Everything must be fulfilled that is written about me in the Law of Moses, the Prophets and the Psalms'" (Luke 24:44). While Moses could only write down the Law as God told Him to, Jesus fulfilled the Law of Moses for us! Now the only thing we have to do to fulfill the Law of Christ is to love the Lord our God with all our soul, all our mind, all our strength, and all of our heart… And "love your neighbor as yourself. All the Law and the Prophets hang on these two commandments" (Matthew 22:39-40). All Jesus truly requires of us after we repent of our sins and acknowledge Him as Savior is that we love God and others as He did. That we follow after Him, dying to ourselves, picking up our crosses, and loving and serving each other just as He did! To fulfill the Law, we are to *love*.

"Let no debt remain outstanding, except the continuing debt to love one another, for whoever loves others has fulfilled the law" (Romans 13:8).

"For the entire law is fulfilled in keeping this one command: 'Love your neighbor as yourself' [Leviticus 19:18]" (Galatians 5:14).

Also, Matthew 5-7 and Matthew 23-25 parallel Deuteronomy 27-30 as they both have blessings and woes to the people. Moses then offers a promise in Deuteronomy 30 that even if a curse comes upon them due to their sins, God will still rescue them out of exile. Jesus was the rescue! He freed His people from exile.

Throughout the New Testament, we see Jesus rebuke the teachers of the Law for being hypocrites. The teachers of the Law would rather observe the Law than help people as Jesus often did on the Sabbath. "'Woe to you, teachers of the law and Pharisees, you hypocrites! You shut the door of the kingdom of heaven in people's faces. You yourselves do not enter, nor will you let those enter who are trying to'" (Matthew 23:13). People who spank children seem to be more concerned with the Law than with the love of Christ that fulfills the Law. We need to love our children the way Christ commands us to in order to fulfill the Law.

Another beautiful illustration of a parent actually doing as Jesus commanded is the story of the prodigal son. Back in those days, it was very shameful for children to ask their parents for their inheritance before the death of their parents. Yet, his father gave his younger son his share of the inheritance and allowed him to leave home. After the son squandered his money, he decided to go back home even though he knew that he could never be treated as a son again because of what he had done to his father. In the Jewish tradition, families would publically shame relatives for shaming them by breaking a pot to show that they had broken ties with the family. So, the son prepared a speech for his father in the hopes of convincing his father to allow him to work as a servant on the family's farm. How did his father respond to his son's returning? Let's look:

But while he was still a long way off, his father saw him and was filled with compassion for him; he ran to his son, threw his arms around him and kissed him.

The son said to him, "Father, I have sinned against heaven and against you. I am no longer worthy to be called your son."

But the father said to his servants, "Quick! Bring the best robe and put it on him. Put a ring on his finger and sandals on his feet. Bring the fattened calf and kill it. Let's have a feast and celebrate. For this son of mine was dead and is alive again; he was lost and is found." So they began to celebrate.

Meanwhile, the older son was in the field. When he came near the house, he heard music and dancing. So he called one of the servants and asked him what was going on. "Your brother has come," he replied, "and your father has killed the fattened calf because he has him back safe and sound."

The older brother became angry and refused to go in. So his father went out and pleaded with him. But he answered his father, "Look! All these years I've been slaving for you and never disobeyed your orders. Yet you never gave me even a young goat so I could celebrate with my friends. But when this son of yours who has squandered your property with prostitutes comes home, you kill the fattened calf for him!"

"My son," the father said, "you are always with me, and everything I have is yours. But we had to celebrate and be glad, because this brother of yours was dead and is alive again; he was lost and is found."

Luke 15:20-32

The father immediately forgave him and welcomed him back into his family. He celebrated his son's return. He didn't punish him or shame him. He had compassion on him. This is how God wants us to treat our children.

References

Brazelton, T. B. & Sparrow, J. (2006). *Touchpoints: Birth to Three.* Cambridge, MA: Da Capo Press.

Erikson, E. H. (1963). *Childhood and Society.* New York, NY: W. W. Norton & Company.

Gerber, M. & Johnson, A. (1998). *Your Self-Confident Baby.* New York, NY: John Wiley & Sons Inc.

Hammond, R. A. (2009). *Respecting Babies: A New Look at Magda Gerber's RIE Approach.* Washington, DC: Zero to Three.

Webb, W. (2011). *Corporal Punishment in the Bible.* Downers Grove, IL: InterVarsity Press.

Chapter 3

Amazing Grace

I wrote this chapter after hearing so many injustices done to children in the name of God. This chapter will help us understand what grace really is and how to treat our children with grace.

Grasping Grace

What is grace? This is the question running through my head as I wrestle with a bit of discouragement as children continue to be harmed by well-meaning people who want so badly to obey God in their parenting. I continue to hear the same comments from prospankers who seem almost desperate to defend themselves for fear of being wrong. I hear on the morning news that two teenagers were shot and killed by their own mother because they were being "mouthy." And, as a book that advocates spanking infants may be being used by people that I know, I wonder what is grace? Who deserves grace? Is the Bible truth or something that can be used however we want in order to support our own beliefs? What does it mean to be Spirit led and to take up our crosses and follow Jesus? Why is there so much division in the body of Christ when God commands us to be "like-minded, having the same love, being one in spirit and of one mind" (Philippians 2:2)?

Another thing that keeps popping up in my mind during my Bible study is the following verse: "So he said to me, 'This is the word of the LORD to Zerubbabel: "Not by might nor by power, but by my Spirit,"' says the LORD Almighty" (Zechariah 4:6).

This verse refers to an angel showing Zechariah a vision seemingly related to the coming of a future Messiah to rescue all people. One Sunday, our pastor discussed the uneventful way that Jesus quietly came on the scene amidst the crowds that were waiting by the Jordan River in order to be baptized by a relative, John the Baptist (Matthew 3:13-17). Everyone thought that the Messiah would come and mightily restore Israel with a mighty sword. But instead, Jesus came as an infant and lived in humble settings. He didn't even look like a powerful king that everyone expected Him to be. Look how Isaiah the prophet described Jesus:

> He grew up before him like a tender shoot, and like a root out of dry ground. He had no beauty or majesty to attract us to him, nothing in his appearance that we should desire him. He was despised and rejected by mankind, a man of suffering, and familiar with pain. Like one from whom people hide their faces he was despised, and we held him in low esteem.
>
> Isaiah 53:2-3

Is this what God meant in Zechariah 4:6b? "Not by might nor by power, but by my Spirit." Possibly. Especially since Christ didn't come on Earth by might nor power. But what about grace? We actually can see the first act of grace given to man by God in Genesis 3 after Adam and Eve were tempted by the devil and ate from the tree of knowledge of good and evil. In the midst of telling Adam and Eve about the consequences that were to come to them and all of mankind because of their sin, God allows them to *live* until their natural lives ran out, and God allowed them to multiply—having children! In all reality, Adam and Eve did not deserve to go on living after sinning against God—*none of us do!* But God let them live and allowed them to multiply. God is huge. He is bigger than any of us can imagine. He is the most powerful being of the entire universe. He could have easily wiped Adam and Eve off the face of the Earth and started over, creating new people who would constantly obey and worship Him like robots, but *He didn't!* Then in Genesis 4 we see Cain murder Abel. Again, grace shows up when God puts a seal of protection on Cain before allowing him to wander out from His Presence—Cain's choice (Genesis 4:13-16)—and marry and have his own children (Genesis 4:13-18). This continues throughout the entire Bible with its climax being Jesus healing, forgiving, loving, extending grace and mercy to people who did *not* deserve it. He bore our punishment for us that we might live!

> Whoever believes in the Son has eternal life, but whoever rejects the Son will not see life, for God's wrath remains on them.
>
> John 3:36

> I give them eternal life, and they shall never perish; no one will snatch them out of my hand.
>
> John 10:28

> Jesus answered, "I am the way and the truth and the life. No one comes to the Father except through me."
>
> John 14:6

But again, what is grace and who deserves it? I think about the Samaritan woman at the well. Jews did not associate with Samaritans. Yet in John 4:1-42, we see Jesus, a Jew, ask a Samaritan woman for a drink of water. Then we see Jesus engage the woman in conversation. Again, this was unheard of for that time period.

When Jesus's disciples come back and find Jesus talking to the Samaritan woman, they were quite surprised (John 4:27). In the midst of Jesus's conversation with the Samaritan woman, her sinful life is revealed. Yet, how does Jesus handle her? Let's look:

> Jesus answered her, "If you knew the gift of God and who it is that asks you for a drink, you would have asked him and he would have given you living water."
>
> "Sir," the woman said, "you have nothing to draw with and the well is deep. Where can you get this living water? Are you greater than our father Jacob, who gave us the well and drank from it himself, as did also his sons and his livestock?"
>
> Jesus answered, "Everyone who drinks this water will be thirsty again, but whoever drinks the water I give them will never thirst. Indeed, the water I give them will become in them a spring of water welling up to eternal life."
>
> The woman said to him, "Sir, give me this water so that I won't get thirsty and have to keep coming here to draw water."
>
> He told her, "Go, call your husband and come back."
>
> "I have no husband," she replied.
>
> Jesus said to her, "You are right when you say you have no husband. The fact is, you have had five husbands, and the man you now have is not your husband. What you have just said is quite true."
>
> "Sir," the woman said, "I can see that you are a prophet. Our ancestors worshiped on this mountain, but you Jews claim that the place where we must worship is in Jerusalem."
>
> "Woman," Jesus replied, "believe me, a time is coming when you will worship the Father neither on this mountain nor in Jerusalem. You Samaritans worship what you do not know; we worship what we do know, for salvation is from the Jews. Yet a time is coming and has now come when the true worshipers will worship the Father in the Spirit and in truth, for they are the kind of worshipers the Father

seeks. God is spirit, and his worshipers must worship in the Spirit and in truth."

The woman said, "I know that Messiah" (called Christ) "is coming. When he comes, he will explain everything to us."

Then Jesus declared, "I, the one speaking to you—I am he."

John 4:10-26

Jesus reveals Himself as the Messiah to her! He did not condemn her because she was a Samaritan or because of the sinful life that she was living. He gracefully offered Himself to her and she not only believed but went and told other Samaritans about Him. They came to see Jesus as well and they too believed (John 4:39-42). He offered forgiveness to all of them despite Him being a Jew and God Himself! Is this grace? I believe so.

But, again, I must ask what is grace? Who deserves grace?

I think of the woman who wiped Jesus's feet with her tears and hair and then anointed Him with sweet perfume in Luke 7:36-38. The woman was a sinner and the Pharisee who had invited Jesus to dine with him was appalled that Christ didn't seem to know who this sinful woman was that was touching Him. "When the Pharisee who had invited him saw this, he said to himself, 'If this man were a prophet, he would know who is touching him and what kind of woman she is—that she is a sinner'" (Luke 7:39). Religious teachers of the Law did not associate with "sinners" like this particular woman who may have been a prostitute. And yet, we see that Jesus didn't shrink away or become angry with her for wiping His feet with her hair. How does He respond knowing exactly who she was and knowing the Pharisee's thoughts about what was happening? Let's look:

Jesus answered him, "Simon, I have something to tell you."

"Tell me, teacher," he said.

"Two people owed money to a certain moneylender. One owed him five hundred denarii, and the other fifty. Neither of them had the money to pay him back, so he forgave the debts of both. Now which of them will love him more?"

Simon replied, "I suppose the one who had the bigger debt forgiven."

"You have judged correctly," Jesus said. Then he turned toward the woman and said to Simon, "Do you see this woman? I came into your house. You did not give me any water for my feet, but she wet my feet with her tears and wiped them with her hair. You did not give me a kiss, but this woman, from the time I entered, has not stopped kissing my feet. You did not put oil on my head, but she has poured perfume on my feet. Therefore, I tell you, her many sins have been forgiven—as her great love has shown. But whoever has been forgiven little loves little." Then Jesus said to her, "Your sins are forgiven."

The other guests began to say among themselves, "Who is this who even forgives sins?"

Jesus said to the woman, "Your faith has saved you; go in peace."

Luke 7:40-50

Allow me to point out that people's feet during New Testament times were quite dirty from walking with sandals on dirt roads. So the fact that this woman was washing Jesus's feet with her hair and tears shows that she more than likely knew that Jesus was more than just a "teacher." But, Jesus, being God, knew *exactly* who this woman was and what she had done. Again, instead of condemning her as the Pharisee did, He *forgave* her and rebuked the Pharisee for his lack of hospitality. He also used this moment to try and teach the Pharisee about forgiveness instead of punishing either the Pharisee or the woman. Grace!

I think of the three-year-old who doesn't pick up when told to by Mommy. Mommy asks, "Are you going to obey or do you want a spanking?" For whatever reason, the child does not obey even though the child knows what's about to happen. Mommy says, "Okay, let's go to your room." The child begins to cry and plead, "Please don't spank me, Mommy!" The child's heart is racing as he cries and struggles to get away. Mommy calmly holds him and says, "You didn't obey me when I asked you to pick up your toys. Jesus wants me to discipline you." Then she calmly slaps the child's bare bottom a few times as the child cries out in pain. Then she holds him and tells him how much she and Jesus love him, but that he must obey Mommy. As the child tries to calm down, his bottom still stinging, he mutters, "I'm sorry." Though the child doesn't truly feel sorry, he has learned that this makes Mommy happy. As they pray and hug again, he's relieved it's over even though deep down the pain is gnawing at him. He happily runs out and plays—until the next time he misbehaves or doesn't obey…

Grace?

I think of a two-year-old in a similar situation. Mommy says, "It's time to pick your toys. Please put them in the bucket."

"No!" says the child.

Mommy says, "I know you were having fun playing with your toys, but it's time to clean up. Please help me." Mommy puts a toy in the bucket as the child watches with somewhat of a defiant look on his face. Mommy asks, "Are you going to pick up your toys or do you need me to help you?"

The child says, "No!" and starts to run off.

Mommy stops him and says, "I see you need help." She picks him up as he struggles and cries. She holds him firmly and says, "I'm sorry this makes you angry. I will hold you for a minute while you calm down, then we will pick up your toys."

The child cries then begins to melt into Mommy's body knowing that he's safe and that she isn't allowing him to spin out of control. She gently puts a toy in his hand while slowly scooting to the bucket. He looks at the toy and then at the bucket, still feeling Mommy's gentle but firm hold on him as he sits in her lap. He slowly drops the toy into the bucket and looks up at Mommy. Mommy smiles and says, "Thank you!" This continues until all his toys are picked up, only laughter becomes louder and louder as they take turns putting toys in the bucket! Then the child proudly gets off Mommy's lap, picks up the bucket, and puts it on the shelf. Then he runs back to Mommy where once again he's embraced in her firm, loving arms. She says, "Thank you for picking up your toys! I love you sooo much and so does Jesus!" Then she begins singing "Jesus Loves Me" with him as he snuggles deeper into her arms.

Grace? I believe so.

> Two other men, both criminals, were also led out with him to be executed. When they came to the place called the Skull, they crucified him there, along with the criminals— one on his right, the other on his left. Jesus said, "Father, forgive them, for they do not know what they are doing." And they divided up his clothes by casting lots.
>
> Luke 23:32-34

> But the gift is not like the trespass. For if the many died by the trespass of the one man, how much more did God's *grace* and the gift that came by the *grace* of the one man, Jesus Christ, overflow to the many.
>
> Romans 5:15

> In him we have redemption through his blood, the forgiveness of sins, in accordance with the riches of God's *grace*.
>
> Ephesians 1:7

> Let us then approach God's throne of *grace* with confidence, so that we may receive mercy and find *grace* to help us in our time of need.
>
> Hebrews 4:16

We are free from sin and the death and pain that comes through sin because of God's amazing grace. Grace that we don't deserve one bit. Shouldn't we pass that on to our children as they learn to obey us?

"I do not set aside the grace of God, for if righteousness could be gained through the law, Christ died for nothing" (Galatians 2:21).

Grace is for *everyone!*

> Amazing grace,
> How sweet the sound,
> That save a wretch like me,
> I once was lost, but now am found,
> Was blind, but now I see!
> (Newton, 1779, http://en.wikipedia.org/wiki/Amazing_Grace)

Chapter 4

What About the Childhoods in Ancient Times and the Rod? Are Children Jesus's Representatives?

Back in New Testament times, children were, in general, loved but viewed as animals that needed to be trained (Strange, 2004). In this chapter, I would like to explore more of the cultural context in which the gospel was written as Jesus's childhood was left out of the Gospels except for His birth in Matthew and Luke, as well as a single brief story of Jesus at age twelve in Luke 2:41-52. While it is obvious that God felt that we do not need to know much about Christ's childhood in order to truly know who He is, I am merely interested in portraying what people thought of childhood as another reason why the Gospel writers left out much of Jesus's childhood. Please note that I am in no way putting the Gospel writers down as they were wholly inspired by God to include what they did in the Gospels. We will also look at more about the rod verses and the Hebrew meaning of the rod. We will see how Jesus's life was much like that of children's and how His very suffering was purposely related to His teachings regarding children. Mark intentionally placed certain passages together to show this.

The Cultural Influences on the Gospel Writers

People in the first century definitely had an interest in children, but when it came to childhood it was not looked upon by the people as an important, valuable time of growth and development within one's lifespan. Unlike today, childhood was not seen as an important part of who a person would eventually become.

> But while people in the ancient world were interested in children, they were not so interested in childhood... Modern people have been taught to see childhood as a time of formation and growth, a time when a person passes through certain crucial stages of development. The ancient world was simply not so reflective about childhood and did not see human personality in the same developmental way.
>
> (Strange, 2004, p. 40)

People in the ancient world did understand that there were certain skills that children needed to be taught in order to be productive adults. But they did not understand the different developmental stages children went through that would allow them to learn these skills. Needless to say, education of children could often be brutal and very unimaginative during the first century (Strange, 2004).

Due to this lack of interest and value of childhood, biographers in the ancient world usually completely ignored people's childhoods or would tell tales of a prodigy child. This seems to be exactly what the Gospel writers did with Jesus, depending on who their intended audiences were. Also, a person's genealogy was seen as more important than how an individual grew up. We see that Matthew and Luke wrote about Jesus's birth as it was so unusual and quite important to understanding Christ. However, Matthew and Luke had very different audiences to whom they were writing. Matthew was writing to a Jewish audience. We see in Matthew 1:1-17 that Matthew begins his gospel with Jesus's genealogy. It is obvious that Matthew expected his readers to be highly familiar with the Old Testament texts, lineages, and prophecies concerning Christ's coming.

> Matthew was writing for readers who assumed that the birth of a great man who would be attended by omens and portents. For this reason, he drew attention to the divinely-ordained dreams of Joseph, which reassured Joseph that he should take Mary as his wife, spoke of the child's future ministry, and directed the movements of the holy family (Matthew 1:20, 21; 2:13, 19, 22). His main story of the birth itself takes a portent as its central theme: the star seen by the magi (Matthew 2:1-12).
>
> (Strange, 2004, p. 42)

Matthew is clearly making connections to the Old Testament for his readers regarding the birth of Jesus Christ. Luke, on the other hand, had a very different audience than Matthew did in writing his gospel. Luke was writing to the Gentiles, who may not have been familiar with the Old Testament Scriptures. "But Gentile readers, too, expected to hear of portents and prophecies surrounding the birth of a great man" (Strange, 2004, p. 42). Luke includes more details of the birth of John the Baptist and Jesus. Luke even includes a story of Joseph and Mary taking baby Jesus to the temple in order to dedicate Him and fulfill the purification rites stated in the Law of Moses in Luke 2:22-40. Although Luke includes the greatest amount of information about Jesus's childhood, he still leaves out much more than he includes on the childhood of Jesus. I find it quite interesting that Luke chooses to include a story of Jesus when He was twelve years old in Luke 2:41-52. I would like to take a closer look at this particular passage, as I believe there are a couple of implications for us. Luke 2:41-52 states:

> Every year Jesus's parents went to Jerusalem for the Festival of the Passover. When he was twelve years old, they went up to the festival, according to the custom. After the festival was over, while his parents were returning home, the boy Jesus stayed behind in Jerusalem, but they were unaware of it. Thinking he was in their company, they traveled on for a day. Then they began looking for him among their relatives and friends. When they did not find him, they went back to Jerusalem to look for him. After three days they found him in the temple courts, sitting among the teachers, listening to them and asking them questions. Everyone who heard him was amazed at his understanding and his answers. When his parents saw him, they were astonished. His mother said to him, "Son, why have you treated us like this? Your father and I have been anxiously searching for you."
>
> "Why were you searching for me?" he asked. "Didn't you know I had to be in my Father's house?" But they did not understand what he was saying to them.
>
> Then he went down to Nazareth with them and was obedient to them. But his mother treasured all these things in her heart. And Jesus grew in wisdom and stature, and in favor with God and man."

The first implication this story has for us is that it shows how people of the ancient world valued stories of prodigy children. This story is indeed an example of a prodigy child as we see twelve-year-old Jesus in the temple courts answering questions that were more than likely very advanced for His age (Luke 2:47). Everyone was amazed at His answers and knowledge of the Torah. While Jesus was at an age that the Jewish boys would be studying under a rabbi, He was still expected to just be learning the things that they were discussing at this particular meeting, but instead Jesus had an advanced knowledge and was blowing the teachers away with it. Little did they know that it was God with whom they were discoursing. This story screams prodigy child!

The second implication this story has for us is the way His parents dealt with their disappointment and anxiety that Jesus did not stay with His family to travel back home. After travelling for a day, Joseph and Mary begin looking for Jesus, figuring He was with another family member or friend. When He was nowhere to be found, they got anxious just as all parents do when a child is not where the parents thought he/she was. I'm sure panic ensued as they made their way back to Jerusalem in order to try and find Jesus. But let's look at how they reacted when they finally found Jesus. In verse 48 we see that not only were they astonished when they found Him, but they were a bit upset with Him for staying behind. It seems clear that Mary thought He remained in Jerusalem on purpose because she asked Him why He treated them in this way. She also tells Him that they were anxiously searching for Him. In verse 49, Jesus gives an almost (especially according to our standards in today's society) sarcastic answer to Mary's question. But His parents don't punish Jesus. Instead, the rest of the story continues like this:

> But they did not understand what he was saying to them.
> Then he went down to Nazareth with them and was obedient to them. But his mother treasured all these things in her heart. And Jesus grew in wisdom and stature, and in favor with God and man.
>
> Luke 2:50-52

Yes, Jewish parents could be heavy-handed with their children. And if they chose to interpret the rod verses literally, Jesus was the age (Na'ar) when parents were to begin physically punishing their sons for disobedience (see Chapter 1 for more info). Yet, Jesus's parents seemed to have just taken Him home with Mary treasuring it in her heart, knowing that their Son was quite special, but not completely understanding everything that was going on. Another thing to point out is that Jesus was obeying His heavenly Father over His earthly parents. We know that Christ was without sin, but His earthly parents could have chosen to interpret this incident as disobedience to them. We will come back to this later.

Coming back to the fact that the Gospel writers left out so much of Jesus's childhood from their Gospels and exploring the cultural reasons for this while fully acknowledging that God did not want it in the Gospel, we see that while Matthew and Luke describe Jesus's birth, Mark and John leave Jesus's childhood out of their gospels completely. Mark and John focus on John the Baptist as a way of introducing Jesus and His ministry. "For Mark and John, it was John the Baptist's ministry, not Jesus's own childhood, which formed the necessary background to help us understand him" (Strange, 2004, p. 43). Despite the fact that childhood was not important during the first century, the Gospel writers did an excellent job of showing us exactly who Jesus was and is.

Due to people eventually wanting more information about Christ's childhood, the "Infancy Gospels" were written some time during the second century. Now, there wasn't much change in how people of the second century viewed childhood. Unfortunately, the "Infancy Gospels" seem to prove this as they tend to paint the child Jesus as a sort of sorcerer.

> In the Gospel of Thomas, for instance, we find some stories which are simply bizarre, like that of Jesus helping Joseph in his carpentry work by pulling a beam of wood so that it stretched to fit the job on which Joseph was engaged. Other stories show a darker aspect, such as the story of a boy who accidently knocked against young Jesus when

running past. Jesus, in this story, cursed the child so that he fell down and died... The fact that later in the story he [Jesus] restored all those whom he had cursed does not remove the impression that in these Infancy Gospels, Jesus has become little more than a powerful sorcerer.

(Strange, 2004, p. 45)

The fact that these Infancy Gospels make the child Jesus as something almost evil has led a great deal of Bible scholars to render the Infancy Gospels totally inaccurate and not authentic. I believe these Infancy Gospels prove that people in the ancient world had a hard time seeing that God could come in the form of a child.

And indeed, some very early Christians did reject the fact that baby Jesus was God at the moment He was conceived. These early Christians believed that Jesus did not become God until He was an adult and baptized. "This was the view known as 'Adoptionism': the baby and child Jesus were merely the human being into whom the divine nature was going to enter" (Strange, 2004, p. 46). A fifth century man named Nestorius had a difficult time with the fact that God entered the world as an infant.

"'I deny,' wrote Nestorius in the early fifth century, 'that God is two months or three months old' (in Cybril of Alexandria, *Epistle* 23). Nestorius, and others, were not crude Adoptionists, but they wanted to believe that the divine nature in Christ was so separate from his human nature that it was spared the experience of infancy."

(Strange, 2004, p. 46)

It is clear that the people of the ancient world did not value childhood.

Here is a poem written by Cecil Frances Alexander in an effort to describe Jesus's childhood and how all children should be like Him:

> And through all his wondrous childhood
> he would honor and obey,
> love, and watch the lowly maiden
> in whose gentle arms he lay;
> Christian children all must be
> Mild, obedient, good as he.
> For he is our childhood's pattern,
> day by day like us he grew;
> he was little, weak and helpless,
> and he feeleth for our sadness,
> and he shareth in our gladness.

(Strange, 2004, p. 39)

Now that we see some of the cultural aspects of why the Gospel writers may have left out Jesus's childhood, let's go back to the rod and see what it truly means.

The Rod

What about the "rod" in the five verses in Proverbs that prospankers take literally to mean spanking young children? In Crystal Lutton's book, *Biblical Parenting*, she includes an in-depth study of the rod as it is used throughout the Old Testament. Interestingly, as I will show in a bit, there are only two verses in the Old Testament in which the rod is used to hit someone. For now, let's look at the Hebrew word for rod.

The Hebrew word for rod is *shebet*. *Shebet* is defined in *Strong's Hebrew Lexicon #7626* as:

a) Rod, staff

b) Shaft (of spear, dart)

c) Club (of shepherd's implement)

d) Truncheon, scepter (mark of authority)

e) Clan, tribe

(Lutton, 2001)

Here is *Strong's* definition of rod: "From an unused root probably meaning to branch off; a scion, for example literally a stick (for punishing, writing, fighting, walking, ruling, etc.) or figuratively a clan."

In the King James Version of the Bible, rod is used for tribe 140 times; rod 34 times; scepter 10 times; staff 2 times; and miscellaneous 4 times (Lutton, 2001). It is quite interesting that *shebet* or *rod* is used to symbolize tribes. Also, while it is considered a tool as shepherds would use it as a weapon to protect their sheep from predators (see Leviticus 27:32, Psalm 23:4, Psalm 2:9, Isaiah 28:27, and Exodus 21:20), in all thirty-four places in which the word *rod* is used, it is in conjunction with the full council of God. It is clear that if we look at all the places in which *shebet* is used for *rod* in the Old Testament, it is used as a symbol of authority the majority of the time. It symbolizes the authority of God, nations, and parents as in Proverbs.

In Exodus 20:21 (NIV), a rod is used to hit someone. Let's take a look at the verse: "Anyone who beats their male or female slave with a rod must be punished if the slave dies as a direct result."

Obviously, the rod is being used to hit an adult, *not* a young child. And if the slave dies from being hit with the rod, which is a heavy instrument, then the person who hit them is to be punished. Obviously, people had slaves back then and God did not want masters beating their slaves to death. The rod can easily cause death in a young child. Even if you measure a stick in proportion to the child as some prospankers suggest doing, with the right force, it could still kill a child. An adult hitting a young child with their hands could also, with the right force and with repetition, severely injure or kill a young child. As many prospankers and psychologists point out, a child who is spanked regularly must be hit harder and harder in order for the spanking to still be effective. This can easily become physical abuse and outright dangerous if the adult hits hard enough to cause injury to the child.

> "In addition, increases in the frequency of spanking are associated with increased odds of abuse, and mothers who report spanking on the buttocks with an object—such as a belt or a switch—are nine times more likely to report abuse, compared to mothers who report no spanking with an object," said Adam J. Zolotor, M.D., the study's lead author and an assistant professor in the department of family medicine in the UNC School of Medicine.
>
> (Zolotor, 2010, http://uncnews.unc.edu/content/view/1487/138/)

In 2 Samuel 7:14, it appears that the rod is again being used to actually hit someone: "I will be his father, and he will be my son. When he does wrong, I will punish him with a rod wielded by men, with floggings inflicted by human hands."

Again, this is talking about an adult, *not* a child. And it isn't even talking about punishment in this sense. God is talking to David about who will build His holy temple. This verse, in the context of 2 Samuel 7:1-17, seems to be talking about Jesus! Even though Jesus did *no* wrong in the eyes of God, He *did* do wrong in the eyes of *men* by not upholding the Law of Moses through His claiming to be God. Therefore, He was still beaten by the hands of men. It is obvious that the rod in this verse is also being used to symbolize the authority of God.

Authority can be used to "beat" people with wisdom of God. In order to drive home a point, God often makes it come up repeatedly in a person's life through His Word, church teachings, the Holy Spirit convictions, and natural and logical consequences. He never beats or spanks His people. The rod verses in the book of Proverbs are not saying to spank children. If it did then prospankers are doing it wrong by not using a rod, which, again, would be very dangerous to use on a small child. As parents and caregivers, God has given us some authority over children in order to teach and guide them with firmness as well as love, gentleness, kindness, and humility.

The Apostle Paul states, "What do you prefer? Shall I come to you with a rod of discipline, or shall I come in love and with a gentle spirit?" (1 Corinthians 4:21). It seems even the Apostle Paul understood that it's better to come in love and gentleness than with harshness.

What is more is that Jesus even made children His representatives. He held them in high esteem compared to the culture of His day.

Children as Representatives of Jesus Christ

The book, *The Child in Christian Thought*, edited by Marcia J. Bunge, gives us an even better glimpse into what life was like for children during New Testament times, and how Jesus's teachings affected them. Given the fact that little information is available on the Christian traditions of childhood, we can gain much insight by looking closely at the different perspectives offered by historical and contemporary Christian theologians. One major concept that seems to play a major role in the view and treatment of children throughout Christianity is original sin. Interestingly, original sin can either lead to the harsh treatment of children or to a gentler treatment. Bunge (2001), page 9, states:

More specifically, it shows that notions of original sin and "breaking the will" are complex and do not automatically lead to the harsh punishment of children, and that the idea of original sin, set within a particular larger theological framework, has in some cases fostered the more humane treatment of children.

It is clear from the Scriptures that we are born with a tendency toward sin, but there is not a precise age at which we become accountable to that sin. The Apostle Paul states: "For I know that good itself does not dwell in me, that is, in my sinful nature. For I have the desire to do what is good, but I cannot carry it out" (Romans 7:14). As we shall soon see, while children are indeed born with a capacity to sin that is not formed until they are older, they are also given immense spiritual knowledge of God by God for His glory.

While some theologians have viewed children as gifts from God, others have viewed children as ignorant and in need of strict discipline and religious education. Many Christians have emphasized the fact that children are to obey their parents in the Lord (Ephesians 6:1 and Colossians 3:20) but seem to ignore Ephesians 6:4 and Colossians 3:21, which states, "Fathers, do not embitter your children, or they will become discouraged." As I mentioned before, "Fathers" can also be translated into "Parents." "It is important to note that grounds for this obedience vary, and in most cases obedience is not absolute" (Bunge, 2001, p. 23). It is dangerous and inappropriate for children to be taught absolute obedience to humans because humans are sinful. The child could be going against God by always obeying a human. Children should be taught to think for themselves in order to "test the spirits to see whether they are from God" (1 John 4:1a). Bunge (2001), page 23, states:

For example, although Barth believes that parents are "God's natural and primary representatives" for children, he claims that raising children "in the discipline of the Lord" excludes provoking them to the anger, resistance and rebellion that emerges through the "assertion of Law, or the execution of judgment." Instead, parents are "joyfully" to invite children to "rejoice" with them in God.

Of all the social institutions with which children come in contact, the family has the highest potential for teaching children about God (Bunge, 2001).

So, how were children viewed and treated in the New Testament? There were two primary social groups that held somewhat conflicting beliefs about children and childhood. The first group was first century Greco-Romans. While the Romans loved and valued their children as heirs of the family and keeping the family's economic status, they also viewed children as non-humans. "The Roman philosopher Cicero wrote concerning childhood, 'the thing itself cannot be praised, only its potential,' and categorically denied the desirability of reverting in any sense to the state of childhood" (Gundry-Volf, 2001, p. 32). Roman law gave fathers full authority and power over their children. Fathers decided whether a newborn lived or was left to die unless another person found the infant and decided to care for him/her (Gundry-Volf, 2001). Because the Romans viewed children so negatively, they were sometimes beaten to death, imprisoned, put in chains, or forced to work in the fields by their fathers. It appears that the Roman society was a violent one with a great deal of power.

The other primary social group in the New Testament period was the Jews. For the most part, Jewish children were viewed positively by their parents. They were seen as blessings from God. To be childless was to be cursed in the Jewish religion. In

Deuteronomy 7:14, it is written, "You will be blessed more than any other people; none of your men or women will be childless, nor will any of your livestock be without young." However, children were also seen as ignorant and in need of strict religious education. Gundry-Volf (2001) explains that they had "a view of children falling short of the ideal represented by the adult male law-observant Israelite. The fundamentally positive significance of children, however, is not thereby negated" (p. 35). The Jewish people rejected the harsh practices of the Romans who were their contemporaries. Jewish fathers had complete power and authority over their children as well, but the "Jews distinguished themselves from many of their contemporaries by rejecting brutal practices toward children, including abortion and exposure of newborns, which can be traced to less positive views of children, and by placing limits on the Jewish father's power over his children" (Gundry-Volf, 2001, p. 35-36).

Jesus changed everything for children. In Matthew 18:1-4, Jesus held children up as models for adults. Matthew 18:1-4 states, "At that time the disciples came to Jesus and asked, "Who, then, is the greatest in the kingdom of heaven?"

He called a little child to him and placed the child among them. And he said: "Truly I tell you, unless you change and become like little children, you will never enter the kingdom of heaven. Therefore, whoever takes the lowly position of this child is the greatest in the kingdom of heaven."

This was quite radical as children were *never* held up in such high esteem in the various cultures of the New Testament.

> Now children shared the social status of the poor, the hun-
> gry, and the suffering, whom Jesus calls "blessed." For this
> reason, apparently, he insists on receiving children into the
> reign of God. John Dominic Crossan may be overstating
> his case when he asserts that Jesus taught a "kingdom of

children" in the sense of a "kingdom of *nobodies*," for "to be a child was to be a *nobody*" [italics added]—an overstatement because children were emphatically not "nobodies" in the Old Testament-Jewish tradition. Nevertheless, it is still probably correct to say that children's vulnerability and powerlessness seem to lie at the heart of Jesus's extension of the reign of God to them.

(Gundry-Volf, 2001, p. 38)

Another interesting thing regarding Jesus holding small children up as models is that children were not required to obey the Law of Moses, and, of course, they did not fulfill it. As usual, Jesus has taken what the Jews believed was required for entering the kingdom of heaven (obedience of the Law) and has completely turned it upside down.

Jesus can be taken to challenge the perception that adults who are under obligation to the Law, and do fulfill it, are thereby qualified to enter the reign of God. Egger thus concludes that the phrase "as a child" means "as one who has neither obedience nor obligation to the Law."

(Gundry-Volf, 2001, p. 39)

It is clear that God wants adults to have humility, love, forgiveness, and openness like children do. We are to treat children, as well as others who are low on the social ladder, with kindness, love, and respect in keeping with God's equal love for all. To mistreat children by spanking and harshly punishing them is to go against God's precepts.

The Apostle Paul states, "For God does not show favoritism" (Romans 2:11).

Also, look at what James writes:

If you really keep the royal law found in Scripture, "Love your neighbor as yourself," you are doing right. But if you show favoritism, you sin and are convicted by the law as lawbreakers. For whoever keeps the whole law and yet stumbles at just one point is guilty of breaking all of it.

James 2:8-10

Caring for children was, and sadly still is, considered a low status job that was primarily for women during the New Testament time period. However, in Mark 9:36-37, it says, "He took a little child whom he placed among them. Taking the child in his arms, he said to them, 'Whoever welcomes one of these little children in my name welcomes me; and whoever welcomes me does not welcome me but the one who sent me.'" Being kind to children in Jesus's name isn't what Jesus is implying here. We are to serve children. "*Receive* or *welcome* (*dechomai*) in the New Testament is used especially for hospitality to guests, which implies serving them (see, e.g. Luke 10:8; 16:4). Jesus taking the child into his arms demonstrates such service. This action is more than a display of affection" (Gundry-Volf, 2001, p. 43).

So, how are we to serve our children in order to be great in the kingdom of God? By sacrificing for them; by patiently teaching them when it would be easier to punish them through spanking or an isolating time-out; by guiding with tender firmness as God does us, especially after redirecting a toddler for the twentieth time in an hour. God implores that the humblest work is what makes us truly great in His eyes for both men and women. We need to treat one another with patience and humility. This includes children. "Therefore, as God's chosen people, holy and dearly loved, clothe yourselves with compassion, kindness, humility, gentleness, and patience" (Colossians 3:12).

The Apostle Paul also writes, "Preach the word; be prepared in season and out of season; correct, rebuke and encourage—with great patience and careful instruction" (2 Timothy 4:2).

Children were, and still are, representatives of Jesus Christ even though they were never sent to speak and heal as were the disciples. Rejecting a child could be related to rejecting Jesus. Why? The reason is, as I pointed out earlier, children were treated with much brutality in the New Testament period, especially by the Romans. If we look at Mark 9:30-32, it states, "They left that place and passed through Galilee. Jesus did not want anyone to know where they were, because he was teaching his disciples. He said to them, 'The Son of Man is going to be delivered into the hands of men. They will kill him, and after three days he will rise.' But they did not understand what he meant and were afraid to ask him about it." It is clear that Jesus is speaking of His own suffering and death. Jesus goes on in Mark 9:33-37 to teach about welcoming children in His name in order to be great in the kingdom of heaven. This is *not* mere coincidence. God's Word is placed where it is throughout the Bible for a specific purpose. The child is weak and needy. *"The child thus represents Jesus as a humble, suffering figure"* [author's italics] (Gundry-Volf, 2001, p. 45). This absolutely brings tears to my eyes. Jesus can relate to the harsh punishment of humble, precious children because He went through it as a humble, suffering servant so that we wouldn't have to.

> In your relationships with one another, have the same mindset as Christ Jesus: Who, being in very nature God, did not consider equality with God something to be used to his own advantage; rather, he made himself nothing by taking the very nature of a servant, being made in human likeness. And being found in appearance as a man, he humbled himself by becoming obedient to death—even death on a cross!
>
> Philippians 2:5-8

As Gundry-Volf (2001) so beautifully states: "To welcome a little child in Jesus's name, I therefore propose, is to welcome

Jesus himself in the sense that he humbled himself like a little child and endured the worst lot of the little child in carrying out his God-given mission" (p. 45). I believe that it is safe to say that Mark, inspired by God, purposely links Jesus's suffering with the child because of that society's awareness of child brutality. It is not surprising that Mark's audience would clearly see this link. When read closely and with open hearts, we too can begin to see this link. This shows that spanking or otherwise harshly punishing children is frowned upon by Christ. "And if anyone gives even a cup of cold water to one of these little ones who is my disciple, truly I tell you, that person will certainly not lose their reward" (Matthew 10:42). Whatever we do to each other, including children, we also do to God Himself.

Children have a miraculous knowledge of who Christ is. This is funny considering that adults in the New Testament thought children were ignorant. Let's look at Matthew 21:14-16:

> The blind and the lame came to him at the temple, and he healed them. But when the chief priests and the teachers of the law saw the wonderful things he did and the children shouting in the temple courts, "Hosanna to the Son of David," they were indignant.
>
> "Do you hear what these children are saying?" they asked him.
>
> "Yes," replied Jesus, "have you never read, 'From the lips of children and infants you, Lord, have called forth your praise'?"

Instead of the chief priests and scribes, who were well educated in the religion, proclaiming Christ as the Son of God and Messiah, it was the supposedly "ignorant" children doing so. We see this throughout the entire Bible. In fact, Jesus even thanks His heavenly Father for hiding godly things from the wise and revealing them to children. "At that time Jesus, full of joy through the Holy Spirit, said, 'I praise you, Father, Lord of heaven and earth, because you have hidden these things from the wise and learned, and revealed them to little children. Yes, Father, for this is what you were pleased to do'" (Luke 10:21).

> In the gospel tradition, children are not mere ignoramuses in terms of spiritual insight. They know Jesus's true identity. They praise him as the Son of David. They have this knowledge from God and not from themselves, and because they do, they are living manifestations that God is the source of all true knowledge about Christ. Jesus's affirmation of the children's praise of him in this periscope is thus an affirmation that children who "know nothing" can also "know divine secrets" and believe in him.
>
> (Gundry-Volf, 2001, p. 47-48)

This is why young children never question if God truly exists. Young children know God is real. Yes, they need to be taught about God through reading developmentally appropriate Bibles, but they are already, in a sense, believers. It isn't until, through exposure to the world and satan's influence, that older children may begin to question God's existence as they struggle with their sinful nature that has now become much more defined in them. This is why spanking them in Jesus's name is so dangerous. Instead of being sinful yet innocent for as long as possible, they are taught and made aware of their sinful natural before they have the power to choose Christ in order to be able to truly fight the constant battle. Children are weak. They may know Christ, but they are not strong enough to fight this battle. Then we inflict pain on them for not winning the battle. Over time, this creates even more sin within them and a very distorted view of God, whether they acknowledge it or not. If adults struggle with sin all the time, is it really fair to punish children for their struggle before they can truly understand it? Look at what Paul says about his own struggle with sin:

> So I find this law at work: Although I want to do good, evil is right there with me. For in my inner being I delight in God's law; but I see another law at work in me, waging war against the law of my mind and making me a prisoner of the law of sin at work within me. What a wretched man I am! Who will rescue me from this body that is subject to death? Thanks be to God, who delivers me through Jesus Christ our Lord!
>
> Romans 7:21-25

We are to use God's Word to *lovingly* admonish each other. "Let the word of Christ dwell in you richly as you teach and admonish one another with all wisdom, and as you sing psalms, hymns and spiritual songs with gratitude in your hearts to God" (Colossians 3:16).

And the Apostle Paul states, "Let us therefore make every effort to do what leads to peace and to mutual edification" (Romans 14:19).

Lastly, yes, children are to obey their parents in the Lord (Ephesians 6:1 and Colossians 3:20). However, as with Ephesians 6:4 and Colossians 3:21 regarding parents not provoking their children to anger, we also leave out Ephesians 5:21 that prefaces the entire section of Christian household behaviors. Ephesians 5:21 states, "Submit to one another out of reverence for Christ." This is exactly what Christ was talking about in Mark 9:36-37. Children are to submit to parents in the Lord. But, parents are also to submit to and serve their children in the Lord by treating them with love, kindness, and respect. "Again, we see that Jesus took children with total seriousness, and that what happens to a child, and to a child's faith, is a matter of great consequence to those who are in the kingdom of God" (Strange, 2004, p. 57).

Conclusion

We have seen in this chapter that the culture of New Testament times did not view childhood as something truly important and special. This very well could explain why so much of Christ's childhood is left out of the Gospels. This was also seen with how children were generally treated, especially by the Romans, during this time period. In fact, Jesus made children His representatives because of their sufferings and His suffering. We see Mark make this inference in Mark 9. However, Jesus radically changed children's social status to one that adults should become like in order to enter the kingdom of heaven. Yes, God wants children to obey their parents in Him, but He desires that parents treat children with respect, kindness, and compassion.

References

Bunge, M. J. (Ed.). (2001). *The Child in Christian Thought.* Grand Rapids, MI: William B. Eerdmans Publishing Company.

Lutton, C. (2001). *Biblical Parenting.* Salt Lake City, UT: Millennial Mind Publishing.

Strange, W. A. (2004). *Children in the Early Church.* Eugene, OR: Wipf and Stock Publishers.

Zolotor, A. J. (2010). UNC Study Shows Link Between Spanking and Physical Abuse. http://uncnews.unc.edu/content/view/1487/138/

Part Two

The Christian History of Spanking

Chapter 5

An Introduction to the Primary Historical Theologies of Spanking in Christianity

In my quest for further understanding as to why so many Christians (and non-Christians, though I am mainly looking at Christians for this study) are adamant prospankers, I have begun a journey into some of the darker history of Christianity and the harsh treatment of children starting as young as infancy. My purpose in doing this part of the book is to uncover some of the main Christian advocates of harsh treatment of children in order to show that spanking came from man and not from God as so many truly believe. In this and the following chapters, we will discover some of the origins of physical punishment. We will also be looking at prominent Christian advocates of physical punishment.

From Where Did the Concept of Spanking Originate in Christian Thought?

Sadly, as I pointed out in chapter 4, brutality of children can be traced back to biblical times, which is why Jesus radicalized the way He wanted society to view and treat children. Despite Jesus placing such a high value on children and never once advising the people to harshly punish young children when He had ample opportunity to do so, Christians have, for centuries, used the Holy Bible to advocate and justify spanking and abusing young children. Physical punishment runs deep within the roots of Christianity, especially within the sects of the Protestants, Fundamentalists, and Evangelicals. It is important for me to note here that I proudly consider myself an Evangelical Christian and have always taken the Bible quite literally. It appears to me as I continue my study of God's Word and the history of this subject that prospankers seem to focus more of their attention on the God of the Old Testament. Yes, "Jesus Christ is the same yesterday and today and forever" (Hebrews 13:8). (See also James 1:17 and Malachi 3:6a). However, some view the God of the Old Testament as quite harsh at times in His righteous anger against humans because of their sins against Him. But, as I point out in chapter 3, we also see God's grace and love for His people. The minute His people cried out to Him in the Old Testament, God forgave them and had mercy on them. "So you, the descendants of Jacob, are not destroyed. Ever since the time of your ancestors you have turned away from my decrees and have not kept them. Return to me, and I will return to you," says the LORD Almighty" (Malachi 3:6b-7). With the coming of Jesus Christ, God allowed His grace, mercy, love, and forgiveness to be much more accessible and evident to mankind. Through Jesus, we can now have a very personal relationship with the God of the Old Testament.

As I have been pointing out throughout part 1 of this book, Christians, as well as secular culture, use primarily the

Old Testament to justify the use of physical punishment with children—especially the book of Proverbs. In fact, the main saying that Christians and non-Christians use to justify and advocate spanking is: "Spare the rod and spoil the child." While this saying sounds very much like a Proverb out of the Bible as many people believe, it is not from the Bible whatsoever. So, where does this saying come from? According to scholar, Philip Greven (1992), "The aphorism is from Samuel Butler's poem 'Hudibras' (1664). See Ian Gibson, The English Vice: Beating, Sex and Shame in Victorian England and After (London: Dukworth, 1978), p. 49" (p. 227). The saying has absolutely nothing to do with God's Word; it only sounds as if it does.

It is concerning that some Christians choose to focus primarily on one aspect of God, His supposed harshness. They have even questioned whether He applied harsh punishment to His own Son. This would basically be saying that God killed Jesus, which is only partial truth and leaves out crucial information regarding Christ's atoning sufferings and death. This feels dangerous to me! It must be pointed out that while Jesus was God's only begotten Son (John 3:16), Jesus was also God Himself (Philippians 2:6a; John 8:58; Revelation 22:13) and chose to suffer and die on the cross for us (Philippians 2:8; John 10:11; Matthew 26:38-39). Yet, many Christians continue to only look at the seeming harshness of God (without understanding cultural norms of the day and taking into account the historical context) instead of looking at all of His aspects, which reveal His true identity as I have just pointed out. Jonathan Edwards, an eighteenth century American theologian, chose to focus much of his attention on the harshness of God depicted in the Old Testament. Because of this viewpoint, he "believed that the Crucifixion 'was willed and ordered by God,' a condition that made 'one of the most heinous things that ever was done' by men, 'one of the most horrid acts,' into 'the most admirable and glorious of all events.' For Edwards, at least, 'the crucifixion of Christ was not evil, but good.' This argument, however, implies that God the Father was directly responsible for the death of his only earthly son" (Greven, 1992, p. 50). That is simply preposterous, as while God allowed the crucifixion and death to happen, He did not bring it on Himself. Instead, God chose to submit Himself into the hands of men in order to bring salvation to humanity. It is sad that people who focus on the harshness of God seem to lose sight of who God is. After all, the Bible couldn't have made it any clearer exactly who God is. "God is love" (1 John 4:16). It is clear from the following Bible passage that God didn't harshly punish His Son (who is God). There was no reason to. God loved us so much that He chose to do something so major in order to make it easy for us to be reconciled to Him and have an intimate relationship with Him. "This is how God showed his love among us: He sent his one and only Son into the world that we might live through him. This is love: not that we loved God, but that he loved us and sent his Son as an atoning sacrifice for our sins" (1 John 4:9-10). To use the seeming harshness of God to justify and advocate the use of physical punishment is completely illogical after seeing all the aspects of God through the same lens.

Eternal Fire

Along the same lines as focusing heavily on the harshness of God, many Christian prospankers have been quite influenced by the threat of eternal punishment—hell—throughout the centuries. They have also been influenced by the feeling of an imminent apocalyptic end (Greven, 1992). Hell has always been a part of Christian theology and teaching. The threat of eternal damnation has terrified many people throughout time. While it is true that eternal punishment does await those that purposely reject Christ's gift of forgiveness and salvation by not asking Him for the forgiveness of sins and accepting Him as Savior (Romans

6:23; Matthew 25:46; Luke 16:19-31), some parents and pastors seem to use this to justify spanking children.

> Michael Wigglesworth, whose parents were among the first generation of settlers in New England, wrote an extraordinarily popular poem about the approaching "Day of Doom." Punishment and affliction were the central themes shaping the obsessions of this anxious and tormented Puritan preacher, whose poem vividly portrays the final days on earth before the Last Judgment and the ultimate separation of the saved from the damned.
>
> (Greven, 1992, p. 55)

Jonathan Edwards was also quite focused on the terrors of eternal punishment during the eighteenth century. They seemed to truly believe that "beating the devil out of them" would somehow save them from hell. This is often based on Proverbs 23:13-14 (KJV), which states: "Withhold not correction from the child: for if thou beatest him with the rod, he shall not die. Thou shalt beat him with the rod, and shalt deliver his soul from hell." Prospankers throughout history have taken these verses quite literally. Please see chapter 1 for the correct interpretation of these verses. Yes, while we are sure that the harsh treatment of children was occurring during Old Testament times, it is unclear if it was done commonly or by those that were naturally prone to violence.

It appears that this focus on the harshness of God and on punishment traces back to Europe. We read throughout our history books that these Puritans convinced the Native Americans to allow their children to go to English boarding schools where they would supposedly get a great education. In reality, the Native American children were treated very harshly and physically punished by these Christians who thought they could beat the evil out of them (Cushner, McClelland, & Safford, 2006). They were not allowed to speak their native language or go back to their parents. See, the Native Americans did not typically use physical punishment with their young children. Therefore, in the eyes of the Christian English settlers who had been taught by their leaders that spanking was an absolute must for obedience to God, the Native Americans were disobeying God and the children needed to be "saved" from their impending doom.

> Anglo-American Protestants have always been among the most vocal public defenders of physical punishments for infants, children, and adolescents. They have provided many generations of listeners and readers with a series of theological and moral justifications for painful blows inflicted by adults upon the bodies, spirits, and wills of children. These defenses remain crucial to any understanding of the earliest sources of suffering and violence in our culture.
>
> (Greven, 1992, p. 60-61)

It makes me wonder why they went wrong in following: "In the same way, let your light shine before others, that they may see your good deeds and glorify your Father in heaven" (Matthew 5:16). I can't imagine spanking children would be truly glorifying God.

What About Breaking Their Wills?

Another theme occurring throughout the centuries among advocates of spanking is the absolute need to break children's wills. It has (still is) been suggested that the breaking of a child's will should happen during the first two years of life. That way the child supposedly will not remember that they had a will. This ideology is tragic because infants and toddlers do not understand the concept of wills. They are mainly concentrating on discovering their abilities. It is important for them to be separate beings from their parents, otherwise they will grow up having a sense of shame and self-doubt (Erikson, 1963). Yet, this breaking of wills seems to dominate many Christian sects. Greven (1992), page 65, states:

> Breaking the child's will has been the central task given to parents by successive generations of preachers, whose biblically based rationales for discipline have reflected the belief that self-will is evil and sinful. From the seventeenth century to present, evangelical and fundamentalist Protestants have persistently advocated the crushing of the will even before a child can remember the painful encounters with punishment that are always necessary to accomplish such goals.

Is breaking a child's will even biblical? Jesus does say, "Whoever wants to be my disciple must deny themselves and take up their cross daily and follow me" (Luke 9:23). We are to die to our flesh (Romans 8:13). God obviously wants us to surrender ourselves to Him. However, He gently brings us into submission through grace, mercy, forgiveness, and natural consequences. Ephesians 5:21 also tells us to submit to each other out of reverence for Christ. Nowhere in the Bible does it say that we must hit each other in order to submit to each other. God doesn't strike us to make us submit to Him. So where exactly does this breaking of a child's will by their parents come from if there's no actual biblical support for this concept?

Susanna Wesley, Jonathan Wesley's mother, was an early proponent of breaking children's wills beginning in infancy through corporal punishment. For example, if her infant son cried too loud, she spanked him (Greven, 1992). Accounts also say that she would not allow her children to eat or drink anything between meals except in the case of illness. If she found that they had asked the slaves for something between meals, she beat the children and harshly reprimanded the slaves. She wrote a letter to her sons regarding her beliefs on child rearing. Sadly, this letter is often quoted by many prospankers today.

> Susanna Wesley was certain in 1732 that "religion is nothing else than doing the will of God and not our own: that the one grand impediment to our temporal and eternal happiness being self-will, no indulgence of it can be trivial, no denial unprofitable. Heaven or hell depends on this alone; so that the parent who studies to subdue it in the child works together with God in the renewing and saving a soul. The parent who indulges it does the devil's work; makes religion impracticable, salvation unattainable, and does all that in him lies to damn his child body and soul forever."
>
> (Greven, 1992, p. 62)

This seems to be saying that salvation lies in how a parent raises his/her child. This is incorrect. Salvation lies in receiving God's gift of Jesus Christ who paid for all of our sins! No human or other god can save us. "For there is one God and one mediator between God and mankind, the man Christ Jesus, who gave himself as a ransom for all people" (1 Timothy 2:5-6). (See also Hebrews 8:6; 1 Thessalonians 5:9; 2 Timothy 3:15).

The thing about breaking children's wills through spanking is: what happens if their wills never break sufficiently? The prospankers say that we must repeat the spanking. Children have been spanked to death with one of the most recent cases occurring in 2010 with seven-year-old Lydia Schatz who was repeatedly spanked with a whip-type instrument during a biblical chastisement (http://whynottrainachild.com/tag/deaths/). In 1982, a two-year-old boy was also spanked to death by his parents.

> On October 3, 1982, two-year-old Joseph Green died from a spanking by his parents, Stuart and Leslie Green. Leslie Green began spanking her son Joseph when he

refused to apologize to another two-year-old after striking him. After a period of spanking, Stuart Green, Joseph's father, entered the room and continued to spank him with a paddle while both parents unsuccessfully tried to force Joseph to apologize to the other boy. After approximately two hours of intermittent spankings, the petitioner— who had been out of the sight and sound of the room where the spanking was occurring throughout the two-hour period—was summoned to the room by another. As soon as petitioner Dorothy McClellan arrived, she told Stuart Green to stop the paddling. Petitioner and others rendered first aid to Joseph, and he was later taken to a local hospital. Shortly thereafter, Joseph Green died from shock and hemorrhaging.

(Greven, 1992, p. 38-39)

These parents were trying to do what they thought was biblical and right in God's eyes.

What is interesting to me is that many of the proverbs that are quoted by prospankers that seem to advocate spanking say the child will not die from spanking ("Withhold not correction from the child: for if thou beatest him with the rod, he shall not die" (Proverbs 23:13, KJV)), and yet, children have died from repetitive and/or the force of the spanking. Every time a child is hit, slight injury can occur as pain is a signal that injury is occurring or is about to. Redness after a spanking shows that the skin has been irritated. Slapping several times can cause the tissue to break down. Over time, this can lead to organ damage and hemorrhaging. Surely, God, who formed us in our mother's wombs (Isaiah 44:24; Jermaiah 1:5; Psalm 139:13-16), knew how hitting affects our bodies—especially a small child's body that is much more vulnerable to force—and did *not* mean hitting in the rod verses. God does not lie to His people. So, to say that a child shall not die from being hit with a big, heavy walking stick (the rod), He must have meant authority and not physical punishment. The Holy Bible is truth—*period!* "For the word of God is alive and active" (Hebrews 4:12a). Yet, satan loves to skew God's Word whenever possible. He is the father of lies (John 8:44b).

Why Do Prospanking Advocates Tell Parents They Are Disobeying God if They Don't Spank?

Throughout history many Christian advocates of spanking claim that if parents don't spank their children then they are disobeying God. They use Proverbs 13:24 to coerce parents into believing that if they don't use physical punishment then they hate their children. Of course, based on the correct interpretation of these rod verses (see part 1 of this book), this couldn't be farther from the truth. And yet, sadly, prospanking advocates continue to teach that spanking is an absolute requirement from God in order to raise obedient, godly children.

> Parents are often advised to tell their children that they are acting as God's surrogates when they inflict pain. As Jack Hyles notes: "So God is like a father and He chooses fathers and mothers to represent Him in the punishing of little children." He advises parents: "Explain to him that you are a child of God and if you refuse to obey God in His judgment upon your children, God will pour out His wrath upon you. For you to be a good child of God requires that you be a good parent to the child. Let him understand this. He will get the idea that God is a holy and just God, One who loves and yet One who wants us to become our best. For this to be so He must punish us when we are deserving."
>
> (Greven, 1992, p. 63)

I must ask where do grace, mercy, and forgiveness come in here? If we are forgiven, then we are saved from God's wrath. "The Word became flesh and made his dwelling among us. We have seen his glory, the glory of the one and only Son, who came from the Father, full of grace and truth" (John 1:14).

The Bible also says, "And all are justified freely by his grace through the redemption that came by Christ Jesus" (Romans 3:23). (See also 1 Timothy 1:14).

It also appears that throughout history advocates of spanking have treated the parent-child relationship as a battleground in which the parent must always win over the child. Susanna Wesley and other early seventeenth- and eighteenth-century evangelical Christians were adamant in regards to using physical punishment to conquer children. The most prominent advocate of spanking in today's Christian society, James Dobson (1970), page 45, states:

> The child may be more strong-willed than the parent, and they both know it. If he can outlast a temporary onslaught, he has won a major battle, eliminating punishment in the parent's repertoire. Even though Mom spanks him, he wins the battle by defying her again. The solution to this situation is obvious: outlast him; win, even if it takes a repeated measure.

Or the child is beaten to death.

Conclusion

It is very sad that somehow all of these seemingly unbiblical themes and misinterpretations have continued so prevalently throughout history. Countless children and families have been harmed, some more visibly than others, by these great misinterpretations of God's Holy Word. My purpose in this quest is to uncover the historic roots of violence against our children, who Jesus so dearly loves. My hope is to show from where some of this came. It seems obvious to me from studying Scripture with an open heart and listening to the Holy Spirit convictions that spanking, hitting, beating, coercing, belittling, and punishing young children did not come from God. Jesus renounced all violence when he came to Earth.

> See to it, brothers and sisters, that none of you has a sinful, unbelieving heart that turns away from the living God. But encourage one another daily, as long as it is called "Today," so that none of you may be hardened by sin's deceitfulness. We have come to share in Christ, if indeed we hold our original conviction firmly to the very end. As has just been said: "Today, if you hear his voice, do not harden your hearts as you did in the rebellion."
>
> Hebrews 3:12-15

References

Dobson, J. (1970). *Dare to Discipline.* Carol Stream, IL: Tyndale House Publishers.

Greven, P. (1992). *Spare the Child.* New York, NY: Vintage Books.

Chapter 6

Susanna Wesley and Her Influence on Spanking

In this chapter, we will be looking at Susanna Wesley and how she has contributed to the belief among Christians that children must be physically punished. We will also see that she believed in breaking children's wills starting at infancy.

Susanna Wesley—Breaking Wills

Susanna Wesley (1669-1742) is held up as the "Mother of Methodism." She married Samuel Wesley who was a pastor. The Wesley's had a total of nineteen children, but only ten of the children survived past infancy. Susanna, as most Puritans, valued education. However, she even taught her daughters as well as her sons how to read and write, which was not common during the eighteenth century (Heitzenrater, 2001). She also allowed each child to do what he/she could for itself starting from birth. Susanna was a very devoted mother.

Before we get too deeply into Susanna's child rearing beliefs and practices, we must take a brief look at how children were viewed by most during the eighteenth century. During this time period, children were seen as miniature adults. They were dressed like adults and were expected to behave like adults at very young ages. The quicker they behaved like adults, the better. Otherwise, children were not to be seen or heard. They were kept out of the rooms occupied by adults. Throughout the eighteenth century, this view of children slowly evolved as a sort of discovery of childhood occurred. This change was not necessarily a positive one for children. Instead of the high expectation for children to be adult-like as soon as possible (which, of course, was negative in and of itself since we now know how important childhood truly is), children were seen as inferior to adults. As Heitzenrater (2001), page 280, states:

> If the previous view put unnecessarily great expectations on young children, the new view gave them very little credit for any good possibilities. Children, now seen as inferior to adults and needing to be governed strictly by them, fell prey to a repressive and tyrannical concept of the family, typified by the harsh Puritan view. Lloyd De Mause characterizes this eighteenth-century stage in the evolving treatment of children in Western civilization as "the intrusive mode."

As I point out in chapters 4 and 5, the viewpoint of children born with original sin seemed to either lead to the harsh treatment of children or compassionate treatment. While the Puritans advocated some of Jesus's views and commands for adults to become like children in order to enter the kingdom of heaven (Matthew 18:1-4), they were quite harsh with their children at times and believed in strict religious education for children (Heitzenrater, 2001; Greven, 1992, Miller, 1990). "In Colonial times, discipline was harsh and children were expected to obey immediately and without question" (Osborn, 1991, p. 23).

Susanna Wesley's child rearing beliefs and practices were in-tune with the time period. Much of John Locke's philosophy can be seen in how Susanna raised her children. John Locke held the belief that children are born "blank slates" and that the environment could completely shape them into the people they would become. He warned that motherly affection toward children was dangerous and that children should be treated as young adults. He also advocated for the use of physical punishment with young children. Susanna taught her infants to cry softly by spanking them. In her letter to her son John, Wesley (1732), page 1, states:

> When they turned a year old (and some before) they were taught to fear the rod, and to cry softly. By this means they escaped abundance of correction they might otherwise have had. That most odious noise of the crying of children, was rarely heard in the house. The family usually lived in as much quietness, as if there had not been a child among them.

I find this quite disturbing as even for older infants and young toddlers crying is the main way of communicating their needs to us. We have much research showing the devastating effects of not responding sensitively to their cries. (See chapter 14 for more information on attachment). I wonder why she felt it was necessary to stifle her infants' cries through hitting them. I also wonder how long this process took since hurting a young child almost always makes him or her cry *louder* and *harder!* The other interesting thing about using physical punishment with infants is that people, including medical professionals, did not believe that infants could feel pain.

What's more is that crying is often seen in the Bible and God comforts those that cry out to Him. "God heard the boy *crying*, and the angel of God called to Hagar from heaven and said to her, 'What is the matter, Hagar? Do not be afraid; God has heard the boy *crying* as he lies there'" (Genesis 21:17). (See also Exodus

3:7; 1 Samuel 7:8; Psalm 55:17; Psalm 145:17-19; and Revelation 21:4). Sadly, I believe hitting her infants to teach them to cry softly had nothing to do with Susanna wanting to be biblical in her parenting and everything to do with her own preferences in parenting. "That most odious noise of the crying of children, was rarely heard in the house. The family usually lived in as much quietness, as if there had not been a child among them" (Wesley, 1732, p. 1). Susanna obviously had an aversion to crying. It is important to remind ourselves again that during the eighteenth century children were to be seen and not heard and that a great deal of Susanna's child-rearing practices were in line with what was common during this particular time period. I am trying to show that these practices were *not* always biblical since many Christians still hold her up as a model for Christian mothers.

We now know from years of research that not providing young children with sensitive, responsive care can lead to failure to thrive, attachment disorders, and even death (Fogel, 2011; Mooney, 2011; Karen, 1994; & Spitz, 1965). Research also shows that pain, especially in the case of a parent hitting a young child, negatively affects brain development in children. Stress hormones are released whenever a child or adult is upset. In adults, these hormones over time can cause heart disease, insomnia, and diabetes. In infants and young children, stress hormones change the way that neurons and synapses are created and formed. (See chapter 13 for more information on how abuse can affect brain development). Infants and toddlers learn through sensorimotor experiences. Hitting them makes them less likely to explore their environments and more likely to withdraw. This withdrawal may seem to make them into good, quiet babies, but this could have dire effects on their health. If a child is afraid to cry because no one will answer him/her or he/she gets hit for crying, the child will stop communicating his/her needs, which could lead to death if no one realizes the child is sick. Plus, stress hormones make infants even more prone to illness. Not to mention the emotional distress children go through when physically punished.

As the children grew older, Susanna Wesley kept them on a very strict schedule. The children were not allowed to play or speak loudly, especially during the six hours of schooling. Susanna homeschooled her children. Even their eating and drinking schedules were extremely strict. In her letter to John Wesley, Susanna (1732), page 1, states:

> Drinking or eating between meals was never allowed, unless in case of sickness, which seldom happened. Nor were they allowed to go into the kitchen to ask anything of the servants when they were eating. If it was known they did, they were certainly punished with the rod and the servants severely reprimanded.

Why would anyone not allow children to drink between meals? I wonder what happened when it was really hot outside. Didn't they get dehydrated? Even for myself, I need drinks between meals. And sometimes I need a snack between meals otherwise I feel sick to my stomach. We all know that children's stomachs are smaller, so they need small snacks between meals. We also know that children become dehydrated quicker than adults so they need drinks throughout the day. I don't understand why Susanna felt it was necessary to keep her children on such a strict schedule and to spank them if she found out they had asked the servants for something to eat or drink between meals. If the family was poor and needed to conserve food, that would be different as far as keeping a strict schedule. However, spanking them for asking for food or drink would still be inexcusable in a poverty situation.

Is keeping food and drink unnecessarily from children, or anyone, for that matter, biblical? In Matthew 10:42, Jesus says, "And if anyone gives even a cup of cold water to one of these little ones who is my disciple, truly I tell you, that person will certainly not lose their reward." In this verse, Jesus is talking about anyone with a low status in society. As chapter 4 shows, children have a very low status in society. Therefore, it seems quite clear that Jesus is including children in this statement. So, denying a child food and drink in a very controlling way is *not* biblical. Just think, everyone who has ever fed a child, a poor person, or even a friend has fed our Lord and Savior, Jesus Christ. Now, I'm not saying that we should allow children, for example, to have a cookie right before supper. What I am saying is to not allow a drink or a small, healthy snack at appropriately spaced intervals between meals is unbiblical and potentially *dangerous* to children. And to spank a child for asking for a drink or a snack is outright *abuse!* Children's bodies are constantly growing and developing, therefore, nutritious meals, snacks, and drinks should be offered to them throughout the day.

Going back to the fact that children were not allowed to play or talk loudly makes me question how much learning was lost for them. Yes, she taught them well and it appears that Samuel, Jr., was quite advanced for his age, but research shows that young children learn best through play and concrete (real) experiences. "Armed with an inborn motivation to learn and explore, they are on a constant quest for knowledge, learning from what they see, hear, feel, taste, and touch. And they do this without the need for prompting" (Lally, 2009, p. 47). Through play and casual interactions, children learn so much, including Math, Science, English, and History. Of course, children should be taught God's Word in similar ways. But it seems Susanna (and others of her day) thought children should be taught in an extremely strict, rigorous manner. As we will see in chapter 7, her child-rearing practices had a strong effect on her son, Jonathan Wesley.

The Wesley family suffered two fires that burned their house down. During the rebuilding of the house, the family was split up and the children lived with other families. It seems that during this time, the children had a bit more freedom than what Susanna would ever allow. Interestingly, here is what Susanna Wesley writes about this time period in the family's life:

> For some years we went on very well. Never were children in better disposed to piety, or in more subjection to their parents until that scattering of them after the fire into several families. In those families, they were left at full liberty to converse with the servants, which before they had always been restrained from, and to run abroad and play with any children, good or bad. They soon learned to neglect a strict observation of the sabbath, and got knowledge of several songs and bad things which before they had no notion of. That civil behaviour which made them admired when at home, by all which saw them, was in great measure lost, and a clownish accent and many rude ways were learned, which were not reformed without some difficulty.
>
> When the house was rebuilt and the children all brought home, we entered upon a strict reform.
>
> (Wesley, 1732, p. 3)

I'm sure that Susanna was grateful that those who survived the fire were safe. I'm also sure (even though she doesn't say so in this particular letter) that she was grateful to the families who took in their children during this very difficult time in the family's life. I'm a bit surprised and saddened that Susanna seemed more concerned about getting her children under her reign once again. Why did she see their freedom as such a negative thing? And if such strict child-rearing is supposed to produce good, obedient Christian children, then why did they disobey their mother when out from under her authority? It seems that Susanna was focused on the Law and legalism more than on true obedience from the heart. Jesus, on many occasions, warned the Pharisees about their legalistic tendencies. "For I tell you that unless your righteousness surpasses that of the Pharisees and the teachers of the law, you will certainly not enter the kingdom of heaven" (Matthew 5:20). (See also Matthew 23:5-7; Matthew 23:13-15; Matthew 23:27-39; and Mark 7:1-23). It is obvious from these verses that God values *true worship from the heart.* I wonder how long it took Susanna's children to truly worship God from their hearts after being raised in such a controlling environment, especially since she taught her children that if they repented to *her* then she would not spank them for their offense. I would guess that when the children repented that they did so out of fear rather than out of true remorse. "On the other hand, some of Susanna's ideas seem very modern, such as not punishing a child more than once for the same infraction…" (Heitzenrater, 2001, p. 284). Jesus does not punish us for our sins, but rather, offers forgiveness, grace, and mercy when we sin. He allows consequences in our lives, but He never punishes us—unless we reject Him forever.

As I mentioned previously, the family appeared to live a nice, quiet life from the outside. But a few sources mentioned that while all her children grew up and continued to love and respect their mother, it seems that they may have all suffered from emotional problems (http://www.gentlechristianmothers.com/community/archive/index.php/t-206124.html). While we cannot know this for sure, I would not be surprised if her children did indeed suffer some negative emotional effects, as this type of parenting puts children at a higher risk for all sorts of problems. (See part 3 of this book for more information about the horrible emotional consequences children who are physically punished often experience).

Also, it seems she struggled with the assurance of her own salvation for many years. From reading some of Susanna's letters, it appears to me that, while she clearly acknowledged human salvation as a result of Christ's sacrifice, she remained in Old Testament philosophical beliefs—that obedience to the Law of Moses was required to maintain salvation. In a letter to her daughter, Susanna Wesley (1709-10 [1997]), page 381, states:

> The soul is immortal and must survive all time, even to eternity, and consequently it must have been miserable to the utmost extent of its duration, had we not had that sacred treasure of knowledge, which is contained in the books of the Old and New Testament. A treasure infinitely more valuable than the whole world, because therein we [find] all *things* [added emphasis by this author] necessary for our salvation.

I am wondering if Susanna ever truly understood that Jesus Christ paid it all for us when He bore our sins on that cross; that the one "thing" that we need for salvation is Jesus Christ. "For God did not appoint us to suffer wrath but to receive salvation through our Lord Jesus Christ" (1 Thessalonians 5:9). I cannot say what was going through Susanna Wesley's head when she wrote her letters. I am trying my best to understand her with extremely limited information in order to show where she may have misunderstood Scripture—something that *all* (including myself) are capable of doing.

Finally, Susanna Wesley seems to contradict herself as she believed a child's will must be conquered in order to submit to his/her parents and ultimately God. However, in a letter to her daughter, Susanna Wesley (1709-10 [1997]), page 380, states:

> For any one which makes a profession of religion only because 'tis the custom of the country in which they live or because their parents do so or their worldly interest is thereby secured or advanced will never be able to stand in the day of temptation, nor shall they ever enter into the kingdom of heaven.

So, why did she treat them so harshly to seemingly raise them in the Lord if she believed that one should never profess faith because their parents do? I admit that I am going on limited information, but this is the overall impression that I have from reading Susanna's letters. Of course, reading and teaching God's Word to the children was extremely important and good. However, I believe that by controlling them so strongly could have set them up to proclaim faith in Christ so as not to disappoint their mother. As we shall see in the next chapter, Jonathan Wesley was an adult before he actually accepted Christ, even though he practiced the "religion" his entire life.

I truly admire Susanna Wesley for being so devoted to her children. She obviously loved her children very much and wanted the best for them. And as I've pointed out, some of her child-rearing practices were common for the eighteenth century. However, I must question holding her up as a model for Christian mothers. Not all of her practices are biblically supported. Children require gentle firmness—something Susanna Wesley apparently was unable to give her children.

We need to remember what the fruit of the Spirit is when we deal with children:

> But the fruit of the Spirit is love, joy, peace, forbearance, kindness, goodness, faithfulness, gentleness and self-control. Against such things there is no law. Those who belong to Christ Jesus have crucified the flesh with its passions and desires. Since we live by the Spirit, let us keep in step with the Spirit. Let us not become conceited, provoking and envying each other. Galatians 5:22-26

References

Bunge, M. J. (Ed.). (2001). *The Child in Christian Thought.* Grand Rapids, MI: William B. Eerdmans Publishing Company.

Greven, P. (1992). *Spare the Child.* New York, NY: Vintage Books.

Lally, J. R. (November 2009). The Science and Psychology of Infant-Toddler Care. How an Understanding of Early Learning Has Transformed Child Care. *Zero to Three, 30*(2), 47-53.

Osborn, D. K. (1991). *Early Childhood Education in Historical Perspective.* Athens, GA: Daye Press.

Wallace Jr, C. (Ed.). (1997). *The Complete Writings of Susanna Wesley.* New York, NY: Oxford University Press.

Chapter 7

Jonathan Wesley and His Schools of Legalism

In this chapter, we will look at Jonathan Wesley (1703-1791). He is known as the founder of Methodism, and for the effects he had (and still has) on the education of children and adults. In chapter 6, I looked at the child-rearing practices of his mother, Susanna Wesley, whom many Christian advocates of spanking hold up as a model for Christian mothers. Susanna gave John special attention as he almost died in one of the house fires. John deeply loved his mother, and it has been said that he didn't think he could ever find a woman like his mother to marry.

Jonathan Wesley—School of Legalism?

Now, before we say that his mother's child-rearing practices couldn't have been that bad if he loved her that much, it is well documented that abused children that have been taken away from their abusive parents will cry and ask, "If I'm really good tomorrow, can I go home to my mommy and daddy?" As I point out in chapter 2, children have a very forgiving nature and love their parents no matter what. That's how I was with my dad despite his physical abuse. He said he was sorry many times throughout my childhood, and I always forgave him. Now some prospankers may argue that there's a line between abuse and spanking. My dad never left marks on my body, but it was indeed abuse as he'd hit and be rough with me for things out of my control. My mom only spanked me once, and though she never apologized, I forgave her within the week. Though both my parents were wrong for hitting me, I've long forgiven both of them and have a great relationship with my mom. So, for all those who claim spankings didn't hurt them, I must ask that they truly think about how they felt right before, during, and afterward because when children are hurt by the closest people in their lives, it *does* harm and hurt, otherwise there wouldn't be so much denial and controversy over using physical punishment with our children. And if spanking (hitting) children was ordained by God, then there would be *no* questions or controversy among Christians *and* the secular world regarding the amount of harm spanking a child receives as Scripture clearly states, "And we know that in all things God works for the good of those who love him, who have been called according to his purpose (Romans 8:28). "Or that all things work together for good to those who love God, who; or that in all things God works together with those who love him to bring about what is good" (NIV, www.biblica.com). Therefore, it is no surprise that John Wesley loved his mother and chose to care for her during her final years of life.

I want to remind us that my purpose in digging into the history of spanking is *not* to point fingers or accuse anyone. My purpose is to show you where some of the topics I brought up in chapter 5 of this part of the book come from—particularly that they are *not from God*. Spanking is from man.

John Wesley did much good in his lifetime. It has been said that he would go out into the country and proclaim Christ to the people who lived in those rural places, winning many souls to Christ. He also started Methodism. And many credit him for the creation of Sunday school. He created schools for children in which they studied many of the traditional subjects as well as the Bible. He made sure poor children were able to be educated in his schools, as well as girls. Sadly, John followed in his mother's footsteps when it came to his beliefs regarding child rearing and the education of children. Though John didn't have any children of his own, we will see these practices in how he ran the schools and in his sermons about children.

First, I want to briefly take a look at common Puritan belief and Calvinism because Susanna and John Wesley's beliefs seem to fit into this belief system. The use of catechisms was the primary way that the Puritans, as well as some other Christian sects, taught doctrine during the eighteenth and nineteenth centuries. They put a high importance on Scripture as authority, which is absolutely correct, as the Bible is an absolute authority given by God. This made literacy training a must for all children. However:

> The Puritans accepted the Calvinistic interpretation of total depravity. This belief carried over to their view of children. Out of concern for the souls of little ones, Puritan ministers sometimes preached sermons particularly for and to children. The aim of these children's sermons was to replace childhood vanity with "early piety."
>
> (Reed & Prevost, 1993, p. 275)

Children do not completely understand sin, nor do they purposely sin until they reach a certain age—that age is different for every child. Plus, in the eighteenth century children were expected to act like adults as soon as possible. People didn't have the knowledge and research of typical child development that we do today. Therefore, developmentally appropriate behaviors of young children were seen as sinful. This usually led to the harsh treatment of children despite Jesus never calling for such treatment. People thought young children went to hell. (See chapters 1 and 4 for more information). While children should indeed be introduced to piety at an early age, to expect that developmentally appropriate behaviors be *replaced* by piety is completely unrealistic and will lead to unnecessary frustration in the child and parent.

Also, during this time period using physical punishment with wives and slaves as well as children was completely acceptable and legal by society. White males were dominant, and anyone weaker or different from them were under their rule and authority. In essence, wives, slaves, children, and servants were considered property of the white male.

> We no longer permit the hitting of servants, apprentices, wives, prisoners, and members of the armed forces. All of these were legal until the late nineteenth or early twentieth century... Research on corporal punishment of children can result in information that may speed up the process of bringing children to the same protection members of the military, employees, servants, wives, and prisoners now have.
>
> (Straus, 2006, p. 10)

Even up until the 1960s, it was totally legal for husbands to hit their wives as long as they didn't leave a mark or injure them.

> Before the late 1960s, a husband's slap of his wife was not regarded as an act of abuse. Today, that same act is unquestionably viewed as abusive (society still has a long way to go before wives are equally regarded as batterers for assaulting their husbands). The "spanking" of children is viewed in the same light today as wife hitting was viewed before the 1960s: NOT abusive by legal standards. Additionally, if an employer "spanked" the buttocks of an employee, it would be grounds for sexual assault.

(Couture, 2007, http://stophitting.blogspot.
com/2006/01/back-in-good-ol-days-and-other.html)

Thus, it appears that children are still considered property of their parents since parents still have the right to spank them as long as they don't leave marks on the children. I find it sad that so many Christians seem to have completely missed the message Jesus Christ brought to us. "So in everything, do to others what you would have them do to you, for this sums up the Law and the Prophets" (Matthew 7:12). It is interesting that throughout history we Christians have failed miserably in applying the Golden Rule, especially when it comes to how children are treated.

Photo credit: Alisson Stoltzfus

I do not believe that the Wesleys took the Golden Rule into account with their child-rearing beliefs and practices. This seemed to have delayed John's salvation, as he did not consider himself a born-again Christian until the date of May 24, 1738.

> Upon arriving back in England, John became involved in a Pietist society organized by Peter Boehler, a Moravian. In 1738, during a meeting on Aldersgate Street in London, John became convinced that salvation came only through faith in Jesus Christ. He called this his conversion, and it profoundly changed his life.
>
> (Reed & Prevost, 1993, p. 275)

Since so many Christian advocates of spanking hold Susanna Wesley's child-rearing philosophy as a model for Christian mothers, I must wonder why John didn't actually receive Christ until he was thirty-five years old. If such a harsh way of parenting our children is supposed to lead them to Christ, or at least make it more likely for them to come to Christ, why did John not feel Christ's love until the age of thirty-five? Yes, every child is different, and no matter what we do the child may not come to Christ, but so many Christian prospankers seem totally convinced that by spanking children it will teach them to respect authority and to be fearfully reverent to God and their parents, and if they learn to submit to authority then they will find it easier to submit to Christ. However, submitting to Christ and authority out of fear is *much* different than submitting out of love, respect, and reverence. While some children who grow up and were "lovingly spanked" by their Christian parents do receive Christ completely, I know of others who seemed to accept Christ at an early age, but the minute they left home, they rebelled and fell away from their faith. For example, I once knew a great Christian family who did their best to raise their three children in the Lord. They were quite strict with them. As teenagers they were not allowed to go to movies, dances, or wear two-piece swimsuits. As children they were "lovingly" spanked. They went to church every Sunday, and the children were involved in youth church activities. They prayed and studied God's Word as a family regularly. These parents did everything in their power to raise their children in the way of the Lord. And while all three of the children accepted Christ as children and were baptized as believers, all three absolutely rebelled against God the minute they left home. Two of them became pregnant the first year after leaving home. One became an alcoholic after leaving home. And what's worse is that they totally abandoned their faith. Today they're all married with children and have semi-returned to their faith as they go to church and occasionally ask for prayer, but Christ is not the center of their lives. I mean we all are sinners and rebel, but to completely abandon our faith as they did the second we leave home sounds like we weren't spiritually healthy. We are supposed to be free in Christ. Why, then, do so many children raised in strict Christian homes feel the need to exercise their newfound freedom through rebellion? Could it be that their parents didn't accurately teach their children what Jesus meant when He proclaimed, "If you hold to my teaching, you are really my disciples. Then you will know the truth, and the truth will set you free" (John 8:31b-32)? (See part 3 of this book for more accounts of children raised in strict, punitive homes, who rejected God as adults).

This seemed to be the case with John Wesley as well, even though he did not rebel against his faith or his parents. Nevertheless, it is clear from his letters that he wrote to his family while at college and graduate school before his conversion that he did not have an accurate understanding of the freedom Christ offers. In a letter to his mother concerning a conversation he had had regarding Christian Liberty, John Wesley (1734 [1915]), page 54, states:

For Liberty as to Rites and Points of Discipline. So Mr. Whiston says: "Though the Stations were constituted by the Apostles, yet the Liberty of the Christian Law dispenses with them on extraordinary Occasions."

For Liberty from denying ourselves in little things; for trifles 'tis commonly thought we may indulge in safely, because Christ hath made us free. This notion I a little doubt, is not sound...

Christian Liberty is taken by some for a Freedom from Restraint as to Sleep or Food. So they would say, Your drinking not one glass of Wine, or my rising at fixed hours was contrary to Christian Liberty.

Lastly, it is taken for Freedom from Rules. If by this he meant making our Rules yield to extraordinary occasions, well: If, the having no Prudential Rules, this Liberty is as yet too high for me, I cannot attain to it.

It seems John believed that in order to be a good Christian, one had to have strict "Prudential Rules." This undoubtedly came from how his mother raised and taught him. This is, as I pointed out in chapter 6, legalism, and Jesus warned the Pharisees and teachers of the Law about legalism time and time again during his ministry. As I point out throughout part 1 of this book, we are free from the Law of Moses. We are now under the law of grace thanks to Jesus's sacrifice for *all* of our sins.

For Christ did not enter a sanctuary made with human hands that was only a copy of the true one; he entered heaven itself, now to appear for us in God's presence. Nor did he enter heaven to offer himself again and again, the way the high priest enters the Most Holy Place every year with blood that is not his own. Otherwise Christ would have had to suffer many times since the creation of the world. But he has appeared once for all at the culmination of the ages to do away with sin by the sacrifice of himself. Just as people are destined to die once, and after that to face judgment, so Christ was sacrificed once to take away the sins of many; and he will appear a second time, not to bear sin, but to bring salvation to those who are waiting for him.

Hebrews 9:24-28

We are free in Christ!

Just four years after John wrote about "Prudential Rules" in a letter to his mother, he came to know Christ. Just a few months before his conversion, John wrote about struggling with darkness and bitterness. "He contrasts it with an earlier day, January 8. Then he was 'in the midst of the great deep' and 'bitterness of soul'" (Eayers, 1915, p. 60). In a letter to his brother and sister where he describes his conversion experience to them, John Wesley (1738 [1915]) states, "But that is all past, and serves only as a dark background for the brightness and beauty of the evening of May 24, when a light shone from heaven upon him" (p. 61). I speculated in chapter 6 that all of the Wesley children may have suffered from emotional problems as adults due to how they were treated. I think what John Wesley described in his letter is proof that he was struggling with emotional problems. Yes, we all battle our own demons, but being raised in such an abusive, controlling, and harsh environment has been proven to put people at a higher risk for emotional problems.

> For a child who can barely walk or talk (the age at which most children are most likely to be hit), it can truly be traumatic if the most loved and trusted figure in the child's life suddenly carries out a painful attack. The consequence can be a post-traumatic stress syndrome that creates deep, lifelong psychological problems such as depression and suicidal thinking.
>
> (Straus, 2006, p. 10)

Now, many parents say that their child is perfectly happy after they've been spanked. Children are usually resilient. They don't dwell on things too long. Therefore, it can be quite difficult to tell exactly how a young child is truly feeling. And children usually act out in order to try to show us how they are feeling, which is misinterpreted as bad (sinful) behavior by parents leading to more punishment for the child.

I once had a good Christian friend who had two young children. One day while I was visiting, her eighteen-month-old happened to touch something that was dangerous. She told him no, but being a typical toddler, he smiled and did it again. She calmly took his hand and swatted it and said, "Dangerous!" He looked at her then at his hand and then smiled and did it again. So she calmly took his hand again, swatted it a little harder than before, and said, "Dangerous!" I could tell that this swat hurt more than the first, but he didn't cry. He looked confused at his mom, got up, walked a little ways, sat down on the floor, and looked as if he was trying to process what had just happened. It broke my heart, and it was all I could do not to say anything. I wonder what his mom was actually thinking watching this. Did she see his confusion, or did she see that hitting got the job done because he didn't touch the dangerous item again? Since she was very prospanking, I wonder if she was in denial about the harm she was doing to her children. Also, the toddler only sat looking confused for about a minute or less before he was up happily playing again. While I knew them, the children seemed happy. The older child was a bit aggressive at times, which concerned me as he was spanked and research shows that children who are spanked have higher rates of aggressive behavior. I wouldn't be surprised if they ended up having some emotional problems now that they are older just as John Wesley seemed to have before his conversion. The children's parents may never know, as teenage and adult children don't always feel comfortable talking to their parents about the emotional problems that they are having.

> Many people who have experienced suffering as children are able to live productive lives. However, these people may harbor self-destructive tendencies, and interpersonal difficulties in that aren't apparent to onlookers. Adults who were mistreated in childhood are often insecure, mistrusting, defensive, authoritarian, passive, withdrawn, apathetic, in denial or quick to sarcasm. Those who transcend childhood suffering are often highly resilient people who have sought to process and understand how their childhood history currently impacts their lives. (Couture, 2007, http://stophitting.blogspot.com/2006/01/back-in-good-ol-days-and-other.html)

After his conversion, John Wesley seemed to really grasp the concept of grace. The night of his conversion, he went quite unwillingly to Aldersgate Street to hear William Holland read a preface written by Luther to the book of Romans. In a letter describing his whole experience that night to his brother and sister, John Wesley (1738 [1915]), page 62, writes:

> With regard to my own character, and my doctrine likewise, I shall answer you plainly. By a Christian I mean one who so believes in Christ as that sin hath no more dominion over him: and in this obvious sense of the word I was not a Christian until May the 24th last past. For till then sin had dominion over me, although I fought with it continually; but surely, then, from that time to this it hath not—such is the free grace of God in Christ. What sins they were which till then reigned over me, and from which, by the grace of God, I am now free, I am ready to declare on the house-top, if it may be for the glory of God...

> My desire of this faith I knew long before, though not
> so clearly till Sunday, January the 8th last, when, being
> in the midst of the great deep, I wrote a few lines, in the
> bitterness of my soul, some of which I have transcribed;
> and may the good of God sanctify them both to you and
> me.

The rest of John's letter regarding his conversion is absolutely beautiful and heartwarming. For the first time in his life, he truly felt and fully grasped God's love and grace for him!

Sadly, I must question why this knowledge of God's grace, love, and mercy that John Wesley gained the night of May 24, 1738, was not applied to his beliefs about child rearing or to the schools he created. He did not have children of his own, but he touched the lives of *many* children through his Methodist schools and his sermons regarding children. In his sermons, which date back to 1783, long after his conversion, he discussed the need for children's wills to be broken beginning in infancy just as did his mother. Because he was a preacher, I expected to see more references to Scripture in order to at least try to back some of his beliefs up with the Word of God, but he used the same verse as his mom: "Start children off on the way they should go, and even when they are old they will not turn from it" (Proverbs 22:6, 2011, NIV). Most of us know this verse as: "Train a child in the way he should go, and when he is old he will not depart from it." Obviously, Bible scholars believe that "start" is more accurate to what God is saying than "train." John Wesley does not use any other verses to back up what he says in his sermon titled "On the Education of Children" (1783) in which Wesley states:

> To humour children is, as far as in us lies, to make their
> disease incurable. A wise parent, on the other hand, should
> begin to break their will the first moment it appears. In the
> whole art of Christian education there is nothing more

important than this. The will of the parent is to a little child in the place of the will of God. Therefore studiously teach them to submit to this while they are children, that they may be ready to submit to his will when they are men. But in order to carry this point, you will need incredible firmness and resolution; for after you have once begun, you must never more give way. You must hold on still in an even course; you must never intermit your attention for one hour; otherwise you lose your labour.

(http://new.gbgm-umc.org/umhistory/wesley/ sermons/95/)

Yes, we must teach our children to submit to our authority, but to break a child's will is not biblical. (See chapter 5 for more information about breaking children's wills). John Wesley goes on in this same sermon to explain how his mother broke their wills as infants. Wesley (1783) states:

My own mother had ten children, each of whom had spirit enough; yet not one of them was ever heard to cry aloud after it was a year old. A gentlewoman of Sheffield (several of whose children I suppose are alive still) assured me she had the same success with regard to her eight children. When some were objecting to the possibility of this, Mr. Parson Greenwood (well-known in the north of England) replied, "This cannot be impossible: I have had the proof of it in my own family. Nay, of more than this. I had six children by my former wife; and she suffered none of them to cry aloud after they were ten months old. And yet none of their spirits were so broken, as to unfit them for any of the offices of life." This, therefore, may be done by any woman of sense, who may thereby save herself abundance of trouble, and prevent that disagreeable noise, the squalling of young children, from being heard under her roof.

(http://new.gbgm-umc.org/umhistory/wesley/ sermons/95/)

Again, nowhere in Scripture does it say to break a child's will. Children are already humble when it comes to believing in Christ or Jesus would not have held them up as models for adults in Matthew 18:1-4. As I continue to point out throughout this book, Ephesians 5:21 says that we are to "submit to one another out of reverence for Christ." Wives are to submit to their husbands (Ephesians 5:22, 24), and yet, this does *not* give husbands the right to treat their wives harshly. Just as Ephesians 6:1-2 says, "Children, obey your parents in the Lord, for this is right. 'Honor your father and mother'—which is the first commandment with a promise—'so that it may go well with you and that you may enjoy long life on the earth'" does *not* give parents the right to treat children harshly. God must have known that humans would have a tendency to treat the weaker (or perceived weaker) one harshly as in both cases He warns that husbands are to love their wives as Christ loves the church (Ephesians 5:25), and for parents not to exasperate their children (Ephesians 6:3). Why didn't John Wesley understand this? Maybe because he couldn't stand to go against what his beloved mother taught. He wasn't strong enough to break the cycle of abuse despite having the power of Christ within him.

John Wesley ran the schools that he created much like his mother ran her home when he was a child. The children at his schools were on an extremely strict schedule and were never allowed to play.

> What others noticed, however, and what is most often remembered is the strong element of religion, and the rigor of the schedule and discipline. The rules for the children at Kingswood meant rising at 4:00 a.m. and retiring at 8:00 p.m.; starting the day with two hours of private and public devotion and an hour of public evening prayers; having no time during the day for play; and spending from 7:00 to 11:00 a.m. and 1:00 to 5:00 p.m. "in school." Students

at all times be in the presence of a teacher and never be allowed to roam free or have contact with the colliers' children in the neighborhood.

(Heitzenrater, 2001, p. 288)

This seems more like a military base than a school for children. And if a child broke a rule or misbehaved, he or she was physically punished. As I pointed out in chapter 6, research shows that young children learn best through play and concrete (real) experiences. How did Jesus teach? He used stories and parables that people who were open to Him could understand and relate to for the most part. He also taught through concrete experiences and miracles. One example that comes to mind of Jesus using a miracle to teach His disciples faith is when Jesus fed five thousand people with five loaves of bread and a couple of fish (John 6:1-15). His disciples said that no one had enough money to buy enough food for all the people, and yet when a boy brought up a basket of food, Jesus blessed the food and all five thousand people had more than enough to eat. This taught exactly what faith in the Lord can do. Jesus also taught by asking open-ended questions to make people think. He was a gentle teacher. He also enjoyed boat rides and hanging out with people. Jesus even went to weddings and turned water into wine (John 2:1-12). Heaven will be one big wedding and party! I can imagine Jesus smiled at children running around playing, otherwise why would He have gotten so angry at His disciples for trying to prevent parents from bringing their children to Him? Also, why did God create children with such a playful nature if He did not intend for children to play? And the Bible continually talks about the joy we are to have in the Lord. Therefore, I do not believe that it was biblically accurate for the Wesleys to require children to follow a very strict schedule. Yes, routines are very important for children, as they need to know what will happen next throughout the day.

Children thrive on routines because routines are flexible in order to meet the children's needs. Schedules are not designed to meet children's needs. They are more for adult's convenience and to keep children under control. While there are stories of revivals and salvation that occurred in John Wesley's schools, I can't help but question whether the good outweighed the potential harm that was done to the children.

John Wesley didn't see children as human beings, but instead, he saw them as a unit for salvation. Gross views Wesley's concept of salvation: "He never considered a child as a child, but rather as a unit for salvation, bred in sin, apt to evil, and altogether as a 'brand to be plucked out of the burning'" (Towns, 1970, p. 323). However, John seemed to contradict himself at times as to whether children were inheritably evil or innocent. Heitzenrater (2001), page 294, states the answer John Wesley gave regarding infants suffering:

> Why do infants suffer? What sin have they to be cured thereby? If you say, "It is to heal the sin of their parents, who sympathize and suffer with them"; in a thousand instances this has no place; the parents are not the better, nor any-way likely to be the better, for all the sufferings of their children. Their sufferings, therefore, yea, and those of all mankind, which are entailed upon them by the sin of Adam, are not the result of mere mercy, but of justice also. In other words, they have in them the nature of punishments, even on us and on our children. Therefore, children themselves are not innocent before God. They suffer; therefore, they deserve to suffer."

To say that infants, or anyone for that matter, deserve to suffer is very unChristlike in my opinion. God made infants and provided crying as their way of communicating with us. This is *not* sinful. John Wesley was also heard saying that children are also innocent. "Take, for example, his observation at the home of an English gentleman and his family in Holland: 'Here were four such children (I suppose seven, six, five, and three years old) as I never saw before in one family: Such inexpressible beauty and innocence shone together'" (Heitzenrater, 2001, p. 294). I wonder if John based this observation either on their outward appearances and/or their behaviors. If the children would have been behaving as typical children, would he have commented on their beauty and innocence?

Overall, from what I have read from and about John Wesley, the impression I get is that he mostly believed that children were evil from birth. As I've pointed out, he believed that children were capable of having a religious life, but that it required that they be strictly educated and harshly punished.

> As it has introduced a new state of things, and so fully informed us of the nature of man, and the end of his creation; as it has fixed all our goods and evils, taught us the means of purifying our souls, of pleasing God, and being happy eternally; one might naturally suppose that every Christian country abounded with schools, not only for teaching a few questions and answers of a catechism, but for the forming, training, and practicing children in such a course of life as the sublimest doctrines of Christianity require.
>
> (Wesley, 1783, http://new.gbgm-umc.org/umhistory/ wesley/sermons/95/)

I wonder what he meant by "sublimest doctrines of Christianity require" because while we are required to teach our children God's Word from a very young age (Deuteronomy 6:6-8), we are not required to be harsh with them. In fact, we are required to teach in a loving, kind manner (Colossians 3:16).

Since John Wesley believed that infants were sinful from birth, he felt that infant baptism was an absolute must in order to wash their sins away and save their souls from hell if they should die.

> Infants are in a state of original sin and they cannot be saved ordinarily unless this is washed away by baptism. They are included in the co-venant with God and capable of solemn consecration to him. This consecration can only be made by baptism. They have the right to come to Christ, to be ingrafted into him and ought to be brought to him for that purpose. Baptism regenerates, justifies and gives the infant all the privileges of the Christian religion.
>
> (Towns, 1970, p. 322)

While many Christians do believe in infant baptism, the Bible seems very clear that baptism is for people who have accepted Christ into their hearts, receiving the gift of salvation offered by Christ. Baptism symbolizes the person's death to sin and his/her rising with Christ as a new person in Christ. "We were therefore buried with him through baptism into death in order that, just as Christ was raised from the dead through the glory of the Father, we too may live a new life" (Romans 6:4). (See also Colossians 2:12 and 1 Peter 3:21). Infant baptism does absolutely nothing as far as salvation is concerned. And I have repeatedly said in chapters 1, 2, and 3 of this book, infants and young children go to heaven if they die since they are not capable of purposely rejecting Christ. They know Him and easily believe in Him. Just as infant baptism does nothing to save children, neither does spanking and controlling them do anything to save them. From all of the research I've pointed out in this book, and from what we know about John Wesley's life, I think it is safe to say that spanking children puts them at a higher risk for rejecting Christ as they are not receiving an accurate portrayal of Christ's love and grace for them.

Conclusion

Jonathan Wesley did much good for the kingdom of God. Many poor children were able to be educated because of him. He also helped a great deal of people come to know Christ as their Savior. However, among all of the truly good things that he did throughout his life, I think it is wise to ask: how much harm did he also do? After all, he did not seem to rely on God's Word for his beliefs on how children should be treated and educated. For this reason, I believe that John Wesley should not be used as a role model for Christians and Christian education. While none of us is perfect, we must remember that the pedestal on which he is often placed among Christians is cracked. Children should be taught through love, gentle firmness, concrete experiences, and much grace. "What do you prefer? Shall I come to you with a rod of discipline, or shall I come in love and with a *gentle spirit?*" (1 Corinthians 4:21)

"Rather, it should be that of your inner self, the unfading beauty of a *gentle* and quiet *spirit*, which is of great worth in God's sight" (1 Peter 3:4).

References

Eayrs, G. (ed.) (1915). *Letters of John Wesley*. London, England: Hodder and Stoughton.

Towns, E. (1970). John Wesley and Religious Education. *Articles*. http://digitalcommons.liberty.edu/towns_articles/16.

Wesley, J. (1783). *Sermon 95. On the Education of Young Children*. http://new.gbgm-umc.org/umhistory/wesley/sermons/95/.

Chapter 8

Calvinism and the Further Belief
that Children are "Little Sinners"
Doomed to Hell

I would like to begin this chapter by discussing some of John Calvin's beliefs in regards to children as many of the people that we have discussed in this part of the book have been highly influenced by his beliefs. After I discuss John Calvin, we will look at Jonathan Edwards as he still influences some Christian advocates of spanking children. It is my hope that you are discovering that spanking is from man, not from God as we go through this historic journey together.

John Calvin

John Calvin (1509-1564) was one of the primary figures in the Protestant Reformation. He became a born again Christian in 1533. He then became a Protestant pastor in Geneva, Switzerland, and created the Geneva Academy after returning from exile in 1542. "Calvin's major institutional contribution to education was his Geneva Academy, which he established upon his return from exile. The academy was divided into two schools.

The private school taught children until about age sixteen, and the public school served as the university" (Reed & Provost, 1993, p. 197). Calvin believed in the strict religious education of children, and the Geneva church controlled the academy. The teachers employed by the church were well versed in Calvin's strict disciplinarian approach that often included physical punishment. The following poem shows exactly how John Calvin felt regarding the use of physical punishment with children:

> Who spares the rod with spirit mild,
> He surely hates and harms his child.
> Stripes and fear are right;
> But who disowns their might,
> And trains his son in tender way,
> Unfits him for life's earnest fray.

> (Reed & Provost, 1993, p. 198)

It seems to me from this poem that Calvin had no understanding of lovingly admonishing children, nor adults, as Colossians 3:16 instructs us. Nor did he seem to fully understand Christ's teaching of forgiveness (Luke 3:3; Luke 24:47). And I must wonder if he knew that gentleness and patience are some of the fruits of the Spirit (Galatians 5:22-23). These perceived misconceptions may have been due, in part, to the available Bible translations of the day. The King James Bible did not appear until 1611, and while more accurate, in many biblical scholars' opinions, versions of the Bible have come out since the King James Version, the King James Version was the first authorized Bible to be printed in English.

Before I get too deeply into Calvin's beliefs about children, I would like to take a look into how society in general viewed children and childhood during the sixteenth century. While most parents loved their children, children were not highly valued during this time period. Parents were unemotional about children as the group took precedence over the individual and therefore children were ignored. Most upperclass parents as well as many of those lower down the social scale, for instance, fostered out their infants, and parents in general were unmoved at the death of infants. Between 1540 and 1660, however, increasing interest was shown in childhood as a state, resulting in "a greater concern for the moral and academic training of children" (Pollock, 1983, p. 6). Pollock (1983) also states that "fifteenth- and sixteenth-century England ("The child as beginning and end," 1976) that children were seen as untrustworthy and as being at the "bottom of the social scale." In fact, "childhood was a state to be endured rather than enjoyed." ...Parents were ambivalent toward their offspring: they were unsure whether to regard them as good or evil and also when to include them in adult society or to exclude them from it" (p. 5).

As I have pointed out, people just did not have the knowledge or understanding of children that we are so blessed to have today. The fact that all of the research and child development knowledge that we have today was gained over the last fifty to one hundred years leads me to believe that children and childhood have not been valued throughout the ages. People have been having children for, perhaps, millions of years on this Earth, and it has taken us this long to really begin to study children in order to see that much more is occurring during childhood than any other time period in the human lifespan. Of course, God has known all of this since the beginning of time as He created us. God did try to tell people this as throughout Scripture we see God speak tenderly and compassionately about His people through images of children and parents. "As a mother comforts her child, so will I comfort you; and you will be comforted over Jerusalem" (Isaiah 66:13). (See also Isaiah 66:11; Isaiah 49:15; Deuteronomy 1:39; Hosea 11:3). And of course, throughout the Gospels of Matthew, Mark, and Luke, Jesus commands the disciples to allow the little children to come to Him. He also holds children up as models for adults and gives a stern warning to anyone who causes them to sin. (See chapter 4 for more information). Even in the rod verses of Proverbs, which so many Christians highly misinterpret, God has tried to tell people that children need to be led with authority, not by being hit. I wonder why it has been so difficult for people to see what God has pointed out throughout the Bible. Obviously, sin and satan have much to do with it.

Coming back to Calvin's beliefs about children, he believed in the total depravity of children and in divine predestination. From my understanding, predestination means that God has predestined some people to go to hell and some people to heaven despite the fact that we are all equal sinners. John Calvin took predestination all the way to infants saying that some infants are destined to hell and some to heaven if they die as infants. Reed and Provost (1993), page 198, state:

> Perhaps the doctrine that was most characteristically associated with Calvin is predestination. He believed that God destined some for eternal life and others for eternal damnation. The nature and reward of the afterlife depended on divine predestination.

Now, Romans 8:28-30 states:

> And we know that in all things God works for the good of those who love him, who have been called according to his purpose. For those God foreknew he also predestined to be conformed to the image of his Son, that he might be the firstborn among many brothers and sisters. And those he predestined, he also called; those he called, he also justified; those he justified, he also glorified.

At first glance, this appears to be supporting Calvin's beliefs, but let's look at Ephesians 1:3-14, which states:

> Praise be to the God and Father of our Lord Jesus Christ, who has blessed us in the heavenly realms with every spiritual blessing in Christ. For he chose us in him before the creation of the world to be holy and blameless in his sight. In love he predestined us for adoption to sonship through Jesus Christ, in accordance with his pleasure and will—to the praise of his glorious grace, which he has freely given us in the One he loves. In him we have redemption through his blood, the forgiveness of sins, in accordance with the riches of God's grace that he lavished on us. With all wisdom and understanding, he made known to us the mystery of his will according to his good pleasure, which he purposed in Christ, to be put into effect when the times reach their fulfillment—to bring unity to all things in heaven and on earth under Christ. In him we were also chosen, having been predestined according to the plan of him who works out everything in conformity with the purpose of his will, in order that we, who were the first to put our hope in Christ, might be for the praise of his glory. And you also were included in Christ when you heard the message of truth, the gospel of your salvation. When you believed, you were marked in him with a seal, the promised Holy Spirit, who is a deposit guaranteeing our inheritance until the redemption of those who are God's possession— to the praise of his glory.

These two passages are not saying that God predestined some to be saved and others to damnation as Calvin seemed to believe. What these passages *are* saying is that before God sent Christ to die for *all* sins once and for all, people had to be Jewish and follow the Law of Moses that God prescribed for His people "to a T." If one was not Jewish, there was little hope of that person being saved—unless, of course, they somehow cried out to God and God chose to save them. But His love and compassion shine through when we read these two passages and see that when God sent His only Son, Jesus Christ, down to Earth to pay for all sins, that God knew that this would allow *all* people the ability to receive salvation through Christ's forgiveness. Therefore, God predestined *all* people the ability to become saved through Jesus instead of one group of people—the Jews (who are still God's chosen people even though they now need to receive Christ in order to be saved)—who followed the Law of Moses. Also, 2 Peter 3:9 states, "The Lord is not slow in keeping his promise, as some understand slowness. Instead he is patient with you, not wanting anyone to perish, but everyone to come to repentance." What's more is what Jesus Himself says regarding the "little ones" in Matthew 18:14 where Jesus had been speaking of children just before He says, "In the same way your Father in heaven is not willing that any of these little ones should perish." God does not randomly pick and choose who will and will not be saved as Calvin seemed to indicate in his teachings. Otherwise, why did Jesus descend to hell before His resurrection and ascension into heaven to bring those who had perished due to not having a way to salvation into heaven (Ephesians 4:9-10)?

Another example of Calvin's beliefs of divine predestination are his comments regarding Genesis 25 where Jacob put on fur in order to trick Isaac into giving him Esau's blessing.

> The third context in which Calvin considers the absolute power of God is provided by the doctrine of predestination. Calvin illustrates this problem with Jacob and Esau as told in Genesis 25 and retold in Romans 9. In the commentary on Genesis, Calvin attacks the idea that Jacob's election was based on foreseen merit or Esau's rejection on foreseen demerit. Calvin repeats the Augustinian argument that since all are unworthy to be saved, election is wholly gratuitous. There is no cause outside the will of God for the election of Jacob and that will, which can never be called to account, is itself "the cause of causes."
>
> And yet Paul does not, by this reasoning, impute tyranny to God, as the sophists trifling allege in speaking

of his absolute power. But whereas dwells in inaccessible light, and his judgments are deeper than the lowest abyss, Paul prudently enjoins acquiescence in God's sole purpose; lest, if men seek to be too inquisitive, this immense chaos should absorb all their senses. (Steinmetz, 1995, p. 199)

I must question what Calvin meant by the fact that Jacob's election was not based on foreseen merit because look how God answers Rebekah when she asks Him about the babies in her womb:

> The babies jostled each other within her, and she said, "Why is this happening to me?" So she went to inquire of the LORD.
> The LORD said to her, "Two nations are in your womb, and two peoples from within you will be separated; one people will be stronger than the other, and the older will serve the younger."
>
> Genesis 25:22-23

While Calvin is correct that God elected Jacob before Jacob could do anything good or bad, God knew that Jacob was going to be major in His ultimate plan for salvation for everyone as Jacob is in Jesus's lineage. God knows who each and every one of us will be. He uses people to do His will. So to say that God does not care about his people by randomly or arbitrarily predestining some to heaven and some to hell is incorrect. God chooses the people that will best carry out His holy and perfect will while not wanting anyone to perish and allowing us free will to choose or reject Him.

Also, this example of God choosing Jacob instead of Esau shows that God has the right to change the rules. The oldest son was always the one who had the birthright. God knew this, but He knew that it was the younger son who would carry out His plan. God often chooses people that most people would not even consider to do His will. As someone with severe cerebral palsy, most people would not think of me as being able to do much good for God's kingdom, and yet, He has chosen me to write this book in order to gain more for His kingdom. I am humbled and grateful to God for choosing me for this particular job.

Calvin believed that infants were not innocent and could have a conversion experience if God chose to save them.

> ...Calvin's insistence on the sinfulness of infants cannot be attributed to his understanding of election, nor can it be considered unique to him or unusually harsh in the premodern era. Even theologians such as Thomas Aquinas (who held that God predestines some people to salvation but actively reprobates no one) understood that newborns were not innocent and without God's predestination would not be saved.
>
> (Pitkin, 2001, p. 168)

Infants and young children do not intently set out to disobey their parents, and, therefore, disobey God. Everything young children do is exploration and testing limits based on where they are in their development. As I pointed out in chapter 4, children cannot control their sinfulness. They cannot call on Jesus when they are being tempted as adults can. Also, the part of the brain that controls our impulses does not fully develop until we are twenty-five years old. God created us, so He is well aware of our abilities and inabilities at each period of our life stages. Look what He says about children in Deuteronomy 1:39:

> "And the little ones that you said would be taken captive, your *children* who do not yet know good from bad—they will enter the land. I will give it to them and they will take possession of it."

God has told us much about children throughout Scripture. We just need to be willing to dig deep into Scripture and open our hearts to the Holy Spirit and God will reveal all we need to know about our children and how to guide them with gentle firmness in order to point their hearts toward Jesus Christ. God is a fair and just God. He knows exactly when each person is going to die. If an infant or young child dies before they can purposely sin against Him and reject Him, He will not punish that child by sending him/her to hell for eternity. He loves children.

If Calvin believed that God predestines some infants and children to heaven and others to hell, then why would he advocate for physical punishment and strict religious education for children in order to "save" them? Of course, he didn't know who'd be saved or not. But if we have no control over salvation as Calvin seemed to believe, then why did Jesus command us to:

> Therefore go and make disciples of all nations, baptizing them in the name of the Father and of the Son and of the Holy Spirit, and teaching them to obey everything I have commanded you. And surely I am with you always, to the very end of the age.
>
> Matthew 28:19-20

The theology of predestination seems to blow a hole into John Calvin's assertions, and, as we are about to see, Jonathan Edwards's regarding how children are to be treated. John Calvin did much good by being a major influence in the Protestant Reformation and other social reformations.

> However, to keep these accomplishments in perspective, the following quote depicts the kind of action that generally follows when church and state unite too tightly: "He united Church and State to such an extent that moral offenses were punishable by the State. During

the first twenty-two years of his rule, fifty-eight people were executed, fourteen witches were burned to death, hundreds were exiled and hundreds more were punished annually for moral offenses. All places of popular pleasure were closed. Dress regulations were severe. Prisoners were tortured to exact confessions of moral offenses"

(Reed & Provost, 1993, p. 199)

Is this someone we want to follow in how we treat children? I think not. Unfortunately, as we've seen throughout this part of the book, many of the people that are currently Christian advocates of spanking hold up as models for Christian parents people who were greatly influenced by John Calvin. Jonathan Edwards was one of them.

Jonathan Edwards

Jonathan Edwards (1703-1758) was the pastor of the Congregational Church in Northampton, Massachusetts, after his grandfather passed away. Edwards is well known for the major movement of revivals called The Great Awakening.

Environmental conditions, low moral actions, and religious practices substantially contributed to the period of revivals, especially from 1720 to 1750. The Great Awakening resulted in the founding of denominational colleges including Princeton, Brown, and Dartmouth.

(Reed & Provost, 1993, p. 303-304)

He wrote many books as well as the well-known sermon called "Sinners in the Hands of an Angry God." He was the president of Princeton University for a very brief period of time before dying due to a smallpox vaccination in 1758. He was a Puritan and was highly influenced by Calvin as were most Puritans during the eighteenth century. (See chapters 5 and 6 for more information regarding this and how the Puritans in general viewed children during the eighteenth century).

> ...It would be a serious error of historical judgment to equate Puritanism with Calvinism. Calvinism was a more pervasive religious and intellectual movement than Puritanism, though Puritanism can be regarded as a special type of Calvinism.
>
> (Steinmete, 1995, p. 5)

Like Calvin, Edwards believed in divine predestination and that some infants and young children would go to hell. He also believed that very young children, including infants, were capable of having conversion experiences if God chose to save them. Brekus, (2001) page 301, in her article about Edwards, states:

> He sternly insisted that "infants are not looked upon by God as sinless, but... are by nature children of wrath." Quoting from the Psalms, he preached, "The wicked are estranged from the womb: They go astray as soon as they be born, speaking lies." Yet on the other hand, Edwards also insisted that an all-powerful, sovereign God could transform even the youngest child into a paragon of Christian virtue.

Berkus (2001), page 301, goes on to explain that:

> To be sure, his hellfire sermons, his belief in the doctrine of infant damnation, and his staunch defense of the patriarchal family made him more conservative than almost all of the other theologians profiled in this book, including Augustine and Calvin. He frequently threatened children with eternal torments in hell if they failed to convert.

Young children do not set out to hit, kick, bite, or throw a temper tantrum. It just happens because they have not learned how to appropriately express how they are feeling, and, as I've mentioned before, young children cannot control their impulses very well without a great deal of guidance and support from adults. Everything an infant or a young child does is purely in exploration.

> Another thing to consider is that toddler defiance is not necessarily a bad thing. It is often a way for children to express their feelings, to assert their budding self-awareness, and to experiment with taking initiative and taking charge. These are all important developmental achievements (Dix et al., 2007). On the other hand, defiance that is aggressive or violent is typically a sign of an emerging vicious cycle implication of parental coercion and aggression (Brook et al., 2001; Calkins, 2002).
>
> (Fogel, 2011, p. 260-261)

Also, a young child who is dealing with anxiety issues may exhibit the anxiety in the form of behavioral problems. Lieberman (1995) states, "Sometimes their anxiety emerges in the form of anger and aggression: hitting, biting, and kicking" (p. 93). I wonder if this is why Jesus warns us about causing children to stumble or sin in Matthew 18:6-9 because when we hit them and treat them harshly, it causes them to feel anger and anxiety, which causes them to act out more in order to express their emotional state. Therefore, it is clear that God does not send them to hell for things they are incapable of or do *not* do with a malicious intent.

As soon as Edwards took over as pastor at the church, he began directing most of his sermons to the children and youth of the church because he believed that they were more malleable and teachable than the adults. While Edwards did talk about heaven, he seemed to focus on hell and condemnation in order to scare both children and adults into conversion. For example, in his well-known sermon, "Sinners in the Hands of an Angry God," pages 98 through 99, Edwards (1741 [1970]) states:

> God has fixed between him and mankind, is gone out against them; and stands against them; so that they are bound over already to hell: John iii. 18, "He that believeth not is condemned already." So that every unconverted man properly belongs to hell; that is his place; from thence he is: John viii. 23, "Ye are from beneath:" and thither he is bound; it is the place that justice, and God's word, and the sentence of his unchangeable law, assign to him.

Yes, as sinners we are destined and deserve to go to hell. And yes, if, when we are capable, choose to reject Christ as our personal Savior, we will go to hell when we die. However, look at what John 3:17-18 says:

> For God did not send his Son into the world to condemn the world, but to save the world through him. Whoever believes in him is not condemned, but whoever does not believe stands condemned already because they have not believed in the name of God's one and only Son.

In the quote above, Edwards chooses to focus on the negative part of John 3:18 in his sermon instead of showing that God chose to send His Son to *save the world and not to condemn it.* I remember when I was a young Christian trying to evangelize to people, I would tell them that they were sinners and would go to hell. I memorized all the famous verses in Romans such as 3:23, 6:23, and 5:8 and spit them out as I tried to lead family and friends to Christ. I was not able to help God win anyone's hearts over to Christ using this approach. What God taught me was that it is much easier to win people's hearts to Him by living in a way that glorifies God, talking about what God's doing in my life, and, most importantly, sharing God's love. That's how I helped my husband open his heart to Christ during our first year of dating. One night, after we'd had many talks about God and he had gone to church with me quite a few times, he was home alone watching a Christian television program and felt Christ's love come over him and prayed to receive Christ as his Savior. My point is that while we need to gently tell people the consequences of rejecting Christ's gift of salvation, it is *much* more effective to share His love, grace, and mercy with non-believers. This includes our children as well. I asked Christ into my heart not because of fear but because I felt His love, and I felt a hunger to be a part of something bigger than myself.

Edwards seemed to understand that children had different needs than adults. He even saw that children went through different stages of development throughout childhood, which was quite unusual for Puritans, as they treated children like miniature adults.

> Following in the footsteps of earlier Christian theologians, he recognized three distinct stages of children's development: infancy (from birth to the age of six or seven), childhood (from seven to between fourteen and sixteen), and youth (from sixteen to twenty-five). For example, in a letter to Thomas Prince, Edwards explained that he had held special religious meetings for "children" who were "under the age of sixteen" as well as for "young people" between the ages of sixteen and twenty-six. Anticipating the arguments of Jean Piaget and other twentieth-century psychologists, he and other Puritans assumed that children reached a crucial turning point around the age of seven in terms of their ability to "reason" and grasp abstract concepts.
>
> (Brekus, 2001, p. 302)

It is true that seven-year-olds are able to reason more and begin to understand some abstract concepts such as conservation (where there are two glasses filled with the same amount of water but one is taller than the other; a seven-year-old knows that just because the taller glass looks like it has more water in it than the shorter glass that they both have the same amount of water in them after watching the same amount of water being poured into them) as they are in Piaget's Concrete Stage of his Stages of Cognitive Development; they go from concrete thinking to more symbolic thinking. They are able to understand that "five crayons" is the same as the symbolic number "5." Yet, they still do not fully grasp abstract concepts. This occurs in Piaget's Formal Operations Stage of Cognitive Development. In the Formal Operations Stage, children no longer need to visualize abstract concepts in order to try and understand them; they can now do everything mentally. Because of Edwards's beliefs about children's different stages of development, he tailored his sermons to each age group and spoke to them in a way that the children could understand. However, he felt that children needed to be introduced to the terrors of hell at a very early age. In the book called *Jonathan Edwards on Heaven and Hell*, pages 62 through 63, John Gerstner (1980) states:

> The fact that hell has its degrees is part of the reason for Edwards's pathetic pleading with children not to start sinning early but to be converted and use their days in the joyous service of their God. If the best doctrine to present to sinners is hell, the best time is childhood. The number of special meetings for children that Edwards held, as well as the diligent attention he gave to the salvation of his own family, shows his persuasion of this point. His approach to children was basically the same as the approach to their parents. They too were in danger of judgment and must learn to flee from the wrath that is to come upon them as well as upon older sinners. They were "young serpents" who had not yet learned to bite, but were full of poison.

Using this doctrine of belief, Edwards would begin by describing heaven to the children with Jesus waiting for them. But then, he would drastically change his tone of voice and vividly describe hell to these children. He would tell them that at any moment they might die and God would send them to hell. Edwards (1741 [1980]), in a private meeting of children, stated, "'Supposing children you could now hear the cries of other wicked children that are gone to hell—Come therefore hearken to me—If you won't hearken but will go to hell...'" (p. 63). "(the sermon outline on Psalm 34:11 abruptly ends here)" (Gerstner, 1980, p. 63). He even went so far as to say that their parents would rejoice as they watched God send their children to hell.

> Stirring up even deeper fears, Edwards insisted that unless they were "born again," their parents would stop loving them. On Judgment Day, as Christ sentence them to eternal punishment in hell, their parents would not "be grieved," but would "praise God for his justice." The same parents who had once tenderly embraced them, soothed their cries, and bandaged their cuts would rejoice to see them in torment.
>
> (Brekus, 2001, p. 316-317)

Can you imagine the psychological impact all of this had on these children, not to mention the confusing view of God Edwards painted on their hearts and minds?

Here is one well-documented story of how one four-year-old girl named Phebe Bartlet was affected by Edwards's fear-inducing sermons. Jonathan Edwards had been called to Phebe's house by her parents.

> According to her parents, who earnestly sought his spiritual counsel, Phebe had undergone a remarkable religious change. Influenced by her eleven-year-old brother, who

recently had been "born again" during a conversion experience, Phebe had begun to disappear into her "closet" to
pray and weep for salvation. "I pray, beg, pardon all my
sins," she was heard crying loudly to God. As her parents
confessed to Edwards, they had assumed that such a young
child was "not capable of understanding" Christianity,
but they had been deeply affected by her anxious prayers
and sobs for mercy. One afternoon, despite her mother's
attempts to soothe her, Phebe "continued exceedingly crying, wreathing her body to and fro, like one in anguish of
spirit," until she finally managed to put her fears into words.
"I am afraid I shall go to hell!" she wept. After another
bout of crying, however, she suddenly fell quiet. Turning
to her mother with a smile, she proclaimed, "Mother, the
kingdom of heaven is come to me!" In the hours and days
afterward, Phebe seemed to have become a "new creature":
she carefully recited her catechism, wept at the thought
that her unconverted sisters might "go to hell," and, like
Augustine, repented for stealing some fruit—a handful of
plums—from a neighbor's tree.

(Brekus, 2001, p. 300)

Now, some people may read this story and ask, "What's so
bad about it?" They might think it was wonderful that a four-
year-old child received Christ at such a young age. If indeed
she did actually receive Christ, and it is great anytime a child
purposefully accepts Christ into their hearts, I must question as
her parents did whether she truly understood exactly what was
happening to her. When we ask Christ for forgiveness and for
Him to come into our hearts, He does so *immediately*. I was given
the wrong impression as a fifteen-year-old that God could save
me at any time. I took that to mean that if I kept asking Him
and read the Bible, He would choose to save me. Since I didn't
feel anything spectacular happen when I prayed for my salvation,
I assumed that it hadn't worked. So I prayed several more times

until one day a friend of mine's mom asked me if I was saved or not. I told her that I didn't know for sure, but that I had been praying for Him to save me. My friend's mom laughed and told me that I was indeed saved. It was a huge relief to know that I was saved and no longer had to wait for God to decide to save me. Therefore, the fact that Phebe kept begging God to forgive her makes me believe that she really did not understand what was happening. All she knew was she was absolutely terrified of being sent to hell and wanted God to love and rescue her. Finally, God must have made His love for her very apparent to her in a way that she could truly understand. Children as young as Phebe are not capable of purposely rejecting Christ because they truly believe us when we tell them about God. As I pointed out in chapter 4, children have a unique knowledge of God as we have seen in Matthew 21:14-16 and Luke 10:21. A conversion experience should *never* be traumatic as it was for Phebe. Children should be made to want to receive Christ because of the unfailing love He has for them, not out of sheer terror! To make a child believe that God wants to punish them or wants their parents to spank them is wrong and is considered spiritual abuse.

While it is true that there were some revivals among the children and youth that Edwards taught, and that some of the children did find these meetings helpful by allowing them to express their fears to Edwards, many of the children were highly affected by them in quite negative ways. They had high amounts of fear and anxiety due to Edwards's teachings.

> Rather than using his ideas to expand their religious authority, they struggled with overwhelming feelings of anxiety and despair. Once again, the evidence comes from Edwards, who proudly reported that children broke down in tears while listening to his sermons. During one of his children's meetings, "the room was filled with cries," and afterward, groups of sobbing children "went home

crying aloud through the streets, to all parts of the town."
Apparently Phebe Bartlet, who feared she might "go to
hell," was not alone.

(Brekus, 2001, p. 320)

It is almost as if Jonathan Edwards delighted in terrifying
children and adults. And from reading some of his work, I also
question whether or not he believed that God enjoys sending
people to hell.

Lately, I have been thinking and dealing with some of what
some people perceive as God's wrath, as my area and areas south
of me have been dealing with wave after wave of severe storm and
tornadoes. Due to weeks of almost nonstop waves of heavy rain,
we have also been dealing with record-breaking flooding. God has
spared my husband and me of any damage due to these horrible
storms and flooding, but many people have lost everything. And
sadly, some people have lost their lives. As my husband and I
thought about why God might be allowing all of this to happen,
we are sure that these are signs of Jesus returning to Earth someday
sooner rather than later. But we also wonder if God is trying to
get people's attention by displaying some of His awesome power
to us to get us to stop thinking about ourselves. I also know that
God enjoys having people cry out to Him so He can help and
comfort them. Whatever His reasons, one thing *is* for sure, God
does not delight in wickedness (Psalm 5:4). His throne is built on
righteousness and justice (Psalm 89:14). And even through times
of destruction, we can see His compassion on us by giving us plenty
of warning in His Word that these things will take place and by
allowing the technology to be created in order to warn people of
a storm so that they can get to the safest place possible before the
storm hits. Despite all of the destruction, there have been numerous
stories of survival against all odds. No one can tell me that God
did not also have His hand in those survival stories. Therefore, to

believe in Edwards's theories about God would lead us to fear that God is angry every time something horrible happens. This is not true. We will discuss this in part 3 of this book in more detail.

I discussed God's grace in chapter 3, when He dealt with Adam and Eve's sin, and I would like to make another point regarding that. How many times do parents discover that their children did something wrong and yell, "Come here right NOW! What did you do? I am going to spank your butt so hard for what you did!" And yet God, who knew *all* consequences of their sin that would occur throughout time, gently asked where they were and about what they had done. He dealt with them with gentle firmness. Do you think Adam and Eve are in hell for all the trouble they caused mankind? The Bible doesn't say either way, but if I had to guess, I'd guess no because God loved them and had compassion on them. How much more compassion He has for young children who believe in Him whole-heartedly with no doubt or hesitation whatsoever and who do not set out to commit sin! How sad it must make God that so many Christians twist His Holy Word around to justify terrifying and punishing children, thereby giving children an inaccurate view of God.

Jonathan Edwards may have had the same inaccurate view of God due to his traumatic childhood. He was abused as a child. He also grew up with a lot of violence in his family.

> His grandmother on his father's side, Elizabeth Tuttle, had been so physically violent and mentally unstable that his grandfather had finally convinced the court to grant him a divorce—a rare event in seventeenth-century Massachusetts. Even more troubling, his great-aunt (Elizabeth Tuttle's sister) had murdered her own son. Given the stories he must have heard as a child, it is not surprising that as an adult, he insisted that Christians owed their first allegiance to God, not humankind.
>
> (Brekus, 2001, p. 320)

Edwards married Sarah Pierpont and they had eleven children, including Esther Edwards Burr. It is well documented that his daughter, Esther, began using physical punishment with her infant daughter.

> Esther Edwards Burr, who became the wife of the Reverend Aaron Burr, president of Princeton. In 1754 she reported to her best friend, Sarah Prince: "I had almost forgot to tell you that I have begun to govourn Sally [her firstborn child]. She has been Whip'd once on *Old Adams* account, and she knows the difference between a smile and a frown as well as I do. When she has done any thing that she Suspects is wrong, will look with concern to see what Mama says, and if I only knit my brow she will cry till I smile, and altho She is not quite Ten months old, yet when she knows so much, I think tis time she should be taught."
>
> By starting her physical discipline of her daughter when the child was nine months old, Esther Burr surely was repeating the experiences she had had as a child herself, thus following her mother's practice of resisting "the first, as well as every subsequent exhibition of temper or disobedience in the child, however young."
>
> (Greven, 1992, p. 21)

How sad, but not uncommon, that the cycle of using fear and abuse with very young children continued throughout the Edwards's family. Also, I must point out that infants do begin social referencing at nine months. This means that as they're exploring their environment they will check in with their parents and/or caregivers, especially when they discover something that they are unsure about in order to see if it's okay to go on exploring or not based on the adults' reaction. What we see with Esther Burr's daughter is *not* your typical social referencing episode. The infant was definitely afraid and unsure of what might bring on another round of physical punishment. The very fact that the infant cried at a wrinkled brow shows, *not* that she was being "well trained" as her mother thought, but that she had been absolutely *traumatized* by her mother's physical aggression toward her! This is not what God had in mind when He said, "Fathers, [Parents] do not embitter your children, or they will become discouraged" (Colossians 3:21).

Conclusion

I must wonder why John Calvin and Jonathan Edwards advocated for the physical punishment, strict religious education, and, in the case of Edwards, put a high amount of fear into children's hearts in order to save them if they believed that God predestines some to heaven and some to hell. Doesn't this seem to, logically, blow a huge hole in their theologies? They may have done some good (though, Edwards ended up being dismissed from his pastoral position in 1750 by the congregation), but these should not be people to whom we look for advice on raising godly children.

References

Bunge, M. J. (Ed.). (2001). *The Child in Christian Thought.* Grand Rapids, MI: William B. Eerdmans Publishing Company.

Fogel, A. (2011). *Infant Development: A Topical Approach.* Hudson, NY: Sloan Publishing.

Gerstner, J. (Ed.). (1980). *Jonathan Edwards on Heaven and Hell.* Grand Rapids, MI: Baker Book House.

Greven, P. (1992). *Spare the Child.* New York, NY: Vintage Books.

Lieberman, A. F. (1993). *The Emotional Life of a Toddler.* New York, NY: The Free Press.

Pollock, L. (1983). *Forgotten Children.* Cambridge, England: Cambridge University Press.

Reed, J. E. & Prevost, R. (1993). *A History of Christian Education.* Nashville, TN: Brodman & Holman Publishers.

Simonson, H. P. (Ed.). (1970). *Edwards: Selected Writings of Jonathan Edwards.* New York, NY: Frederick Ungar Publishing Company.

Steinmetz, D. C. (1995). *Calvin in Context.* Oxford, England: Oxford University Press.

Chapter 9

Control, Catholicism, and the "Rules for Spanking"

This chapter will conclude this part of this book in which we have explored and discovered some of the origins of spanking children within Christianity. It was my goal to show that spanking is from man and *not* God, as so many well-meaning Christians have believed throughout the ages. In this chapter, I will reveal how the idea of controlling children dates back to the early church in the ancient world, look at how Catholicism has advocated and used physical punishment with children, show the likely origin of the "Christian rules of how to spank children," and will conclude with explaining behaviorism and how physical punishment falls under that very old and outdated branch of psychology.

The Origins of the Christian Need to Control Children

Many Christian advocates of spanking, as well as the parents who follow these advocates, are often quite concerned with controlling their children's behavior, and, really, one could say controlling their children. Advocates such as James Dobson, the Ezzos, the

Pearls, and others teach parents that they must be in control of their children from birth. They claim that newborn infants must be taught that their parents are the bosses, not them. If this sounds familiar, it is because control and breaking children's wills go hand in hand. We've seen how breaking the child's will has been advocated for and done by Christians throughout history despite there being no biblical grounds for doing such a thing (See chapters 5, 6, and 7 for more information on breaking children's wills). This need for adults to control their children dates back to New Testament times. In fact, certain verses of the New Testament are used to try and justify controlling one's children.

The books of 1 Timothy and Titus are known as the Pastoral Epistles. However, like Ephesians and Colossians, these books have passages about family relations. Unlike Ephesians and Colossians, 1 Timothy and Titus have qualifications that leaders of the church must meet in order to be considered for such leadership positions. In particular, 1 Timothy 3:4-12 and Titus 1:6 say that leaders of the church must manage their family well and "see that his children obey him" (1 Timothy 3:4a). At this point, we must look at a bit of historical context in which all four of these books, written by the Apostle Paul, were written. In the New Testament period, after Jesus ascended into heaven, followers of Christ began gathering in homes in order to worship Jesus and be taught from the Word as the disciples and apostles wrote the letters and books that now comprise the New Testament. Some books and letters were written for certain groups, churches, and people based on the circumstances of the time and geographical locations. The books of Ephesians and Colossians were clearly written to be read aloud to congregations that would meet in homes of certain people to worship:

> ...as we are reminded by Colossians 4:16: "Once this letter has been read among you, see that it is read also to the

church at Laodicea, and that you in turn read my letter to Laodicea." Each group in these ethical lists—husbands, wives, children, and slaves—was addressed because these people were present in the meeting for worship and would hear the letter being read out.

(Strange, 2004, p. 73-74)

The author of Ephesians and Colossians clearly expected every group of people regardless of age and occupation to be present at worship meetings. Therefore, the teachings of these two books for the Christian household address both sides of these relationships. And as I've pointed out throughout part 1 of this book, the verse in Ephesians that prefaces the Christian household teachings is 5:21, which states: "Submit to one another out of reverence for Christ." It is clear that Paul had Christ's radical teachings about everyone being equal and the great being last and the servant being first in the kingdom of heaven (Matthew 19:30; Mark 9:35) when he wrote Ephesians and Colossians because although there is a hierarchical order in each of these relationships, there is also mutuality. Husbands are not to dominate their wives just as parents are not to dominate their children. There's a sense of equal responsibility to each other in each relationship.

In at least some congregations, therefore, children were not merely passive spectators on the edge of what was going on, but were taught and encouraged alongside adults during the course of the church's meeting for worship... Significantly also, Colossians and Ephesians make the responsibilities of parents and children *mutual* (Emphasis added by this author). If children owe their parents the duty of respect, no less do parents their children of consideration. This was quite a radical idea in the culture of the time, where a far more one-way relationship would be the norm.

(Strange, 2004, p. 74)

I would like to point out another great example of Jesus teaching equality when it comes to the kingdom of heaven. Let's look at Matthew 20:1-16. In this parable told by Jesus, a landowner goes out and finds servants that have not been hired. The first servants are hired early in the day and agree to do a full day's work in the fields for a denarii. As the day goes on, the landowner continues to hire servants to work in his fields, each agreeing to work for a denarii. At the end of the day, all of the hired servants come to be paid by the landowner. Every servant received a denarii for his work. When the servants that had worked all day in the field saw that the servants that had only worked for a few hours or less in the field received the same amount of pay as them, they were quite frustrated with the landowner and questioned him about this. Look how the landowner answered the servants:

> But he answered one of them, "I am not being unfair to you, friend. Didn't you agree to work for a denarius? Take your pay and go. I want to give the one who was hired last the same as I gave you. Don't I have the right to do what I want with my own money? Or are you envious because I am generous?"
>
> Matthew 20:13-15

It is clear that Jesus does not favor those who have been following Him longer. Nor is anyone a worse sinner than another. Yes, we will all be judged and receive different rewards based on our own relationship with God, but He views and loves everyone equally. Jesus has called us into a new way of living in which family life is no longer absolute, "but moulded by the demands of the kingdom" (Strange, 2004, p. 75). As we have seen in chapter 4, fathers had unlimited authority during the first century and more than likely in the previous centuries leading up to the first century. Discipline was often heavy-handed with the use of physical punishment (Bunge, 2001; Strange, 2004). But Christ changed all of that when He came. His message was one of peace, mercy, and forgiveness instead of violence.

> Here in Colossians and Ephesians, we see a practical expression of Jesus's vision for the family and the kingdom of God. Here the family is no longer an autocratic institution, but a place for all members to grow together in their common life in Christ. Something similar could be said about the way the relationship of masters and slaves is made mutual in Colossians and Ephesians (Col. 3:22-4.1, Eph. 6:5-9).
>
> (Strange, 2004, p. 75)

Christ values mutuality over dominance.

Sadly, it seems that many Christians do not understand this, as throughout the centuries paternal control over the family is what is often emphasized in most fundamental and even some evangelical churches. I believe the Scriptures in which these churches tend to focus to justify paternal control of the family are 1 Timothy 3:1-15 and Titus 1:6. Since 1 and 2 Timothy and Titus were also written by the Apostle Paul, we might begin to wonder if Paul is contradicting himself because these books have a very different feel when it comes to instructions for the Christian family. The answer to this question is no. Why? Because 1 and 2 Timothy and Titus were written for pastors and other leaders of the church. That is why these books are referred to as the Pastoral Epistles. They were not read aloud to the congregation during worship meetings as were Ephesians and Colossians. These books were also more in line with the cultural norms of the first century, as well as were meant to aid in the management of the church.

> It is often remarked by commentators that the Pastoral Epistles conform to the received ethical opinions and

dominant social expectations of the surrounding culture of the day... Of the two ways of understanding the Christian family, it was that of the Pastoral Epistles which predominated in early Christianity.

(Strange, 2004, p. 77)

Just as the view of how the Christian families were dominant in the ancient world, they still are dominant today.

People, in general, seem to have a superiority complex. It wasn't until the 1960s that we had the Civil Rights Movement, making black and white people equal when it came to the U.S. laws. It wasn't until 1990 that the Americans with Disabilities Act was passed in order to protect people with disabilities from discrimination. And although this country has made great progress in providing people with equal rights, we have a long way to go as racism, discrimination, and ageism are still very much alive in this country and all over the world. Due to our sinful nature, we have a tendency to want to be in control. Therefore, it is understandable that some Christians tend to ignore what Ephesians and Colossians have to say about family life, except for the verses that tell children to obey their parents, and focus on what 1 Timothy and Titus say about how a Christian family should be run. In 1 Timothy and Titus, dominance over the people lower on the hierarchical chain is now emphasized rather than a mutual relationship. Children are left out of the picture except for how leaders of the church are to manage them.

In 1 Timothy 3:4f, we are told that the bishop or overseer must control his children without losing his dignity, and that the way he manages his household is a mark of his ability to manage a congregation. A similar quality is also required in a deacon (1 Tim. 3:12), and, as Titus lays down, in an elder (Tit. 1:6).

(Strange, 2004, p. 75)

While this type of management works well within the church itself, it is quite harmful for individual Christian families, as each member of that family should have a respectful, mutual relationship with each other. I am in no way implying that the husband is not the head of the household, he certainly is (Ephesians 5:23). While the church is God's household as 1 Timothy 3:15 states, it is important to remember that "the letters themselves are in the form of an address to church leaders, rather than to the whole congregation" (Strange, 2004, p. 76). These passages should not be used to justify parental control as some Christians try to do.

> Children's discipleship, which was given its own place in Colossians and Ephesians, was absent from the Pastoral Epistles. Children have become part of their parents' discipleship; they make their appearance only on the margin as objects of control and as problems requiring proper management.
>
> (Strange, 2004, p. 76)

Taken alone, it is quite easy to misuse these passages to justify the need to control children. This is why we must understand the context in which they were written and for whom they were written. However, as I said with the husband being the head of the household, this does not mean parents are not to be over the children. God has given authority to parents to guide and correct their children, but this does not mean the parents have a right to abuse their leadership roles. The children also submit to parental authority when parents submit to their children by giving appropriate care, love, respect, and guidance.

Shepherds must control their herds. Control in this context means to oversee, guard, and steer the flock to abundant food and water. This is exactly what our church leaders, as well as parents, should be doing. Shepherds also protect their flocks from harm.

Jesus does this with us if we allow Him (John 10:1-5). He even laid down His life for us. We must follow His example. Acts 20: 28-30 states: "Keep watch over yourselves and all the flock of which the Holy Spirit has made you overseers. Be shepherds of the church of God, which he bought with his own blood." And most importantly, 1 Timothy 3:2-5 says that while a church leader must manage his family well and see to it that his children obey him, he must also be:

> ...above reproach, faithful to his wife, temperate, self-controlled, respectable, hospitable, able to teach, not given to drunkenness, *not violent but gentle*, not quarrelsome, not a lover of money. He must manage his own family well and see that his children obey him, and he must do so in a manner worthy of *full respect*. (If anyone does not know how to manage his own family, how can he take care of God's church?)

I have bolded two important phrases that some Christians seem to ignore. The leader is to be *gentle* and see that his children obey him in a way that is worthy of *respect*. Somehow I don't think spanking a child or using other forms of harsh punishment meets these particular qualifications.

Over the centuries, people have always seemed to equate respect with fear as if these two words are interchangeable. The Bible often says to fear the Lord (see chapter 2 for more information regarding what fear the Lord actually means). I would like to look at the definitions of fear and respect. Dictionary.com defines fear as "a distressing emotion aroused by impending danger, evil, pain, etc., whether the threat is real or imagined; the feeling or condition of being afraid." The definition of respect according to Dictionary.com is "esteem for or a sense of the worth or excellence of a person, a personal quality or ability, or something considered as a manifestation of a personal quality or ability." And "to hold in esteem or honor." As we can clearly see, fear and respect have absolutely *nothing* to do with each other. What I find even more interesting is that the definition for fear contains the words "evil" and "pain" whereas respect does not. This makes sense because fear is not from God as 2 Timothy 1:7 states, "For the Spirit God gave us does not make us timid, but gives us power, love and self-discipline." It makes me wonder why so many Christians believe that fear and respect are one in the same. People, especially children, that fear someone will often do something not because they want to or respect the person but because they are afraid of the person and want to avoid painful punishment. Sadly, some parents do not care why their children obey them, just as long as they do. Unfortunately, parents who use fear and punishment to make their children obey them are actually teaching their children to be selfish as the child is not thinking about doing something for another person but rather protecting him/herself from punishment. We should *not* be teaching our children to only do things to avoid punishment, as the Bible says, "Do nothing out of selfish ambition or vain conceit. Rather, in humility value others above yourselves" (Philippians 2:3). Craig Hart is the author of the article called, "Three Essential Parenting Principles" that was published in the Spring 2003 issue of *BYU Magazine*. He is quoted in Janet Heimlich's book, *Breaking Their Will*, which states:

> "While coercion often leads to immediate conformance by the child, research indicates it rarely results in a long-term solution and often leads to the child's being more defiant, depressed, aggressive or withdrawn, and manipulative in the home and with peers," writes Hart.
>
> (Heimlich, 2011, p. 86)

While the passages in 1 Timothy and Titus are important for how churches are to be run and provide some guidance on family life issues, they should not be our sole references of how families should be run. Sadly, since ancient times, Christians have had a need to control their children. Christian advocates have taught parents to do this through harsh treatment and punishment of children despite Christ's radical teachings regarding family and children.

> The *Didache*, or *Teaching of the Apostles* (date uncertain, but probably early second century) speaks to parents about the need not to "withold your hand" [in punishment] from your son or daughter, but to bring them up in the fear of the Lord (*Didache* 4.9). Polycarp, Bishop of Smyrna (c. 69-c. 155), wrote to the Philippians with moral instruction, which, like Clement's before him, spoke to the men about how they were to instruct their wives. Among the wife's duties was "to educate the children in the education of the fear of God" (Polycarp, *Philippians* 4.2).
>
> (Strange, 2004, p. 77)

I believe the following passage from Strange (2004), page 82, sums up the cultural and Christian origins of the need to control children and minorities:

> The modern observer is likely to have little sympathy with what can be seen the way in which the second-century church treated its women and children members. The emergence of the patriarchal structure which we see in the writings of the Apostolic Fathers (Clement, Polycarp, Ignatius) may look, from our point of view, like a decline—both from the teaching and example of Jesus and from the insights of Paul about the child's inclusion among God's people.
>
> But before we dismiss the course taken by the church, we should bear two things in mind. The first is that the

church adopted a form of existence which would allow it to work with the grain of the surrounding culture, which, as we saw in chapter one, was markedly patriarchal. This adaptation, which seems to have well under way by the time the Pastoral Epistles were written, was perhaps a necessary evolution for the church to maintain its witness. Further, as a matter of principle, we recall that Jesus' own ministry to children was through their parents. The second century church was therefore developing in a line with the precedent of Jesus's own ministry.

We have been focusing on Fundamentalist Protestant Christians throughout this part on the Christian history of spanking children. However, fundamental Christians are not the only ones to have a long history of control, fear of hell and satan, and the breaking of the will through the use of physical punishment with their children. As we will see in this next section, Roman Catholics also contribute to the dark history of hitting children in the name of God.

Catholicism and Spanking

The Roman Catholic Church has a long history of using physical punishment with children. This should not be surprising considering how violent the first-century Romans were (see chapter 5 for more information). In fact, it wasn't until 1980 that most Catholic schools banned the use of corporal punishment. Unfortunately, some Catholic schools, as well as some public schools, still permit the use of corporal punishment. These schools are primarily in the southern United States. The use of spanking children in schools dates back to colonial times as the Puritans were not the only ones that took Native American children from their families in order to "civilize" them. In fact, there was a Catholic mission boarding school called St. Francis located in South Dakota that had a long history of using harsh physical punishment, as well as other abuses, with the Native American children that were literally torn from their families and forced to attend this school. In an article published in 1990 in *Lakota Woman* called, "Civilize Them with a Stick," one Native American woman describes her family's experiences in St. Francis:

> They used a horse buggy whip on my grandmother then she was put back into the attic—for two weeks.
>
> My mother had much the same experiences but never wanted to talk about them, and then there I was, in the same place. The school is now run by the BIA—- The Bureau of Indian Affairs—but only since about 15 years ago. When I was there, during the 1960s, it was still run by the church. The Jesuit fathers ran the boys wing and the sisters of the Sacred Heart ran us—with the help of the strap. Nothing had changed since my grandmother's days. I've been told recently that even in the 70s they were still beating children at that school. All I got out of school was being taught how to pray. I learned quickly that I would be beaten if I failed in my devotions or, God forbid, prayed the wrong way, especially prayed in Indian to Wakan Tanka, the Indian Creator.
>
> (Dog & Erdoes, 1990, p. 565-566)

Most Christian parents, Catholics included, spank their children for the remissions of sins, meaning that the spanking is to cleanse the child from the sin that they have committed by disobeying their parents. After a child is spanked, the child is supposedly free from the guilt of his/her sin since he/she has paid the penalty for his/her sin and can be forgiven by his/her parents and God. In an article written by Crystal Lutton, author of the book, *Biblical Parenting*, she suggests that one of the origins of the practice of spanking may be with the Catholics. In her article entitled, "The History of Spanking," Crystal Lutton (2011) states:

> There is an interesting history of spanking. From its earliest practice, in Ancient Greece, spankings were administered to adults. It was a pagan practice for increasing fertility in barren women who were spanked by the pagan priests and later was introduced into the Catholic Church as a means of adult women having their sins removed through the spankings of the priest after confession.
>
> (http://aolff.org/spare-the-rod/the-spanking-files-2/history-of-spanking)

While I trust Crystal Lutton's vast knowledge in this area, I personally have no other references that say the same thing, therefore, hesitate to guarantee this as absolute fact. At the same time, I do believe that we must consider this as a possibility. At the very least, this shows how far back spanking goes in the history of Catholicism.

The Catholics have their own version of the Bible in which they tout as "God's Word." The Catholic Bible contains all of the books of the Holy Bible, which Protestants use, but it also contains some other books that are not in the Protestant Holy Bible. One such book is Sirach. Sirach seems to be quite similar to the book of Proverbs and is located in the Old Testament of the Catholic Bible. Like Proverbs, there is a verse in Sirach that seems to strongly advocate for the use of physical punishment with young children. Sirach 30:12 states: "Bow down his neck while he is young, and beat his sides while he is a child, lest he grow stubborn, and regard thee not, and so be a sorrow of heart to thee" (DRA 1899 American Version). The next verse in Sirach seems to indicate that a child should not play but be put to work in order to control his behavior. "Instruct thy son, and labour about him, lest his lewd behaviour be an offence to thee" (DRA 1899 American Version). As an evangelical, Bible-based Christian, I don't know if Catholics take these verses literally or what exactly is meant by them. Given the fact that Catholicism has a long history of using physical punishment with children both at school and in the home, I would guess that the majority of Catholics have taken these verses as well as the rod verses in Proverbs literally. At many of the Catholic schools, children have been hit with rulers. Their hands, heads, and bottoms are some of the locations on which children have been hit with rulers as a form of "discipline" at school.

> Not willing to wait for God or the devil to get us, the Church had its own brand of punishment. Humiliation tactics were a specialty of the Church. Corporal punishment was quite common. Anyone who ever went to a Catholic grammar school can vouch for that. Guilt and anxiety were always favorites of the Nuns. As if the fear of God they laid on you was not enough, the Nuns took matters into their own hands. More than a few children were hoping the devil got to them before the Nuns and their Rosary's did. (Cooney, 2003, http://fspp.net/Articles/crumbling_walls.htm)

How sad that, again, children were turned off to God due to how they were treated. Not only that, children were often hit in these Catholic schools for every little act that was considered an act of defiance as we saw in the Native American woman's description.

> According to Irwin A. Hyman, author of *Reading, Writing, and the Hickory Stick: The Appalling Story of Physical and Psychological Abuse in America's Schools*, Catholic schools have a long history of using physical punishment for just about every perceived act of defiance on the part of students. Speaking about disciplinary methods that were widespread decades ago, Hyman notes, "No restraint was considered prudent in the vigorous application of the yardstick on open hands, across knuckles, and to derrieres in an effort to save the souls of errant youth."
>
> (Heimlich, 2011, p. 89)

And while corporal punishment, as I mentioned previously, has been banned in most Catholic schools, children attending the more conservative Catholic schools in the South are at a higher risk of being spanked while in school.

Much like fundamental Christians, Catholics have often feared hell and the devil when it comes to one of the reasons they spank their children. They have often believed that they could "beat the devil" out of their children. As we have seen throughout this part of the book, fear of hell and satan is a common thread among Christian prospankers.

> For a very long time, Christians have associated demons and the devil with sinfulness. In the late 1500s, each of the seven deadly sins was paired with a demon. Many Christians speak of sin as what separates believers from God—a separation that makes a person vulnerable to being possessed by satan or demons. Therefore, some Christians believe that when a child misbehaves—thereby exposing his or her sinfulness—a proper remedy is to drive out the evil forces that might have taken over the child's soul.
>
> (Heimlich, 2011, p. 103)

In case anyone is wondering what exactly are the seven deadly sins, they are: wrath, greed, sloth, pride, lust, envy, and gluttony. It seems that the Catholic Church divides these sins into two categories: venial and mortal sins. Sacraments are often used to restore the relationship between a Catholic who has committed one of these sins, especially if he/she committed one in the mortal sins category, and God. Otherwise, a Catholic may face eternal damnation according to the Catholic Church. The Protestant Holy Bible mentions seven things that God hates and detests in Proverbs 6:16-19. And interestingly, the opposite of the fruits of the Spirit described in Galatians 5:19-21 seem to highly correspond with these seven deadly sins.

The fear of satan is exactly what drove Matt's mother to use physical punishment with him when he was a child. Janet Heimlich interviewed sixty-year-old Matt in her book, *Breaking Their Will*. His story is a perfect example of how Christian parents can allow fear from satan dictate how they raise and treat their children:

> She would take me into the utility room, her domain, and pull this big belt off of the wall which she had hung in the closet. I think it was my uncle's Marine belt—one of those big wide leather belts with the big brass buckle on it—and she'd whale on me, on my bottom and the backs of my thighs. Every once in a while she would ask me to pull down my pants and do it on my bare skin. I do remember a couple of times that she was hitting me so hard and flailing so hard that she lost control of the belt, and the buckle hit me a couple of times and made these gashes in my skin. Generally, I'd start crying and yelling, and then she'd say "Okay, go to your room." And I'd go to my room, and not only would I close the door to my room, but I'd go in my closet, and I'd close the door to my closet so I had double protection. And then I would cry, and say things like, "Nobody loves me," and "I hate my mom."
>
> Matt's mother likely had a problem controlling her anger, yet there was another force at play: her religious beliefs. The woman was a devout Catholic and was petrified of the devil.
>
> (Heimlich, 2011, p. 75)

Sadly, many Christian parents who are trying so hard to save their children from the devil by using physical punishment with them don't realize that they are playing right into satan's hands. satan knows our weaknesses. He also knows that children believe in God at birth and, therefore, wants to do everything he can to destroy their natural faith in God by having their parents teach a wrong and distorted view of who God truly is through hitting the children in His name. We must remember that satan is the father of lies (John 8:44) and that the "devil prowls around like a roaring lion looking for someone to devour" (1 Peter 5:8).

This leads me to a well-known ritual practiced primarily by Catholics but is also practiced by some Protestant groups called exorcism. "What is *exorcism*? Dictionary.com defines it as 'to seek to expel (an evil spirit) by adjuration or religious or solemn ceremonies'" (Heimlich, 2011, p. 269). When we think of exorcism, we usually think of Jesus commanding an evil spirit or demon to come out of a person as well as a Catholic priest doing the same thing. We also think of the movie, *The Exorcist*. We usually don't think of anything physical being done to the person with the evil spirit except for maybe being restrained so the demon doesn't throw the person around and/or the laying of hands on the person in order to bless them. I never thought beatings could be a part of an exorcism. I also didn't know exactly how many children have undergone exorcisms until I began researching physical punishment in the Roman Catholic Church. Sadly, physical punishment seems to be done during exorcisms in which a child is involved because, as I have been pointing out all throughout this part of the book, many prospankers truly believe that spanking and beating children can purify their souls. "For this matter, repeated corporal punishment designed to 'beat the devil' out of children...can constitute a form of ritual abuse" (Heimlich, 2011, p. 269).

Many children have had an exorcism done to them for any number of reasons, including typical developmentally appropriate behaviors, challenging behavioral problems, certain physical conditions or disabilities such as epilepsy, mental or emotional problems or conditions, and even sleepwalking. Of course, children with special needs and behavioral problems are at a much greater risk for both physical punishment and exorcism.

> We should also be concerned that children with special
> needs or behavioral or psychological problems are not
> getting help because they are mistakenly viewed as being
> possessed by demons. In these cases, children may be
> denied access to specialists and undergo exorcisms.
>
> (Heimlich, 2011, p. 275)

Unfortunately, being beaten during an exorcism not only causes physical and psychological harm to children, but in some cases it has caused death.

> On April 14, 2008, authorities said that twenty-five-year-
> old Nelly Vasquez-Salazar of Waukegan, Illinois, confessed
> to brutally slashing to death her 6-year-old daughter,
> Evelyn Vasquez, because she believed that the child was
> possessed by the devil. The child reportedly had been
> stabbed eleven times. What apparently led the mother to
> suspect demons was her daughter's habit of sleepwalking.
> According to police, Vasquez-Salazar told her mother that
> she would wake up and find Evelyn standing by her bed.
> Her mother then reportedly told her that the child was
> possessed.
>
> (Heimlich, 2011, p. 268)

Now before we shrug this off as one of the more extreme cases, another example of a child dying from an exorcism is Terrance Cottrell. Terrance had autism and had undergone many exorcisms in order to rid him of the supposed evil spirit causing his autism. Autism causes children to usually not want to be touched or to make eye contact with another person. Therefore, we can imagine how upset Terrance would get during exorcisms with people touching him, surrounding him, chanting, and praying. During his final exorcism, the pastor sat on Terrance's chest in order to restrain him, "which led to his being suffocated by the pastor" (Heimlich, 2011, p. 275). It is important to note that these parents who physically punish and have their children go through exorcisms, for the most part, truly believe that what they are doing is truly right and good. As I've said throughout this book, parents want to obey God in order to raise godly children. It's just too bad that "experts and authorities" that use their weaknesses to gain these parents' trust are leading these parents down the wrong path. It is also too bad that our focus isn't more on God's Word and its true meaning.

What I find even more interesting when it comes to exorcism is the following verse found in Matthew 8:16, which states, "When evening came, many who were demon-possessed were brought to him, and he drove out the spirits with a word and healed all the sick." Jesus drove out demons not by beating the person with the demon, but as the verse says, with *a word!* And we see this all throughout the New Testament that demons and evil spirits are rebuked and driven out verbally! Also, while there are demons and evil spirits on this Earth wreaking havoc for satan, we must be cautious in determining whether someone is absolutely possessed by a demon because God is the only One truly "trained" and able to cast out demons and evil spirits. He will guide the correct person to expel the demon out with a *word* if absolutely necessary. Therefore, it is quite clear from Scripture that "beating the devil out of them" is not biblical. As I've shown:

> Parents who frequently spank their children due to beliefs that this treatment can rid a child of evil spirits can cause serious, even deadly, injury... The tragic death of Josef Smith, the eight-year-old boy who died from having been physically abused by his parents... As it turns out, the parents' fear of Josef being possessed by a demon likely played a role in his death.
>
> (Heimlich, 2011, p. 275)

In conclusion of this section about Catholicism and the use of physical punishment with children, I would like to take a brief look at St. Augustine as he had a major influence over some of the people that I have discussed in this part of the book. St. Augustine (354-430) was a great theologian. He was extremely interested in children, especially infants. He believed in original sin and that every child was born with a sinful nature.

> Augustine watched infants closely and attempted to put into words this world without language. Augustine described tenderly the smiles of sleep and the comfort of nursing but juxtaposed these occasions of serenity with a newborn's jealous rage when, even after it had been fed, it saw another infant at a nurse's breast.
>
> (Stortz, 2001, p. 83 & 84)

Despite his belief in a child's sinfulness beginning at birth, as well as his being physically punished as a child, St. Augustine did not believe that children ought to be spanked by adults.

> While children in this age of life can exhibit temper tantrums and extreme acts which many modern Christian smacking advocates have urged parents to repress with corporal punishment, Augustine gave no such advice.
>
> (Martin, 2006, p. 159)

Also, Augustine didn't like the inequity between adults and children as they both sinned, but yet, children were the ones getting punished for it.

> That basic inequity between children and adults marked his childhood: "The schoolmaster who caned me was behaving no better than I was." Though childhood was full of reprehensible actions, Augustine did not favour punishing children as severely as adults.
>
> (Martin, 2006, p. 160)

It is clear from what we've seen throughout this section that the Roman Catholics have a dark history of using fear, control, and physical punishment in the name of God just as do fundamental Christians. We have also seen a possibility that the origins of spanking for the remissions of sins may have begun with ancient Catholicism. And finally, we've seen that using physical punishment to rid children of evil spirits has been done throughout history even though it has no biblical basis. While not all Catholics have advocated for nor used corporal punishment with children, sadly, a great deal have.

In the next section, we will discover the origins of the "rules" for "lovingly" spanking.

From Where the "Rules" for a "Loving Christian Spanking" Come

I have often wondered where the current, as well as historical, Christian advocates of spanking came up with the rules of a "loving, godly" spanking. After all, there are supposedly two types of spankings in our current culture—the godly spanking versus the cultural spanking. According to many Christian prospankers, the cultural spanking is when non-believers spank their children out of anger or frustration. Of course, Christians are also capable of spanking their children out of anger or frustration. According to the Christian advocates of spanking children who claim to be biblical and child "experts," spanking in anger is what causes all the adverse effects of spanking in children. They claim that a "godly" spanking done without anger and "lovingly" is not harmful to children in any way. In fact, James Dobson (1996), page 25, states:

> For example, a dime sized bruise on the buttocks of a fair-skinned child may or may not indicate an abusive situation. It all depends. In an otherwise secure and loving home,

that bruise may have no greater psychological impact than a skinned knee or a stubbed toe. Again the issue in not the small abrasion; it is the meaning behind it.

Therefore, as long as the child is physically punished in the "correct and loving way," even if the spanking leaves marks and bruises on the child's bottom, legs, or hands (the most common places for children to be spanked), it will not do any psychological or emotional harm to the child. We'll come back to this in the next part of this book called, "The Effects of Spanking."

So, what exactly are some of these "rules" for a "loving, godly, Christian" spanking? They are:

1. Never spank in anger.
2. Always spank lovingly.
3. Spank only for outright disobedience or harmful behavior.
4. Tell the child exactly why he/she is being spanked before and after the spanking.
5. Explain to the child that Jesus wants the parent to discipline him/her because the child sinned by disobeying the parent.
6. Hug and comfort the child after the spanking.

Of course, there are different variations of these rules depending on which Christian prospanking advocate one consults. Another "rule" that often varies among Christian advocates of spanking is whether or not to use one's hand or an object to spank the child because for some the hand is part of the parent and should symbolize love and care to the child. However, what I find quite interesting is that there are no such "rules" in the Bible on how to correctly spank a child. God *always* provides instructions on important subjects such as prayer, marriage, sex, and forgiveness for us to follow. Jesus has provided us with numerous parables that illustrate the numerous important topics about which He spoke. Since spanking a child is supposedly very important, why are there no specific biblical instructions or examples for how to appropriately spank children? Some Christians use Psalm 4:4 and Ephesians 4:26, which states, "In your anger do not sin" in order to say that these "rules" for spanking children are indeed biblically based. However, this verse is not a direct instruction on how to spank. Yes, it *can* be applied to spanking, but this is the only verse, besides the rod verses, that *can* be applied as the rest of Scripture is more against than for spanking.

To answer our original question of where do the "rules" for the "loving and godly" spanking originate, I found an article that shows one of the origins of these "rules" for spanking. There is a book that was written by Dorothy Spencer that was published in 1936 that explains domestic adult discipline. It is called *The Spencer Spanking Plan.* As part of the domestic adult discipline, husbands are instructed on how to appropriately spank their wives.

> Dorothy Spencer advocates that the key to a happy marriage is for the disobedient partner to be spanked. Spanking in this context is to administer punishment in a timely manner and then move forward with a clean slate. The punishment should be administered as soon as offense occurs.
>
> Here is an example that Dorothy Spencer gives for how a spanking can be given immediately even if you are not at home:
>
> The two of you are on a drive down the highway and you notice that your partner is driving far beyond the speed limit. You *mention that* it would be appropriate to pull over to the next exit with a convenience store. Once at the store, you and your partner go to the bathroom where the deserved discipline is administered. Since this is being

given with immediacy, the session will not need to be that severe.

Because of noise and privacy considerations, use a switch or similar quiet instrument and give enough to make sure your partner sees the error in his or her ways, but let it be done in ten minutes or less. If you feel that you should be more forceful, explain to your partner that you are not finished and he or she can expect the rest once you get to a place where you can finish.

(Minnicks, 2011, http://www.examiner.com/article/ spanking-an-unconventional-way-of-handling-marital- disputes)

Other rules from *The Spencer Spanking Plan* include not spanking in anger, not injuring the wife, and hugging the spouse afterward and making sure she knows she is very loved. Isn't it interesting that these "rules" for spanking wives are quite similar to the "rules" for spanking children in a "Christian" way? It seems very obvious to me that the Christian advocates of spanking children such as Dobson, Tripp, the Pearls, Lessin, and the like have adapted these Spencer rules to rules for spanking children. And yet, there is absolutely *nothing* in the Bible that resembles these rules. In fact, if we are to take the rod verses in the book of Proverbs literally, we are to beat children across the *back*, not bottom, legs, or hands, with a *staff/walking stick*. It does not provide us with any more instructions than that. People have interpreted these verses in a way that works for them. They try to cover their guilt by making up rules and using objects that *they* deem appropriate to inflict harm on their children in Jesus's name.

Just as spanking is man-made, so are the "rules" for a "Christian, godly, loving" spanking. There is no biblical support for such rules just as the Bible does not support using control and fear to break children's wills. In the final section of this chapter, we shall see how spanking and harsh punishment was, and still is, put under the guise of the first offshoot of the field of psychology.

The Guise of Behaviorism

In the late nineteenth and early twentieth centuries, the field of psychology began to be of interest to many people. They wanted to know the science behind animal and human behavior, such as what caused or stopped behavior. This brought a great deal of experiments with both animals and humans in order to understand the human mind better. Behaviorism was the first branch of the field of psychology. Ivan Pavlov, John B. Watson, and B. F. Skinner were among the first behaviorists who observed that behavior can be controlled through rewards and punishments. "Behaviorism is the view that behavior should be explained by observable experiences, not by mental processes" (Santrock, 2008, p. 227). As one can see, behaviorism is very black and white as it focuses solely on what is seen and totally ignores what is unseen.

For example, behaviorists believe that to get a toddler to stop throwing temper tantrums, negative reinforcement or punishment, such as spanking, must be used to stop the child from having a fit. On the other hand, if one wants a toddler to keep picking up his/her toys, then according to a behaviorist, positive reinforcement or reward must be administered to the child such as praise or candy. E. L. Thorndike was another one of the early behaviorists and he summed this idea up into what is known as the Law of Effect.

> The Law of Effect says behaviors that are followed by pleasant consequences are more likely to occur in the future while behaviors that are followed by unpleasant consequences are less likely to occur in the future.
>
> (Preston, 2011, http://www.angelfire.com/zine2/defense_ of_spanking/why_punishment_is_needed.html)

Behaviorists, in general, do not take into account children's emotions, ages, developmental stages or abilities, or anything else going on within the child or family when it comes to behavior. "For the behaviorist, these thoughts, feelings, and motives are not appropriate subject matter for a science of behavior because they cannot be directly observed" (Santrock, 2008, p. 227). Behaviorism aims to externally control all behavior without taking into account or looking for the root of the behavior. As we shall see in part 4 of this book that is entitled, "Discipline without Harm," children act up for a variety of reasons, and there is usually a need behind the behavior being exhibited. If we can address the need behind the behavior, the behavior will usually go away. Also, behaviorists don't seem to take into account that children may not know the appropriate way to behave and/or may just be learning the appropriate behavior. As I continue to point out throughout this book, punishment aims to *stop* behavior, it does *not teach* more appropriate behavior. People argue that they always tell the child how to appropriately behave next time after the spanking or other punishment, but they fail to realize that the child is too busy trying to recover from the spanking or other punishment that they are not capable of truly hearing the parent or of doing any learning—especially if the child is in pain.

Spanking has been hidden under the guise of behaviorism for fifty to one hundred years now. Because of this, many prospankers such as James Dobson, who is a psychologist, use the fact that it has been proven by psychology that spanking and other forms of punishment work to control children's behavior. This helps justify hitting and shaming children because a branch of psychology claims it is necessary. As I said in the section about the origins of control in this chapter, spanking is all about control and not about how to *truly* teach children how to behave. And spanking has been shown to lead to even more unwanted behavior.

> All too often, aversive stimuli are not effective punishments,
> in that they do not decrease the unwanted behavior and

indeed sometimes increase the unwanted behavior over time. One recent study found that when parents used spanking to discipline 4- to 5-year-old children, the problem behavior increased over time (McLoyd & Smith, 2002). Another recent longitudinal study found that spanking before age 2 was related to behavioral problems in middle and late childhood (Slade & Wissow, 2004).

(Santrock, 2008, p. 240)

Unfortunately, Christian advocates of spanking, such as Dobson and others, claim that studies such as these are biased and inaccurate. They truly believe that using behaviorist methods in order to control children, as long as they are done in a "loving, godly way," are an "effective" way to keep sin and satan out of children. We must remember that behaviorism is outdated and is only another guise to promote the harsh, unbiblical act of spanking children. As we shall see in the next two parts of this book, we know a great deal more about the human mind, especially when it comes to child development. We must not base childcare and rearing on a quite old, narrow-minded branch of psychology!

Conclusion

Throughout this part of the book, we have explored where different concepts such as breaking a child's will, fear of death and hell, control, and behaviorism originated and how they have influenced Christians to spank their children. We have also looked at historical figures that have advocated for spanking children and have tested their theologies against what the Bible actually says regarding the treatment of children. And finally, we have read some horrific true stories about Christian parents harming, and even killing, their children in order to do their best to raise their children in a godly manner. Most of them were trying to do so out of love. It is my hope that as you have read this part, as well as part 1, that God is showing us that hitting and punishing children was never what He intended. Please be open to His true will.

I would like to end this part of the book on a positive note. While there have been many throughout history who have spanked and have advocated for spanking, there also has been many who have not, such as: D. L. Moody, Martin Luther, St. Augustine, and Martin Luther King, Jr. They understood that the rod verses do not mean to hit children but to use proper authority in order to discipline them in a way that will lead them to God. I conclude this with the following passage from the book called, *Children in the Early Church* by W. A. Strange:

> Here is the advice of the so-called *Teaching of the Apostles* (*Didascalia Apostolorum*), a Syrian Christian church order of the early third century, on the subject of disciplining children:
>
> Do not hesitate to reprove them [your children], reasoning with them and chastising them and arguing; for you will not kill them by chastising them, but rather give them life, since this is his hope; beat him with a rod, you will free his soul from hell [Prov. 29:17; 25:14]. Our "rod" is the word of Jesus Christ, as Jeremiah saw a branch of an almond tree [Jer. 1:11]. Everyone therefore who hesitates to speak a word of chastisement to his son, hates his son. (*Didascalia* 4.11; Funk 1906 1 230, 232).
>
> (Strange, 2004, p. 78)

May we discipline our children with the Word of our living God!

References

Bunge, M. J. (Ed.). (2001). *The Child in Christian Thought*. Grand Rapids, MI: William B. Eerdmans Publishing Company.

Cooney, T. (2003). *The Crumbling Walls of the Roman Catholic Church*. http://fspp.net/Articles/crumbling_walls.htm

Dobson, J. (1996). *The New Dare to Discipline*. Carol Stream, IL: Tyndale House Publishers, Inc.

Dog, M. C. & Erdoes, R. (1990). Civilize Them With a Stick. *Lakota Woman*, 28-37, 38-39, and 40-41.

Heimlich, J. (2011). *Breaking Their Will*. Amherst, NY: Prometheus Books.

Lutton, C. (2011). *The History of Spanking*. http://aolff.org/spare-the-rod/the-spanking-files-2/history-of-spanking

Martin, S. (2006). *Thy Rod and Thy Staff They Comfort Me*. Jerusalem, Israel: Sorensic.

Minnicks, M. (2011). *Spanking: An Unconventional Way of Handling Marital Disputes*. http://www.examiner.com/article/spanking-an-unconventional-way-of-handling-marital-disputes

Preston, P. (2011). *Why Punishment is Needed*. http://www.angelfire.com/zine2/defense_of_spanking/why_punishment_is_needed.html

Santrock, J. (2008). *Educational Psychology (Illinois Version)*. Boston, MA: The McGraw-Hill Companies.

Strange, W. A. (2004). *Children in the Early Church*. Eugene, OR: Wipf and Stock Publishers.

Part Three

The Effects of Spanking

Chapter 10

My Story

What are the effects of spanking? Is it true that as long as one does it the "right, loving, godly" way that there are no harmful effects to the child? Are the research studies claiming that spanking is harmful biased and inaccurate? What about the studies claiming that not all spankings are harmful? These are just a few of the questions I will explore throughout this part of the book. We have already explored why God, through Scripture, does not support using physical punishment with our children despite what many Christian prospankers say. We have read many stories of parents trying to do the right thing for their children but harmed or killed them in the process all because satan had tricked them into believing that using physical punishment was what God wanted. In the following chapters, we will hear from many who were spanked as children and how it affected them and their relationships with God. If God hasn't spoken to your heart in my previous chapters, I pray He will with this part of the book. Please, allow God to speak to you as you read this. He will not condemn you.

My Story

I have touched on my story throughout the book, but I haven't actually told my story until now. What I am about to write is quite difficult for me. Parts of it my own husband didn't even know. But I am trusting God to use my pain for His glory. I grew up in a non-active Christian home. We had Jesus figurines and the Ten Commandments on the wall, but we didn't go to church. I had Bibles and Bible storybooks, but God was not emphasized. I was born with severe cerebral palsy. When I was born, I did not breathe for roughly forty minutes. The doctors were about to give up on me, but my dad about punched one of them and told them not to give up on me. I'm grateful God did not let my dad allow the doctors to give up on me. God had/has a plan for me.

I have three half-siblings. We grew up with my parents but with my siblings visiting their mom every other weekend. My childhood was, overall, okay. I had a lot of love for my parents and they loved me. They raised me as "normally" as possible, despite my severe physical disability. I have a lot of happy memories with my mom and my dad (my dad died in 2003 of a massive heart attack) and would not trade them for anything. They believed in me and encouraged me to be all that I could be. And they fought hard to make sure I got the services and education that I needed and deserved. I will always be grateful to them for that!

But, my childhood also had a very dark side. My dad had quite a temper at times. My first memory of his temper was when I was quite young. I was no more than three or four years old and we were eating supper. I do not remember what made him angry, but I remember him throwing my plate of food on the floor. He kept throwing stuff, and I just remember screaming and crying.

I do not remember the first time my dad hit or got rough with me. I seem to remember a man hitting me at a family member's workplace. I do not know who did it. All I remember is fussing in a playpen and being hit rather hard. Being hit was a common occurrence throughout my childhood by my dad. Due to my cerebral palsy, I have a great deal of spastic, involuntary movements. If Dad felt I wasn't doing my best to relax and cooperate during my care, he'd get angry and hit me or get rough with me—forceful. I remember being afraid to be left alone with him sometimes if I knew he'd have to do something with me in which I had trouble relaxing. Once he hit me in the face while giving me a shower for a reason I cannot remember. The mark didn't last more than an hour or so. Due to my dad's violent temper, no one could exercise any control over him. He would not listen to *anyone*.

I remember Dad hitting me a few times for actual misbehavior, but I tried not to push him that far. My siblings are all older than me and I saw how Dad treated them when they did something wrong, so all he had to do was yell and I'd cry. Sometimes he'd tell me not to cry or else. One time, he made a wooden paddle with holes in it to use on my siblings. Although he never used it on me, I was absolutely terrified of it.

Despite all of this, I was a happy child for the most part, as well as extremely determined. I did not act up all that much. However, outside of the fear that I had, I also dealt with some aggressiveness. I'm not sure if anyone knew this, but, though I've always loved children, as a child, I remember sometimes hitting them on purpose as they walked by at my babysitter's house. I was between five and eight years old at that time. This makes me sad, but I would always hit the younger ones. Thankfully, I didn't hit them for very long before I stopped on my own. Believe it or not, I never got caught hitting the children and I didn't enjoy it all that much. I believe it was my way of dealing with being hit and seeing my siblings get hit even worse than I did. Another way I remember dealing with the aggression was when I was playing with my Cabbage Patch Kids dolls. I had one named Elroy that I'd pretend got into trouble a lot. I would yell at him (quietly since

I'd sometimes cuss) then spank him hard. After I'd spank him, I'd hold him and pretend to comfort him. I don't know why, but I believe I only did this routine with that doll. I had *many* Cabbage Patch Kids dolls. I was good at hiding my aggressiveness.

Now, don't get me wrong, I did not spend every waking minute terrified of my dad. I loved sitting by him in his chair. I loved playing with him and going places with him. When I was little, I also wanted him to put me to bed because he also made me feel safe at times. That's how parents are; no matter how badly he hurt me, I still loved him and knew he'd protect me. I also missed him so much when he went away on business trips. Even though I was relieved that I didn't have to worry about making him angry during the time he was away, I still counted the days until he'd come home and was so excited to see him when he arrived home. I truly loved my dad.

Dad ended up driving my siblings out of the house when they were teenagers. My siblings all rebelled and lived hard lives. Two of them managed to get past the abuse and have created good lives for themselves now. The other is still struggling. After my siblings left, my parents divorced as a result of my dad's continuing violent temper. I was in seventh grade at the time. I was very upset about the divorce, but I also remember being relieved that I no longer had to worry about making him mad until the visits, as I'd visit him every other weekend. I remember soon after visiting him, I realized that no one could rescue me when he got angry with me anymore. Also, Dad would have probably fought hard if he had not been given visitation rights, making things worse for me. I soon began always dreading the weekends spent with him. On the Fridays before I visited him, I'd get a sense of sickening dread as people told me to have a good weekend as I left school. I never told anyone exactly how I felt due to a feeling of shame. I also loved him and didn't want to hurt him. I actually would have been more upset if I were kept away from him. And, of course, fear. He could also make one feel very guilty. When he did hit me or get rough with me, he would apologize, especially after the divorce. I believe he truly was sorry most of the time. The older I got, the more I dealt with anxiety and depression. While I don't attribute all of my anxiety and depression to my dad as I had a lot of other issues going on, I am sure some of it was indeed due to him.

I did go through a rebellious stage between the ages of thirteen and fifteen where I wanted to get drunk, high, and have sex like a lot of my friends were doing. Thankfully, God kept me from being able to do those things due to never being able to be left alone or able to sneak out. If I could have, I definitely would have just as my siblings did—anything to forget the pain and fear and to be "normal" like everyone else. At that point, I probably would have stopped visiting Dad regularly, but my disability left me no choice. I do remember getting angry with him and hitting him back during one visit around that time. He didn't do anything, thankfully.

I came to Christ at the age of fifteen thanks to one of my babysitters. Going to church with friends was a huge comfort to me. I felt God's love for me and I know He is how I survived the rest of my childhood because Dad did not stop hitting me until I was seventeen and *I* was the one who finally got up the courage to make it stop. My husband and I actually began dating when I was seventeen. We hid our relationship from everyone for several months because he was older than me. Besides Jesus, he is the *best* thing that ever happened to me! We emailed for a couple of months before going on our first date. Believe it or not, he was one of my dad's best friends and was a part of my life since I was a young child. He was younger than my dad and was nothing like him except for sharing certain hobbies. He had no idea that my dad was abusive to my siblings and me. See, my dad knew how to make himself look good and would tell people how "hard" his life was. I believe very few people knew the truth about who my dad really was. We didn't tell my dad until I was eighteen because we were afraid of his reaction, especially me, though no one completely knew why—my then-boyfriend included. It wasn't until six months into our relationship that he finally found out exactly who my dad was.

I suffered from low self-esteem back then with the abuse, not being able to do the "normal" things that teenagers do, being hurt by guys my age who couldn't see past my disability, people telling me I would never accomplish my goals and dreams that I had set for myself, etc. I'm certain that I would not have survived without God and then my husband. As my now-husband became my boyfriend during my senior year of high school, he showed me that I was beautiful and worthy of love. Being hit throughout one's childhood usually ruins one's self-esteem. Well, pile that with disability and others putting one down, and one's got even less of a sense of worth. Yet, I was a good actor, so no one but God knew exactly how much I struggled. As my boyfriend loved me, I got stronger. Then one weekend in May, I'd had it. I was especially spastic that weekend and my dad hit me and got rough with me for the *last time*. The next time I saw my boyfriend, I had to tell him. It was the *hardest* thing I've ever had to do except for writing this. See, being hit always brings a sense of shame no matter from whom it comes or how it's done. I felt like I was always partly to blame. I should have been better to prevent it. I really didn't know how my boyfriend was going to take it. I didn't want him to beat Dad up nor did I want him to think I was somehow defective either. He was quite upset that my dad had been hitting me. He had no idea. And yes, he wanted to beat up my dad but didn't.

After my eighteenth birthday, we told everyone about our relationship. My dad refused to accept it. In my opinion, he disowned me. I also believe that he couldn't handle the truth about the abuse finally being out. I reached out to him several times but he absolutely refused to admit he was wrong about anything. We invited him to our wedding in 2003, but he refused to come. He did send us a card. It hurt that he refused to accept me or apologize. Then, three months after our wedding, he suddenly died. At first, I thought he had gone to hell, but later I found out he was a Christian even though he *never* acted like one. The year after his death was hell for me. At first I was very angry and sad. I remember looking at his picture at the memorial service and being so angry with him for leaving and hurting his children yet again. Then the severe anxiety set in. I was having many, many panic attacks. I thought I was going to die. My doctor put me on Zoloft, which made it even worse. I just couldn't deal with the pain while getting used to married life and living on my own for the first time. And I couldn't talk about it because it was too painful. Finally, God led us to the program called, *Attacking Anxiety and Depression* by Lucinda Bassett. By doing that self-help program, I began to heal.

I still deal with anger and anxiety issues. My husband doesn't get angry often, but it always makes me anxious when he does and raises his voice, though he has *never* and would *never* hurt me. Sadly, I hit him in anger when we were first married, which made me very angry with my dad for creating that aggressive tendency within me. It has never happened since then. I also still have nightmares once in a while of Dad hurting me. I never tell my husband about those. And I get very anxious and upset when a child is threatened and spanked, even "lovingly." It hurts me too. So when I see a child beginning to act up in a store or at a gathering, I get tense and pray the child stops before he/she gets spanked.

I have forgiven my dad for everything. I do miss him at times. It is important for me to note that my dad was physically abused as a child. Both of my parents had Christian mothers. I do not blame God for allowing me to go through all that I have because

He is using me to help children, which brings Him glory and saves lives. Some of you may read this and think, "Well, that was abuse. If he would have lovingly spanked you, it wouldn't have harmed you." I know myself very well, and if my parents would have spanked me in Christ's name and told me that this was God's will, I would *not* be a Christian. It would have *scared* me away from God! People will blow me off and/or criticize me for writing this book, but everything that I've written is true. Hitting children is harmful no matter *how* it is done.

The following chapters within this part of this book will show how harmful any form of physical punishment is for all children. May we "have nothing to do with the fruitless deeds of darkness, but rather expose them" (Ephesians 5:11).

Chapter 11

Denial, and the Continuum of Violence Toward Children

In the last chapter, you read my very personal story. I can't begin to put into words how difficult that was for my family and me. As I said in chapter 10, the purpose of this part of the book is to explore all of the effects of using physical punishment with children. In this chapter, I will be discussing denial as one of the many effects of spanking (hitting) children. I will also share a couple of definitions of physical abuse and will discuss the continuum of violence against children.

Denial: "I Was Spanked and I Turned Out Okay"

One of the many and most visible, if one looks closely enough, effects of spanking and physical abuse is denial. Denial is a psychological defense mechanism to any traumatizing or painful event. This is why denial is one of the first steps in the grieving process. It is easier to deny that something very painful has occurred than to deal directly with the pain. How many times have we heard, "I was spanked and I'm okay," from prospankers?

Google "spanking children" and we get an array of prospankers arguing intensely with antispankers about how spanking isn't harmful. They base their arguments on their personal experiences. They are often quick to become defensive and even get downright angry when antispankers try to gently point out how and why they are wrong. This is due to the fact that it is very difficult to admit that their parents hurt them as children, or that they are now hurting their own children. Instead, they come back with the same arguments as to why spanking cannot possibly be harmful.

> One reason the harmful effects [of spanking] are ignored is because many of us (including those of us who are social scientists) are reluctant to admit that their own parents did something wrong and even more reluctant to admit that we have been doing something wrong with our own children. But the most important reason may be that it is difficult to see the harm. Most of the harmful effects do not become visible right away, often not for years. In addition, only a relatively small percentage of spanked children experience obviously harmful effects.
>
> (Straus, 2006, p. 152-153)

Therefore, since the effects of physical punishment are rarely visible to parents and other adults, it makes it even easier to deny that they exist.

Denial begins at a young age when the physical punishment begins, whether it's "lovingly" done or done in anger because they are taught that physical punishment is something parents do to children and that it is for the children's own good. When children grow up being physically punished, they assume that all children are treated this way. Spanking becomes a normal part of childhood until the children become old enough to find out that not all children are spanked. Instead of admitting their parents were wrong, some children have internalized the painful message that they deserved to be hit and that it was for their own good and that they use denial to deal with their pain. Of course, guilt and shame also factor into denial. I will be discussing guilt and shame in chapter 14. Of course, this is often compounded when the child sees that society accepts the hitting of children, and when he/she is taught that God also "accepts" or even "commands" that children be hit in His name and in the name of "discipline."

I like how Alice Miller, author of *For Your Own Good*, explains how denial can begin to develop in children when force and coercion are used with them from a young age. Miller (1994), pages 8 and 9, states:

> We justifiably resist new exhortations if moral demands were frequently imposed upon us at too young an age. Love of one's neighbor, altruism, willingness to sacrifice— how splendid these words sound and yet what cruelty can be hidden in them simply because they are forced upon a child at a time when the prerequisites for altruism cannot possibly be present. Coercion often nips the development of these prerequisites in the bud and what then remains is a lifelong condition of strain. This is like soil too hard for anything to grow in, and the only hope at all of forcibly producing the love demanded of one as a child lies in the upbringing given one's own children, from whom one then demands love in the same merciless fashion.

We can see that the cycle of denial can continue throughout many generations as children grow up denying that their parents mistreated them by hitting them and, therefore, treat their children the same way that their parents did. Also, "Children do not want to be a burden to their parents, nor do they want to be the cause of pain and suffering" (Quinn, 1988, p. 44). The passage from Miller reminds me of the parable Jesus taught about planting the seed (God's Word) in different soils in Matthew 13:1-9, 18-23. If the seed doesn't fall on good, healthy soil, then it cannot take root. When children are taught from a young age that physical punishment is a normal part of life in the parent-child relationship, it can be very difficult for them to accept the truth later on that this indeed is not normal or even correct.

Going back to the idea that God "approves" of parents hitting their children, the children begin to believe that they are somehow evil, dirty, and that they deserve to be punished for their sins despite the fact that Jesus Christ has already paid the penalty for humanity's sins. For example, Lisa, a contributor of the Broken Daughters website shared her story. She grew up in a Fundamental Christian home. When, as a toddler, she began displaying developmentally appropriate (typical) behaviors for her age, her parents sought the advice of their pastor. Their pastor convinced Lisa's parents that Lisa's developmentally appropriate behaviors were actually from the evil one and were sinful and that her parents needed to harshly physically punish Lisa for them in order to free her from satan's influence. By then, Lisa's parents had been reading other books such as *To Train Up a Child* in which the same advice was echoed. In her story on the Broken Daughters website, Lisa describes the first time her parents beat her as a toddler. Yes, she clearly remembers it despite being so young. But what caught my attention even more and made me even sadder is what Lisa says after describing this horribly traumatizing experience. She writes:

> This wasn't my only beating and by far not my severest, but it is one of the most prominent ones in my mind. It is hard for me to see the injustice in this until today. I was a bratty child. An evil child. That's what I learned all my life. I find it hard to say that my parents beating me back then was wrong. I have been told by outsiders that it was, but it's still a concept hard to grasp for me.
>
> (Lisa, 2011,
> http://brokendaughters.wordpress.com/2011/06/18/
> training-up-this-child-part-2-who-let-the-dogs-out/)

It is clear that Lisa, like many other children who are physically punished from a young age and throughout their childhood, internalized the message that she deserved to be beaten for her sinful behavior and finds it difficult to completely renounce her parents' treatment of her even though she is fighting against the denial.

As I previously mentioned, children are quick to pick up on the societal and cultural norms in which they live. Children, when made to feel safe and unjudged, will admit that physical punishment is indeed quite painful emotionally in addition to physically.

> In 2006, the final report was published of the UN Secretary-General's Study on Violence against Children, the first comprehensive global study into the nature and extent of the problem. The Independent Expert leading the Study, Professor Paulo Sérgio Pinheiro, wrote in the report: "Throughout the study process, children have consistently expressed the urgent need to stop all this violence. Children testify to the hurt—not only physical, but "the hurt inside"—which this violence causes them, compounded by adult acceptance, even approval of it."
>
> (Global Initiative to End All Corporal Punishment of Children-FAQ, 2011, http://www. endcorporalpunishment.org/pages/frame.html)

However, due to the fact that societal and cultural norms accept the use of physical punishment with children, compounded by the fact that even God "accepts" this, children's cries for help go unheard, thereby, convincing children that this must be a good thing. We've seen in the historical part of this book that children haven't been valued as they should, though there have been some improvements along the way. Sadly, society still tends to take the side of the adult rather than the child; thus, making the child feel as if he/she has no choice but to also take the side of the adult or otherwise face possible, or even more, rejection from the family, society, and God.

Society takes the side of the adult and blames the child for what has been done to him or her. The victimization of the child has historically been denied and is still being denied, even today. This denial has made it possible for society to ignore the devastating effects of the victimization of the child for such a long time.

(Miller, 2010, http://www.squidoo.com/alice-miller)

Repression often coincides with denial as part of denial is repressing painful events in order to not have to deal with them. Children are taught, even forced, at very young ages to repress their negative feelings. For example, many great, loving parents will often shush their baby when the baby cries. Or, parents will tell the infant, "You're okay." These parents mean well and are doing their best to comfort the infant, but they are actually teaching their child that crying and having negative feelings are bad. Some Christian prospankers will go so far as to spank infants for crying too much. As children get older, many Christian prospankers, such as James Dobson, Tedd Tripp, the Pearls, and Roy Lessin, tell parents to spank the child again if they cry too long after the first spanking, act angry, or try to defend themselves during the spanking. In his book, *Shepherding a Child's Heart*, page 149, Tripp (1995) states:

After you have spanked, take the child up on your lap and hug him, telling him how much you love him, how much it grieves you to spank him, and how you hope that it will not be necessary again. Then if he is still not restored, you are to check your own spirit to see if you have handled him roughly... [or] brought unholy anger on this holy mission, and if you have, seek forgiveness from God. If your child is still angry, it's time for another round, "Daddy has spanked you, but you are not sweet enough yet. We are going to have to go back upstairs for another spanking.

Lisa, who I previously mentioned, was spanked for being in a bad mood one day. She writes on the Broken Daughters website:

> So, on that one day, I was in a very frustrated, grumpy mood. I barked at my siblings. I didn't do my chores as thoroughly as I should and normally did. Come dinner time, I sat on my chair with a sour face, poking around in the mashed potatoes and not really eating. My mother told me to straighten up, which I did only half-heartedly. My dad asked me what happened, and I told him I didn't know, I was just feeling a bad mood. Silence. Chewing. Let's get over it.
>
> After dinner, I was quick to clean up the dishes with my mom. I wanted some alone time. I was trying to carry the dishes as fast as I could. In my hurry, I dropped a glass. That wouldn't have been a big deal on its own. But my mom was so stressed—so stressed. She started yelling at me, yelling away her day's worth of frustration. After a few minutes of this, my dad came storming out of the living room, yelling at us both for disturbing his peace. My mom started crying and yelled back at him that I was impossible to raise and she needed him, that he was never around to be the strong leader he would like to be. That pushed my dad over the edge. He grabbed my arm and pulled me out of the room. I heard my mom yell behind me that when I got back, she wanted a happy child and not this grumpy lump of clothes I was. My dad pulled me into the kid's bedroom, got his cane off the closet and started beating me in fury. I was screaming my life out. My siblings started crying outside. My dad ran to the door, grabbed the first child he could get a hold of, which was Jacob, pulled him in too and gave him a spanking as well.
>
> (Lisa, 2011,
> http://brokendaughters.wordpress.com/2011/06/21/
> training-up-this-child-part-5-the-pearl-song/)

Sometimes, as children grow up learning to repress and deny the pain in which their parents have inflicted upon them, they actually begin to idolize their parents. I know two women who were physically punished by their fathers and to this day neither women will admit that their fathers did anything wrong. However, their brothers disagree with them as their fathers also physically punished their brothers. "Fantasies always serve to conceal or minimize unbearable childhood reality for the sake of the child's survival; therefore, the so-called invented trauma is a less harmful version of the real, repressed one" (Miller, 2010, http://www.squidoo.com/alice-miller). The fact that, as I mentioned previously, so many prospankers—Christian and non-Christian alike—get so defensive whenever someone tries to lovingly point out the truth about spanking and that it is harmful only further proves the harm. We usually only get defensive and upset when we don't want to admit we are wrong, or when something is painful. It can be quite difficult to face facts rather than hold onto what we have been taught to believe from a young child. The Bible tells us that God speaks to us in a still, small voice (1 Kings 19:11-13). Look at what God says in Isaiah 30:21: "Whether you turn to the right or to the left, your ears will hear a voice behind you, saying, 'This is the way; walk in it.'" How can we hear God speak to us if we don't allow Him to help us undo the denial and repression that our parents inflicted upon us because their parents did the same to them and so on? If we choose not to listen to God and allow Him to help us break free from this denial and repression, then the cycle of abuse, physical punishment, and the use of other degrading methods of punishment will continue. As Alice Miller (2010) states:

> As beaten children are not allowed to defend themselves, they must suppress their anger and rage against their parents who have humiliated them, killed their inborn

empathy, and insulted their dignity. They will take out this rage later, as adults, on scapegoats, mostly on their own children. Deprived of empathy, some of them will direct their anger against themselves (in eating disorders, drug addiction, depression etc.), or against other adults (in wars, terrorism, delinquency etc.).

(http://www.squidoo.com/alice-miller)

If we don't allow God to truly work in our lives, satan will attack us. Condemnation, denial, and repression are from satan. Please pray to God for help if one of your first reactions to this is defensiveness as satan may be attacking you. God forgives and does *not* condemn.

Is All Hitting Violence Toward Children?

There seems to be a continuum of violence when it comes to spanking children. Look at the following diagram. On the left hand of the line/continuum is a light slap or swat on a child's covered bottom or on the child's hand. As we move toward the right side of this continuum, we have severe beating that leave the children seriously injured or dead. In the middle of the continuum are things such as hitting the child's bottom a few times with an open hand, hitting a child's bare bottom with an open hand, using an object to hit a child's bare bottom, and so on. Many people see absolutely no problem with the "light hitting" that begins the continuum, as that is often considered "loving discipline" and a parent's "duty" in raising children. But as we move toward the right side of the continuum, most people would agree that beating children to death is wrong. In the middle of the continuum is where arguments within the prospanking community often begin as they don't agree where the line between "discipline" and abuse should be placed. As Phil E. Quinn (1988) points out in his book, *Spare the Rod,* page 19:

Contemporary society tends to believe that *some* hitting of children is good and acceptable as a parenting technique—but certainly not *all* hitting. The good hitting, we euphemistically call spanking. The bad hitting, we call child abuse. The dilemma, as always, is, Where does spanking end and beating begin? For too many parents, a spanking ends when bleeding begins.

The Continum of Violence Toward Children

There are some definitions at which I would like us to take a look. First, let's look at the definition of the word *spank*:

1. Verb: "to strike (a person, usually a child) with the open hand, a slipper, etc., especially on the buttocks, as in punishment."

2. Noun: "a blow given in spanking; a smart or resounding slap" (www.dictionary.com).

Here is the definition of the word hit:

1. Verb: "to deal a blow or stroke to."

2. Verb: "to come into violent contact with" (www.dictionary. com).

Here is the definition of the word abuse:

> Abuse is defined as any thing that is harmful, injurious, or offensive. Abuse also includes excessive and wrongful misuse of anything.
>
> (Gulli & Nasser, 2002, http://www.ask.com/health/
> galecontent/abuse)

As we can see, these definitions are quite similar to each other. Many prospankers try to claim that spanking and hitting children are two completely different things. Yet, we see that the only difference between the definitions of hitting and spanking is that spanking says it is done on the child's buttocks. Other than that, there is no difference. When we look at the definition of abuse, we see that it is anything harmful or offensive. Because spanking and hitting is always intended to inflict pain on a child, it is covered under the definition of abuse. Pain means harm *is* being done to the body. As I pointed out in chapter 5, the body uses pain to alert us that injury is either taking place or is about to take place. Plus, there is emotional pain that always occurs when a person—child or adult—is hit against his or her will. That's why we run away from both physical and emotional pain. It isn't fun unless one needs it for sexual pleasure, which we will discuss in chapter 14. There are two more definitions of abuse that we need to consider. In the first, Phil E. Quinn (1988) defines abuse as "any assault, whether verbal, sexual, or physical, or any deprivation of basic health and welfare necessities—regardless of severity, parental intention, or observable effects on the child" (p. 18).

The second definition of abuse is by Alice Miller. Miller (2010) defines abuse as:

> Humiliations, spankings and beatings, slaps in the face, betrayal, sexual exploitation, derision, neglect, etc. are all forms of mistreatment, because they injure the integrity and dignity of a child, even if their consequences are not visible right away.
>
> (http://www.squidoo.com/alice-miller)

I understand that these definitions will upset many people because no parent wants to think that he/she is or has abused his/her children. And most grown children do not want to think that their parents abused them. This is very painful and difficult to face and accept. But, all of these definitions are meant to be preventive. They are not meant to condemn anyone. However, if we allow light hitting of children, then light hitting could easily, and usually does, lead to more severe hitting—even if it is totally unintentional. The reason for this is that children tend to build up a tolerance to spanking depending on their personalities. So, a light slap on the hand or bottom might work well for a toddler but is usually not effective enough for a three- or four-year-old. Children deserve the same rights as adults when it comes to being hit. If we lightly slap another adult against his/her will, we can be arrested and charged with assault! It shouldn't matter how old or big someone is, he/she should be protected from having harm inflicted on him/her by another person. It should *not* be left up to parents concerning how much pain can be inflicted on their children because "children can be subjected to an incredible amount of pain and suffering before our perception of parental prerogative changes to one of parental abuse" (Quinn, 1988, p.19).

Conclusion

The effects of spanking/abuse are very real; otherwise people wouldn't need to get defensive when their beliefs that spanking is not harmful are challenged. Look at any article on the Internet, such as, http://www.volunteertv.com/mobi?storyid=124072014, and we see many angry comments from prospankers about how good spanking is. This is denial as it is too painful for some people to admit that hitting children is wrong and causes harm. Yet, their comments only testify to the harm that spanking causes. Repressing, denying, and projecting the pain from spanking/abuse only causes the cycle of physical punishment to continue. God *never* intended this for His children—big and small, young and old! We must face the truth, even when it hurts, and walk into the light instead of stumbling around in the darkness.

> Light has come into the world, but people loved darkness instead of light because their deeds were evil. Everyone who does evil hates the light, and will not come into the light for fear that their deeds will be exposed. But whoever lives by the truth comes into the light, so that it may be seen plainly that what they have done has been done in the sight of God.
>
> John 3:19b-21

References

Broken Daughters-Lisa. (2011). http://brokendaughters. wordpress.com/2011/06/18/training-up-this-child-part-2-who-let-the-dogs-out/

Broken Daughters-Lisa. (2011). http://brokendaughters. wordpress.com/2011/06/21/training-up-this-child-part-5-the-pearl-song/

Global Initiative to End All Corporal Punishment of Children. (2011). *FAQ*. http://www.endcorporalpunishment.org/pages/frame.html

Gulli & Nasser. (2002). *Abuse*. http://www.ask.com/health/galecontent/abuse

Miller, A. (1994). *For Your Own Good*. New York, NY: The Noonday Press.

Miller, A. (2010). *How is Emotional Blindness Created?* http://www.squidoo.com/alice-miller

Quinn, P. E. (1988). *Spare the Rod*. Nashville, TN: Abingdon Press.

Straus, M. A. (2006). *Beating the Devil Out of Them*. New Brunswick, NJ: Transaction Publishers.

Tripp, T. (1995). *Shepherding a Child's Heart*. Wapwallopen, PA: Shepherd Press.

Chapter 12

Lack of Empathy Allows for Anger and Aggression to Come More Easily

In the last chapter, I discussed one of the major effects of spanking, which is denial. We also looked at repression and the continuum of violence against children. If a swat or light slap on a child's hand or bottom is intended to cause pain to the child, then it is a form of violence against the child just as it is for adults. Children are not subhumans and do not deserve to have pain inflicted upon them because they are *unable* to behave like adults. As we've seen in the last two parts of this book, God never intended us to spank our children. This chapter further proves this as it is showing the very harmful effects of spanking children—even if it's done "lovingly" and by Christian parents. In this chapter, I will be discussing how spanking effects empathy, anger, and aggression in children and adults.

Empathy—"That Child
Needs a Good Spanking!"

We hear the above statement, "That child needs a good spanking," by many advocates of spanking as if they have no empathy for what the child is actually experiencing or the pain a "good spanking" will cause the child both physically and emotionally. As we saw in chapter 11, many prospankers were spanked/abused as children themselves but have repressed their pain and are now in denial that hitting children does in fact cause harm. This denial can often, and does indeed, lead to a lack of empathy when it comes to children as well as other adults.

So, what is empathy? Empathy is the ability to put oneself in another's shoes. The ability to share in another's joy or pain. An example of this is when a close friend gets hurt in some way and because we can share in his or her pain, we want to do anything we can to help ease his or her pain. We may not completely understand how our friend feels, but we know what it is like to hurt. As Christians, we share in Christ's sufferings (Romans 8:17; 2 Corinthians 1:5; and Philippians 3:5). Even though we do not know exactly what it was like for Christ to be beaten and then nailed to a cross in order to bear all of humanities' sins, just thinking about it breaks my heart, humbles me, and fills me with gratitude for Him. The Bible also says that we are to "Rejoice with those who rejoice; mourn with those who mourn" in Romans 12:15. Empathy is obviously important to God!

Despite empathy being important to God as it allows us to love our enemies (Matthew 5:44 & Luke 6:35), which is not easy to do, we are not born with empathy. Empathy is learned. An infant is not capable of empathizing, but this is *not* because of *purposeful* sin as some Christian prospankers believe. This is because an infant's brain is not developed enough to allow the infant to think beyond his/her world. This does *not* mean that the infant is evil. This just means that infants are not at that developmental stage and won't be for four or five more years (or longer if these children are not treated with respect and gently told about other's feelings). The young brain is designed by God to first learn what the child's body can do. During the first three months infants are learning exactly how their bodies work. In fact, infants and toddlers are in Jean Piaget's first stage of his cognitive development theory, which is sensorimotor development. While children this age do learn a great deal through social interactions, all of their learning is happening through their five senses and movements. Piaget and Inhelder (1969) state, "We call it the 'sensorimotor' period because the infant lacks symbolic function; that is, he does not have representations by which he can evoke persons or objects in their absence" (p. 3). Infants do not have a strong concept of self. That begins to develop as infants grow into toddlers. Late in the first year of life, infants begin to discover that they are separate beings from their parents. All throughout the first year, infants discover that they can make things happen. "The emergent self is the sense of familiar experience of the body and of the familiarity in the way others respond to those experiences" (Fogel, 2011, p. 202). During the second year of life, toddlers' sense of self develops much more. They now know that they are independent from their parents. Toddlers are really discovering exactly who they are outside of their parents. They have a very strong desire for independence even though they are way too young to handle much independence as the very thing that they so strongly desire is also often very overwhelming for them. This is why toddlers have so many "behavioral issues." Actually, these "behavioral issues" are developmentally appropriate as they discover who they are, how they fit within their families and their world, and try to strike a balance between dependence and independence. For this reason, toddlers are still focused on themselves, although they are a bit more aware of others and may comment when they see or hear someone cry. They may even try to comfort the person who is crying. However, toddlers will think the reason the other person is crying is for the same reason they cry. "A happy and well-adjusted little girl, watching a lion roar in the zoo, reflected: 'He's roaring because he wants to eat me for breakfast.' She could not imagine that the lion had his own private reasons to roar" (Lieberman, 1993, p. 179). Let me make myself clear. Infants and toddlers are very aware of their parents' emotions from birth and are affected by them, but this does not mean that infants and toddlers can empathize with the parents.

Young children from birth until somewhere around the age of four or five years are what Piaget calls egocentric. Again, this may be due to our sinful nature but it does *not* mean that young children are evil. God designed children exactly how they are. There's a reason He made young children egocentric, probably for survival in this harsh, sinful world.

> Piaget referred to this feature of early thinking as "egocentrism," not because children are selfish but because they understand an event subjectively, through their own reactions to it. Their understanding of the relation between cause and effect is centered on their own capacity to make things happen. As a result, young children react to an event in terms of how it affects them. In other words, children reason by applying to themselves the real or imagined consequences of an event.
>
> (Lieberman, 1993, p. 179)

This is why young children have a very hard time sharing with other children. They can't imagine the other child wanting the toy as much as they do. I will be discussing how to appropriately teach young children empathy and how to encourage turn taking in the next part of this book about using gentle discipline.

Since empathy is a learned behavior, how does the use of physical punishment affect the development of empathy in children? If we read books and comments written by prospankers, whether they are Christian or non-believers, there's always a certain sense of coldness and harshness as they try to convince others that spanking is an absolute must for raising respectful and/or "godly" children. They may try to sugar coat it by explaining how to spank "lovingly," but it is still harsh as they also use seemingly harsh Bible verses that are taken completely out of context to back themselves up. In fact, the very phrase that I discussed in chapter 11, "I was spanked and I'm okay," further shows not just denial but a lack of empathy. They assume that because they are "okay" after being spanked (hit) as children that the same will be true for all children. This seems very egotistical. Also, when they read about someone who *isn't* ok after being hit as a child, they often blow off that person and/or say that the person's parents didn't spank "the right and lovingly" way. I continue to hear the exact same argument from prospankers that if spankings are done "the right way," then no emotional harm is done to the child. Only research and the very actions of prospankers show otherwise. *All* spankings are harmful to children! This is true when it comes to empathy.

Given the fact that children are naturally egocentric, when we hit children in order to teach them a lesson, children focus on the pain, fear, and anger they are feeling from being spanked, and, therefore, are unable to truly internalize the message. Yes, parents may tell the child before and after the spanking why he/she is being spanked, but the child does not truly hear the parent's words. Pain does stop the behavior temporarily, but pain highly interferes with the learning process as children are more focused on the pain than anything else. Yes, children may act like they truly understand why they were spanked, but this is simply to please their parents in order to avoid further spankings. Many parents spank when children are "malicious" or disrespectful such as when a three-year-old hits his brother or sister. He gets spanked for hitting, which makes no sense because children can see clearly that hitting and spanking are the same—only adults "spank"—but being spanked for hitting does not teach him how to appropriately interact with his siblings. He may be forced to apologize to his sibling, but he is so focused on how *he* was hurt that he is unable to even try to learn how his sibling felt when he hit him/her. This hinders the development of empathy in the child. "One of the most enduring consequences of corporal punishments—and yet one of the least appreciated and studied— is the stifling of empathy and compassion for oneself and others" (Greven, 1992, p. 127). Yet, God requires us to be empathic and compassionate with other people. "If you had known what these words mean, 'I desire mercy, not sacrifice,' you would not have condemned the innocent" (Matthew 12:7). (See also Hosea 6:6; Ephesians 4:32; Colossians 3:12). As Greven (1992), page 127, states:

> The ability to put oneself in the place of others and to understand how they feel and experience life, and the ability to grasp sympathetically both their suffering and their joy is one of the greatest human achievements.

Sadly, as their parents, the very people who are supposed to be loving and teaching them empathy purposely and intentionally hurt the children and the children begin to develop immunity to empathy. They are so focused on their own pain and how to avoid being physically punished that they are unable to fully grasp or appropriately relate to other's suffering and pain. We see this mostly in adults who were physically punished or harshly punished in other ways and grow up to become prospankers and advocates of spanking. But, we can also sometimes see a lack of empathy in children. On August 20, 2011, Amy shared with me how being spanked caused her to struggle with a lack of empathy throughout her childhood. Amy stated:

> I personally struggled in my childhood with empathy. I would often spank my younger siblings even when I was very young. I would get angry with them and erupt just as my parents did with aggression, and would act out a spanking ritual on my younger sibs. Then afterwards I would feel little to no guilt or remorse. I felt justified since that was how adults resolved their issues when they became angry at me. I had lost sight of an ability to empathize with my siblings who most unfortunately were getting doubly spanked. I was also unable to make friends because when I became angry I would become aggressive. It really does change the course of one's attitude and in a strange twist of fate their ability to know or trust oneself.

It is clear that Amy's parents taught her a "lesson in indifference to suffering" (Greven, 1992, p. 127). Going back to all of the books written by prospankers, as I said, they all lack empathy and compassion for children. In fact, they advise parents, especially mothers, to stifle their empathy and natural desire to protect their children in order to "discipline them with the rod." Here is one such example of an advocate of spanking telling mothers to stifle their empathy in order for their children to be spanked:

> J. Richard Fugate, an advocate of the rod, recognizes the impulse toward empathy and compassion in some parents, especially mothers: "A mother naturally cringes at the thought of switching her own child. The reality of intentionally inflicting pain, especially in using a rod that can make a mark (which will quickly go away), goes against the natural tendency to protect, comfort, and nurture her child. Uninformed mothers may even try to interfere with the father's proper use of a rod." His advice is for mothers

to think of the long-term consequences of their use of the
rod in obtaining the obedience of their children, however
much they may feel the need "to protect, comfort, and
nurture" their children.

(Greven, 1993, p. 127-128)

I find this quite interesting as throughout the Bible God says
He will love, nurture, and protect His children. Yes, there were
times in the Old Testament when God got angry with people
for turning their backs on Him, and yet, He would always have
compassion on His people. He created mothers with a natural
instinct to nurture and protect their children. Just as He made
young children egocentric, He also made mothers nurturers and
protectors of their children. This is all for survival in a world
that is broken by sin. God is love. I can't imagine the Holy
Spirit instructing parents to ignore their God-given instincts
in order to intentionally inflict pain on their children. In fact,
God commands us to take off our sinful nature and put on love
and peace.

Put to death, therefore, whatever belongs to your earthly
nature: sexual immorality, impurity, lust, evil desires and
greed, which is idolatry…Therefore, as God's chosen
people, holy and dearly loved, clothe yourselves with
compassion, kindness, humility, gentleness and patience.
Bear with each other and forgive one another if any of
you has a grievance against someone. Forgive as the Lord
forgave you. And over all these virtues put on love, which
binds them all together in perfect unity.

Colossians 3:5, 12-14

What prospankers don't seem to understand is that it is our
sinful nature that allows us to intentionally inflict harm on children
and other people. Prospankers rely on the same five- or six-rod

verses in Scripture to justify allowing their sinful nature to inflict pain on their children and then further justify it by saying they comforted the child after the spanking. I would like to ask you, if you're a prospanker, do you actually feel the Holy Spirit jumping for joy inside you while you're hitting your child? Do you feel that warm glow we feel when God is pleased with us while your child is crying out in pain inflicted by you? These are tough questions, but if we are honest with ourselves, the answers to these questions are "no." We may think that after we spank our children and are busy loving and comforting them that God is pleased. However, is that *really* the Holy Spirit or is it a combination of endorphins being released as well as our minds trying to justify our actions? Some Christians reading this may not have a strong sensitivity to the Holy Spirit. After all, how do we know it is the Holy Spirit speaking to us? First, one must be a born-again Christian in order for the Holy Spirit to dwell inside you. "Therefore I want you to know that no one who is speaking by the Spirit of God says, 'Jesus be cursed,' and no one can say, 'Jesus is Lord,' except by the Holy Spirit" (1 Corinthians 12:3). Second, the Holy Spirit *never* tells us to do anything evil. Everything that the Holy Spirit tells us is good and glorifies God. Thirdly, everything the Holy Spirit tells us to do will not only benefit us but will benefit others. I will be discussing godly sorrow versus worldly sorrow in chapter 14 on guilt and shame, but, for now, I want to point out that the Holy Spirit always promotes godly sorrow in that we are more concerned about how our mistakes affected others and/ or our relationship with God instead of how our mistakes have affected us. Therefore, the Holy Spirit encourages empathy, peace, and love, which are the fruits of the Spirit of which Galatians 5:22 speaks. The Holy Spirit does *not* promote pain and violence in Jesus's name. In fact, the Holy Spirit reminds us of Christ's teachings, which are peaceful and gentle. "But the Advocate, the Holy Spirit, whom the Father will send in my name, will teach you all things and will remind you of everything I have said to you" (John 14:26). Finally, Scripture warns us not to do anything that will "grieve the Holy Spirit of God, with whom you were sealed for the day of redemption" (Ephesians 4:30). Since we must stifle empathy, compassion, and gentleness when we spank (hit) our children, this grieves the Holy Spirit.

Another reason physical punishment hinders the development of empathy in children is that it does not show respect for the body, mind, feelings, and spirit of the child. Therefore, the child does not learn to respect his/herself or others. Thus, the cycle of physical punishment/abuse, which are one in the same (see Chapter 11), continues unless the person recognizes that it is wrong and against God's will and works against it. Also, physical punishment causes children to become passive, which, despite what many Christian prospankers say, *is not* good! This can lead to children not getting the help they need both in and out of school. It also leads to apathy. Greven (1992), pages 128 through 129, states:

> Equally enduring are the apathy and passivity so often experienced by children who are physically punished and abused. Ruth and Henry Kemp point out: "Another outstanding characteristic of young abused children is their compliance and acceptance of whatever happens. They are passive and obedient, even when in the hospital they are required to submit to painful procedures, or when in the process of an evaluation they are taken away from their parents by a stranger. They will remain in uncomfortable positions for a long time if asked to do so, or sit quietly while their mothers talk for a long time. That this truly is compliance is proved by their gradual growth of assertiveness and resistance, if they are removed to a more permissive environment."

This may sound great to some parents. Who wouldn't want an easy, compliant child? But what people such as the Pearls fail to understand is these children are *not* truly happy. They've learned to stop feeling, to stop caring about themselves and others in order to survive lest they get beaten again. This is no way for anyone to live, much less a child. In severe cases such as these, children do not learn empathy at all as they are so focused on just surviving. This is exactly what happened to Phil E. Quinn. Quinn (1988) begins by stating the fact that "Empathy makes us so uncomfortable with someone else's suffering that we are motivated to do something about it. Parents unable to empathize with the hurts of their children are likely to do little to relieve the suffering" (p. 55).

Quinn goes on to describe how he never learned empathy as a child due to the severe abuse he endured throughout his childhood. He explains:

> Empathy is learned most easily in childhood. The tragedy for me, as for many others, is that I was never provided the opportunity to develop empathy. My childhood was spent trying to survive—not only the abuse, but my own incredible feelings. I was too preoccupied with my own feelings to be concerned about those of others. It took all my concentration and effort to avoid being overwhelmed by a childhood that threatened almost daily to destroy me. Even at the age of twenty-three it was difficult to vicariously experience what someone else might be thinking or feeling.
>
> (Quinn, 1988, p. 55)

Due to not being able to learn empathy as a child, it wasn't until he started having children that Quinn was force to teach himself how to be empathetic toward his children. Quinn (1988), pages 55 through 56, states:

Like other survivors of child abuse, I tended to measure the suffering of others—particularly my children—by my own experience. If what they seemed to be experiencing fell within the range of my own negative experience, then no empathetic response would result. Like all children learning to walk and run and play, my children would occasionally fall down and skin their elbows and knees. Also like most children, they would turn to me for comfort. At first. But after a while they stopped coming to me for comfort. Why? I was totally oblivious to their suffering! Seeing their little skinned elbows and knees provoked no emotional reaction in me at all...To be an effective parent, I literally had to resensitize myself to the experiences of my children; to realize that skinned elbows and knees *do* hurt and that it was important to respond with empathy and caring. It took time and conscious effort to develop these empathetic skills, but I made it.

Sadly, not everyone is as successful at retraining themselves to become more empathetic toward others—especially toward their children, as Quinn was. Denial and repression often set in making one oblivious to the need to have more empathy. Then satan further hardens our hearts by having us read books and articles that say children must be spanked in order to become God-fearing adults. Since children learn by example and experience, it can sometimes be difficult to break out of the cycle of using physical punishment/abuse with their own children. After all:

> If it was good enough for my parents and me, they reason, then it is good enough for me and my child. It is one way to parent, or at least it is the way it has always been done in my family. This is one reason abused children tend to become abusive parents.

> (Quinn, 1988, p. 56)

It is clear that children are learning more through their parents' *actions* toward them than by their words. Parents can tell their children until they're blue in the face that violence is unacceptable, but if they are hitting their children in order to drive home the message, the children will get the exact *opposite* message. Children are too focused on the pain to internalize a message of peace and love from their parents' words. Thus, the age-old saying, "Actions speak louder than words," is quite true when it comes to children.

> From the research of Straus and others, we've learned quite a bit about the effects of spanking. We've learned that spanking teaches kids that hitting others is morally correct. In other words, hitting is okay if the other person is doing something wrong and won't stop it.
>
> (Sprain, 2000, http://www.parentingthoughts.org/
> Spanking.htm)

Children will often imitate how their parents treat them and other people. When they see and/or experience adults hitting children, they will often act it out during play either with a doll or a sibling.

> The mom of one of my patients once told me that she thought she had to spank her child to be a good disciplinarian—until one day she observed her 3-year-old daughter hitting her younger brother. When the mom intervened, the daughter said, 'I'm just playing mommy.' Obviously, there was no more spanking in that house.
>
> (Sears, 2010, http://www.parenting.com/article/
> ask-dr-sears-spanking—yay-or-nay)

I have witnessed similar situations in which a physically punished child hits their sibling during play. They really have no idea why what they did was wrong nor do they understand how they've hurt their sibling. "Spanking sabotages empathy. A child is likely to haul off and hit another child without considering whether his actions are going to hurt the other person" (Sears, 2010, http://www.parenting.com/article/ask-dr-sears-spanking—yay-or-nay).

Finally, there have been Facebook postings in which people joke about how they were spanked and it didn't affect them. Here's an example of one such post:

> I have to laugh at people who are against spanking... My parents whipped my butt like there was no tomorrow... I didn't hate them... I didn't have trust issues with them because of it... I didn't fear them... But I darn sure respected them! And I learned what my boundaries were and knew what would happen if I broke them... I wasn't abused... I was disciplined... *Re-post if you got your butt smacked and survived it... God put extra padding back there for a reason.*

I am sickened and saddened by the harsh, mocking tone of such a post as if being hit and/or hitting a child is not serious. It also further proves that prospankers lack empathy and compassion. To truly believe that children need a "good whipping or spanking" in order to learn limits and boundaries shows a lack of regard for the fruits of the Spirit, the child's feelings and dignity, and for people who were spanked and did *not* turn out "just fine." Yes, children who are physically punished/abused can learn empathy, but it is much more difficult for them, and they often learn it from someone other than their parents. The research and actions of prospankers clearly demonstrates that physical punishment/abuse limits the development of empathy in children.

"Do not seek revenge or bear a grudge against anyone among your people, but love your neighbor as yourself. I am the LORD" (Leviticus 19:18).

In the next section of this chapter, I will be discussing how spanking/abusing children often leads to anger and aggression at some point in their lives. Also, the physical punishment/abuse in the name of God often leads some to become angry with God and/or the church.

Anger and Aggression: "I Refuse to Follow a God that Promotes and Inflicts Violence!"

The above statement, "I refuse to follow a God that promotes and inflicts violence," saddens me greatly. I have been hearing it a lot lately from non-believers after the airing of the interview with Michael and Debi Pearl from No Greater Joy Ministries on CNN. The parents of Lydia Schatz were convicted of murder after beating Lydia to death by following the Pearl's child training "wisdom" found in their book, *To Train Up a Child*. We will be discussing how people—including those that grow up in Christian homes—can become so angry that they reject God forever.

As we saw in the previous section on empathy, a lack of empathy makes becoming angry and aggressive with others— especially with children—much easier. After all, as we saw, some prospankers tell parents to suppress their God-given instinct to love, nurture, and protect their children in order to inflict pain on them in the name of "godly discipline." Empathy works to inhibit anger and aggression in people (Quinn, 1988). People who lack and/or suppress empathy and compassion are much more likely to believe that spanking children is perfectly fine. The reason for this is that being hit by one's parents not only makes one feel weak and helpless, but it also teaches the child that the stronger adult is allowed to hit the weaker child. Children are never allowed to defend themselves during spankings lest they endure further spankings with possibly even more force being applied by the parents. These memories are stored either consciously or subconsciously in their minds. When these children become adults, many of them crave the power that they lacked as children, therefore misusing the power they now have over their children. "Only now, when someone weaker than they is involved, do they finally fight back, often quite fiercely. There are countless rationalizations, still used today, to justify their behavior" (Miller, 1994, p. 16).

Anger and aggression are two very common effects of physical punishment/abuse with children because children have a very black and white view of justice and fairness. Even when children are spanked the "right, loving" way, anger and aggression pop up as they try to cope with the confusion and unfairness of being intentionally hurt by their parents who are supposed to love them. Greven (1992) states, "Being assaulted violently in the name of discipline invariably produces anger and often rage in children, just as it does in most adults" (p. 123). Because young children cannot express their anger verbally due to a limited vocabulary, they will often act out aggressively. Also, some children may become more defiant as a way to seek revenge for being hit by their parents. "In fact, research shows that children who are spanked tend to grow defiant and aggressive" (Heimlich, 2011, p. 78). Despite what many Christian advocates of spanking claim, the anger, aggression, and the other harmful effects of physical punishment are actually *worse* when it is done in the name of Jesus,

Psychology professor, Bette L. Bottoms (2003), at the University of Illinois-Chicago, conducted psychological tests on two groups of subjects to see if it was indeed more harmful to use physical punishment within a religious or non-religious context. One group experienced physical punishment/abuse in the name of religion. The other group experienced their physical punishment/abuse in a non-religious context. The results were clear. The subjects who had experienced physical punishment/abuse in the name of God "more severely suffered from such psychological problems as depression, anxiety, hostility, and psychotic personality disorders" (Heimlich, 2011, p. 31). Heimlich (2011), page 31, goes on to state:

> In that study, Bottoms opines as to why abuse involving religion might be more traumatic than abuse in which religion is not a factor: "Religious contexts and justifications may add an additional layer of complexity and harm to the experience of child physical abuse... We speculate that there is an additional sense of betrayal involved and much internal cognitive dissonance and perhaps guilt as victims deal, not only with the physically abusive actions, but also with the confusing relation of the actions to religion, which they are taught to believe and follow."

This is further illustrated by MC's experiences as a child. MC was brought up in a Fundamentalist Christian family where spanking is used quite commonly as parents are taught that God "commands" that children be spanked. MC was spanked by his father on his bare bottom throughout his childhood with his father using his hand, belt, or paddle. As a child, MC repressed his anger because he was taught that he deserved to be hurt by his father for disobeying; that his father spanked him because he loved him; that the spanking was for his own good; and that God commanded his father to spank him as this was a sign of love. While there were occasions where MC did get angry as a child due to his own spanking or friends and siblings being spanked, much of his anger cropped up when MC became a young adult. He found out that everything he had been taught as a child was all lies. He felt betrayed. In an electronic message sent on August 28, 2011, MC conveyed the following to me:

> The main out-let of my anger is unfortunately the church. The church may not have personally whacked my bare skin with a paddle or belt, but they certainly passed along the false teachings that caused my father to do it. I resent the teachings and practices of the church I grew up in, and I resent any Christian organization that passes along, or accepts, such teachings today. My blood boils when I think of how what the church taught impacted my sexual development, leading to an orientation that eroticizes spanking. If my orientation is a sin, then the church helped lead me into that sin by passing along their pro-spanking message. I also find it difficult to trust the church; and as much as I have tried to separate my anger at the church from God, I sometimes find myself unable to trust God, and often feel angry at God. I feel like the church failed me, and now my relationship with God is strained and filled with tension.

How very sad that MC struggles with anger for the church and with God because of the pain he experienced as a child. This is quite common of people who have been hurt in the Name of God. How can a child grow up to truly trust in the Lord when He "wanted" the child to be hurt for his/her sin? I find it interesting that so many Christians truly believe in spanking to discourage their children from sinning and lead them to God, but we've been seeing throughout this part of this book that the opposite seems to happen in most cases of physical punishment.

> Some parents even believe that it is their Christian duty to administer physical punishment—to build character, discourage sin, and instill a sense of submission and obedience to the will of God, as represented through

parental authority. They take what God has created in his own image and refashion it so their children will grow up to be just like them.

(Quinn, 1988, p. 156-157)

Many Christian and non-Christian prospankers constantly claim that spankings done "lovingly" are never harmful in any way to the child; this obviously is *not* the case. Look what Quinn (1988) goes on to say: "My adoptive parents told me hundreds of times, during the endless beatings, that they loved me. If that was their way to love, they very nearly loved me to death" (p. 157).

Olivia grew up in England in the 1950s when physical punishment was rarely questioned. She was physically punished regularly as a child. On August 27, 2011, Olivia shared with me via electronic mail how angry she felt whenever her parents would hit her. It was even worse if her dad tried to be loving afterward. Here's what Olivia stated:

> I would be in my room and Dad would go and fetch his large slipper with the leather sole…yelling of course… He would wrestle me over his lap while he sat on my bed, pulling my panties down while pinning both my hands with one of his above my head, while I told him and begged him to stop to no avail. He would then use that pinning technique with one leg to make sure I couldn't get away and then start spanking. Down would come that leather slipper over and over on my bottom while I screamed the place down. I was terrified, ANGRY, I hated him…them… How DARE he/she hit me? How DARE they hit anyone? On and on it would go…not just say ten strikes but on and on. Honestly I don't know how long. All I know was that I was left a seething, angry, distraught mess, almost "thrown" onto my bed to stay there until I was "ready to come down and behave." Most of the time I stayed there. A lot of the time I was told to stay there as further punishment. [He

tried once with the "oh we love you" and tried to cuddle me. I was having none of it… I couldn't bear him near me. I hated him! How DARE he want to hold me and tell me he loved me! HE was LYING… How could you hit and hurt someone like that and then tell them you LOVED THEM? That is how I felt then! How did I usually feel? I…distraught is not strong enough. I really do NOT have the words. As I have said before, I learned fear, pain, anger, hate, and resentment. I really DID hate them at that time. I prayed to God to send me away. [A common threat to children in those days was to be "sent to boarding school," which was supposed to be a terrible place]. I prayed that they WOULD send me to boarding school because I was never in trouble at school, my teachers all liked/loved me! I can remember blubbering bubbles and snot and almost being sick with the…anger, the…fear…the…unfairness… the…audacity of it for hours… My bottom bright red again with white streaks where the slipper had fallen. Or my mum's fingers…hard, hot ridges… I was always asking to go and stay with my paternal grandparents for "the weekend" or a week. My grandmother was only too pleased to have me…and I think she knew why from the way she spoke to me. My mum never knew but there were a few times when, although I was only perhaps eight to eleven I went out into the night when she was asleep and sat on the front garden wall sobbing at the stars and moon and sky, begging God to help me. This would have been HOURS after being spanked…and after her bedtime…

Again, while Olivia sought comfort from God in most cases throughout her childhood, the very thing that was supposed to help discourage sinfulness in her actually was what created her anger, hate, and resentfulness toward her parents who thought they were doing the right thing. I wonder if some prospankers are not only in denial and lack a certain amount of empathy but are also so filled with anger that they get revenge by twisting Scripture around in order to justify hurting their own children. After all:

> Beatings, which are only one form of mistreatment, are always degrading, because the child not only is unable to defend him- or herself but is also supposed to show gratitude and respect to the parents in return. And along with corporal punishment there is a whole gamut of ingenious measures applied 'for the child's own good' which are difficult for a child to comprehend and which for that very reason often have devastating effects later in life.
>
> (Miller, 1994, p. 17)

Sadly, the devastating effects that Miller is describing are the very ones that keep the cycle of physical punishment/ abuse continuing.

While some research shows that an occasional spanking done "lovingly" is a *bit* less harmful (we will discuss spanking "in love" more in-depth in chapters 13 and 14), it is still damaging as it teaches children to equate hitting with love. This creates a higher risk for domestic violence as children who were hit grow into teenagers and adults. Simons, Lin, and Gordon conducted a research study in 1998 to see if physical punishment did indeed increase the risk of dating violence later on. They studied 113 boys in rural Iowa that were in seventh grade and/or were thirteen years old. They asked these boys' parents how often the boys were spanked, and how often a belt or a paddle was used to administer the spankings. The questions were repeated in three intervals during this five-year study. Over half of the boys in this study experienced physical punishment during these five years. "Consequently, the findings about corporal punishment apply to the majority of boys in that community, not just to the children of a small group of violent parents" (Straus, 2006, p. 201). During this study, the boys were also asked if they had hit, pushed, or shoved their girlfriends in the last year during a disagreement. The boys were asked about any other delinquent acts they may have been involved with as well. The study took into account whether the boys' parents were loving, consistent, and supervised their children. Here are the findings from this study:

> Simons and his colleagues found that the more corporal punishment experienced by these boys, the greater the probability of their physically assaulting a girlfriend. Moreover, like the other prospective studies, the analysis took into account the misbehavior that led parents to use corporal punishment, and also for the quality of parenting. This means that the relation of corporal punishment to violence against a girlfriend is very unlikely to be due to poor parenting. Rather, it is another study showing that the long run effect of corporal punishment is to engender more rather than less misbehavior. In short, spanking boomerangs.
>
> (Straus, 2006, p. 201)

Yet another study done with young children shows that corporal punishment "was associated with an increased probability of a child assaulting the parent a year and a half later. Thus, while it is true that corporal punishment teaches the child a lesson, it is certainly not the lesson intended by the parents" (Straus, 2006, p. 200). Some prospankers claim that consistently spanking does not make children any more aggressive than other children, and that the key is to be consistent. I must challenge this because there are just too many other studies showing the opposite to be true. Also, if physical punishment does not create an aggressive tendency in children, then why do a great deal of these children grow up to follow in their parents' footsteps? It just does not line up with the research or the societal norms. While I will be discussing "lovingly" hitting children in chapters 13 and 14, I want to share what Wendy conveyed to me about how it was when she was in grade school. Corporal punishment was allowed during the time she was in grade school. However, there still was a great deal of aggressiveness at the school. Here is what Wendy observed as written via an electronic message dated August 27, 2011:

> Since physical punishment was used both at home and at the school I went to from K-4, violence just seemed like a normal way to solve problems. There was some concern about aggressive behavior, but not enough knowledge at the time to realize that spanking might not be the best response to it.

Katie also went to a Christian grade school where corporal punishment was used. However, the teachers and principal were not allowed to spank the children if they were angry. Here are Katie's thoughts about seeing calm teachers spanking children at school as conveyed to me via an electronic message on September 3, 2011:

> I can tell you that at our DND schools the teacher who was angry wasn't supposed to spank—it was meant to be an "impartial" teacher to administer a "reasonable" beating. I was a good girl and never got hit at school though. I thought it was creepier to have someone who wasn't angry do the hitting—it seemed worse to me than someone who had lost their marbles. Calculated.

It seems that spanking children "in love" is worse than being hit in anger. Either way, hitting children teaches them how to behave aggressively and violently toward loved ones. It also can teach children to submit to domestic violence. In a study written in the *Journal of the American Academy of Pediatrics* in 2010 examined 2,000 families to see if the use of physical punishment with three-year-old children was related with physical violence used between the parents. Over half of the three-year-olds in this study had been spanked at least once during the previous month. The results of this study showed that, "The odds of using physical punishment doubled in households where parents used aggression against each other. This is not surprising since physical punishment is a form of interpersonal aggression" (Lopez-Duran, 2010, http://www.drmomma.org/2010/09/why-spanking-is-never-okay.html). Sadly, most hitting of children begins at the extremely young age of one year old, with some infants being hit before they are even a year old. Infants *never* understand being hit! This is far beyond their comprehension. It is the same for toddlers! Research shows that "children who were spanked at age one had more aggressive behaviors at age two and performed worse on measures of thinking abilities at age three" (Thomas, 2009, http://www.drmomma.org/2009/09/early-spanking-increases-toddler.html). And finally, in yet another study that was done to see if spanking infants and toddlers made them more aggressive as they got older:

> Slade and Wissow found that, compared with children who were never spanked, children who were frequently spanked (five times a week) before age two were four times more likely to have behavioral problems by the time they started school. (Slade E., Wissow L. *Spanking in Early Childhood and Later Behavior Problems: A Prospective Study of Infants and Young Toddlers*, Pediatrics, vol. 113, no. 5, May 2004).
>
> (Klebanov, 2011, http://www.examiner.
> com/parenting-in-san-francisco/
> the-ministry-of-michael-and-debbie-pearl)

It is clear that physical punishment does increase aggression in children.

A great number of prospankers claim that the world is much more violent than it was back in the "good old days" because children are being spanked less. They believe that children who are not physically punished are not as respectful. These two claims are actually incorrect. "Straus (1994) and Gershoff (2002) report that over 90 percent of parents still report using corporal punishment on their children" (Couture, 2007, http://stophitting. blogspot.com/2006/01/back-in-good-ol-days-and-other.html). Sadly, the majority of children today will be hit at some point during their childhoods. Ever since Adam and Eve sinned, there has been violence as violence is due to sin entering the world. The only true difference between now and then is that we are almost constantly exposed to violence thanks to the media. Besides sex, violence is a common theme in our movies, television shows, music, and videogames. Plus, the news is constantly reporting acts of violence. We are so much more aware of violence whereas back then people were not as exposed or aware of the violence that was occurring and they could shelter themselves and their children from violence because there was no television or Internet. Children didn't watch cartoons or play videogames filled with violent images like they do today. Because so many parents have to work full-time in order to survive today, children are being left alone with all this access to violent media with little guidance from busy, stressed out parents. Research shows that all of this exposure to violence is desensitizing children and adults to violence. Greven (1992), page 129, states:

> "Research has demonstrated that television must be considered one of the major socializers of children's aggressive behavior. Two major behavioral effects of heavy viewing of televised violence are: (1) an increase in children's level of aggression; and (2) an increase in children's passive acceptance of the use of aggression by others." Both aggression and apathy thus are intensified by an immersion in television violence although the roots of both undoubtedly are to be found in the life histories of punishment and abuse of those who view such violence with either indifference or enthusiasm.

It is clear that between being spanked (hit) from young ages and being exposed to so much violence via the media that children are learning that violence is how we solve problems. And they learn that a certain amount of aggressive behavior is acceptable and even expected in today's society. However, Jesus is very much against any type of violence. Look what He says in Matthew 11:13: "From the days of John the Baptist until now, the kingdom of heaven has been subjected to violence, and violent people have been raiding it." Not only does this show that Jesus is against violence, but that violence has always been in the world.

Since aggression and anger are closely related as they feed off each other, I would like to conclude this chapter by taking one last look at anger. While anger can be used in a productive manner, it is often allowed to fester, leading to rage, bitterness, and resentment. Scripture warns us not to sin in our anger (Ephesians 4:26). Jesus also gives a very stern warning in Matthew 5:21-26 about allowing anger to get out of control. He also tells us to be quick to reconcile with each other in this same passage. As we've seen throughout this section, physical punishment often creates a strong feeling of anger in children even if it is done in the "correct, godly, loving way." As we saw with MC, anger may not appear until the child becomes an adult. Anger is a common response to being hurt in any way. As Greven (1992), page 124, states:

> Anger is a child's best (and often only) defense, for it arises out of a powerful sense of self, a self being violated and abused by painful blows and hurtful words. The child has been hurt on *purpose [bolding for emphasis done by Steph]* by an adult in order to teach a lesson in discipline, but the child experiences this pain and reproach as an assault upon the self as well as upon the body. Often the result is not only anger but also hatred and a powerful desire for revenge, which often takes the form of imagined

mutilation or murder of the person who inflicted the pain. These powerful emotions are permanently stored in unconscious memories, but sometimes people also remember them quite consciously, years after the events that provoked the feelings.

Here is an example written by a child of how being spanked caused him to have angry, violent thoughts:

Boy, Age 13, Illinois

'Many adults spank their children. Sometimes, they think it is the best way to punish a child. I believe spanking isn't effective because all you're doing is hitting a child. When I get a spanking (mainly from my mom) it doesn't hurt… it just makes me very mad… It can give a kid violent thoughts… Everyone should stop harsh spankings on kids'

(Block & Gomez, 2011, p. 25)

If spanking is so right and godly, then why do adults still deal with the anger created in them from being spanked by their Christian parents? Here is yet another story of a child being hit by his father who was a pastor, and, after many years, still vividly remembers the anger he felt toward his father:

When in his early fifties, Edmund Gosse recalled in his famous autobiography, *Father and Son* (1907), his one encounter with corporal punishment as vividly as if it just happened. Gosse was the only child of two intensely apocalyptic parents, English members of the sect of Plymouth Brethren. He recollected: "It was about the date of my sixth birthday that I did something very naughty, some act of direct disobedience, for which my Father, after a solemn sermon, chastised me, sacrificially, by giving me several cuts with a cane. This action was justified, as everything he did was justified, by reference to Scripture."

Gosse also had vivid memories of his own reactions and feelings to this encounter with corporal punishment. He recollected "being made, not contrite or humble, but furiously angry by this caning. I cannot account for the flame of rage which it awakened in my bosom," he wrote, but added that "I have to confess with shame that I went about the house for some days with a murderous hatred of my Father locked inside my bosom."

(Greven, 1992, p. 124)

Some may say that it is a child's will that causes the child to become angry and aggressive after a "godly" spanking. I must disagree with this because a "godly" spanking is supposed to help rid the child of sin, but instead it sows a seed of sin into a child's heart. It is obvious that this is *not* what God intended! This is why Jesus warns against causing children, and anyone weaker, to sin in Matthew 18:6-9 and Mark 9:42. This is also why Ephesians 6:4 and Colossians 3:21 commands parents not to embitter their children. Yes, a lack of discipline causes children to sin and become embittered, but so does physical punishment and other types of harsh punishment.

Going back to CNN's interview with the Pearls, authors of *To Train Up a Child*, with which I began this section, many non-believers have been leaving many angry comments on Christian websites that advocate against the Pearl's teachings and the use of any type of physical punishment, saying, "I refuse to follow a God that advocates and promotes violence!" After hearing about the abusive and deadly teachings of the Pearls, who truly believe that their teachings are ordained by God, atheists and other non-Christians have been absolutely tearing apart God's Word by taking certain verses and passages completely out of context in order to show how violent and bad God is. They are angry because instead of seeing our true God, they are seeing an evil, hateful god. They are not seeing God's amazing grace, mercy, love, and forgiveness because we Christians are not doing well with showing our broken world God's love for them. Matthew 5:13-16 states:

> You are the salt of the earth. But if the salt loses its saltiness, how can it be made salty again? It is no longer good for anything, except to be thrown out and trampled underfoot. You are the light of the world. A town built on a hill cannot be hidden. Neither do people light a lamp and put it under a bowl. Instead they put it on its stand, and it gives light to everyone in the house. In the same way, let your light shine before others, that they may see your good deeds and glorify your Father in heaven.

We are supposed to be the salt and light of the world in order to bring people into the kingdom of God, but yet, we hit children in God's name, murder people in God's name, say, "God hates fags," while appearing to act better than others. It really is no wonder so many people are rejecting God and are so against Christians. They are getting a completely inaccurate view of who God is from the very people who are representing Him.

This anger is causing people to perish because they refuse to come to Him for salvation. This is *not* what God wants at all. He loves everyone so much and is not willing that any should perish (2 Peter 3:9). It is clear from all of the research and personal stories that children remember being physically punished and abused more than parents realize. Do we really want our children to grow up to be angry, unempathetic people who become aggressive toward weaker people? Or do we want our children to grow up displaying the fruits of the Spirit in order to help turn more people to God that they may know His wonderful peace, love, and joy that we can only get through a personal relationship with Him? It's up to us. Please open your hearts to the truth! God does *not* promote, condone, or command the use of physical punishment with children. Please open your eyes and look around the world in order to see what is happening because precious children are being hurt.

> Do not repay anyone evil for evil. Be careful to do what is right in the eyes of everyone. If it is possible, as far as it depends on you, live at peace with everyone. Do not take revenge, my dear friends, but leave room for God's wrath, for it is written: "It is mine to avenge; I will repay," says the Lord.
>
> Romans 12:17-19

References

Block, N. A. & Gomez, M. Y. (2011). *This Hurts Me More Than It Hurts You: In Words and Pictures.* Lexington, KY: Center for Effective Discipline.

Couture, L. (2007). *Back in the Good Ol' Days.* http://stophitting. blogspot.com/2006/01/back-in-good-ol-days-and-other. html

Fogel, A. (2011). *Infant Development: A Topical Approach.* Hudson, NY: Sloan Publishing.

Greven, P. (1992). *Spare the Child.* New York, NY: Vintage Books.

Heimlich, J. (2011). *Breaking Their Will.* Amherst, NY: Prometheus Books.

Klebanov, M. (2011). *The "Ministry" of Michael and Debi Pearl.* http://www.examiner.com/parenting-in-san-francisco/ the-ministry-of-michael-and-debbie-pearl

Lieberman, A. F. (1993). *The Emotional Life of the Toddler.* New York, NY: The Free Press.

Lopez-Duran, N. (2010). *Why Spanking is Never Okay* http:// www.drmomma.org/2010/09/why-spanking-is-never-okay. html

Miller, A. (1994). *For Your Own Good*. New York, NY: The Noonday Press.

Piaget, J. & Inhelder, B. (1969). *Psychology of the Child*. Washington D. C.: Basic Books, Inc.

Quinn, P. E. (1988). *Spare the Rod*. Nashville, TN: Abingdon Press.

Sears, W. (2010). *Spanking—Yay or Nay*. http://www.parenting.com/article/ask-dr-sears-spanking—yay-or-nay

Sprain, J. (2000). *Spanking-What Research Says*. http://www.parentingthoughts.org/Spanking.htm

Straus, M. A. (2006). *Beating the Devil Out of Them*. New Brunswick, NJ: Transaction Publishers.

Thomas, J. (2009). *Early Spanking Increases Toddler Aggression, Lowers IQ*. http://www.drmomma.org/2009/09/early-spanking-increases-toddler.html

Chapter 13

What Does Fear and Love Got to Do with It?

In the previous chapter we looked at how spanking/abuse negatively effects the development of empathy in children. We also saw that any type of physical punishment can cause aggressive tendencies in children and adults. Physical punishment also leads to anger in children and adults due to being hurt intentionally by the very people that are supposed to love and protect them. In this chapter, we will see that fear is the main effect of hitting children. We will see that by teaching children that God wants them to be spanked, they often develop a fear of God that either strains their relationships with God or causes them to reject Him altogether. Finally, we will see that spanking "in love" is indeed harmful despite what many prospankers claim.

Fear: "That Child Needs the Fear of the Lord Put in Him!"

We have all heard that line from prospankers a number of times. As I pointed out in chapter 2, putting the fear of God into a child is one of the primary reasons people spank children. They use fear and respect as interchangeable concepts when they have *no* similarities in their meanings. (See chapter 9 for more info). Fear is indeed the primary effect experienced by *all* children who are physically punished whether mildly or severely. Pain is why physical punishment is effective, though only temporarily, as most humans are afraid of pain and will usually do everything in their power to avoid it. It usually takes only one or two times of a young child being hit for him/her to become afraid of getting spanked. Most prospankers, especially Christians, view this fear as a good thing, and even a must, in order to teach children to obey them and ultimately God. Yet, 2 Timothy 1:7 states, "For the Spirit God gave us does not make us timid, but gives us power, love and self-discipline." And 1 John 4:18 says that there is no fear in love. Fear comes from satan. "Courage comes from God, while fear is what satan tries to give us" (Meyer, 2011, p. 272). Throughout the Bible God tells His people not to be afraid of Him.

Greven (1992), page 122, states:

> Once a child is struck, the memory remains encoded in the brain and body for life. Even those who were struck only once or twice can often remember the pain and shock years afterward. For those children who are punished more frequently, however, the anticipation of pain itself becomes part of the punishment, and the anxiety and even dread generated by experiential knowledge of the burning sting of a hand, or a belt, or a rod, or any other implement, cannot easily be quelled.

Children will begin to cry, have an elevated heart rate, and shallow breathing—all symptoms of fear—before their parents even begin to spank them. MC, who we met in chapter 12, relayed to me on September 29, 2011, via electronic message how he felt right before he was spanked by his father. MC states, "The stomach sinking dread of impending punishment was used as a motivator."

Olivia, from chapter 12, also felt a similar fear before she was spanked. On August 27, 2011, Olivia conveyed to me in an electronic message the following:

> Sometimes I would be either sent to my room...or taken there [I can remember one time when it was in their room] more like dragged there. There was NO way this quiet child was going to allow herself to be hit...even knowing it would make it worse. I had to "fight back" and defend myself. Even terrified of the outcome I would NOT just "give in."

Sadly, tears of fear turn into tears of pain as most Christian advocates of spanking advise parents not to let a child's crying and/or pleading dissuade them from implementing the physical punishment. As Greven (1992), page 123, states:

> Children cry when they are hurt and when they are frightened, and corporal punishments entail both pain and fear. Tears of anticipation, which are ineffectual efforts to ward off or delay the pains to come, are usually followed by tears of suffering, as Christenson, Dobson, Fugate, Lessin, and others have noted... The big and powerful always find ways of intimidating and dominating the small and powerless, and pain is the most compelling method of all for forcing children to submit their wills and selves to the wills and commands of adults. The pain generates fear, as so many corporal-punishment advocates readily acknowledge, and the fear never disappears entirely.

It is clear that being hit by someone the child loves and is reliant on is quite scary for the child. This is especially true because most children begin being hit at the age of one year old, or, in some cases, even before he/she is a year old. Infants and toddlers are just learning cause and effect, so they have no understanding as to why they're being hit or what may cause them to be hit again. Can we imagine exploring a new world and being purposely hurt every time we touched the "wrong" thing or went the "wrong" direction not knowing why it is wrong or what else is "wrong?" What an absolutely terrifying experience that would be for us. I wouldn't want to do much exploring after a while for fear of making a mistake. And yet, all too often, this is the new world that a great deal of infants and toddlers come into. Here is one such example. Phil E. Quinn's one-year-old daughter kept touching a breakable object on his parent's coffee table. He told her "No" several times but every time he'd go back to talking to his parents she'd reach for it again. Until finally:

> My mother counseled sweetly, "You'd better teach her who's boss right now, or you'll be in big trouble later!" It was the same voice so often used to rationalize the beatings she had inflicted upon me. As if on cue, I reached out and smashed the child's tiny hand flat on the surface of the table. In that instant I saw the confusion in her eyes turn to hurt and then to pain as they filled with tears. I also saw my parents relax. It was obvious that I had won their approval, but at the expense of my infant daughter. My parents smiled. I felt sick. I had become like them. Many times since that day I have asked myself why I did not just move the objects out of her reach. (Quinn, 1988, p. 76)

Thankfully, Quinn knew what he did to his daughter was wrong, and, therefore, worked to stop it. But for many prospankers, they focus more on the fact that the hitting worked, which enables them to squelch any empathy they may have for their child's pain, thus enabling them to continue hitting their child whenever he/she doesn't or, more likely, is *unable* to comply with the parent's command. This creates an environment of fear for the child even if he/she doesn't show it in obvious ways. Research shows that infants and toddlers who are physically punished do not explore their environments as much as their peers who are not physically punished.

> Psychologists studied a group of sixteen fourteen-month-olds playing with their mothers. When one group of toddlers tried to grab a forbidden object, they received a slap on the hand; the other group of toddlers did not receive physical punishment. In follow-up studies of these children seven months later, the punished babies were found to be less skilled at exploring their environment. Better to separate the child from the object or supervise his exploration and leave little hands unhurt.
>
> (Sears, 2011,
> http://www.askdrsears.com/topics/discipline-behavior/
> spanking/10-reasons-not-hit-your-child)

Quinn (1988) puts it quite well when he states that "the fear of punishment or retaliation becomes the inhibiting force in these situations" (p. 76). As we can see, fear inhibits learning in children and adults because fear narrows brain receptors. If we don't feel safe, we have trouble concentrating and/or taking healthy risks for fear we will be punished if we make a mistake. "Abundant research has shown that negative emotions, such as anxiety, fear, irritation, shame, and guilt hinder learning, because they temporarily narrow the scope of attention, cognition, and action (Pekrun & Perry, 2002)" (Boekaerts, 2002, http://www.sciencedirect.com/science/article/pii/S0959475202000105). However, many prospankers seem to ignore and/or be in denial about how all forms of hitting children are harmful due to the fear it instills in children.

Research has shown that physical punishment can lower children's IQ scores because instead of learning critical thinking skills, they learn not to question authority—even when doing so would help them come up with a correct solution to the problem. "Over decades it has come to be agreed upon by psychologists and learning theorists that punishment is generally an ineffectual and problematic learning tool" (Grille, 2005, p. 182). In fact, this can lead children and adults to a form of learned helplessness. Children grow up learning that they are punished every time they don't succeed in meeting their parents' high expectations for them, so they quit trying. This can lead to struggling in their occupational pursuits.

> So, even if no single instance is traumatizing, they may be similar to the laboratory animals in Seligman's experiments on "learned helplessness" who became passive and withdrawn as a way of adapting to punishment they could not escape (Seligman and Garbor, 1982).
>
> (Straus, 2006, p. 138)

On the other side of this spectrum are children who are quite successful throughout their schooling and careers because they are perfectionists. They are also afraid to fail due to fear of punishment, so they become overachievers stressing themselves out beyond what is necessary in order to *always* succeed and *always* please others. This can cause them to hide their sins and quirks deep within their hearts in order to prevent anyone from knowing what is truly going on inside of them. Here is a perfect example of a child who was spanked consistently in the "right, loving" way, and how she quickly learned to hide her sins and became a perfectionist:

> The little girl's parents were careful not to spank in anger. They followed a procedure of talking to the little girl before

and after each spanking. The little girl always seemed so repentant before the spanking. After the spanking, she appeared to be relieved of a heavy burden of guilt that she had been carrying.

The little girl grew up to be an excellent teenager. She was easy to get along with and quick to please. She was upheld in her church as a model of good behavior for younger girls.

Though on the outside this little girl was a model daughter, on the inside things were different. You see, spankings taught this girl a very important lesson: as long as you conceal all sin and human weakness, including negative emotions, you will be acceptable and valued, and you will escape punishment...

As a teen, this girl hated to be called "sweet" or a "role-model." She knew that in her heart she was imperfect, weak, sinful. She was terrified that those who put her on a pedestal would one day be disappointed in her when they found out she wasn't her they thought she was. She hated herself. She often wanted to rebel to escape from the pressure...

You see, spankings taught this little girl to hide her true self, to exhibit perfection. They taught her that to be acceptable, she must never be negative, never be disobedient, never question authority. She knew that she must never tell her parents how spankings made her feel. She knew that after a spanking, she should act repentant and remorseful, but she also knew that she shouldn't cry for too long or sound angry when she cried after a spanking, or that would be reason for another round.

(Robinson, 2011, http://richlyforgiven.blogspot. com/2011/07/lock-em-up-throw-away-key.html)

Like this girl, fear due to physical punishment teaches children to try to do whatever it takes to avoid being hit by their parents. Not only are these children desperate to avoid the physical pain of physical punishment but also the emotional pain and fear that goes along with being hit by loved ones. Sometimes this means only behaving around parents and other adults instead of doing what is right, whether or not an adult is around. "For some children, the lessons learned through spanking include the idea that they only need to be good if Mommy or Daddy is watching or will know about it" (Straus, 2006, p. 151). I did this myself as a child and have witnessed a great deal of children do this throughout my work with young children. They always look so guilty and a little afraid when they find out that I saw what they did. Because I use positive guidance techniques with them, we have always worked it out in a positive manner. (I will be discussing positive, gentle discipline in part 4 of this book). Phil E. Quinn, from whom we have been hearing throughout this part of the book, learned early on in his childhood to try to do whatever it took to avoid being beaten by his parents. Quinn (1988), page 83, explains:

> I had long ago learned to do or say whatever my parents demanded of me. It was the only chance I had. In my dangerous world there were no such things as right or wrong, good or bad, truth or deceit. Reality was what my parents told me was real. Truth and good and right were what they wanted at the moment. Believing anything else was a threat to my survival.

While I understand, and even Quinn admits, that what he suffered as a child was a severe case of abuse, many people who were spanked a bit more mildly than what Quinn experienced admit to still having similar feelings as Quinn. The fear, anger, and pain are the same for every child who is intentionally hurt by their parents and other adults—that is unless the children have repressed and denied their true feelings (see chapter 11). Sometimes parents set up children so that they will be physically punished no matter how they try to respond correctly to their parents. Quinn experienced this when his mother asked him what his name was. Quinn (1988) states, pages 84-85 and 88-89, that:

> Confused and frightened, I did not know what to answer. If I agreed with her that my name was Joe, then I would be lying. And how many times had I been told that lying would not be tolerated? Lying was a punishable offense. And yet, if I did not agree with her, I took the risk of appearing defiant and contradicting her. That also was an offense sure to bring punishment. What was I to do? I was desperate as the seconds ticked off... With a deep sigh of despair, I surrendered my will to the inevitable. Unable to change what was happening, I withdrew deeply into that private inner world I had created for myself... My adoptive parents' choice of teaching methods may be attributed to ignorance of the possible short- and long-term effects. In their well-intentioned attempt to fortify my character, their method actually weakened whatever moral strength I might have had and resulted in serious emotional damage that in the long run had an effect opposite to the one they had intended. It did not build character—it destroyed it.

In chapter 12, I introduced the concept of godly sorrow versus worldly sorrow. I would like to take a deeper look at these two concepts here as fear and guilt often lead people of all ages to have worldly sorrow instead godly sorrow. Let's first take a look at what the Bible has to say about godly sorrow and worldly sorrow. In 2 Corinthians 7:8-11, it states:

> Even if I caused you sorrow by my letter, I do not regret it. Though I did regret it—I see that my letter hurt you, but only for a little while—yet now I am happy, not because you were made sorry, but because your sorrow led you to repentance. For you became sorrowful as God intended and so were not harmed in any way by us. Godly sorrow

brings repentance that leads to salvation and leaves no regret, but worldly sorrow brings death. See what this godly sorrow has produced in you: what earnestness, what eagerness to clear yourselves, what indignation, what alarm, what longing, what concern, what readiness to see justice done. At every point you have proved yourselves to be innocent in this matter.

What the Apostle Paul is saying here is that godly sorrow makes us think beyond ourselves to how our actions have hurt or affected other people and our relationship with God. We look past whatever consequences our actions caused us and want to do everything in our power to repent and seek forgiveness from God and the person we have hurt. This is why Paul says that godly sorrow brings life as we seek to be forgiven. On the other hand, worldly sorrow brings death according to what Paul says in this verse. Due to fear of punishment as well as guilt, people of all ages will focus on the consequences that are happening to them because of their actions rather than how they've hurt God and the other person. This is worldly sorrow. Being afraid of punishment and rejection causes worldly sorrow. Also, feeling so guilty and bad about oneself that one feels that he/she deserves whatever punishment he/she has coming to him/her leads to worldly sorrow. There is a difference between the conviction of the Holy Spirit that usually makes us *want* to seek forgiveness and repent and guilt, which makes us feel worthless and fearful, hence, making us *not* want to seek forgiveness or repent. The Holy Spirit *never* threatens us or puts us down when He convicts us. He gently but firmly makes us aware of our sins in a way that we focus outwardly instead of inwardly. Physical punishment *does not* lead children to godly sorrow despite what all of the Christian advocates of spanking may say. As the stories and research show, physical punishment causes children to become fearful and to hide their sins from their parents and ultimately from God. Of course, God sees everything and knows our hearts (Psalm 44:21; Psalm 139:23), but we can still act as though God does not see what is really going on. This causes children not to come to God or their parents for help when they make mistakes.

In a groundbreaking book entitled, *This Hurts Me More Than It Hurts You: In Words and Pictures, Children Share How Spanking Hurts and What to Do Instead,* by Nadine A. Block and Madeleine Y. Gomez, children wrote and drew about how being hit *really* makes them feel. Two stories written by a thirteen-year-old girl and a twelve-year-old boy regarding the fear and other emotions spanking has caused illustrate how children become fearful when they are hit. The twelve-year-old even recognizes that spanking is indeed abuse. Here's what they have to say about spanking:

Girl, Age 13, Illinois

"Say No to Spanking. Parents shouldn't spank their children because it affects your child's feeling. When a child gets a spanking, they only experience the anger their parent has towards them. It makes kids afraid to talk to their parents about their problem because they're afraid of the consequence. Also, spanking can leave marks and bruises on the bodies of innocent children. Spanking is one of the harshest punishments a parent can do to their child. I think parents should think of different ways to deal with family problems other than spanking their kids. Children that are hit will become adults that will hit. We need to try to end this violence so every child can feel safe in his or her home. Let's break the silence!" (Block & Gomez, 2011, p. 9).

Boy, Age 14 [12], New Hampshire

"I am twelve years old, and I am homeschooled. I am going to tell you a child's perspective of corporal punishment. When I talk about corporal punishment, I'm talking about child abuse because that's exactly what it is. If a husband hits a wife or a wife hits a husband, it's illegal, but if a mother or a father hits a child, it's legal. Why is there a difference when two spouses hit each other than when a parent is violent toward a child?

"What is the difference?

"Some adults like to use the word 'spanking' so the child gets the impression that what the adult is doing is right. But if the adult uses the word 'hit,' the child knows something is wrong. I believe that we need to start calling 'spanking' what it really is. Spanking is HITTING!

"Now I am going to tell you a child's perspective…I was in several foster families. When I was in my biological family I got hit all the time. I also saw my brothers get hit, and I hated it. Sometimes at night my stepfather would come in to 'spank' us and we'd all dart under the bed. The only emotion I felt was fear…sheer and utter fear! And sometimes when one of my brothers would do something 'wrong' my birth mother and stepfather would tell me to hit him. I even got hit in one of my foster homes, a place that was supposed to be protecting me from abuse!

"When a child is getting hit, he feels like he is hated and no one loves him. He really feels like no one loves him. Over time, children start putting up bricks around their heart. They start shutting everyone out and they learn to dissociate. When they get older they may become a cold and callous person who can't love. Hitting really does not help their behavior. When people really do tell them wrong from right, they ignore it all. Prisoners may have emotional problems from being hit. Not everyone turns out like that because they may have one person that really loves them.

"When children get hit, the first feeling is fear. 'I'm going to get pain.' It is fear because it means violence. A kid's definition of it is pain. They get that fear that clutches their heart like an iron grip. And that iron grip stays and it hardens over their heart and just shuts them down. They feel angry, rage. They feel like they just want to get revenge and inflict pain on the one that inflicted pain on them. They feel sadness. The one who gave them the pain is the one who is supposed to protect them from pain. They feel distrust, they can't trust anyone. Their natural feeling when they are with someone who cares is to trust, but when that very person that is supposed to protect them from pain, hurt, and sadness hits them, the trust just disappears. They destroy all that trust. Unless someone shows they care who doesn't hurt them, who uses strong but caring words, unless children have that type of person, they are going to stay that way.

"So if you stop hurting children, then they won't close their heart. They will be more accepting and trusting and they will give that love to another person. They will be more loving so the next generation and then the next and the next will do the same thing. Then there will be peace. If you start with the children a whole chain link starts of love, care, give and take. They won't have all that anger stocked up in them and no one will be angry enough to start wars.

"So, you see, to save the world, you need to save the children!"

(Block & Gomez, 2011, pps. 13-15)

As we can see, fear is a common thread in these children's stories. They both mentioned hiding and not talking to their parents due to fear. Is this what we really want for our children? Does God want us to teach them worldly sorrow by hitting them in His name? But, there are times when children will try to admit their sins and wind up getting punished for practicing godly sorrow. Quinn calls this a double bind because even though the child did do wrong, the child admits to it and tries to tell the truth only to be hit anyway. This is quite confusing for a child who gets spanked for telling the truth.

> Few life experiences are as potentially damaging to the mental and emotional health of a developing child as the "double bind," a dilemma in which a child is forced to make a choice but will be punished regardless of the choice made. It is a situation in which a child is powerless to avoid punishment.
>
> (Quinn, 1988, p. 92)

> Having told Katie that if she ever got into the makeup again she would be spanked, the mother then told her that if she did not tell the truth she would be spanked. The child was going to be spanked whether she told the truth or not! Katie was trapped. There was no way to avoid punishment. It was a no-win situation, a double bind.
>
> (Quinn, 1988, p. 96)

What did Katie learn from this experience? That one gets hit for telling the truth. This double bind causes confusion, feelings of helplessness, fear, and distorted thinking in the young, developing minds of children. I can guarantee that this will *not* lead children to godly sorrow! (I will be discussing a much more appropriate and positive way of handling this type of situation in the next part of this book about discipline). As Quinn (1988) states, "Spanking children when they tell the truth is not the way to teach them to be honest" (p. 96).

Some prospankers such as the Pearls take this double bind to the extreme by advising parents to spank the child for not obeying immediately. Given that young children take longer to process information, it is totally unreasonable to expect them to obey us immediately. Plus, it is healthy and developmentally appropriate for young children to explore and test their limits.

Therefore, hitting a child for getting out of bed and hearing the parent coming and getting back in bed before or as the parent reaches the room is downright confusing to the child. It teaches children to always have some fear because they never know what may cause their parents to hit them—especially when the children are actually trying to do the right thing. It's not fun living with a certain amount of fear and anxiety throughout one's childhood.

Prospankers will spank children for crying and/or crying too long after a spanking. Many of us have heard, or even been told as children—I was—"Stop crying or I'll give you something to cry about!" What prospankers either forget or are in denial about is that when we, as children, and even as adults sometimes, are so hurt and upset, we really can't stop crying. It is truly awful to be crying and have that awful fear that if we don't stop crying, we will be hurt even more. I speak from personal experience. I am not the only one who has dealt with this threat and fear. Darlene has also experienced this threat as well as the typical fear that goes along with being hit as a child. Here is what she writes in her blog, "Emerging From Broken":

> I became afraid to cry. I remember trying to stop…trying to control my breathing and slow it down and trying to stifle that hiccup sound that comes from heavy sobbing. I was so afraid of the consequences of NOT being able to stop the tears. I don't even remember if I ever got a second beating for not stopping; all I remember is being told to stop and trying to comply and that the fear of the consequences made it very hard to get any kind of a grip on the situation.
>
> I became so afraid to cry that even today it is very rare that I do cry. But it isn't just being told to stop crying that caused all the problems around that statement. There is more to the communication, "Stop crying or I will give you something to cry about." That statement means that

the speaker, the adult looming over me, told me that I had "nothing" to cry about.

What happens to a child who is not allowed to express emotional hurt or pain? What happens when the communication (covert OR overt) is that you should NOT express your emotions?

I began to invalidate my own physical and emotional pain.

There is fear that comes with this dynamic too. I am crying. I'm told that I have no reason to cry and then told that if I don't STOP crying, I will GET something to cry about. Since I am already in pain, usually in both emotional and physical pain, and I am really afraid of what they might do that would give me a "real and valid" reason to cry.

(Darlene, 2011, http://emergingfrombroken.com/stop-that-crying-or-i-will-give-you-something-to-cry-about/)

Punishing a child for their negative feelings or their personalities is quite harmful. Basically, parents who do this are teaching their children not to be or feel who they really are and how they truly feel. Instead, parents send the message to their children that they are only loveable and accepted by their parents when they are who their parents want them to be. For example, parents will sometimes punish their children for being "wimps" or for being shy.

This is a dramatic example of another kind of double bind—threatening to punish a child for losing. Or for not being good enough. Or for not being what we want. Instead of physical punishment, others of us threaten to withhold love or approval or acceptance.

(Quinn, 1988, p. 94)

I know of a parent who made her preschooler exercise every time the child acted shy around other adults. It is extremely sad that this parent just could not accept her child for who the child was and used a mild yet damaging form of punishment to force the child to change who he really was. As we are about to see, this fear and anxiety gets even worse as Christians bring God into the equation. Some Christian parents who punish their children for being shy or anything other than who their parents want them to be will make their children afraid that God will also disprove of them. Here is an example of a child growing up with this exact fear.

> Rose spent much of elementary school hiding in the bathroom and suffering from stomachaches. A shy child, she was terrified at the prospect of carrying out her Pentecostal Christian parents' stern wishes that she "save the souls" of her classmates and teachers. Her failure to convince others to "give their lives over to Jesus" led Rose to develop fears that God would be angry at her and that demons would possess her.
>
> (Heimlich, 2011, p. 26)

Teaching children that God will reject them for not living up to His standards is not supported by God's Word. Psalm 66:20 says, "Praise be to God, who has not rejected my prayer or withheld his love from me!" And Romans 5:8 states, "But God demonstrates his own love for us in this: While we were still sinners, Christ died for us." And throughout the Bible, we see many verses talking about God's unfailing love for us.

We will return to discussing how teaching children that God wants them spanked can, and often does, lead children to grow up and either reject God or struggle with their relationships with Him due to being afraid of Him. For now, I want us to see that having overly high expectations for children and hitting them can cause children to have anxiety issues. Due to a great deal of Christian advocates of spanking teaching parents that many of the typical, developmentally appropriate behaviors that young children display—especially behaviors that come across as defiant—are sinful and require punishment, many Christian parents either are not aware of their children's needs or choose to ignore these needs in order to purge their children from their sins. Robin Grille (2005), author of *Parenting for a Peaceful World*, page 199, states:

> The researchers found that members of literalist denominations were significantly more inclined to hit their children. What's more, literalist parents had more inappropriate expectations from their children, and showed less empathy toward their needs.
>
> In 1998 in the United Kingdom, the National Children's Bureau asked a large group of five to seven year old children how they felt when they got smacked. All of them spoke of wounded feelings, hurt, embarrassment, and shock. The children's responses, reproduced in their own words, are a moving testimony to the violation they experience at the receiving end of parental "discipline." It would take a very thick skin for anyone to read these children's messages, and continue to deny that smacking or spanking constitute violence.
>
> (Grille, 2005, p. 183)

I am quite certain that fear also ran through all of the children's responses. Joan shared with me on October 11, 2011, via an electronic message how being spanked, physically abused, and verbally abused caused her to have extreme anxiety and panic attacks that she continues to deal with even though she is well into adulthood. Joan writes:

I am a recipient to spanking and verbal and physical abuse. My father was an alcoholic; he was a very miserable and unhappy person and ran a very tight ship, so to speak. He verbally and physically abused my mother and for some reason out of all the children, he chose me to abuse. Yes, I left home and my school to escape being at the hands of my father. Oh yes, I went to another school and graduated. I tried not to comment on certain posts especially of yours, because of your topic, because even years later I still have those memories, and I still break down and cry for what he had done to me. I am crying as I write this, because I am begging people to think about the consequences of their actions. I started to experience different things about twelve years after I left home, but at the time I didn't know what I was dealing with. Whenever he wanted to release any anger, or things didn't go his way, I seemed to be his punching bag and more. To this day, I remember my father spanking me for no reason, or kicking me down the stairs. He would sit in the basement every night drinking a case of warm beer or whatever he had available. My bedroom was directly above the basement where he would sit and drink. I could hear everything through a baseboard heating vent. I knew when he was getting drunk and I would lie in bed in fear because I knew he was coming up soon and I would be his target. Oh yes, I would lock the door, but it was easily opened with a metal fingernail file. I was finally diagnosed with anxiety and panic attacks due to the trauma I went through as a child. I used to see the commercials on television for anxiety and panic attacks, and I wondered why people couldn't control them. You can't even imagine how frightening anxiety or panic is. Is there anybody here that knows what the many symptoms of anxiety or panic are? Here are just a few: allergy problems, increase in allergies (number, sensitivity, reactions, lengthier reactions), shortness of breath, pounding heart, terror, a loss of control, back pain, stiffness, tension, pressure, soreness, spasms, immobility in the back or back muscles, chest pain, chest tightness—which at times you think you may be having a heart attack—choking, difficulty speaking, talking, dizziness, feeling lightheaded, excess of energy, you feel you can't relax, falling sensation, feel like your are falling or dropping even though you aren't, feel like you are going to pass out or faint, chronic fatigue, exhaustion, super tired, worn out, heart palpitations, racing heart, hyperactivity, excess energy, nervous energy, nausea, neck, back, shoulder pain, tightness/stiffness, night sweats, waking up in a sweat, no energy, feeling lethargic, tired, numbness tingling. OMG it is horrible, you just can't imagine what my world is like at times.

Research backs up what Joan and many others—including myself—experience due to being spanked and abused as children. Anxiety is quite common in people who have experienced physical punishment and abuse as children.

> Corporal punishment has been linked to a host of psychological problems. A history of harsh punishment has been found to underlie "conduct disorder," and anxiety disorders in children. Adults who were physically punished as adolescents are more likely to suffer from depressive symptoms, suicidal thoughts and alcohol abuse.
>
> (Grille, 2005, p. 184)

Boys and men are more likely to conceal the fact that they're struggling with anxiety issues because they are afraid of looking weak, but both males and females are more likely to experience anxiety issues from being physically punished as children. That fear that begins at a very young age when the child is first hit often manifests itself into generalized anxiety disorder. That fear children experience the moments leading up to a spanking is a panic attack for children. Their brains release stress hormones, which cause children's heart rates to rise, breathing to become shallow, their muscles tense, and they are in a fight or flight mode. This is why children often cry before the parent spanks them; they're already in pain and distress! The spanking just elevates all these symptoms to greater intensity. But, because the body cannot sustain this anxious state for very long, once the pain of the spanking subsides, relief takes over the child. That is why many parents can say that their child is perfectly happy after the spanking. But what parents can't see are the lingering symptoms after the body has gone through all of this. Now imagine what life must be like for children who face multiple spankings throughout a day. It *does* take a huge toll on a child's body, mind, and spirit. This can turn into always having some anxiety as the child is always afraid of doing something wrong. For young children, it can either cause them to become somewhat withdrawn or cause them to act out more as they try to cope with their feelings with a limited vocabulary. This is serious stuff as young minds and bodies are trying to develop. Fear leads to anxiety. There are no two ways about it. Like Joan, MC also experienced anxiety as he became an adult and now has generalized anxiety disorder. MC, in an electronic message dated September 29, 2011, stated:

> I also discovered that my past belief, that I was spanked and turned out fine, was not true. I had been suppressing the harm that spanking had done to me because I did not want to face the truth that my father and the church, two strong influences in my youth (for better or worse), were responsible for hurting me. Spanking likely had a strong influence on my young adult, and adult struggles, with Generalized Anxiety Disorder and perfectionism. I could never fail. I could never accept myself for failing. I felt my worth was dependent on being the good son who got A's and B's, who never got into any trouble. Failure was connected with punishment in my childhood experiences.

As I said in my own personal story in chapter 10, I have my own anxiety issues from the physical abuse that I suffered under my dad. Is it any wonder when one is forced to live with a certain amount of fear throughout one's entire childhood? As I have shown in chapters 11 and 12, for some, the fear and pain of being hit by their parents causes them to repress and deny their true feelings, which often leads to hardened hearts regarding the harm spanking does to children. But for others it can cause them to become timid and hypersensitive toward other's pain.

> A "tough skin" grows over the wound, which obscures or masks the depth of the pain that throbs beneath. The feelings of pain and betrayal are sealed off, minimised, trivialised, or denied. Deafness to one's own pain entails indifference to the pain of others. Those whose anger boils over become bullies, those who are paralysed with fear, the victims. While some children of violent parents become desensitised, others become hypersensitive. They grow up to be timid, unsure of themselves, they are easily intimidated, downtrodden and manipulated.
>
> (Grille, 2005, p. 186)

This means that for some children and adults, the fear and anxiety from being intentionally hurt by their parents is too much for them to take. It was for me as a young adult, especially after my dad died. The panic attacks were intense and paralyzing. The same is obviously true for Joan and MC as they finally were free from the control of their parents. I know of a woman, who I'll call Ginger, that was spanked the "loving, correct, godly" way and still dealt with much fear and anxiety as she became a young adult. And yet, despite all the research showing that spanking— no matter how mildly, "lovingly," or intensely it is done—causes anxiety and other harmful effects in children and adults, many prospankers still eagerly claim that fear in children is a good thing. But it isn't whatsoever! This is especially true for young children as they're hit the most due to their need to explore, lack of vocabulary, and lack of impulse control as their brains are just developing. It also hurts the parent-child bond as I've pointed out throughout this book.

> Spanking creates fear in the child: The message a toddler gets from a slap or spanking is that a parent or other loved and trusted adult is prepared to induce pain and even do physical harm to force unquestioning obedience. That's terrifying to a little kid... However well-intentioned, a slap registers as the shattering of the whole deal between parent and child. Young children are left awash in feelings of fear, shame, rage, hostility, self-destructiveness and betrayal that they can't yet resolve or manage.
>
> (Robinson, 2002, http://www.religioustolerance.org/
> spankin4.htm)

As we can clearly see, the only "good," if one can even call it "good," that this fear due to being physically punished does for children is forces them to comply quickly. Psychologist Elizabeth Thompson Gershoff of the National Center for Children in Poverty at Columbia University did a meta-analysis of eighty-eight studies of the effects of corporal punishment. Gershoff (2002) states:

> For one, corporal punishment on its own does not teach children right from wrong. Secondly, although it makes children afraid to disobey when parents are present, when parents are not present to administer the punishment those same children will misbehave.
>
> (http://www.apa.org/news/press/releases/2002/06/
> spanking.aspx).

Many parents want their children to love and respect them, but it is clear that forcing children to do this through pain and fear does *not* equal *true* love and respect. I believe Olivia sums this up quite nicely in her comment to me on September 25, 2011, via an electronic message. She says, "If a giant stands over me an adult, beating me and asks me whether I 'love them' and will 'obey them' I will probably say 'oh yes!' …and what has that giant earned? REAL love? REAL obedience? REAL RESPECT? No…in every single case." This goes for God as well.

After spanking the child, many Christian parents will have their children pray with them in order to have children seek God's forgiveness and then parents may read or cite Scripture to their children. These parents follow the rules for "loving, godly" spanking as I discussed in chapter 9. After all, this is how all of the major Christian advocates tell parents to spank as "mandated" by the Bible. Heimlich (2011), page 113, states the following regarding this:

> All the while, though, these advocates are sure that God wants parents to physically punish their kids. Spanking "is God's idea," writes Roy Lessin in *Spanking: A Loving Discipline*. "He is the one who has commanded parents use this type of discipline as an expression of love…Do we love God enough to obey him? Do we love our children enough to bring correction into their lives when it is needed?" Even more frightening, Larry Christenson states in *The Christian Family* that parents' failure to physically punish children will incur God's wrath.

We do need to discipline our children, but we do not need to physically punish them. If we don't discipline children then they will cause us shame, but if we do discipline them, they will bring us peace (Proverbs 29:17). Discipline brings peace whereas punishment brings fear and anxiety to the entire family.

MC was taught throughout his childhood that it was God's will for him to be spanked. In an electronic message dated September 29, 2011, MC conveyed to me how being brought up believing that God wanted him to be spanked negatively affected his relationship with God. He writes:

> During one of our AWANA messages, a leader summed up this philosophy of love, fear, and punishment by telling us, "My father showed me his love with his belt, and if your parents love you then they will show it the same way." Sunday school teachers would talk about spanking their own children and how it was good for them to be spanked. Once, a smart boy raised his hand and asked the teacher why we get spanked when we sin, but our parents never get spanked when they make mistakes or do something wrong. Our teacher told us that even though our parents did not get physical spankings, God gave them spiritual spankings when they needed it. Pain, fear, and love became an unholy trinity held together with God's infallible hands.
>
> Another aspect that makes my relationship with God difficult is the fact that the Bible refers to God as a father. My dad was the spanker in our household. The combination of fear and pain, at my father's hands, caused me to have a very distanced relationship with my dad. This is not unusual, as I am told that most who were negatively affected by corporal punishment have a strained relationship with the parent who administered the spankings. The comparison of God to a father has some unintentional baggage for me. If my earthly father is a representation of God as a father, then I see a relationship that is built on pain and fear of punishment. Sometimes when I would pray as a child, I would actually envision God as being a mother instead of a father. To me it was more believable to see God in this role because my mother was very affectionate, protective, and she did not use the pain of a spanking to discipline me. Thinking of God as a father and thinking about the fear and pain that my father imposed on me with his belt,

hand, or paddle did not inspire a close relationship with God. If I got too close to God, I was afraid he might hurt me or punish me. However, the fear of being ultimately punished by God through torture in hell motivated me to try to maintain some sort of fear-based relationship with God. Fear is tiring. It wears you out. I feel burned out from fear.

Between the manipulation of pain and punishment, my disillusionment, and my inability to trust the church, I obviously do not have a stellar relationship with God. What relationship I may still have is marred by the pain of the church's role in my subjection to corporal punishment, the lies that I was told in God's name, a sense of betrayal, and disappointment with the church's resistance to accept the truth about a practice that harmed me. I have tried to separate my negative feelings toward the church from my perceptions of God, but that is extremely difficult.

MC is not the only one who struggles with their relationship with God due to being taught that spanking is God's will. Ginger also did for quite a while. In a face to face conversation with me on September 20, 2011, Ginger told me that her Christian mother, who spanked her regularly until Ginger was fourteen, taught her that not only did God want her mother to spank her, but that God also spanks using natural consequences. Basically, Ginger was taught that whenever something bad happened to her that it was God spanking her for a sin she committed. For a while, Ginger believed that God was punishing her whenever things went wrong in her life. Thankfully, a biblically-sound pastor helped Ginger understand that this was not how God worked at all and helped Ginger to see God as a loving and merciful God. How sad it is that children are getting a scary image of God instead of a true representation of Him. Lisa, who we met in chapter 11, also was taught an incorrect image of God by her fundamentalist Christian parents and now she isn't sure whether or not she still believes in God. In her blog, Broken Daughters, she discusses her images of God she now has due to her upbringing. Lisa writes:

Why does God make us so we need teaching? I thought creation was good; creation was perfect. After all, God is perfect. Why did he make us *defect beings* who need teaching like a pack of naughty kids? There's only one answer I can give: *God is a mean boy.*

He likes watching us suffer, he likes us as defect beings, because that's the only way we can humor him with our sad attempts to get through life. God used to show that a lot more back in the day, when he ran around punishing people for wearing the wrong pair of shoes, screaming and yelling at them because they weren't worth a second of his precious time. He would come down and "spank" the humans, because remember? *Spanking = love.*

That's really all I'm getting from the God I have been taught to believe in.

It reminds me a bit of ants. Remember playing in the garden, watching an ant colony, deciding to kill one and let the other escape? You would catch some and put them some place else to see where they would go, if they'd make their way back. You kill some random ones to see the reaction of the others. I sometimes feel like God is just a mean boy, enjoying the power he has over a bunch of ants. Would the boy be sad if all ants died? Certainly not.

But then there's Jesus. He's so different, no wonder that bunch of spanked kids loved him, viewed him as the Messiah. He is loving, caring, not judging, not punishing. *Sometimes I feel like God and Jesus are from two separate religions.*

Jesus is really the only reason why I haven't abandoned religion all together yet.

(Lisa, 2011,
http://brokendaughters.wordpress.com/2011/07/18/
when-good-things-happen-to-bad-people-wait-what/)

This makes me so sad, but yet I can't blame Lisa for having these images of God considering what her parents and church ingrained in her throughout her childhood. As I pointed out in my personal story in chapter 10, had my dad hit me in the name of Jesus, I wouldn't be a Christian today due to being afraid of God and having a totally warped image of Him based on my dad's behavior toward me.

> Victims of religious child maltreatment often suffer a spiritual loss. For example, experts say children may feel angry at, or terrified of, a deity if their abuser is active in the victim's place of worship. Many victims are unable to pray and can reject their faith altogether. In a 1995 study by Bottoms, she notes that a significant number of alleged victims of childhood religion-related abuse changed their faith or became atheists.
>
> (Heimlich, 2011, p. 31)

To make matters worse, on top of parents and children being taught that God requires spankings, many of these Christian fundamentalist organizations and churches are so authoritarian that members face being kicked out if they choose to challenge the beliefs of the organization or church.

> Fear abounds in religious authoritarian cultures, as members understand that they will pay a price if they do not behave or believe correctly. For example, they might believe that harboring religious doubts jeopardizes their chances to be "saved" in the next life. If members do not abide by certain social norms, they can be formally or informally ostracized.
>
> (Heimlich, 2011, p. 50)

But many children grow up and do leave their faith. Sammy grew up in a fundamental Christian home where harsh physical punishment was the norm. Sammy writes:

> While my parents were Southern Baptist, not Independent Fundamentalist Baptist, they still believed the Bible command them to spank their children in the name of God. Their "discipline" could be quite harsh. My step-dad would hit me on the back and legs with a belt or a flyswatter, leaving stripes of marks and, sometimes, bruises. Afterwards, it would be painful to sit for days at a time. I have permanent scars from those years...
>
> For me personally, the worst result of growing up in such a home was the twisted view of God it created, one I've talked about on this blog before. Believing that God hates you and is going to abandon you to hell forever creates a hell here on Earth, one that I wouldn't wish on my greatest enemies. While time and a new perception of God has healed some scars, some blemishes will never fully disappear.
>
> (Sammy, 2011, http://scientificuniversalist.blogspot. com/2011/09/ungodly-discipline.html)

Sammy is not the only one to reject the "god" that their parents represented to them. Wendy and Nadia found themselves questioning if God was real or outright leaving their churches. Wendy conveyed to me via an electronic message dated September 23, 2011, the following:

> I remember growing up Catholic with a mother who was more religious than my father and also used physical punishment more. My aunt and uncle weren't into religion at all, and spanking seemed to be reserved for extreme stuff. Their family seemed a lot happier than ours, and I was kind of envious. Once when I was 10, my mom apparently didn't like my facial expression and she reached

out and smacked me in the face. My cousin, who'd seen what happened, seemed to be appalled and asked me later if my mom was nuts. Not too surprisingly, I stopped going to church as soon as I left home and have never cared to return.

It is very sad that while Wendy may consider herself a Christian, she has completely stopped going to *any* church due to her upbringing. It is also sad that she often envied her aunt and uncle's family because they didn't believe in God and rarely spanked their children. God wants *everyone* to be saved and have a loving, personal relationship with Him. But how can that happen when children raised in a Christian home see a non-Christian home as happier and more peaceful? Didn't God intend for this to be the exact opposite? Nadia had a similar experience as a child as she went to a Christian school and was spanked there because her P.E. teacher thought that she was being defiant by wearing her new watch to gym class. While she understood that students couldn't wear jewelry to gym class, she was truly unaware that watches were also considered jewelry. Even though she tried to tell her P.E. teacher this, she still got spanked.

> My personal experiences with spanking were absolutely terrifying. Every teacher had the power to spank, and the offenses that called for spanking were at the discretion of the teacher. Since none of my peers knew what could provoke a spanking, we went to school in constant fear...
> Having had a first-hand experience with spanking, I can say with a measure of authority that spanking does not produce results, neither short nor long-term. After leaving that school, I personally left the church, and refused to attend throughout my school years. Why? I felt that if a school like that could condone and embrace abuse, then I did not want to have any part of the religion or God associated with it. It wasn't until I was much older that

I realized that God is not about punishment, abuse, and humiliation. God is, in short, love.

But there are many children from Christian households who get spanked, and I don't doubt for a second that a majority of these children will grow up to either forsake religion, or they will become adults who are angry, scared, or both. After all, as the joke goes, the quickest way for a Catholic to leave the religion is to send him to a Catholic school. I can't tell you how many of my friends, having equated Christianity with hate and intolerance, stopped believing merely because their instructors in religious practice were angry people concerned only with physically and psychologically subduing those younger and weaker than them.

(Nadia, 2011, http://whynottrainachild.com/?s=Nadia)

I am very grateful that Nadia eventually was able to find out exactly who God truly is over time just as Ginger did. But as we have seen throughout this chapter, fear of God often drives children *away* from Him. This is *not* what God intended for us. Look at what Ephesians 3:12 says: "In him and through faith in him we may approach God with freedom and confidence."

And Hebrews 4:16 states: "Let us then approach God's throne of grace with confidence, so that we may receive mercy and find grace to help us in our time of need."

And finally, 1 John 5:14 says: "This is the confidence we have in approaching God: that if we ask anything according to his will, he hears us."

It is obvious that God wants us to have confidence and boldness when we approach Him. Yes, we are to be humble and reverent toward God, but *never* afraid of Him. We are not to be paranoid that God will strike us down every time we make a mistake. Out of love and godly sorrow, God wants us to come to Him seeking forgiveness, knowing that our sins will be forgiven.

"Like other forms of post-traumatic stress, paranoia is a delayed and transformed re-experience of earlier threats and dangers to the self, to the will, and to the body" (Greven, 1992, p. 172). Daniel Paul Schreber suffered extreme abuse from his devout Christian parents. "Dr. Schreber's methods of discipline and control mirror those rationales for corporal punishment explored earlier" (Greven, 1992, p. 170). Dr. Schreber was a pastor and justified his abusive behaviors toward his son with Scripture. He advocated for extreme measures of control for children beginning in infancy.

> He recommended, for instance, that, when a small child cried for no apparent reason, the remedy was to "step forward in a positive manner: by quick distraction of the attention, stern words, threatening gestures, rapping against the bed…or when all this is no avail—by moderate, intermittent, bodily admonishments consistently repeated until the child calms down or falls asleep." The goal was clear: "Such a procedure is necessary only once or at most twice and—one is master of the child *forever*."
>
> (Greven, 1992, p. 171)

Sadly, Daniel Schreber turned the fear that his father instilled in him into paranoia as an adult. He believed that God and his doctor were out to harm him but that his father had nothing to do with his severe paranoia.

> Schreber believed even as an adult that he adored his father. But he also believed that God and his doctor were intent upon harming or destroying his very soul. He was absolutely right in his assumption that his self and soul were in grave danger, but he could not acknowledge from whom. Like other victims of violence, assault, and abuse, he identified with his abuser and forgot himself in the process.
>
> (Greven, 1992, p. 172)

Granted, Schreber's abuse from his minister father took place in the late 1800s to early 1900s, but like so many Christian parents, past and present, his father truly believed that what he did to his son was biblical and not abusive.

Anxiety and paranoia are not uncommon in children who have been physically punished/abused as children, especially when it is done in the name of Jesus! MC, Ginger, the others I've mentioned in this chapter, including myself, have experienced a less severe form of paranoia or panic attacks. For Ginger and MC, it had to do with believing God was ready to punish them every time they made a mistake since they were physically punished in the name of God. For myself, I suffer from a more generalized anxiety. I usually do not have panic attacks anymore, but I often worry about my health beyond what is necessary or normal. I also get very anxious with storms, thinking that a tornado will come blow our house apart. Granted, we have experienced some pretty severe weather during the writing of this book, but even as a child I was terrified of storms. I truly believe that a great deal of my anxiety issues comes from being physically abused by my dad. The fear instilled in children from being hit by adults in their lives whether it is done "lovingly" or not does indeed negatively affect children as they grow up—even if they try to deny or repress it. Greven (1992) states:

> The roots of paranoia…are to be found in struggles over the will, of being forced to give in to superior force and power and, we must add, pain and fear. The pervasive sense of being threatened with harm, of being forced to surrender, of being manipulated or coerced into compliance with the will of another person or persons, persistent in paranoia, is rooted in the experience of aggression by adults against the wills, bodies, and selves of children. The pervasive suspiciousness and fear of subversion and of conspiracies, so characteristic of paranoia, reflect earlier battles over the

child's willfulness and autonomy, long submerged in the unconscious but still present in the minds of many people for the rest of their lives.

(Greven, 1992, p. 173)

For some children who are physically punished, they may not come to be afraid of God, but they question why God isn't answering their cries for help.

> In a booklet that aims to educate the public about child maltreatment in Amish communities, one woman writes about the beatings she received as a girl: "Where was God when those awful beatings occurred? Did He care? How would I know? God is Our Father, the Bible says, but is He also like my earthly father—ready to strike me down and call me 'worthless' when I fail. How could I trust God? ... Many times I've tried to persuade God to just let me die."
>
> (Heimlich, 2011, p. 32)

Olivia also would sometimes wonder why God wasn't answering her cries for help. Perhaps God knew that through our physical and emotional pain we would rise up and take a firm stance against the hitting of children. Or, maybe God did try to speak to our parents' hearts but they were too hardened to truly hear Him. If God really wanted us to obey Him out of fear, He would have created little robots that He could easily subdue. But our God is a relational God. He wants us to obey and worship Him because we *love* Him.

I want to take a look at the third commandment, which states: "You shall not misuse the name of the LORD your God, for the LORD will not hold anyone guiltless who misuses his name" (Exodus 20:7). Most people, as I did, think this means not using God's name in a flippant manner or to curse. But, as I recently learned, this commandment also means not using God's name to justify doing evil.

> Rabbi Joseph Telushkin wrote the following in his book Jewish Literacy.
>
> "Many people think that this means that you have to write God as G-d, or that it is blasphemous to say words such as goddamn. Even if these assumptions are correct, it's still hard to figure out what makes this offense so heinous that it's included in the document that forbids murdering, stealing, idolatry, and adultery. However, the Hebrew, Lo Tisa, literally means 'you shall not carry God's name in vain."
>
> In other words, don't use God as your justification in selfish causes.
>
> According to Telushkin, the prohibition is not in merely using God's name. The prohibition is the actions you take in the name of God.
>
> Let me see if I can drive this point home more clearly.
>
> We are not permitted to justify illegal or evil acts by saying that they mandated by God. We can never use God as an excuse or justification to do evil, to otherwise violate the laws of civilization and the laws of the Torah.
>
> (Simon, 2010, http://simonsense.blogspot.com/2010/02/some-thoughts-on-third-commandment.html)

This is very important as we are never to use God's name when we do evil. Since hitting a child is evil and causes so many negative effects in children and adults, we should *never* spank (hit) children in God's name, telling them that this is God's will for them, because when we do this, we are breaking the third commandment. Not only do we break the third commandment by telling children that Jesus wants them to be hurt when they sin, but we are also emotionally abusing our children. It is obvious from all the research, personal stories, and Scripture that using God to justify intentionally inflicting pain on children causes them to be afraid of Him. This is more damaging than just hitting them. They are being taught that they are worthless and must suffer physical pain before God will forgive them. Parents who do this to their children, and Christians leaders who advocate for this, are playing head games with vulnerable and impressionable young minds with damages being quite high to deadly if the child grows up to reject God forever!

> As harmful as other forms of abuse and neglect can be, emotional maltreatment is often the most damaging. As one psychologist put it, when various forms of abuse are present, children are most affected by the perpetrator's "psychological stance." Write the authors of the APSAC handbook, "Empirical research suggests that the most common and lasting effects of physical abuse, sexual abuse, and neglect tend to be related to associated and embedded psychological experiences" (Heimlich, 2011, p. 126)

Do we really want children to grow up equating fear and pain with love and God? Do we want children to grow up and feel as MC conveyed to me via an electronic message dated September 29, 2011, where he states:

> I learned once, from a speaker at an Intervarsity Christian Fellowship conference, that in a relationship with Jesus one can either be a son/ daughter or an orphan. The individual who is a son or daughter of Jesus is motivated to follow out of love; the orphan is ruled and motivated by fear. For most of my life, I feel like I have been the orphan?

It is obvious that Jesus wants us to obey Him out of love and *not* fear when He states:

Anyone who loves me will obey my teaching. My Father will love them, and we will come to them and make our home with them. Anyone who does not love me will not obey my teaching. These words you hear are not my own; they belong to the Father who sent me.

John 14:23-24

Fear and love never go together, and as we shall see in the next section, spanking "in love" is quite harmful.

"Lovingly" Spanking: "If Children Are Spanked 'Lovingly,' it Isn't Harmful!"

I can't tell you how many times I've heard this argument throughout the writing of this book. Prospankers truly believe that if they follow the "rules" for "godly, loving" spanking, as I discussed in chapter 9, that no harm will ever be done to a child. But many people have been spanked "lovingly" and *were* harmed by it. MC is quick to point out in an electronic message written on September 29, 2011, that:

> I will sum up these experiences with the observation that none of these spankings struck me as being abusive, or out of the ordinary, by the standards adopted by authority figures in the time period of my childhood (the 80s), or the church culture I was raised in. By all standards, I was punished by the "Spank in love" misnomer that permeated evangelical and fundamentalist thought and was accepted by a majority of 80s society. My father did not wail on me in a fit of rage, he did not leave me black and blue, break my bones, break my skin, or leave me covered in red welts. My torment was delivered in a cool manner, with calculated precision, and was sanctioned with appeals of biblical obedience to god and an empty mantra explaining that I was being treated this way for my own good, that I was

being treated this way because I was loved, and that what was being done to me actually hurt my father more than it hurt me. By all standards of the culture, and the time period, I was not abused. However, such treatment impacted deeply in a host of negative ways, which leads me to conclude that all forms of hitting, from the more mild to the more severe, are all stepping stones that lead down the slippery slope into various degrees of mistreatment and abuse. There is no such thing as a right way to hit somebody.

Ginger, as we saw previously, was also spanked the "godly, loving" way. Some of my critics often claim that my research is based on abuse and not spanking. I would like to remind everyone that many of the children and parents call this "abuse" spanking. All the Christian advocates call this "abuse" spanking as they say leaving red marks that are temporary is okay, and that the spanking must cause the child a considerable amount of pain in order to be effective. Pain is pain no matter what one chooses to call it. Since many prospankers argue over where to draw the line between spanking and abuse, as I pointed out in chapter 11, I must take a firm stand and as a preventive measure, call *all* hitting of children abuse. After all, intentionally inflicting pain on adults is considered abuse. Hitting the elderly is elder abuse. Hitting a child is child abuse. Children are human beings just as adults are.

> Unfortunately, it simply is not a biblical concept (if Christians view their discipline practices as biblical because they are based on the concrete-specific teaching of the Bible's rod texts). Of course, the notion of physical beatings as an expression of parental love is very biblical. But the contemporary banning of parental anger is highly problematic. In fact, the restriction of "no anger" in spanking goes directly against a biblical and theological development of corporal punishment.
>
> (Webb, 2011, p. 49)

Anger in the Old Testament went along with most punishments. In fact, when God chose to punish His people in the Old Testament, He was quite angry with them and would usually unleash His wrath upon them until they cried out to Him and He would have compassion on them. As William Webb (2011), author of *Corporal Punishment in the Bible: A Redemptive-Movement Hermeneutic for Troubling Texts*, page 50, states:

> Now the difficulty with a no-anger policy for spanking, if it is indeed based on the Bible, is that when God practices corporal punishment, his use of the rod and whip clearly does involve anger. Numerous texts speak of (1) God disciplining his people in anger, and more specifically of (2) God disciplining his children with the rod or whip as an expression of his anger and wrath. In fact, the emotive connection between anger and the rod of discipline is so direct that the Bible sometimes describes divine corporal punishment with the short-form idiom (3) God's "rod of anger" or "rod of wrath."

Neither Webb nor I are saying that God wants us to spank and that we are to spank in anger. Webb and I are just further pointing out that the contemporary method advocated by Christian prospankers is not supported in the Bible. Now, while having some love in the home is preferable than a home that uses harsh punishments without ever showing love and affection to the children, it is a very misleading statement made by prospankers to say that if children are spanked "lovingly" then it is not harmful. Love and pain are contradictory to each other. And there is no such thing as a "gentle spanking." A mild swat is intended to cause mild pain to the child as well as create fear in the child, otherwise, why would one bother to swat the child? I truly believe that "love spanking" can actually be *more* harmful to children than spanking in anger (which, as I said, I would *never* recommend) because we are teaching them to equate being hit and intentionally hurt with love.

Children are able to sense and recognize other's emotions from infancy. They know the difference between an angry look and/or voice and a happy look and/or voice. But it is extremely confusing to children when our faces or tone of voice don't match our feelings. Say, for example, a two-year-old is throwing a tantrum in public and the parent, trying to be perceived as a "good parent," forces a smile as she angrily tells her child to stop it. Outside of the toddler being too out of control to hear her (we'll discuss this in the next part of this book on discipline), if the parent looks happy, it is very difficult for the child to tell whether the parent is happy or angry. This is quite true of children who are spanked by a calm, unemotional parent. This method of physically punishing children is sending them a very confusing, mixed message to them. Due to the spanking being delivered by a calm, loving parent, young children process it as premeditated and calculated and then as an extension of love. While it may be redemptive for Christian advocates of spanking to teach parents not to spank in anger but to do so "in love," teaching young children to equate love with pain is very dangerous and damaging.

> In addition, while all can agree that parents should be affectionate with their children, as many conservative Protestants seem to be, one wonders if children in these families would do even better if they received that affection and were *not* spanked. Some worry about the potentially damaging psychological effects of children being made to endure pain inflicted by parents with whom they share a loving relationship. "If you are both very affectionate with your children and you're physically punitive with them, that's a very mixed message, and I think it has long-term consequences," Phillip Greven told me in our interview.
>
> (Heimlich, 2011, p. 112)

My dad was very affectionate with me throughout my childhood, but he was always angry with me when he hit me. I think that was a Godsend because had he been calm when he hit me, I may have had even more fear of him growing up, and it would have been much harder for me to acknowledge that what he did to me was wrong and to forgive him. If someone close to us hurts us when he/she is angry, it is easier to forgive him/her because we know it was more than likely due to the anger. But if the person is calm and unemotional when he/she hurts us, we don't know what his/her motive is. This is scarier and more damaging to the relationship. This is quite true when it comes to young children who are often shocked and confused when their loving parents physically punish them. They often do not understand what is going on. To associate love with hitting and pain is not a healthy thing.

> The first of these unintended consequences is the association of love with violence. Corporal punishment typically begins in infancy with slaps to correct and teach. Mommy and Daddy are the first and usually the only ones to hit an infant. And for the most part this continues throughout childhood. The child therefore learns that those who love him or her the most are those who hit.
>
> (Straus, 2006, p. 123)

This is extremely sad and unfortunate.

Beth Fenimore's family was close friends with Roy Lessin, author of the 1979 book entitled, *Spanking: Why, When, How*, when she was growing up. Her parents followed his advice to "lovingly" spank children. Despite being spanked the "godly, loving" way, Beth was traumatized by the spankings and suffered psychological damage. Here is a portion of a letter she wrote to Roy Lessin regarding the negative effects his advice to parents had on her:

Beth Fenimore, September 7, 2005

Open Letter to Roy Lessin, Author of *Spanking: Why, When, How*

Dear Roy,

After 19 years I have found the courage to write you this letter declaring how your choice to teach and write about spanking has affected me. My purpose in writing you this open letter is to share with you and others that the spanking approach you recommend is harmful. My parents both know my view on this issue. I have talked to them, as well, about how their decision to implement your spanking recommendations affected me. I have a mission. My mission is to warn new parents who are innocently trying to raise happy, healthy children. Should just one parent spare their child the kind of pain that I endured at the hands of my parents implementing your spanking recommendations, my pain will have more meaning than it does now. I want to begin by talking about your spanking approach so that we'll both be using the same language. In your book, you describe a process by which a parent performs a spanking on their child.

The first step is to use the right instrument; if a parent uses their hand, the child might become fearful of the parent's hand.

The second step is to spank promptly. The third step is to find a private place in which the parent can conduct the spanking.

The fourth step is for the parent to explain to the child why they are going to be spanked.

The fifth step is to get the child into a good spanking position (when my parents and other adults—such as your wife, Char—spanked me, the ritual involved removing the child's clothing); you recommend bending the child over a bed, or bending a smaller child over the parent's lap.

The sixth step is to hit the child on the buttocks with a stick or other spanking implement.

The seventh step is to continue spanking until the child yields a broken cry, which indicates a broken will.

The eighth step is reconciliation. You recommend that parents comfort the child until sufficient time has passed, and then ask the child to stop crying. You recommend that parents spank a child who displays a "wrong attitude" by continuing to cry too long after a spanking.

The language in your book is much more "sugary" than what I've just written. But my description does not come close to what it feels like to receive a Roy Lessin spanking. So I'll describe what a Roy Lessin spanking is like.

My first spanking was when I was six months old. My mother spanked me for crying after she put me to bed. She had to spank me repeatedly to teach me to not cry when she put me down. I know about this incident because my mother used to tell all new mothers about how young I was when she started spanking me. My last spanking occurred when I was thirteen years old. The Roy Lessin spankings that I remember most vividly took place between the ages of three and seven, because I hardly went a few days without a spanking at that time. I'd like to share with you, and others, what it was like receiving a Roy Lessin spanking.

The moment I found out I was going to get a Roy Lessin spanking, I felt physically ill. Because the Roy Lessin spanking is a ritual, the ordeal could take a long time. (When I refer to a spanking ritual, I'm referring to the steps you outline in your book.) This was hard for me because I had a child's sense of time. The dread bubbled up and consumed me, and stayed with me until the spanking ritual was over. My parents usually sent me to a private room, such as my own room, and there I would wait until one of my parents came. (My dad spanked me the most, so in my illustration let's assume my father is conducting the Roy Lessin spanking.) My father would explain the reason for the spanking. This was an excruciating process because I had to listen while knowing what was coming. Since I might face back-to-back Roy Lessin spankings, I had to be careful not to be disrespectful in my listening to my father. I had already developed irritable bowel syndrome (IBS), and would feel my guts cramp up with anxiety during his speech. Then he would ask me to take off my pants and underwear. I would feel deeply embarrassed because my father was not supposed to see me naked. (My family had a high standard for modesty.) My humiliation and fear would grow immeasurably as I leaned over the bed, my father's knee, or whatever was around. My private parts were helplessly exposed as my dad laid his hand on my back. Trying to pull away and defend myself would only mean that the spanking would be longer, or I'd get a back-to-back spanking. The stick, paddle inscribed with scripture verses, or belt would swish violently through the air before slapping painfully on my buttocks or thighs. I would scream in pain and anguish. I cannot remember a moment of thinking of resisting, rebelling, or trying to "win" anything, as you recommend parents should watch for as they hit their children. I just tried to survive the best way I knew how. The screaming, the hitting, and the pain would continue for unknown amounts of time. When the gruesome pain ended, I would begin to battle with my emotions and my body. I knew that crying too much could mean that my father would start a Roy Lessin spanking ritual all over again to correct my "wrong attitude."

One aspect of receiving a Roy Lessin spanking is the sexual aspect. It's taken me years to even begin to allow myself to speak of this aspect. You see, as a child I had no idea what sex was. I just had this funny sensation that came and went during the Roy Lessin spanking ritual. To my great dismay, I learned that sexual stimulation can be cross-wired with the painful ritual of spankings. This cross-wiring was a real problem for me. Because I couldn't cope with the double message of love and pain, I avoided developing an intimate relationship with a man for a very long time. It took years for me to find a healthy sexuality outside the memories I have of the Roy Lessin spankings. I struggled with this double message as a child. I feel a deep sense of shame as I remember hitting and torturing my dolls and Barbies when no one was around. I needed some way to express the fear, pain, and sexual confusion I felt inside; yet my childish mind couldn't comprehend the significance of what I was doing.

My parents were your "A" students. They followed your eight steps occasionally reducing the entire Roy Lessin spanking ritual to a few swats—not very often, though. My butt and thighs would sting for a long time after a Roy Lessin spanking ritual, so I'd go into the bathroom and use my mother's mirror to look at my behind. I remember seeing red stripes crisscrossing my buttocks and my thighs. At times, I had old marks underneath the new marks. My parents conducted several Roy Lessin spanking rituals a day when I was a young child. I remember a teacher at school asking me one day why I didn't just sit still. I couldn't tell her that it was because the marks on my butt hurt so bad sitting in the little wooden chair.

The second point about "wrong attitudes" is that you tell parents that their children will be happy with your mode of discipline, or even prefer being spanked. I want to say that I didn't experience that joy. I built myself a cheerful, obedient shell. I lived in that shell, only peeking my head out when I felt safe, for 30 years. It took me another seven years to actually try taking the cheerful, obedient shell off—only to run back into it when something felt like the "old fears of my childhood." I have not been happy living in this shell, constantly pretending to be happy when I felt miserable inside. When I think of a happy child, I think of a child who feels free to express their ideas, thoughts, and emotions. I think that a parent's job is to teach a child how to express their emotions, not hit them with a stick until the child displays the emotion of the parent's choosing.

For most of my life, I worried that I'd remembered all this wrong. About eleven years ago I called Char and asked her to listen to while I recalled a Roy Lessin spanking for her. I described to her in as much detail as I could remember the beatings I endured again and again. Char told me that my memories were exactly what you and she had taught my parents. I had not remembered wrong!

I read your book a few weeks ago. I was again surprised to realize I knew and remembered your teachings very well. After the years of growing up around your family and hearing you preach at Outreach, your book brought back your painful teachings and the painful memories I've been trying so hard to live with. I kept wanting to grab my cheerful, obedient shell because to this day I feel scared when I think of all the Roy Lessin spankings and teachings.

Both Char, during my call with her, and you, in your first book, talk about spankings having a higher purpose in saving the soul. You reference Proverbs 20:30: "Blows that wound cleanse away evil; strokes make clean the innermost parts." Those "blows" left horrible marks on my body that made sitting difficult and bathing with soap sting horribly, and they terrified my spirit.

As a grown woman I still fear Roy Lessin spankings. I sometimes wake up in the middle of the night begging my husband to "not let them get me."

My father and I have talked several times about Roy Lessin spankings. He has asked for forgiveness, and is horrified by what he has done. These conversations have been incredibly painful for both of us, and I'm now 37 years old! I believe that he thought he was doing the right thing. You were a leader in the church he believed in, and you were his friend. Our families socialized together. This was not some teaching he picked up somewhere, and then went off to make the best of it.

I hope that by this point you begin to see how your simple, sweet words about raising children are actually harmful. Perhaps you're wondering if I want to have a dialogue with you, and talk about what you really meant by your early book. Perhaps you've adopted a policy of grace, and now recommend that parents spank less and not on bare skin? The truth is, I don't want to know. If I needed justification or reasoning for your teachings, I could use your book as a reference. What I'd like you to do is reconsider your position after carefully looking at how your teachings affected me. Would a loving parent really want to raise a child to fear people, to wear a cheerful and obedient shell, or to live with PTSD and other ailments? I hope the answer you come to is No. I hope that you realize that hitting a child for any reason is not loving. Then, I hope, you join the cause to end corporal punishment in the homes of children. I came into this world a happy, healthy baby. For no other reason than the Roy Lessin spankings, I now fight for my physical and mental health. Please help others and me so this doesn't happen to any more children. Help end corporal punishment. Help end child abuse. If Jesus said, "Whoever causes one of these little ones who believe in me to sin, it would be better for him if a great millstone were hung round his neck and he were thrown into the sea" (Mark 9:42), I can't image that God would condone such behavior in people who claim to be loving parents.

Sincerely,
Bethany A. Fenimore
(Fenimore, 2005, http://nospank.net/fenimore.htm)

It is obvious from this heartbreaking letter written by Beth that even if parents spank their children in the "loving, godly" manner that it still does much harm to the children. In fact, teaching children to equate love with hitting not only teaches children that hitting a loved one is acceptable as I showed in chapter 12, but as Gershoff, who I mentioned previously in this chapter, also found that "spanking can lead children to think that aggression is common in relationships with loved ones. Gershoff in fact did find that CP (corporal punishment) is associated with increased risk of victimization from abusive relationships in adulthood" (Niolon, 2010, http://www.psychpage.com/family/disc.html). In fact, many of the women that I know who were spanked "lovingly" became victims of spousal abuse because they equated love with being hit. This is a very dangerous cycle for any person to become entangled. God never intended for this to happen.

As I have continued to discuss throughout this book, teaching children that God wants them to be hit not only makes children become afraid of Him and is blasphemous, but it does not accurately teach children God's true love for them. "What value is there, for example, in teaching our children that God loves them if they learn that love is something that hurts or makes them feel guilty" (Quinn, 1988, p. 92). As I pointed out in part 1 of this book, many prospankers misinterpret Proverbs 13:24, which states, "Whoever spares the rod hates their children, but the one who loves their children is careful to discipline them," to mean that they *must* spank in order to show their love for their children. (See part 1 of this book for the correct interpretation of the rod verses). This is *not* a mandate from God to spank children in order to show love to them. Love and this type of pain *never* go together. What this is saying is that parents who love their children will discipline (teach and guide) children in a manner that will enable the children to thrive and will ultimately lead them to Christ. Spanking and permissive parenting do the exact opposite of what this verse is saying. Being hit or not being disciplined at all does not make children feel loved by their parents. Hurting children intentionally never accurately shows love for them. God does not intentionally hurt us to show His love for us as God is love. The Bible is also quite clear on what love is and is not. As Quinn (1988), page 98, beautifully states:

Nowhere in I Corinthians 13—the great chapter on love—is hitting listed as an act of love. It tells us clearly that love is patient and kind, is never jealous or envious, never boastful or proud, never haughty or selfish or rude. Love is a state of mind, a quality of the spirit that manifests itself in human relationships. Love holds the other person in highest esteem; it does everything possible to uplift the other. Love never hurts; it helps. It never tears down; it builds. Love never punishes; it disciplines! To equate love with violence is a serious mistake that can have devastating consequences. Love and violence are two entirely different things. If we hit children because we love them, we must be careful we do not love them to death.

Research shows that physically punishing children hurts the parent-child bond as most people can vividly remember the first time their parents slapped them. A study was done with students regarding how corporal punishment chips away at the parent-child bond. Straus (2006), pages 154 through 155, states:

> Part of the process by which corporal punishment eats away at the parent-child bond is shown in the study of 270 students... We asked the students for their reactions to "the first time you can remember being hit by one of your parents" and the most recent instance. We used a check list of 33 items, one of which was "hated him or her." That item was checked by 42 percent for both the first and most recent instance of corporal punishment they could remember. The large percentage who hated their parents for hitting them is important because it is evidence that corporal punishment does chip away at the bond between child and parent.

Yes, children may *look* and *seem* happy after being physically punished, but this is usually a facade in order to please their parents. Their parents obviously won't allow their children to show their true emotions. This is not healthy nor is it true love. I want to end this chapter with one last story of a woman who was spanked the "loving, right" way but still was negatively affected by it.

> When I was a little girl and my mother thought I required discipline, she would pull me face down across her lap and give me a series of stinging slaps of her hand on my bare buttocks while I cried. In fifteen seconds it was over. I would be in tears and clutching my bottom for a minute or so, but it didn't really hurt much after that, just a hot itch. My rear end would be a solid pink right afterwards. But in a few hours it would be back to normal. And that was that.
>
> I was not "abused" as a child, just "spanked with love." She never left a bruise when she "lovingly spanked" me. The permanent marks were inside, not outside.
>
> Mother firmly believed in spankings as discipline for her children because they "worked" so well. All she needed to do if my behavior displeased her was say, "Carol, do you want a spanking?" and that would frighten me into obeying her. And if she told me to do the dishes and I didn't do them very well and got spanked for it you can bet those dishes were unusually spotless for the next couple of days. But spankings also left me with lifelong emotional and sexual problems that I still don't know how to fix despite years of therapy. My mother got an obedient daughter and cleaner dishes and I got a lifelong mess inside.
>
> (Neddermeyer, 2006, http://ezinearticles. com/?Loving-Spankings—Part-I&id=373269)

Conclusion

It is clear that fear is the main effect of spanking no matter how it is done. Believing that God wants children to be hit often leads many children to struggle with their relationships with God or to be so afraid of Him that they totally reject Him. Even when children are spanked the "loving, godly" way, there is much harm done to them. Sadly, spanking is so ingrained in our society, especially among Christians, that the majority of people have a very difficult time admitting that *all* physical punishment is harmful to children. As Straus (2006), page 146, states:

> Conversely, almost everyone thinks that spanking children is not harmful, despite the studies showing that it is. Eighty four percent of American adults, including most practicing psychologists, believe that corporal punishment is sometimes necessary. The remarkable thing is that the members of the Family Research Laboratory seminar are social scientists who, presumably, are against hitting children. Yet the idea that "moderate corporal punishment" is harmless is so deeply ingrained in American culture that even this group was more skeptical of the idea that it could adversely affect a person's occupation and income.

This is very sad because the research and personal testimonies I am presenting further prove that physical punishment is indeed very harmful to children. Any amount of Bible study further shows that spanking is not from God otherwise there would be *no* harmful effects! Fear is not from God. I love this quote from Gandhi because it is more biblical than he probably realized. "Power is of two kinds. One is obtained by the fear of punishment and the other by acts of love. Power based on love is a thousand times more effective and permanent than the one derived from fear of punishment" (Mahatma Gandhi). Yes, physical punishment "in love" has other harmful effects that many people don't know about that we will discuss in the next chapter—one of which is sexuality. Again, I ask, is this really what God wants for our children?

> Love is patient, love is kind. It does not envy, it does not boast, it is not proud. It does not dishonor others, it is not self-seeking, it is not easily angered, it keeps no record

of wrongs. Love does not delight in evil but rejoices with the truth. It always protects, always trusts, always hopes, always perseveres. Love never fails.

(1 Corinthians 13:4-8)

References

Block, N. A. & Gomez, M. Y. (2011). *This Hurts Me More Than it Hurts You: In Words and Pictures.* Columbus, OH: The Center for Effective Discipline.

Boekaerts, M. (2002). Bringing About Change in the Classroom: Strengths and Weaknesses of the Self-Regulated Learning Approach—EARLI Presidential Address, 2001. http://www.sciencedirect.com/science/article/pii/S0959475202000105

Darlene. (2011). Stop That Crying or I Will Give You Something to Cry About. http://emergingfrombroken.com/stop-that-crying-or-i-will-give-you-something-to-cry-about/

Fenimore, B. (2005). Open Letter to Roy Lessin. http://nospank.net/fenimore.htm

Gershoff, E. T. (2002). Is Corporal Punishment an Effective Means of Discipline? http://www.apa.org/news/press/releases/2002/06/spanking.aspx

Greven, P. (1992). *Spare the Child.* New York, NY: Vintage Books.

Grille, R. (2005). *Parenting for a Peaceful World.* New South Wales, Australia: Longueville Media.

Heimlich, J. (2011). *Breaking Their Will.* Amherst, NY: Prometheus Books.

Lisa. (2011). When Good Things Happen to Bad People…Wait, What? http://brokendaughters.wordpress.com/2011/07/18/when-good-things-happen-to-bad-people-wait-what/

Meyer, J. (2011). *The Confident Woman Devotional.* New York, NY: FaithWords.

Nadia. (2011). There is No Fear in Love: Why Spanking Doesn't Work. http://whynottrainachild.com/?s=Nadia

Neddermeyer, D. M. (2006). Loving Spankings – Part 1. http://ezinearticles.com/?Loving-Spankings—Part-I&id=373269

Niolon, R. (2010). Corporal Punishment in Children – What Does it Accomplish? http://www.psychpage.com/family/disc.html

Quinn, P. E. (1988). *Spare the Rod.* Nashville, TN: Abingdon Press.

Robinson, B. A. (2002). The Anti-Spanking Position. http://www.religioustolerance.org/spankin4.htm

Robinson, C. (2011). Lock Them Up and Throw Away the Key. http://richlyforgiven.blogspot.com/2011/07/lock-em-up-throw-away-key.html

Sammy. (2011). Ungodly Discipline. http://scientificuniversalist.blogspot.com/2011/09/ungodly-discipline.html

Sears, W. (2011). 10 Reasons Not to Hit Your Child. http://www.askdrsears.com/topics/discipline-behavior/spanking/10-reasons-not-hit-your-child

Simon, M. (2010). Some Thoughts on the Third Commandment. http://simonsense.blogspot.com/2010/02/some-thoughts-on-third- commandment.html

Straus, M. A. (2006). *Beating the Devil Out of Them.* New Brunswick, NJ: Transaction Publishers

Chapter 14

※❀❀❀❀

Sexuality, Guilt, and Depression

In the previous chapter we discovered that fear is the main effect of corporal punishment that *all* children experience despite the Bible clearly stating that fear is not from God. We also saw that "loving, godly" spankings are indeed harmful to children despite what many prospankers continue to claim. The research and numerous anecdotes (personal stories) show that hitting "in love" and in the name of God often has damaging effects on children even if they deny and repress these effects. In this chapter we will be discussing an effect of "lovingly" spanking that has, since researching for this book, come to my attention. Many people are unaware of the fact that "love" spankings causes sexual problems for children and adults as they seek to turn something painful and out of their control into something pleasant and somewhat controllable. This brief discussion may cause discomfort. We will also discuss how physical punishment often leads to depression, shame, and guilt as spanking never makes one feel good about oneself.

"Love" Spankings Continued: "Children Are Not Sexual Beings"

Many people, in general, believe the above statement to be true. While children do not understand sexuality in the way that adults do, they have the ability at birth to become somewhat aroused and to feel pleasure. This is why young children very innocently explore their bodies during diaper changes and baths. This is a very normal and healthy part of the young child's development. By the age of two, most young children are beginning to notice the differences between males and females and will ask questions out of pure curiosity. Simple, honest answers are all that young children want and need. While a child's budding sexuality should be respected, their innocence and purity must be protected.

But does spanking respect and protect them in this vulnerable area of their development? It does not appear to as research shows that spanking "in love" can cause children to become sadomasochistic as they grow up. Here is the definition of sadomasochism from dictionary.com:

1. interaction, especially sexual activity, in which one person enjoys inflicting physical or mental suffering on another person, who derives pleasure from experiencing pain.

2. gratification, especially sexual, gained through inflicting or receiving pain; sadism and masochism combined. (www. dictionary.com)

While I am no human sexuality expert, knowing what I do know about how young children learn and process information with their constantly developing young brains, I can see why this is a very real effect of physical punishment for many children. Also, if we need further proof of this effect, all we have to do is type "spanking" into Google without specifying children in the query and a whole slew of pornographic sites and images pop up portraying lovers spanking each other. Getting back to how young children learn and process things, everything a child experiences is a learning experience for him/her. They must act on things or experience them to completely understand a concept. If the concept is not made real and concrete to the child, he/she will not truly understand it despite the ability to rattle off memorized rote facts. The facts are virtually meaningless to the young child without the ability to somehow see, hear, smell, taste, or touch what the child is learning. John William Money—a psychologist, sexologist, and author—studied how lovemaps are formed. Lovemaps are how the brain determines what is sexually pleasurable (Straus, 2006).

> Money argues that because the centers of the brain that process feelings of sexual arousal and feelings of pain are in such close proximity, when they are stimulated simultaneously many times over a long period of time, the brain can no longer separate the two. So feelings of sexual arousal and pain become forever woven together. This fusion is especially likely because the most common age for spanking is two to six, which substantially overlaps the age that Money regards as most vulnerable for lovemap vandalism.
>
> (Straus, 2006, p. 124-125)

We will return to how physical punishment often affects brain development, but I want to explain that young children crave some control over their lives. This is developmentally appropriate, and young children should be given an appropriate amount of control when possible—not too much, as it will overwhelm them—but not too little or they will do everything in their power to gain control even if it is only mentally. So, as children continue to learn that physical punishment is done by their parents out of "love" for them, children may begin to use their often-vivid imaginations to turn something that is painful and scary into something pleasurable as well as something that they can control. What many parents and advocates of spanking fail to realize or acknowledge is that the buttocks is connected to the genitals—physically and mentally. The buttocks contains many highly sensitive nerve endings, which is precisely why advocates of spanking advise parents to spank their children on the bare bottom in order to cause the most pain to the child. Despite the pain that physical punishment causes children, because the buttocks is connected to the genitals, arousal can occur during the spanking. If we make children bend over to spank them, we could easily be hitting their genitals in addition to their buttocks.

> Corporal punishment commonly focuses upon a child's buttocks, the anal area in the back being the most frequently beaten part of the body. However, the anus, as Freud and many others have known, is one of the most erotic zones of the body, closely linked with the genitals and responsive to orgasms and erotic pleasures, a source of pleasure and pain for children and adults alike. The assault upon the buttocks thus becomes far more consequential than most of us ever recognize.
>
> (Greven, 1992, p. 184)

This is quite true because, as with the other effects of physical punishment, children, adolescents, and adult children are not likely to tell their parents how spanking has affected them. This is especially the case if the child winds up becoming a sadomasochist. What child discusses their sexual preferences with their parents even if they are normal, healthy preferences?

As I pointed out at the beginning of this section, many parents and advocates of spanking are either ignorant about or are in denial of children's normal, healthy sexual development.

By using physical punishment with their young children, parents may very well inadvertently force the rewiring of their children's brains. As Greven (1992), page 183 through 184, states:

> The absence of sexuality as always been one of the central illusions of advocates of corporal punishments for children. Most advocates of physical punishment appear oblivious to the sexuality of children at any age prior to puberty. Having spent many centuries denying or prohibiting all forms of sexual experience or expression in children, Christian advocates of corporal punishment generally overlook the dimension of children's experience with punishment that subsequently transforms pain into pleasure: the erotic component of the assaults upon the buttocks and other parts of the body by people who say they love the child they are beating.

MC, who has been graciously telling me how being spanked by his Christian father throughout his childhood has affected him for the purpose of this book, struggles with sexual problems as a direct result of being "lovingly" spanked. In an electronic message dated September 29, 2011, MC conveyed the following to me:

> My full understanding and acknowledgment of this harm remained insidiously buried in my subconscious, until I began to come to awareness in my junior and senior years of college. Before my junior year, I still lived under the delusion that I was spanked and turned out fine. I also believed that if I wanted to be a Christian parent, in the future, I would have to spank my children. To hold these delusions, I had to repress a lot of what I have now acknowledged as truth. The downfall of this repression occurred when I had the epiphany that spanking had always had an odd sexual meaning to me. From the time I was five, I can remember playing with myself, while thinking about being spanked. When I was a teenager, I

had always masturbated to thoughts about spanking, or being spanked. I used to seek out stimuli, to cater to this interest, through scenes of corporal punishment in books, movies, etc.... And yet it took me until college to come to the realization that corporal punishment had a sexual meaning to me. When I had this epiphany, I realized that I could never justify using corporal punishment on a child, when CP was a part of my sexual orientation.

This epiphany was both a blessing and a curse. It was a blessing because it led me to seek out research. It caused me to understand how my childhood experiences with CP distorted my sexual development, and it led me to become the staunch anti-spanking advocate that I am today. However, this also became a curse, because it threw into doubt my basic trust of anything that the church had ever taught me. I now knew that the church had lied to me. I discovered that there is no biblical basis for the corporal punishment of children, even though countless of adults, Sunday school teachers, AWANA leaders, and pastors had taught me that it was God's will for parents to spank their children. I realized that I had been mistreated with the church's blessing, and that such mistreatment had violated my sexual development. Obviously, this infuriated me.

MC isn't the only one who struggles sexually as a direct result of receiving "love" spankings as children; Carol, whom we met in chapter 13, also struggles with sadomasochistic tendencies.

I tried so hard to be good. But sooner or later I always found myself face down across my mother's lap getting yet another spanking. I just couldn't control it—except in my fantasies. In fantasy I could make everything happen just so, as if it really were under my control. My mother's preferred discipline method emotionally upset me so much that I sexualized it—everything about it: the kind of clothing she wore and I wore, the things she would say before and after my spanking, the position she put me in, on and on. Fantasy let me cope with my trauma and get a pretend feeling of control over something really out of my control. When I imagined myself as a naughty girl over her mommy's lap getting her bare little bottom spanked, I pictured myself crying and begging the Mommy to stop. Yet it was my fantasy so really I had total control. And by eroticizing, I made something awful and frightening into something delightful and pleasant.

And it worked. Becoming a spankophile at an early age kept me from falling apart. It comforted me when nothing else could. It made me feel in control when I wasn't. And it gave me a make-believe escape from something for which there was no true escape. (How do you escape when it's your very own Mommy who is hurting you?) And now I am stuck with it for the rest of my life.

Parents who say "it didn't do me any harm so it can't do my child any harm" just don't get it. Everyone is different. My mother got spanked when she was little, and she carried on the same tradition with my sister and me. But my mother didn't become a spankophile. And although my sister got the same kinds of punishments as I did—across the same lap and from the same palm—she didn't become a spankophile either. But I did. There is no way you can tell beforehand which of your spanked children will have a guilty sexualized fixation for the rest of her life. So any parent who spanks their child is putting them at risk. Punishing your child with spankings is just like playing a lottery where if you "win" you mess up your kid for life. Most spanked kids don't turn out as obsessed as me. But some of us do. And we aren't rare. Growing up I knew two other little girls who both got spanked by their parents and who both loved to play House the same way I did: with play spankings, play spankings, and more play spankings all afternoon without ever getting bored. (At least two of us were strict disciplinarians of our dolls, too!) One girl would even get me to pretend to be her real life mother so we could reenact actual episodes for which she had been disciplined in her home. For me to meet two others so like myself in this way would be almost impossible if kids like me were rare.

Now I am retired, unmarried, childless, and on medication for depression. At a tender age I used my budding sexuality to cope with something I didn't know how else to cope with. And it has left its mark on me forever. I've been paying the price all my life and I will never stop paying. I am unmarried because the circuits in my brain that should have been used for romance were vandalized by spankings instead. I am childless because I never married. So there is a direct link between my spankings, how I coped with them, and my being sexually abnormal, and hence never marrying and having any children of my own.

(Neddermeyer, 2006, http://ezinearticles. com/?Loving-Spankings—Part-I&id=373269)

It is extremely egotistical to assume that all children come out undamaged after years of being physically punished. While not all children will become sadomasochistic, it is obvious that some do. While we never know which of these effects that I have discussed in this part of this book will affect children and to what degree, it is obvious that *all* children are affected negatively by physical punishment.

We need to remember that God created each and every one of us in our mother's womb (Psalm 139:13-15). He created our bodies to enjoy sex in the context of marriage between a husband and a wife.

"Haven't you read," he replied, "that at the beginning the Creator 'made them male and female,' and said, 'For this reason a man will leave his father and mother and be united to his wife, and the two will become one flesh'? So they are no longer two, but one flesh.'"

Matthew 19:4-6

If God created our bodies to develop how He intended over time, then He obviously knows what will harm or inhibit healthy growth and development. Therefore, God would *never* command us to beat our children with a rod that He knows will affect brain development and lead to sin.

As Straus (2006), page 124, states:

> Under average childhood conditions, the lovemap is heterosexual and relatively uncomplicated. But when lovemaps are "vandalized," the child comes to connect erotic arousal with acts that for most people have no sexual connotations.

If we are honest, much of what many Christian advocates of spanking tell parents to do to their children would be highly frowned upon if the child was replaced by another adult. Do we really want to risk creating a seed in our children that may lead them to struggle with sin for the rest of their lives? Whether or not children develop this sadomasochistic tendency, many children who are spanked often deal with guilt, shame, and depression throughout their lives.

Guilt, Shame, and Depression: "Spanking Relieves Children of Their Guilt"

Many Christian advocates claim that physical punishment is supposed to relieve children of their guilt from the sin that they committed, but this is often not the case. MC dealt with guilt and shame from his sexual struggles as a child, and the spankings he received only made him feel worse. MC conveyed to me in an electronic message dated September 29, 2011, the following:

> I experienced this difficulty most vividly between the ages of eleven to high school, when I felt constant shame and

guilt over the natural act of masturbation. I felt like this was a horrible sin based on my father's reaction when he barged into my room, without knocking, to catch my eleven-year-old self in the act. I had no knowledge about sex and was absolutely terrified and shamed when my father blasted me in front of my mother. He accused me of being sexually active, a term I did not understand, and kept threatening to take me to the doctor to have me examined in order to see if I was guilty of what he was accusing me of. Therefore, every time I would masturbate I would be struck with this horrible sense of guilt and shame. I would get down on my knees, pray for forgiveness, and promise never to do it again. But I broke all those promises every time I felt the natural urge. I could not accept any grace on this issue. I felt like I must not truly love God if I could not stop. I began to doubt whether I was saved, or whether I was elect (a new theological concept that I was being introduced to in my high school). I kept expecting punishment. Every time I gave in I imagined that that was one more strike against me in God's Book, and that when I finally did meet God he was really going to let me have it.

How sad that MC was never taught about God's amazing grace and forgiveness as a child, and obviously he did not feel a sense of relief from his guilt and shame through the spankings that he received. Is this relieving guilt through punishment even biblical? I have touched on this subject somewhat in part 1 of this book. Let's delve a bit deeper into this subject now since shame, guilt, and depression are some of the main effects of physical punishment. Jesus Christ suffered and died for all of humanity's sins—this was done for *all* ages and *all* groups of people—past, present, and future! Because of what Christ did for us on the cross, all that is required of us is that we come to Him and accept His gift of forgiveness and grace by repenting of our sins. He does not require us to be punished before we can be forgiven of all of our sins and alleviated from the guilt and shame our sins cause us. There is no condemnation in Christ. "Therefore, there is now no condemnation for those who are in Christ Jesus" (Romans 8:1).

When children grow up believing that they deserve painful punishment for their sins, it makes it much more difficult for them to accept grace. Physical punishment does *not* teach children about the loving, gentle yet firm discipline that our heavenly Father provides us. While none of us are worthy of the grace and forgiveness that God so freely gives us through Christ, there comes a point when children that are physically punished in Jesus's name feel so unworthy and unlovable that they reject God's gift of salvation. They think things such as: "How could God ever love me?" or "I am unforgivable by God." It is true that God wants us to be humble (Psalm 147:6; Proverbs 3:34; Matthew 23:12), but He does not want us to feel badly about ourselves or feel worthless (Psalm 103:10-12). In fact, look at what Jesus says as He prays to His Father in John 17:13, "'I am coming to you now, but I say these things while I am still in the world, so that they may have the full measure of my joy within them.'" He wants us to have His joy and have it to the fullest!

Despite what many Christian prospankers claim, physical punishment does not create joyful children and adults. It may seem to make children happy and cheerful, but this is because the children have learned that they must always be happy and cheerful around their parents in order to avoid more physical punishment. It's hard to believe that parents "slap their children silly," but, sadly, they do. However, when given the opportunity to be honest about how being spanked truly makes them feel, children will testify that spanking makes them feel badly about themselves. Here are two testimonies from the wonderful book entitled, *This Hurts Me More Than It Hurts You* by Nadine A. Block and Madeleine Y. Gomez:

Girl, Age 13, Ohio

I feel so stupid when I get spanked for things I forget are bad... When my mom hits me, I feel like running away, and I have often planned to run away.

(Block & Gomez, 2011, p. 9)

— ∽ —

Boy, Age 16, Ohio

Why does he want to hit me? I never do anything bad... I work hard and study and have no friends... I stay out of his way... I feel real bad inside...

(Block & Gomez, 2011, p. 9)

The research backs up what these children are saying. Children that are spanked, even "lovingly," have higher rates of depression.

Based on a sample of 649 students from 3 New England colleges, this study examined the long-term effects of childhood corporal punishment on symptoms of depression and considered factors that may moderate or mediate the association. Similar to national studies, approximately 40 percent of the sample reported experiencing some level of corporal punishment when they were 13 years old. Findings indicated that level of corporal punishment is positively related to depressive symptoms, independent of any history of abuse and the frequency of other forms of punishment.

(Turner & Muller, 2004, http://jfi.sagepub.com/ content/25/6/761.abstract)

Another study conducted by the National Family Violence Survey shows a clear link between corporal punishment and depression. Here are the findings of this study:

The National Family Violence Survey involved 6,002 adults respondents, including adults who were living with a spouse, living common law, or a single parent living with one or more children. They were asked the question: 'Thinking about when you yourself were a teenager, about how often would you say your mother or stepmother used corporal punishment, like slapping or hitting you?' A second question was asked concerning their father or stepfather. About half of the subjects reported memories of having been hit during adolescence. Respondents were asked five questions to find out if they had suffered sadness, depression, feelings of worthlessness, hopelessness, feelings that nothing was worthwhile, or suicidal thoughts during the past year.

For the men, [in the study], there is a clear tendency for depressive symptoms to increase with each increment of corporal punishment. For the women in the sample, the slope starts out even more steeply than for the men, but then declines for the highest categories of corporal punishment…the significant effect of corporal punishment occurs despite controlling for possible confounding with five other variables – SES, gender of the child, husband to wife violence, excessive drinking and witnessing violence between parents. The data showed that 'with increasing amounts of corporal punishment [during teen years], … thinking about suicide [in adulthood] increased.

(Robinson, 2009,
http://www.religioustolerance.org/spankin5.htm)

Because of the ways in which young children learn and process things, even if parents are trying to focus on correcting behavior, when we physically punish young children, it is conveying to them that they are "bad" and deserve to be in pain. As I have pointed out so many times throughout this book, pain and fear inhibit a child's learning process, so even if parents do tell the child what to do instead, it will not completely sink in. Plus, young children learn through repetition, so it is unrealistic to expect a child to remember what to do next time. Therefore, the message that young children hear repeatedly as they get spanked is a very negative message about *who* they *are* instead of about *what* they *did*. Young children are just gaining self-awareness, so being physically punished is an assault on their entire beings. They cannot separate their behavior from who they are. Because of this, young children often feel anger, confusion, and much anxiety from this assault done to them by people that that they love. When they display these negative feelings through crying too long or acting out, they usually get punished again. This teaches them to deny and/or repress their true feelings. But when anger and anxiety are not properly worked through, this can, and often does, lead to depression as the child grows and internalizes all of his/her negative feelings as well as the repetitive negative message he/she receives from his/her parents from being hit. This buried anger and anxiety causes one to become aggressive toward oneself by repeating the message, "I deserve pain because I'm bad and worthless." This is so sad because the child grows up truly believing the age-old adage of so many prospankers, "I was spanked and I deserved it." Greven (1992), page 132, states:

> While the etiology undoubtedly is complex, punishment in childhood always has been one of the most powerful generators of depression in adulthood...depression often is a delayed response to the suppression of childhood anger that usually results from being physically hit and hurt in the act of discipline by adults whom the child loves and on whom he or she depends for nurturance and life itself.

This is very sad since God has entrusted us to help His little ones grow up in His love, grace, and joy.

What is even more interesting, considering that Jesus wants us to have His joy to the fullest is that history shows that the conservative and fundamental sects of Christianity have a persistent theme of depression. Of course, it is these sects that also consistently advocate and practice physical punishment in order to break their children's wills. Greven (1992), page 132, explains the following:

> Melancholy and depression have been persistent themes in the family history, religious experience, and emotional lives of Puritans, evangelicals, fundamentalists and Pentecostals for centuries. Assaults on the self and on self-will are the central obsession of vast numbers of men and women from the early seventeenth century to the present. Suicidal impulses frequently appear in these Protestants' self-portraits as well, although those who write memoirs and autobiographies are usually survivors, not suicides. They may have successfully thwarted their inner impulses toward self-destruction, but the experience of conversion and the new birth rarely relieved them fully of their depressive symptoms.

While no one can be happy all the time, God gives us a sense of joy that should never stop. Happiness is circumstantial, but joy is continual as it is based on the hope we have in Christ, knowing that there is so much more to this life than what is seen. Let's look at what the Bible says about joy despite the trials and sufferings that all Christians go through. Romans 12:12 says, "Be joyful in hope, patient in affliction, faithful in prayer." In 1 Peter 1:8, it states, "Though you have not seen him, you love him; and even though you do not see him now, you believe in him and are filled with an inexpressible and glorious joy." And finally, Philippians 4:4-7 says to:

> Rejoice in the Lord always. I will say it again: Rejoice! Let your gentleness be evident to all. The Lord is near. Do not be anxious about anything, but in every situation, by prayer and petition, with thanksgiving, present your

requests to God. And the peace of God, which transcends all understanding, will guard your hearts and your minds in Christ Jesus.

Therefore, no matter what our circumstances are, Christians should have a certain amount of joy and peace within them. Chronic depression should not be plaguing Christ followers as it has for centuries. All we have to do to see this plague of depression is to pick up biographies of certain Christian historical figures. As Greven (1992), page 132 through 133, states:

> Many evangelicals, generation after generation, voiced their anxiety and depression in their diaries, letters, and autobiographies. In some families, such as the Mathers, melancholy afflicted fathers and sons for at least three successive generations. The persistence and, indeed, the centrality of melancholy and depression for an understanding of religious and secular experience in America from early-seventeenth-century Puritans to late-nineteenth-century Victorians has been explored brilliantly by John Owen King in his illuminating book, *The Iron of Melancholy*. Some of the most compelling historical evidence we possess concerning the nature and history of depression comes from the religious tradition associated most directly with Calvinism and evangelical Protestantism over the past four centuries.

Of course, I do realize that there are many other causes for depression. But we cannot deny the fact that corporal punishment is a main theme when it comes to depression in conservative and fundamental Christians. Due to the fact that many Christian prospankers believe in the necessity of breaking a child's will at a young age, they fail and/or refuse to realize that they are also breaking the child's spirit. Young children are just learning cause and effect. As I explained earlier in this chapter, young children learn through experience—i.e., sight, sound, touch, smell, and taste. But unless the experience of cause and effect is logical to young children—such as the fact that blowing a toy windmill makes it spin or that dropping a block on a hard surface makes a loud sound—they will fail to process it as something that makes sense to them. Therefore, being hit by a parent who loves them for random things that the parent deems wrong or bad is not logical for young children, especially for infants and toddlers. Yes, they may learn to avoid these things that the parent says are bad or wrong, but it isn't because the children truly understand; it is because they are afraid of being hit and hurt by their parents. Being forced to become broken by their parents hinders their natural development and causes feelings of anger, rage, and self-doubt in children, which then become feelings of unworthiness and hopelessness later on in life.

> Depression rooted in anger remains so potent because it often begins so early—in the first three years of life, precisely the period corporal punishment advocates have always stressed as critical for the start of physical punishments and the suppression of children's wills and self-assertion. The first assaults upon children's bodies and spirits generally commence before conscious memory can recall them later. The unconscious thus becomes the repository for the rage, resistance, and desire for revenge that small children feel when being struck by the adults they love. The impact of pain and physical violence is most severe because the children are unable to protect themselves from the blows. Though they cannot remember consciously what happened to them during the first three or four years of life, the ancient angers persist while the adult conscience directs rage inward upon the self. The psyches of so many Puritans, evangelicals, and others who have suffered from adult depressions bear witness to this process.
>
> (Greven, 1992, p. 134)

Sadly, throughout history, and even in today's society, a child's self-worth often depends upon their behavior in many fundamental Christian families who use spanking as a way to control their children.

> Obedience was the be-all and end-all—parenting relations were based on authority and control, rather than affection. The word *love* is almost never mentioned, in reference to children, in surviving documents from this era. Literature produced before the late 18th century tended to refer to children with annoyance. Few violent means were spared in extracting obedience from the "little devils."
>
> (Grille, 2005, p. 52)

Heimlich (2011), page 87, states:

> "The Bible states that obedience must be complete... Children are not to obey their parents only when and if they feel like it. God wants them to respond to their parents' authority and to learn to obey them in every area," writes Roy Lessin in *Spanking: A Loving Discipline.* Along the same vein, *The Secret of Family Happiness*, a book published by the Watchtower and Tract Society, tells Jehovah's Witness parents that children need discipline "constantly." Also, an article in the Witness magazine *Awake!* states that "permissiveness is hateful." Meanwhile, others also state that parents should rule their homes with a commanding presence. "God has established the institution of the parent as one of His ruling authorities on earth," writes J. Richard Fugate in *What the Bible Says about... Child Training.* "To this position has been delegated both the right to rule children and all the power necessary to succeed in training children according to God's plan." To drive this point home, he quotes Deuteronomy 21:18-21, which states that parents of a rebellious and drunken son should have him publicly stoned to death. "As you can

see," Fugate writes, "God is very serious about children being obedient."

Obviously, these Christian advocates of spanking do not understand God's unconditional love for us, nor do they understand that nowhere in the Bible does God give parents such absolute "commanding authority" over their children. This is like saying that husbands have absolute "commanding authority" over their wives. Neither statement is biblically true. Parents are not supposed to force children to obey them but are to teach children how to do this and to provide help to children when they are having a hard time following this biblical instruction. This teaches children that their parents and God love them unconditionally even when they are struggling. God lovingly corrects us and gives us natural consequences when necessary, but He does not punish us or withdraw His love from us. Look at how the Apostle Paul puts it in Romans 5:16-18:

> Nor can the gift of God be compared with the result of one man's sin: The judgment followed one sin and brought condemnation, but the gift followed many trespasses and brought justification. For if, by the trespass of the one man, death reigned through that one man, how much more will those who receive God's abundant provision of grace and of the gift of righteousness reign in life through the one man, Jesus Christ! Consequently, just as one trespass resulted in condemnation for all people, so also one righteous act resulted in justification and life for all people.

What an awesome God we have!

When children are physically punished, it does not make them feel loved unconditionally by anyone. Here is one such example. Heimlich (2011), page 89, states:

An example is thirty-six-year-old Alex Byrd, who grew up in a fundamental Pentecostal household in the southeast part of the country. As Byrd told me on November 23, 2009, he was spanked just about any time he was seen as being "bad." "And by 'bad,' says Byrd, 'I mean pretty much anything from laughing at specific words during mandatory family Bible reading to wrestling with my sister in a way that the parents did not approve of to not going to bed at a specific time or going outside of the yard or talking to people my mom did not want me talking with.' These tough standards meant Alex was sometimes spanked four or five times a day. 'I would be made to pull a switch off of a tree, be whipped with it, basically be told in some cases that I had sinned against God because I had disobeyed my parents, and would pretty much be made to pray and essentially repent to God.'"

Another reason that physical punishment does not relieve guilt and causes children to feel badly about themselves is that verbal shaming is used along with physical punishment as seen in the above example with Alex Byrd as his parents would tell him how he had sinned against God whenever he made a mistake. Sometimes shaming is used to threaten the child before physical punishment is applied. Some parents who may not use physical punishment with their children but believe that children deserve some type of punishment use shaming to control their children's behavior.

> Verbal punishment is common in almost every home and school. It relies on shame as the deterrent, in the same way that corporal punishment relies on pain. Shaming is one of the most common methods used to regulate children's behaviour.
>
> (Grille, 2005, p. 194)

Like spanking, shaming gives children negative messages about *who* they are instead of what they did. It's no wonder children who are spanked have higher incidences of depression with both a physical and emotional assault on their entire beings. And even if children are not hit, being punished with shaming is still an assault against their entire beings.

> Shaming is designed to cause children to curtail behaviour through negative thoughts and feelings about themselves. It involves a comment—direct or indirect—about what the child *is*. Shaming operates by giving children a negative image about their *selves*—rather than about the impact of their behaviour.
>
> (Grille, 2005, p. 194)

All of this makes children feel very shameful and guilty inside. They truly begin to believe that they deserve to feel a great deal of pain in order to try and resolve some of the guilt and shame as they grow older. What ends up happening to some children as they enter adolescence is that they feel so poorly about themselves because they have internalized the negative message that they deserve to feel pain when they make mistakes so they begin to intentionally inflict physical pain upon themselves after being spanked. Lisa, who we met in chapter 11, began inflicting pain upon herself after her dad would spank her to help her feel relieved of her guilty feelings. Lisa writes:

> My parents, who followed Pearl's advice, spanked in this very Pearl-esque way, where the children are talked to prior to the spanking and told that the parents hate to hurt them but they have no other choice. That it hurts them more than it would hurt me. This particular sentence inflicted tons of guilt on me. I hated to be spanked or hit, obviously, but I loved it at the same time. I needed it. I hated myself so much, so deeply, that I sometimes wished

my dad would really hurt me, really beat me, in order to be free of that guilt. It's very hard to explain how I felt.

I started this self-destructive behaviour around the age of eight or nine. I remember that my mother cried a lot because she felt overwhelmed by all the kids. She cried even more when there was a spanking, and they were daily business at our house. My dad would hit me and I still hated myself for doing this to them. Once the spanking was over, I was given some quiet time to calm down and freshen up. I went to the bathroom and cried endlessly, not that much because of the spanking but because I felt my mistake wasn't punished properly. I felt the need to feel more pain, and I didn't want to burden my parents with spanking me. I decided to do it myself. I looked for some sort of thing, a hard thing, to cause myself more pain and to remove the guilt I felt. It could be anything really, like a hairbrush, a stick, a wooden spoon, whatever was at hand. At first I started hitting myself on the legs and thighs until it really hurt. For some time, it was enough to do this three or four times to remove the guilt, but as I grew older, more and more pain was needed to calm my conflicts.

Sometimes I didn't do it for weeks, then I did it every day, then stopped it for some weeks again. It really depended on my emotional situation. I never felt like I was doing something wrong. After all, I wasn't cutting myself, so I was much better than those people. What I did was right. It was the Holy Spirit leading me to do this. How else could I feel so much relief in it?

Time passed and my self-punishments on my legs grew harder, more severe, more painful. One day my mother saw my bruised legs after a really tough session and asked me what that was all about. I told her I fell really bad playing outside in the garden and didn't realize I was so bruised up.

I had to hide it much better, find a better way to do it. More pain, less bruises. It took me just a few days to figure out a part of my body where nobody could see my bruises. My head. All the bruises and bumps would be hidden under my long hair. I felt like I had found the Holy Grail. It was the perfect plan. But it didn't last long. The pain inflicted by my hands beating on my head was really severe, and I was twelve or thirteen at that point. But this pain wasn't enough. I went back to anything hard to increase the pain level. And when that wasn't enough anymore, I really hated myself. I hated myself for having no way of causing such severe pain as to fulfill my need for feeling really repentant. This anger caused me to be even harder on myself, try it any way I could. I went on for minutes, hitting myself on the head with a hairbrush and crying, and it wasn't enough pain. I started tearing my hair out and screaming at myself, the most vicious things I could imagine, using words which would set me up for another spanking if my parents heard me say them.

I remember a day where I had gotten a spanking and it didn't satisfy my need to feel real pain. I sat in the bathroom, hitting my head with a hairbrush, not feeling the pain I wanted to feel, shrieking out in shrill screams then cursing at myself. *You are a piece of* (expletive deleted), *everybody hates you, you are worthless, you can't do anything, you will go to hell and marry the devil and God will laugh at you, your parents hate you, you're going to hell anyway so kill yourself right now and release them from this burden, you piece of dirty dog* (expletive deleted). I whispered these things to myself in a snakelike manner so my parents wouldn't hear, but they certainly heard the screaming. My Dad came knocking on the door, telling me that I needed to stop the screaming or else I'd get another spanking. I hushed up quickly and answered "Yes, Dad" as cheerful as I could. I started tearing my hair out, hitting myself with everything that wasn't nailed to the ground, and it didn't satisfy, so I hit my head against the wall, hoping it will finally start bleeding so I could stop. But it didn't bleed. It never did. After fifteen or twenty minutes, I gave up. I was defeated. I couldn't cause enough pain. My head was dizzy, spinning and painful, but it still wasn't enough.

(Lisa, 2011,
http://brokendaughters.wordpress.com/2011/09/07/
cutting-eating-disorders-selfdestructive-behaviours/)

Sadly, Lisa isn't the only one who felt the need to inflict more pain on herself in order to try and resolve the guilt that she felt. MC would often think about intentionally inflicting pain on himself due to feeling so poorly about himself after internalizing the message that he deserved to feel pain whenever he made a mistake. In an electronic message dated September 29, 2011, MC conveyed the following to me:

> Sometimes, I would think about hurting myself. I had this weird idea that if I hurt myself, then maybe God would have pity on me, and would forgive me, and save me. Basically, I was conditioned with this idea that I had to be punished and hurt before I could be accepted and forgiven. Therefore, a large part of my Christian experience has been fear based, rather than love based. Fear has motivated me rather than love, and that is why I am more of an orphan than a son, when it comes down to my relationship with God.

Research shows that depression, guilt, and shame from being harshly punished as young children often leads to self-destructive tendencies later on in childhood and adulthood.

> All absurd behavior has its roots in early childhood, but the cause will not be detected as long as the adult's manipulation of the child's psychic and physical needs is interpreted as an essential technique of child-rearing instead of as the cruelty it really is. Since most professionals themselves are not yet free from this mistaken belief, sometimes what is called therapy is only a continuation of early, unintended cruelty.
>
> (Miller, 1994, p. 132)

It is also true that if children are not taught to treat themselves with love and kindness as young children, they will have a difficult time doing so as adults.

The way we were treated as young children is the way we treat ourselves the rest of our lives. And we often impose our most agonizing suffering upon ourselves. We can never escape the tormentor within ourselves, who is often disguised as a pedagogue, someone who takes full control in illness; for example, in anorexia.

(Miller, 1994, p. 133)

This message of not being good enough often begins in infancy when most parents who believe in control use shaming to control infants' crying and other behaviors that are typical and developmentally appropriate for infants. "A five-month-old baby is lying in his mother's arms. He is close to sleep, then wakes and begins to grizzle. His mother tells him that he should stop being a naughty boy, and that she will be cross with him if he doesn't sleep" (Grille, 2005, p. 193). Unfortunately, many prospankers and people who use shame don't understand just how impressionable and vulnerable young children are when it comes to such negative messages that punishment instills in them. I know for myself, I still often put myself down much of the time in my head. It is extremely difficult to escape such negative messages about oneself, which are imparted by the very people children love and by whom they want approval and acceptance. Grille (2005), page 196 and 197, states the following:

Since children are more vulnerable and impressionable than adults, shaming messages received in childhood are significantly more difficult to erase... To understand the damage wrought by shame, we need to look deeper than the goal of "good" behaviour. If we think that verbal [or physical-added by author] punishment has "worked" because it changed what the child is doing, then we have dangerously limited our view of the child to the *behaviours* that we can *see*. It is too easy to overlook the inner world of children; the emotions that underlie their behaviour, and the suffering caused by shame. It is also easy to miss what the child does once out of range of the shamer.

Finally, being spanked and taught that any negative emotion and opinion one has deserves punishment leads some adults who were raised in this manner to later struggle in their marriages. This is exactly what is happening with Dave who was raised in a strict Amish home as a child. Dave's wife explained to me in an electronic message dated November 10, 2011, the following:

> For the first few years of our marriage I almost worshiped him because he was just so awesome. I kid you not I thought he was "perfect."
>
> One thing I noticed right away, though I overlooked for a while, about my amazing man was that he wouldn't argue with me…about anything!
>
> My husband's parents were Old Order Amish and Mennonite. He was always punished with a belt when he did anything "wrong." And speaking his mind was in the "wrong" category. He was expected to always "be respectful" to adults and telling his mom that (for example) he didn't like what she'd prepared for lunch was disrespect and punishable with the belt. Squirming (showing any boredom) in church was punishable by the belt. Arguing with his parents or questioning them in any way was punishable with the belt.
>
> According to him his parents never did it in anger or did anything he felt was "abusive." He said he always got a "talking to" beforehand and that his dad always had this demeanor that said he was really not happy having to do it. He said his dad even cried once in a while afterward and often said he hated doing it. (This is sad for his parents!) So, this is why I think that as far as followers of *To Train Up a Child* would look at my husband's parents and give him an "A+" and say he did everything "right."

Because my husband actually had an extraordinary relationship with his parents and lived that kind of old fashioned life on the mission field where his work in the family was "necessary" for the family's survival, he never felt any desire to "rebel" against his parents. He ate when he was told. He got up when he was told and went to bed when he was told. He sat still no matter how long the church service was. He didn't complain about sleeping on dirt floors in village huts or about having to eat weird food. Living on the mission field, he ate food at least once a week that made him want to gag without expressing anything. Sometimes they went without food. But he never complained. He never disagreed with his parents. He never questioned his parents. He never challenged them. He was the "model child." Had the Pearls known the family they'd have looked at my husband as a shining example of how their parenting practices are right and God's way because my husband was so obedient!

So, he grows up and gets married to me and he treats me exactly the way he was trained to treat people: Don't argue. Don't express dislike. Don't complain. And, it is not working. Every year that we've been married has just been this slow steady progression from awesome to where we are now in total separateness and depression. We have like "no" relationship at this point.

His parents maybe wanted a child who'd never ever give them any "trouble" and preferred him to be complacent and obedient, but that doesn't work for a spouse. You can't ever get to know someone who has no opinion. I don't know what he actually thinks about things or what he thinks about what I think. I don't even know what he actually thinks about anything, because he was trained to agree with whoever he was talking to or it was being disrespectful. He thinks he is "keeping the peace" and that things "aren't worth fighting about."

Now, had his parents had the attitude that he should not do or say the same things, but had taken a totally different approach to it by talking to him and discussing the things he said with him, then they would have learned things about their son. They would have gotten to know him and even if they'd have ultimately said, "Look, mom has limited things to choose for us to eat and even if you don't like what she's made you need to just eat it," it would have taught him a totally different lesson and would not have made him just simply shut down. That approach would have taught him that his opinions mattered and they were ok to have but sometimes we need to do things we don't like. The way he was taught he learned that to express a negative opinion was "disrespect" and that expressing it was painful. He learned that his opinions didn't matter and that trying to do anything with them would not change his world at all and so it's better just to not have them at all.

I believe that being spanked changed everything in the world and his whole future for him. It changed everything about him. And, now it's destroying our relationship and though we don't fight (because he can't) our kids sense that we have no relationship and they don't like it. My oldest daughter cries and says if this is how it is she never wants to even get married because it's terrible.

Did this consistent use of the rod produce a happy child like the Pearls say? I'd say he's miserable. I'd say he knows he's missing out on life. I'd say he feels alone all the time. I'd say he feels frustrated and sad because he's not running thru houses every day saving little kids but he is facing me every day and can't connect with me. On the one side of him he's a hero and on the daily side of him he's a total failure in his eyes. He is still that same little boy lying awake at night paralyzed unable to get up and go to anyone for help when he's uncomfortable. He does what he was "trained" to do to be "a good boy" but it doesn't work anymore. Now, his wife wants from him exactly what his parents punished him for: for him to think on his own and to be himSELF. And, he just can't do it. He has...no joy in life. He is a man who would literally give you the shirt off his back and would do anything for you, but, he has no joy. The whole situation makes me so angry every day because if you "raise a child up in the way you think they should go and you do it all wrong...when they are old..." they will struggle like heck to depart from it...

It is quite clear spanking and shame do *not* produce truly happy people, and it is extremely sad how Dave and his wife, as well as a great deal of others who have been raised to be obedient robots, struggle greatly as adults. "Many studies have indicated that shame causes a host of relationship difficulties. This is not surprising, since relationship skills depend on emotional intelligence" (Grille, 2005, p. 198).

As with the sexual problems from being spanked "lovingly," children, whose young brains are in the midst of critical development, that are exposed to high levels of stress, anxiety, and pain on a daily basis causes stress hormones that forever change children's brain structure that can lead to a lifelong struggle with depression—sometimes leading some to commit suicide. Straus (2006), pages 78 through 79, states:

> At a 1991 conference attended by specialists on depression, there was wide agreement that depression is a mental health problem with many causes, but that it probably involves a biological process in which there are lasting changes in the structure and chemistry of the brain (Holden, 1991). A speaker at the conference reported that "One fact that could play a role in such long-term changes is stress. Both animals and people who experience chronic stress respond by secreting 'stress hormones' [that are] the most robust biological concomitant of depression—showing in up to 50 percent of cases, especially severe ones" (Holden, 1991, p. 1,451). Several other *permanent* changes in brain function were reported in both animals and humans who experience

continuing stress. For children, one such continuing stress may be corporal punishment by their parents. It often begins in infancy and is particularly frequent for toddlers, many of whom are hit almost daily. Moreover, we have seen that corporal punishment continues into the teen years for a majority of American children. The changes in brain structure and function associated with the stress of having been physically assaulted for 13 or more years might explain the link between corporal punishment and depression.

Conclusion

It becomes clearer and clearer that physically punishing children "in love" is nothing but harmful. It sends the message that love and pain go together, which is very dangerous for the host of reasons I have discussed throughout this part of the book thus far. It is also clear that physical punishment does not relieve children of their guilt and that this is not even biblical because Jesus has paid for all of our sins once and for all. Instead, physical punishment eats away at a child's self-worth, putting children at risk for depression as they become adolescents and adults. Finally, spanking has been shown to cause permanent changes in the brain that can lead children to struggle with sexual problems and depression. God never intended for all of this. We continue to see that spanking implants seeds of sin rather than discouraging sin. Sin does not lead to joyfulness in Jesus. As 1 Thessalonians 5:16-22 states, we are to:

> Rejoice always, pray continually, give thanks in all circumstances; for this is God's will for you in Christ Jesus.
> Do not quench the Spirit. Do not treat prophecies with contempt but test them all; hold on to what is good, reject every kind of evil.

In the next chapter, we will learn about Stockholm Syndrome, the cycle of abuse, more on how pain and stress affects the young child's brain, and how we can know that the anti-spanking research is *not* biased as prospankers strongly claim.

References

Block, N. A. & Gomez, M. Y. (2011). *This Hurts Me More Than it Hurts You: In Words and Pictures.* Columbus, OH: The Center for Effective Discipline.

Greven, P. (1992). *Spare the Child.* New York, NY: Vintage Books.

Grille, R. (2005). *Parenting for a Peaceful World.* New South Wales, Australia: Longueville Media.

Heimlich, J. (2011). *Breaking Their Will.* Amherst, NY: Prometheus Books.

Lisa. (2011). *Cutting, Eating Disorders, Self-Destructive Behaviours.* http://brokendaughters.wordpress.com/2011/09/07/cutting-eating-disorders-selfdestructive-behaviours/

Miller, A. (1994). *For Your Own Good.* New York, NY: The Noonday Press.

Neddermeyer, D. M. (2006). Loving Spankings – Part 1. http://ezinearticles.com/?Loving-Spankings—Part-I&id=373269

Robinson, B. A. (2009). *Child Corporal Punishment: Spanking Results from Studies in 1985 & 1986.* http://www.religioustolerance.org/spankin5.htm

Straus, M. A. (2006). *Beating the Devil Out of Them.* New Brunswick, NJ: Transaction Publishers Publishers.

Turner, P. A. & Muller, H. A. (2004). Long-Term Effects of Child Corporal Punishment on Depressive Symptoms in Young Adults. *Journal of Family Issues.* 25 (6), 761-782. http://jfi.sagepub.com/content/25/6/761.abstract

Chapter 15

The Vicious Cycle of Abuse, Brain Damage, and Research Credibility

In the last chapter we saw how teaching children to equate love with pain can cause them to become sadomasochistic. We also saw how spanking children, even when done "lovingly" and the "right way," causes many children to struggle with depression, guilt, and shame because having pain intentionally inflicted on them by their parents never makes them feel positive about themselves. In this chapter, we will see how spanking keeps the vicious cycle of abuse and authoritarian parenting going for generations unless one fights against it. New research shows that children that are physically punished/abused can develop a form of Stockholm Syndrome as they deny and repress their pain. Also, I will be showing that intentionally inflicting pain on children causes brain damage as the brain gets rewired due to experiencing pain and trauma throughout childhood. Many parents do not realize how vulnerable the young, developing brain is. Finally, I will be explaining the scientific method of conducting research in order to disprove the claim of a great deal of prospankers that all the research proving spanking is harmful is somehow biased. I hope this part of the book further proves that spanking did *not* come from God, otherwise *none* of these harmful effects would ever occur.

The Cycle of Abuse and Authoritarian Parenting: "My Parents Spanked Me and I Survived and So Will My Children!"

Many prospankers often make this statement. They've learned that physically punishing children is an acceptable manner of child rearing as it is what their parents did to them. Also, Christian advocates of spanking have incorrectly taught them that God mandates the use of physical punishment in order to have godly children. As these people have grown up learning never to question authority figures, it makes it easy for them to blindly obey the Christian advocates of spanking who claim that they are "experts" on child rearing such as Dobson, the Pearls, Lessin, Tripp, the Ezzos, and Christenson. Plus, many well-meaning, everyday church pastors teach that the rod verses in Proverbs mean that we are to hit children in order to "discipline" them. The way parents were treated as children is most often the way parents will go on to treat their children.

> If you are harsh and demanding, it is very likely your children will rebel and turn away from your value system sometime down the road. In addition, you are setting up your children to reap a lifetime of emotional pain and rejection, and the cycle of abuse continues.
>
> (Kuzma, 2006, p. 9)

Many people confuse the three parenting styles. The three parenting styles are authoritarian, authoritative, and permissive. If parents physically punish their children, they are authoritarian, even if they do some of the things that authoritative parents do such as listening to their children at times or offer some choices to the children. This is because authoritarian parenting stresses obedience without question, first-time obedience, strictness, and the use of punishment, especially corporal punishment, with their children. Authoritarian parents also have very high (usually beyond what the children are developmentally capable of) expectations for their children. While authoritarian parents, in general, love their children very much and simply want the best for them, these parents tend to focus more on keeping control of their children than on using effective discipline strategies that respect the actual needs of the individual child. Janet Heimlich (2011), page 46, explains authoritarianism this way:

> What is *authoritarianism*? Usually this term refers to an oppressive form of government where leaders have great control over their subjects. Dictionary.com describes authoritarianism as "favoring complete obedience or subjection to authorities as opposed to individual freedom."

Fear is the primary way authoritarian parents gain and maintain control over their children. Most of these parents are fundamental Christians in which their church leaders also use authoritarianism tactics to maintain control over their congregations. "Fear and authoritarianism often go hand in hand, as religious leaders can use terror tactics to maintain order and control" (Heimlich, 2011, p. 48).

Is authoritarianism biblical? One could say it was during Old Testament times as God was not easily accessible and people had to obey all God's commandments in order to be accepted by Him. But, as I continue to point out throughout all of this book, God saw that His people were not able to live up to His extremely high expectations and chose to send His Son, Who was God, to die for all of humanity's sins. God humbled Himself to the lowliest of lows and chose to come to Earth as an infant, be born naturally as every other baby was born, drink milk from His mother's breasts, and then suffer and die like a common criminal for us. Our great and mighty God did all of this for us. As soon as Christ died, the veil that was across the temple tore in two, symbolizing that we now have full and complete access to God (Matthew 27:51). The God of all creation did that for us. We now live in grace. "But now he has reconciled you by Christ's physical body through death to present you holy in his sight, without blemish and free from accusation" (Colossians 1:22). What's more is that God is singing over us (Zephaniah 3:14-17)! Therefore, authoritarianism is not biblical.

Sadly, if all one has ever experienced is authoritarianism and being physically punished throughout childhood, it can make it very difficult for the person to break out of that cycle because he or she does not know any other way to be a parent toward his or her child. Thus, the same patterns take place within the parent-child relationship. Here is an example of the patterns that generally occur in authoritarian and abusive homes.

> The Cycle of Abuse follows a certain predictable pattern that begins when the child is young and gets progressively worse as the child becomes a teenager. Here are the steps you will see:
> 1. The child misbehaves. 2. The parent notices the child's misbehavior and gives him instructions to correct it. 3. The child does not comply. He may ignore the instructions, argue, or even refuse to do what the parent says. 4. The parent feels angry. The parent feels that his authority is being threatened. The parent yells at the child, shakes him, insults him, or hits him. 5. The child feels angry, resentful, and worthless. 6. The child's misbehavior becomes more ingrained and is now based on feelings of revenge and/or worthlessness. 7. The parent becomes more and more frustrated with the continued misbehavior

and the entire cycle escalates until someone intervenes or someone gets hurt badly.

You can see the potential for this cycle to occur in any family.

(Keith, 2011, http://childparenting.about.com/cs/
familyissues/a/childabusecycle.htm)

This is particularly true in homes where obedience to authority is of the upmost importance. As obedience becomes ingrained in the child's mind, as with Dave who we met in chapter 14, he or she may become afraid to question anyone and may begin to crave the healthy amount of control that he or she lacked throughout childhood that when he or she finally has a child, he or she may begin to enforce the control onto the child. These people feel so angry, resentful, and guilty that they misuse their authority over their child because they are finally in a position of power over someone reliant on them. Miller (1994), page 78, states:

When someone suddenly gives vent to his or her rage, it is usually an expression of deep despair, but the ideology of child beating and the belief that beating is not harmful serve the function of covering up the consequences of the act and making them unrecognizable. The result of a child becoming dulled to pain is that access to the truth about himself will be denied him all his life. Only consciously experienced feelings would be powerful enough to subdue the guard at the gates, but these are exactly what he is not allowed to have.

Another reason why using authoritarian parenting and physical punishment with children tends to keep the cycle of abuse going is that, as I discussed in chapter 13, a great deal of children who are physically punished struggle with a lack of empathy as they deny their own pain and become a proud survivor of physical punishment. This sense of pride makes them deaf toward other's pain and suffering, especially that of their children. Also, they have become accustomed to obeying authority, especially when they believe that it is "godly," and will obey even when it causes severe pain to a child. Alice Miller (1994), page 81, states:

> The other explanation—that these were people who worshipped authority and were accustomed to obey—is not wrong, but neither is it adequate to explain a phenomenon like the Holocaust, if by obeying we mean the carrying out of commands that we consciously regard as being forced upon us. People with any sensitivity cannot be turned into mass murderers overnight. But the men and women who carried out "the final solution" did not let feelings stand in their way for the simple reason that they had been raised from infancy not to have any feelings of their own but to experience their parents' wishes as their own. These were people who, as children, had been proud of being tough and not crying, of carrying out all their duties "gladly," of not being afraid—that is, at bottom, of not having an inner life at all.

This very well might explain why Michael Pearl and other Christian as well as non-Christian prospankers seem so proud of what they are advocating and doing to their children. Their hearts have been hardened by the pain they experienced as children, thus, continuing this vicious cycle by not only doing it to their children, but teaching other parents to do it to their children in order to "obey God" and raise "godly children." Studies have been done showing this pride and willingness to obey authority even when it causes another to be in severe pain.

One such study was conducted by Stanley Milgram, which was published in 1974 as *Obedience to Authority*. In this study, Milgram wanted to see the lengths that people would go in obeying someone they perceived as having authority over them.

To conduct his experiment, he set up a situation in which there was a "teacher" and a "learner." The teacher would ask the learner a question, and if the learner answered the teacher's question incorrectly or failed to respond at all, a shock ranging from 0 to 450 volts would be administered to the learner at increasingly voltage each time the shock was administered by the teacher. In reality, no shocks were actually given to the learner, but this fact was kept from the teacher.

> The experiment's true purpose was to discover the point at which an individual would refuse to obey and then actively disobey the insistent commands of the experimenter. Milgram found that in experimental situations in which the "learner" voiced his response to the increasing shocks, from mild discomfort to agonizing screams and pleas to be released from the straps binding him to his chair, many of the "teachers" nevertheless continued to inflict the shocks.
>
> (Greven, 1992, p. 201)

What's more is many of these "teachers" continued administering the shocks until the "learner" finally grew silent as the higher voltage shocks could cause serious harm and even death. This concerned Milgram and his colleagues. Greven (1992), page 202, goes on to state:

> What astonished Milgram and his colleagues was the proportion of individuals willing to obey the command to inflict pain right to the limit even when, in at least one instant, the person inflicting the shock believed that the person being shocked had died. After the termination of the experiment, this man commented: "Well, I faithfully believed the man was dead until we opened the door. When I saw him, I said, 'Great, this is great.' But it didn't bother me even to find that he was dead. I did a job."

It is important to note that the study used people from all different backgrounds and different walks of life, and yet, half of the participants still continued to give shocks up to the maximum limit. I found this very interesting and disturbing, as did Milgram. Why would so many seemingly good people obey authority to the point of inflicting such severe pain and even death on another person? Knowing the research in child development, I suspect it had something to do with how these people were treated as children. Also, these people believed that the shocks that they were administering to the "learner" were for his own good.

> In most of the experiments, Milgram found that approximately half the people who volunteered to give the shocks were willing to obey the authority to the limit despite the anguished pleas, and subsequent silence, of the person they were helping to "teach."
>
> (Greven, 1992, p. 202)

While Stanley Milgram never considered the childhoods of the people who obeyed unwaveringly, I believe that this study shows what happens when pain, fear, and coercion are used with children; they lose a major part of themselves. Christians think broken wills are a good thing for children, but in reality, a broken will means an inability to think or feel for oneself. A broken will eventually turns into a hardened, calloused, prideful heart that is willing to listen to only the Christian teachers that align with their beliefs rather than taking the time to really study God's Word and hear His still, small voice. This also allows children to relate and defend their parents' hurtful and abusive actions, and, therefore, keeping the cycle of abuse and authoritarianism going despite hearing their children's cries of pain.

Stockholm Syndrome

Most people are familiar with Stockholm Syndrome from the two well-covered cases of it. The first case of Stockholm Syndrome happened in Stockholm, Sweden, on August 23, 1973. Bank robbers held three women and a man hostage for 131 hours. The robbers strapped dynamite to all of the hostages. At the end of the hostage situation, the hostages wound up defending their captors.

The second well-known case of Stockholm Syndrome is what happened with Patty Hearst. Patty Hearst was kidnapped by the Symbionese Liberation Army on February 4, 1974. When two months later the group robbed a bank in San Francisco, it was observed on the bank's surveillance camera that Patty was with the group and holding a gun during the robbery. She had become attached to her captors and voluntarily aided them in their criminal activity. Here are a few more details of the situation that Patty Hearst was in so that we can understand the psychological aspects of how people can develop Stockholm Syndrome:

> The apparent leader, Donald DeFreeze, called himself Field Marshall Cinque Mtume. Like Charles Manson only five years before, he wanted to start a revolution of the underprivileged, and he intended to do that by declaring war on those with status and money. From his followers he commanded total obedience and worship.
>
> By her account, Patty was kept blindfolded for two months in a closet at the group's headquarters, unable even to use the bathroom in privacy. DeFreeze realized that her visibility as a social figure that had gained the nation's sympathy would showcase his cause, so he worked to turn her into an angry revolutionary.
>
> From her report, DeFreeze relied on harsh psychological techniques:

She was isolated and made to feel that no one was going to rescue her.

She was physically and sexually abused by various members of the gang.

She was told that she might die.

She was fed lies about how the gang was oppressed by the establishment.

She was forced to record messages that blasted those she loved.

By early April, she had a new identity and was deemed ready to accompany the gang on their next daring foray.

(Ramsland, 2011,
http://www.trutv.com/library/crime/terrorists_spies/
terrorists/hearst/1.html)

Many people don't realize that Stockholm Syndrome occurs in domestic situations as well, such as spousal abuse and child abuse. With the main dynamic occurring in cases of Stockholm Syndrome being that the person is reliant on the captor/abuser for survival, many times the victim will end up becoming attached to the captor/abuser and begins to truly believe the captor/abuser has his or her best interests at heart as he or she believes the lies that the captor/abuser feeds him or her. Also, the abuser holds absolute power over the victim. "Because survival depends upon the good will of the oppressor, the abused become infatuated with and bonded to them" (Levy, 2009, http://www.psychologytoday.com/blog/tribal-intelligence/200909/mackenzie-phillips-and-the-stockholm-syndrome). This is how it is with children and their parents. Children have no choice but to be totally reliant on their parents for survival. Most parents that physically and emotionally harm their children truly love their children and will do just enough things correctly—such as comfort their children, be responsive to some of their children's needs, and play with their children—that the children form an attachment to their parents, even if it isn't a secure attachment. (See chapter 16 for more information on attachment). As children grow up being fed lies by their parents about physical punishment being "for their own good," being done "out of love," children begin to deny and repress their pain allowing them to truly believe these lies. They begin to identify with their parents, thus, believing their parents have done nothing wrong to them.

Michael Pearl seems to be a perfect example of Stockholm Syndrome occurring because of child abuse. As I mentioned in the previous section of this chapter, he talks proudly of the whippings that he received as a child. And now he proudly teaches parents to do the same to their children beginning in early infancy. He truly sees nothing wrong with his teachings despite three children dying because their parents followed his teachings. Interestingly, it appears that the more severely the parents abuse a child, the more likely it is for the child to develop this form of Stockholm Syndrome.

> In the book, Traumatic Experience and the Brain, author David Ziegler, the director of a treatment program for abused children, writes that "I have often noticed that the degree of loyalty from a child to an abusive parent seems to be in direct proportion to the seriousness of the abuse the child received. In this counterintuitive way, the stronger or more life-threatening the treatment, the stronger the loyalty from the child."
>
> (Levy, 2009, http://www.psychologytoday. com/blog/tribal-intelligence/200909/ mackenzie-phillips-and-the-stockholm-syndrome)

Since children can never escape from their parents on their own, they cannot completely withdraw from their parents. Therefore, children will develop unique ways of coping with harsh treatment.

If the betrayed person is a child and the betrayer is a parent, it is especially essential the child does not stop behaving in such a way that will inspire attachment. For the child to withdraw from a caregiver he is dependent on would further threaten his life, both physically and mentally. Thus the trauma of child abuse by the very nature of it requires that information about the abuse be blocked from mental mechanisms that control attachment and attachment behavior.

(Freyd, 2009,
http://dynamic.uoregon.edu/~jjf/defineBT.html)

Blocking the pain from physical punishment and abuse is known as dissociation. Dissociation is where the child mentally removes him/herself from the situation so that he or she can no longer feel the pain. It is like an out of body experience. During a spanking, a child might pretend to be hovering over the scene where his or her parent is hitting him or her. This allows children to cope with the pain without risking their ability to survive by maintaining a bond with their parents. I believe Stockholm Syndrome is a very real negative effect of corporal punishment. It may explain why so many prospankers are proud that they survived being physically punished and see nothing wrong with continuing the cycle with their children. Sadly, as we've seen throughout this part of this book, messing with little minds and bodies leads to big consequences that are permanent. In the next section, we will see that physical punishment leads to young brains being harmed.

How Spanking Hurts Brain Development

The first seven years of a child's life is when the majority of brain development and growth occurs. The first three are even more vulnerable because the foundations of brain and personality growth happen during these first few years. Yes, infants are born with a certain personality, but what happens to infants after birth often has long-term consequences on whom they will become. The brain is developing very fast during this time and all experiences will either enhance or harm this critical time of brain development.

> In early childhood, the brain develops faster than any other organ in the body. By age 5, the brain reaches about 90 percent of its adult weight, and by 7, it is fully grown. This makes early childhood a very sensitive and critical period in brain development.
>
> (Riak, 2011, http://www.nospank.net/pt2009.htm)

What's more is that many Christian advocates of spanking infants claim that the infants are purposely trying to manipulate their parents, but this is not true because the way that the infant's brain works makes them incapable of manipulating their parents.

> Because children lack abstract reasoning and analytical abilities until they approach the age of twelve, they lack the ability and the mental wiring to be able to plot "diabolically." This website offers an easily understood description and more detail about how the brain of a child develops over time, noting how brain function starts out as rudimentary and becomes more sophisticated as the child matures. Children learn as they grow and grow as they learn, but that learning process differs greatly from the way an adult learns. The Pearls created the idea of the child as the natural adversary of the parent, an idea that does not arise from Biblical or scientific fact. Their concept of the "diabolical will" of the child attempts to spiritualize and rationalize *the Pearls' own intolerance* of the natural immaturity and the limited function of a young and developing child.
>
> (Kunsman, 2012, http://undermuchgrace.blogspot. com/2012/02/what-its-like-to-experience-only-right. html)

Sadly, people just don't know how vulnerable the young brain is and that spanking, no matter how it is done, has been shown to affect brain development in a highly negative manner. Most children begin getting physically punished before they are one year old. And most Christian prospankers claim that it is best to spank children between the ages of two and six years old. This is precisely when the brain is the most vulnerable to stress and trauma. The pain of being physically punished is unlike other types of pain that young children experience because their parents, to punish them, intentionally inflict this pain on them. It is usually accompanied by verbal shamings from the parent. Therefore, whether the spanking is administered "lovingly" or in anger, the child, even as an infant, knows that the parent's intention is to inflict pain on him or her even if the child does not understand why the parent is hitting him or her. The trauma of being intentionally hurt by the very people children love and on whom they are reliant is what causes negative effects on young children's brains.

Recent research has studied the brains of people who were abused as children using fMRIs. One such study was conducted by Psychologist Eamon McCroy. It was published in *Current Biology* on December 5, 2011, and it showed that the brains of abused children looked similar to those of soldiers who had been in combat.

> His team compared fMRIs from abused children to those of 23 non-abused but demographically similar children from a control group. In the abused children, angry faces provoked distinct activation patterns in their anterior insula and right amygdala, parts of the brain involved in processing threat and pain. Similar patterns have been measured in soldiers who've seen combat.
>
> (Keim, 2011, http://www.wired.com/ wiredscience/2011/12/neurology-of-abuse/)

As I pointed out in chapter 14, children begin to become stressed and fearful before a spanking takes place. They release stress hormones into their bodies as their heart rates and blood pressures rise. The pain of being hit only causes their bodies to further secrete stress hormones. This huge release of stress negatively affects the child's entire body. Given that young children are incapable of controlling their emotions and impulses, spankings are likely to occur quite frequently and, sadly, more than once a day. Having chronic stress is not good for brain development.

> Stress caused by pain and fear of spanking can negatively affect the development and function of a child's brain. It is precisely during this period of great plasticity and vulnerability that many children are subjected to physical punishment. The effect can be a derailing of natural, healthy brain growth, resulting in life-long and irreversible abnormalities.
>
> (Riak, 2011, http://www.nospank.net/pt2009.htm)

Now, before I get blamed for not citing Christian research with regard to how physical punishment negatively affects brain development of young children, Dr. Kay Kuzma, Christian author of *The First Seven Years* who has a background and doctorate degree in Early Childhood Education, states the following:

> If, however, early spankings are given frequently, emotional pain is laid down in the limbic system of the brain that can affect the child's later behavior. There is startling new evidence against inflicting pain on children reported in a special issue of *Newsweek*, titled "Your Child," (Spring/ Summer 1997). It has to do with the vulnerability of the brain to trauma during the first few years. If the brain's organization reflects its experience, and the experience of the traumatized child is fear and stress, then the

neurochemical responses to fear and stress become the most powerful architects of the brain. "If you have experiences that are overwhelming, and have them again and again, it changes the structure of the brain," says Dr. Linda Mayers of the Yale Child Study Center. Here's how:

Trauma elevates stress hormones, such as cortisol, that wash over tender brains like acid. As a result, regions in the cortex and in the limbic system (responsible for emotions, including attachment) are 20 to 30 percent smaller in abused children than in normal kids, finds Dr. Bruce Perry of Baylor College of Medicine. These regions also have fewer synapses.

In adults who were abused as children, the memory-making hippocampus is smaller than in nonabused adults. This effect, too, is believed to be the result of the toxic effects of cortisol.

High cortisol levels during the vulnerable years of zero to three increase activity in the brain structure involved in vigilance and arousal. (It's called the locus cerulean.) As a result the brain is wired to be on hair-trigger alert, explains Perry. Regions that were activated by the original trauma are immediately reactivated whenever the child dreams of, thinks about, or is reminded of the trauma (as by the mere presence of the abusive person). The slightest stress, the most inchoate (early stage) fear, unleashes a new surge of stress hormones. This causes hyperactivity, anxiety, and impulsive behavior. "Kids with higher cortisol levels score lowest on inhibitory control," says neurologist Megan Gunnar of the University of Minnesota. "Kids from high-stress environments (have) problems in attention regulation and self-control" (p. 32).

(Kuzma, 2006, p. 412-413)

We can see a cycle here. The more trauma that happens to the young, developing brain from being physically punished, the more likely the child will misbehave due to this harm. The more young children misbehave, the more frequently they will get hit. At least until the child is old enough to start using psychological coping skills and their minds, spirits, wills, and brains are totally broken.

It is clear that using corporal punishment with children has detrimental effects on their brains and minds, and, therefore, should *never* be used with them. As I continue to point out throughout all of this book, it is God who created us. He knows exactly how our bodies work from conception. Since He knows how harmful spanking is to His youngest children, surely He never intended the rod verses to be taken literally. If He had then *none* of these detrimental effects would occur no matter how the physical punishment is administered. I would like to share Dr. Kay Kuzma's suggestion of how we are to interpret these rod verses. Kuzma (2006), page 416, states:

> Some suggest that the biblical "rod of correction" was a common measuring instrument to determine certain standards. The analogy could be made that if children didn't meet standards, the "rod" would be used to make the necessary corrections—not by beating, but by pointing out error.

Given the biblical explanations to the rod verses that I have provided throughout this book, and the fact that the Bible does in fact speak of using a rod to measure things (Ezekiel 40:5-6; 42:16-19; Revelation 11:1; 21:15-16), I believe this is another accurate way to interpret these rod verses. After all, God continues to lovingly discipline His people as He freely offers and grants us forgiveness. "But with you there is forgiveness, so that we can, with reverence, serve you" (Psalm 130:4).

How Do We Know the Research Against Corporal Punishment is Reliable and Valid?

Many prospankers, especially Christians, often claim that the research proving that all corporal punishment is harmful is biased and inaccurate. They also claim that corporal punishment and physical abuse get lumped together in many of these anti-spanking studies.

So, how can we be sure that these studies showing corporal punishment to be harmful are accurate? All valid and reliable studies are done using the scientific method. The experimenter, who is an experienced professional in the field, comes up with a hypothesis to be tested. A hypothesis is a hunch or idea that the experimenter wants to see if it's true. Using the scientific method, the experimenter conducts the study in order to maintain objectivity. This means keeping all biases out of the research being conducted. There are three main things that the scientific method requires of all research. The first is reliability. Reliability means conducting the study in a manner that guarantees accurate results each time it is conducted with the same subjects but using different methods. The second is validity. Validity means that the test or instrument used in the study measures precisely for which it is intended. For example, many studies done on corporal punishment use surveys or other high tech instruments to measure the amount of harm done to children and/or adults participating in the studies, and special care was taken to ensure these instruments measured the results accurately. Finally, replicability guarantees that other researchers can perform the exact experiment and have similar results.

Assessing objectivity, reliability, validity, and replicability of studies prevents the dissemination of inaccurate or untrue information that can result from such research pitfalls as poor research design, researcher bias, inappropriate or inaccurate use of statistical methods, insufficient size of population studied, or inadequate or unclear instructions and procedures for research subjects. (Puckett, Black, Wittmer, & Petersen, 2009, p. 25)

I believe all of the research studies that I have presented throughout this part of the book meet the criteria of the scientific method. And all of the research presented in these studies is from credible, well-known scholars in this field. Yes, there have been a few studies released that claim corporal punishment isn't harmful to children, but the overwhelming majority of studies done say that it is. The studies that claim corporal punishment isn't harmful are conducted primarily by advocates of spanking, especially Christians. These studies are small and have a specific sample of individuals in order to gain the desired results. And, because corporal punishment is still widely accepted in our society, the people who do reliable studies showing corporal punishment is harmful have nothing to gain, whereas the people doing a few studies showing corporal punishment is not harmful have everything to gain. Plus, all of the true stories that we have read throughout this part of the book further prove that the research is correct. Many of these anti-spanking studies are done by Christians as well as by non-Christians. As Joan Durant, a professor at the University of Minnesota, states after completing a recent twenty-year study in Canada, "Here, we have more than 80 studies, I would say more than 100, that show the same thing (about corporal punishment), and yet we keep calling it controversial" (French & Wilson, 2012, http://health.yahoo.net/news/s/nm/spanking-kids-can-cause-long-term-harm-canada-study). It's due time we begin to take all this research seriously!

Conclusion

In this part of the book, we have seen the many negative effects of using physical punishment, such as: denial and repression, lack of empathy, anger, aggression, fear and anxiety, fear of God, sadomasochism, guilt and shame, low self-esteem, depression, higher risk for domestic violence, Stockholm Syndrome, inhibited brain development, and the continuing cycle of abuse. I pray that all of these chapters have further proven that God does *not* want children to be physically punished. To end this part of the book, I would like to share two more stories. One is straight from the Bible.

Rehoboam was the son of King Solomon. King Solomon may have been blessed by God with wisdom, but he also sinned against God by having many wives and building altars for his wives' gods. Children were even sacrificed on these altars. King Solomon treated Rehoboam very harshly as a child and physically punished him. How did Rehoboam turn out when he became king after his father died? Not too well according to 1 Kings 12:1-24. I am only going to cite 1 Kings 12:10-14 for our purposes. I highly recommend reading this entire passage because it seems clear that Solomon treated children rather poorly from the way the young men who grew up with Rehoboam advised him. In 1 Kings 12:10-14, it states:

> The young men who had grown up with him replied, "These people have said to you, 'Your father put a heavy yoke on us, but make our yoke lighter.' Now tell them, 'My little finger is thicker than my father's waist. My father laid on you a heavy yoke; I will make it even heavier. My father scourged you with whips; I will scourge you with scorpions.'" Three days later Jeroboam and all the people returned to Rehoboam, as the king had said, "Come back to me in three days." The king answered the people harshly. Rejecting the advice given him by the elders, he

followed the advice of the young men and said, "My father made your yoke heavy; I will make it even heavier. My father scourged you with whips; I will scourge you with scorpions."

Obviously, Rehoboam turned out even worse than his father. Yes, this was all part of God's ultimate plan for us (v. 15), but this does not mean that God was pleased. And we must ask why God put Rehoboam's story in the Bible if He was prospanking? I believe God was trying to show His people what happens when parents treat their children harshly. Remember Solomon eventually fell away from God, so even though he may have been the wisest man, he ended up disobeying God.

The second story I want to share with you also sums up everything that I have presented to you in this part of the book. Though Chloe was only spanked once as a child, it affected her quite negatively. Her brothers were spanked much more than she was, but, sadly, she also fell victim to the very negative effects the spankings had on them. Here is what Chloe relayed to me in an electronic message dated February 10, 2012:

> I come from a white, upper middle-class family. Though neither of my parents graduated from college, both of them were lucky enough to find incredible jobs and raised their family in comfort, if not leisure. They had four children, two boys followed by myself, a girl, and another girl. At least two of their children (the oldest and youngest) were mistakes due to lack of family planning. My parents spoke of divorce quietly, mulling the idea over, unbeknownst to their children, for over ten years while the middle two children (myself and my brother) primarily grew up. They were not happy with each other. My father worked long hours, six or seven days out of the week, and drank excessive amounts of alcohol when he arrived home. My mother was suffering from mild depression coupled with

a thyroid disease that was later improved by surgery. This hormonal complication led to impatience and exhaustion and she had no energy to deal with the four of us. She left it up to our father to "deal" with us when he got home.

My father loved us when we were young. As a young child, I adored him and went to such lengths as to wait for him outside of the bathroom when he showered in the morning just so I could be the first one there when he opened the door. Maybe my father loved my older brothers as much when they were young, but all I remember of the interactions between the three of them was rage. My brothers constantly fought and needlessly were mean to me, and my father only dealt with this one way—he would drag the boys into his office and spank them with his belt. Our father was never one to talk to us before or after we had disobeyed him or made him angry. We always knew what we had done to upset him and apparently that was enough communication. Although my brothers were seemingly always in some form of trouble, I never was. I was an obedient child by nature, aiming to please, and my parents disapproval of my actions through one glance was more than enough for me to repent any misdeed or stop any tantrum. Later into my adolescence, it was confirmed to me that both of my parents knew how sensitive I was— and my older brother, similarly—and this knowledge enrages me further.

When I was seven, in the 2nd grade, either at the very beginning or the very end of the school year, I made a new friend in class. She was a new student and she made me promise that I would visit her that night at her house, a block away from my own home, or else she wouldn't consider me her friend any longer. Swayed by peer pressure, I asked to go ride my bike that evening after school and though I knew it was against the rules to go off our street, I turned off of our road and peddled down four houses to her new residence to play with her. We jumped on her trampoline with her older sister, distracted by our game until I noticed it was growing dark. At the same moment, I spotted my father's truck rushing past the front of the house. He did not notice my bike lying in their driveway, but I knew with an ache and a jolt that it was time for me to go home. I raced down the street and hopped off my bike in the front yard of my house, tracing through the unkempt grass of our front yard diagonally as we always did when coming up to the front door. My father barreled out onto the front porch and demanded where I had been, not waiting for an answer. He told me he had been out to the major, traffic heavy road looking for me. I was not to go anywhere the next day. I leaned my bike against the brick siding, and, unable as always to meet his eyes, I snuck past him into the house. I caught my mother's eye in the hallway just as my father struck me for the first and only time in my life. I was in the second grade, barely 50lbs, and my father was 6"2 and 220lbs. I was wearing jeans and he only hit me once, on my bottom, open handed, and yet my bladder lost control as I ran up the stairs into my bedroom. I remember crying, and initially I'm sure it was from pain but I was still crying after I changed and went to bed. This is a normal, all American 1990s scene. I was a willfully disobedient child and my father, in a non-abusive manner, disciplined me as he saw fit to teach me never to scare him and Mom like that ever again. I am positive that he hit me because he had been so afraid of never seeing me again, and he had my best interests at heart, just as with every other time he hit my brothers and younger sister. I understand in so many ways that I have nothing to complain about when compared to other children in abusive homes. But I will say a number of things: My parents knew that all of us were sensitive children and we could have learned better if they had had a little more patience with us, even if that patience just staved off hitting us. All three of my siblings and I are still angry about the way our father physically disciplined us, and we've talked this over as adults. Further, my father admits to being sorry about spanking us. Not just "the way" he punished us but the fact that he hit us at all. Also, my brother, three years my elder, was the most angry about it, far angrier than I could ever be. He expressed his anger over our father's spankings by taking it out on me. My brother beat the ever loving (expletive deleted) out of me when we were children and well into our teenage years, and it escalated to my brother raping me when I was 15. I am not saying that this is a math equation; that our father hitting my brother directly caused this event that tore my family apart in 2003, but it certainly was a root of the problem. And while my brother lashed out with his anger, I kept mine hidden.

Ever since I was a very small child, I found spankings sexual. As an adult woman with sexual relationships in my past and present (although they are continually a work in process, given my history) spanking in the bedroom has always been a desire of mine that has thankfully been fulfilled by generous young men. In no way am I saying that my father meant anything sexual by spanking me, nor do I perceive that event in any way sexual. However, being spanked as a child and wanting that specific sensation as a sexually active adult does tend to complicate and convolute my sex life in a very unpleasant way. I would also like to address the stereotype that childhood spanking leads to adulthood fetishes: I am not saying that. I'm not saying there is much of a connection between the two. I am, however, saying that if your child is predestined by nature and temperament (as I was and am) to enjoy that type of sexual conduct, I assure anyone that spanking that child when they are young will not help them in any way, shape, or form. It will only confuse them.

Overall, my parents raised us right. I love them both. But I know I could love my dad so much more than I do. But my trust was broken as a seven-year-old. He was supposed to love me unconditionally. He had all the tools necessary at hand; all he needed to do was not give in to the temptation to hit a child in front of him that scared him and pissed him off. In his heart, he did have my best interests. But he caved into his own interests—he caved into the relief that he would feel after dishing out his anger on me. And, believe me, I have looked at this from all angles. Some might say that if my father had sat me down, explained why I was being punished, and then calmly spanked me after having me wait in my room, I would feel different. Less violated. Less angry. I assure you, no; I would feel more violated, more angry. I am glad my father lost control with us. If he had the nerve to come to the conclusion that I would somehow benefit from being hit in a logical manner, he would be entirely mistaken. The way I would have learned my lesson would have been this: I had raced home after seeing my father driving in his truck and saw him approach me on the front porch. From there, if he had bent down to my level at four feet from the ground and told me that he had been so worried that I had been hurt, or taken from him, or lost or scared. If he had told me that he had been so frightened that he was about to call the police and have them search for me...I would have cried and clung to him and told him I was sorry and that I hadn't meant to disappoint him or worry him or scare him because I thought the world of him. I loved him and it was scaring me to see him so scared. I would have understood that. And I wouldn't have spent the next ten years of my life wondering why I was so afraid of my father. He is a good man, like most men who spank their children. But I beg of anyone to remember how strong and important and loved you are in the eyes of your children, and understand what power you hold in your hands, and at what expense.

I am a twenty-four-year-old woman, and when I look at my father I see a man who would scratch my back while lying together in front of the TV watching Star Trek and I see a man who sacrificed his dream to study history in college to work his entire life and who spent that money on my college education, and I love this man. I wish I could shake this distrust of him, and this sadness that follows my siblings and I from our childhoods. My brothers both have children and neither of them have laid a hand on the very well behaved 9, 4, 3, and 2 year olds. And every time my father talks to any one of us about our childhoods, the regret always shines through. This is how spanking has affected my entire family.

Maybe you have read all of this part of the book and have already spanked your children. Is it too late to change? No, it is not! If your children are still young, I urge you to take them in your arms and apologize for spanking them. Trust me, they will forgive you! Then tell them that you will no longer spank them, but that they will have consequences for their actions. Doing this will undo some of the damage that has been done to them. Be prepared for them to act out more at first as they finally feel safe with you to show you their big emotions. Be patient with them and yourself as you make this transition with them. Pray often. If your children are grown, I still strongly urge you to apologize to them and tell them you were wrong. This will help them to hopefully stop the cycle with their children. Whatever happens, never give up on your children! Grace is for parents too!

God does *not* want children to be hit. I pray that people will open their hearts to His truth! In my next part of this book entitled, "Discipline without Harm," we will discuss how to discipline children in gentle but firm ways in order that they may be led toward our loving God instead of away from Him. For now, I leave us with this touching imagery by Dr. Kay Kuzma as we turn our focus away from punishment and toward discipline as God intended:

> If I focus on Jesus as a disciplinarian, I see Him calling to a disobedient child, "Come unto Me." Then I see Him gently lifting that child into His arms, establishing eye

contact, and talking to him seriously. I hear Jesus pointing out the folly of disobedience and the consequences that will result. I see Jesus taking time to listen to the child's feelings. Then I see Jesus pointing out the love that God has for His erring children and how God established limits so they wouldn't hurt themselves, others, or things. Then with tears in His eyes, I see Jesus praying with the child that he will turn from his disobedience and be willing to obey his parents' reasonable rules and God's rules. I can even see Jesus imposing a meaningful consequence if the lesson needs reinforcing. And then as the little one runs off to play, I see Jesus noticing the good things he does and giving the child a smile of approval. For your children's sake, I invite you to discipline as you think Jesus would.

(Kuzma, 2006, p. 416-417)

I say amen to that!

References

French, C. & Wilson, R. (2012). Spanking Kids Can Cause Long-Term Harm: Canada Study. http://health.yahoo.net/news/s/nm/spanking-kids-can-cause-long-term-harm-canada-study

Freyd, J. J. (2009). What is a Betrayal Trauma? What is Betrayal Trauma Theory? http://dynamic.uoregon.edu/~jjf/defineBT.html

Greven, P. (1992). *Spare the Child.* New York, NY: Vintage Books.

Heimlich, J. (2011). *Breaking Their Will.* Amherst, NY: Prometheus Books.

Keim, B. (2011). How Abuse Changes a Child's Brain. http://www.wired.com/wiredscience/2011/12/neurology-of-abuse/

Keith, K. L. (2011). The Cycle of Abuse. http://childparenting.about.com/cs/familyissues/a/childabusecycle.htm

Kunsman, C. (2012). What It's Like to Experience Only the Right Side of the Brain in the Way that Children Do (A Neuroscientist Experiences a Stroke on the Left, Analytical Side of the Brain). http://undermuchgrace.blogspot. com/2012/02/what-its-like-to-experience-only-right.html

Kuzma, K. (2006). *The First 7 Years.* West Frankfort, IL: Three Angels Broadcasting Network.

Levy, A. R. (2009). Tribal Intelligence. http://www.psy-chologytoday.com/blog/tribal- i intelligence/200909/ mackenzie-phillips-and-the-stockholm-syndrome

Miller, A. (1994). *For Your Own Good.* New York, NY: The Noonday Press.

Puckett, M. B., Black, J. K., Wittmer, D. S., Peterson, S. H. (2009). *The Young Child* (5th ed.). Upper Saddle River, NJ: Pearson.

Ramsland, K. (2011). Hearst, Soliah and the S.L.A. http://www. trutv.com/library/crime/terrorists_spies/terrorists/hearst/1. html

Riak, J. (2011). Plain Talk About Spanking. http://www.nospank. net/pt2009.htm

Part Four

Discipline without Harm

Chapter 16

Attachment Theory:
Why Not Train a Baby?

In this part of the book we will be looking at how to biblically discipline our children without inflicting pain on them or harming them in any way. Some of the discipline strategies that we will be discussing throughout this part are modeling, child-proofing, validating feelings, fulfilling the child's physical and emotional needs, setting realistic limits and boundaries, helping children comply, giving choices, and using natural and logical consequences with children. The Bible says that we are to encourage each other (2 Corinthians 13:11).

The first year of life is an important and vulnerable time. Infants are learning a great deal about themselves, their world, and the people in their world. While so much development takes place throughout the first year of life in regard to all four developmental domains, one of the main things infants are concentrating on is forming secure attachments with a few primary caregivers who provide them with consistent, responsive care. This chapter will look at some historic theories and figures associated with attachment, such as: Rene Spitz, Harry Harlow, Erik Erikson, Mary Ainsworth, and John Bowlby. It will then describe some of the contemporary attachment figures and theories that have been deemed developmentally appropriate by many in the field of infant development. After this, some highly considered developmentally inappropriate methods of infant care such as baby training will be looked at with regards to the harmful effects they have on infants and attachment.

Historical Roots of Attachment

Prior to and on into the 1800s and early 1900s, not a great deal of accurate knowledge or research had been gained in attachment. A very common belief held by most people during this time period was that infants' affection toward their mothers was due to the milk the mothers supplied to them. The people did not believe that infants needed or were capable of giving human love (Karen, 1994). There were three major viewpoints on infants during this time period. The first was that of the eugenics who claimed that infants were genetic constructions and believed that a perfect human race could be created through not allowing society's outcasts to reproduce. "The genetic view achieved its greatest respectability in Arnold Gesell, the eminent American pediatrician in developmental psychology, who first brought attention to the child's inborn maturational timetables" (Karen, 1994, p. 2). Gesell asserted that genetics were in total control of how children turned out no matter the environment in which they were raised.

The second viewpoint of this time period was that of the behaviorists. Robert Karen (1994), page 3, states:

> In his famous 1928 book on child rearing, Watson wrote: "Treat them as though they were young adults. Dress them, bathe them with care and circumspection. Let your behavior always be objective and kindly firm. Never hug and kiss them, never let them sit on your lap. If you must,

kiss them once on the forehead when they say goodnight. Shake hands with them in the morning. Give them a pat on the head if they have made an extraordinary good job of a difficult task."

The behaviorists were perhaps the first "baby trainers" believing that as long as the infant's physical needs were met within a strict schedule, the infant should not be coddled. Sadly, some people still hold this belief in today's society as shall be discussed later.

The third viewpoint, which led to the first experiments and the birth of attachment theory, was that of the psychoanalysts. Psychoanalysts placed a high importance on loving relationships in the development of healthy social-emotional behaviors in infants and children. Psychoanalysts considered themselves environmentalists like the behaviorists but felt that the environment should be a very loving and affectionate one. John Bowlby was the main figure in psychoanalysis and is considered to be the founder of attachment theory (Karen, 1994) as will be discussed a bit later. While Bowlby may have founded attachment theory, it was Rene Spitz's research on infant hospitalism and Harry Harlow's experiment with rhesus monkeys that delivered one of the first scientific blows to the common beliefs held by the majority of people of this time.

Rene Spitz: Hospitalism

In the 1940s, Rene Spitz did a study on infant hospitalism. A total of ninety-one infants were placed in the Foundling Home located just outside of the United States. For the first three months of the infants' lives, they were breastfed by their mothers in the Foundling Home. If an infant's mother was not available, one of the other mothers would also breastfeed that infant. The infants enjoyed the affection given by their mothers during this initial three-month period. After three months, all of the infants were separated from their mothers. The infants were cared for by nurses and received high quality physical and medical care. Each nurse was in charge of eight to twelve infants, making it almost impossible for the infants to have any need except for the physical/medical need met. As Spitz (1965) states, "To put it drastically, they got approximately one tenth of the normal affective supplies provided in the usual mother-child relationship" (p. 279). In other words, no love or social support was given to these infants.

It wasn't long before a rapid decline was seen in the infants' development. Just after three months of the separation, the infants' motor development had completely halted and they became totally passive. They'd stopped crying. The infants just lied on their backs and did not have the motivation to roll over or sit up.

> The face became vacuous, eye coordination defective, the expression often imbecile. When mobility reappeared after a while, it took the form of spasmus mutans in some of the children; others showed bizarre finger movements reminiscent of decerebrate or athetotic movements (Spitz, 1945a).
>
> (Spitz, 1965, p. 279)

Sadly, these infants were failing to thrive and were severely stunted in all aspects of development.

By the end of the children's second year of life, those who had survived, their development was "forty-five percent of the normal" (Spitz, 1965, p. 279). This was after they had been placed back into loving homes. These children had become severely disabled both physically and mentally. Even the children who survived and were checked on again at age four, the majority still could not sit unassisted, walk, or talk (Spitz, 1965). It was a horrific example of how social-emotional depravation severely affects infants. Many of the infants did not survive. The death rates of these children were extremely high compared with other children in institutions in which loving care was provided. According to Spitz (1965), "of the 91 children originally observed in the Foundling Home, 34 had died by the end of the second year; 57 survived" (p. 281). It was speculated by Spitz that the death rate might have been even higher due to the fact he lost touch with some of these children after the study. It was also noted by Spitz that only two of the infants died of disease (Spitz, 1965).

Spitz wasn't the only one in the 1940s that observed hospitalism and deaths occurring in institutionalized infants. Hungarian pediatrician, Dr. Emmi Pikler, was noticing much of what Spitz did. She, thus, created a model of care for these infants in order to avoid the devastating effects of hospitalism (Gerber & Johnson, 1998; Hammond, 2009). This chapter will look at Dr. Pikler's work later. First, Harry Harlow's experiment with the rhesus monkeys was a chance to duplicate Spitz's study. It shed a great deal of light on infant needs and attachment.

Harry Harlow and the Rhesus Monkeys

In 1958 Harry Harlow conducted a series of experiments with rhesus monkeys in order to try to understand the conditions in which human infants wither away and to come up with some preventive measures. He also wanted to disprove the common idea that infants love their mothers because of the food they provide for their infants. "Regarding mother-love, sociologists and psychologists were in accordance with psychoanalysts: The baby loves the mother because she feeds it. Harlow found this implausible" (Karen, 1994, p. 123). Harlow conducted his research at the University of Wisconsin in Madison. He was the president of the American Psychological Association at the time of his experiments.

Harlow used the rhesus monkeys for his experiments because they were quite similar to human infants. He took eight newborn rhesus monkeys and separated them from their mothers. He raised them in cages outfitted with surrogate mothers, which were contraptions inside the cages. In one cage, there was a block of wood covered with soft sponge rubber that had been covered with a terry cloth. Attached to it was a circular face with a light bulb behind it for warmth, and a feeding nipple. In the other cage was a wire mesh with a feeding nipple attached to it. The monkeys spent all of their time with one of the surrogate mothers. Harlow observed that no matter which surrogate mother "fed" the baby monkeys, they spent up to eighteen hours a day clinging to the terry cloth mother (Karen, 1994).

> The monkeys affectional ties to their cloth mother were sustained even after long separations. And when the infant monkeys were placed in a strange situation, a room filled with a variety of stimuli known to arouse monkey interest, they always rushed initially to the cloth mother when she was available, clung to her until their fear dissipated, and rubbed their bodies against her.
>
> (Karen, 1994, p. 124)

This clearly demonstrates that monkey and human infants love their mothers for the comfort and love they provide and not for food.

Interestingly, Harlow also found that the infant monkeys preferred the familiar face drawn on the surrogate mother to a new face or no face. Sadly, all of the monkeys in these studies ended up having some devastating social-emotional problems due to not having an actual live mother to give them the love and interaction they needed as infants. They could not easily relate to their peers and raising their offspring proved to be even more difficult with abuse and murder occurring.

Cross and Harlow (1965) reported the syndrome of compulsive behaviors which become ever more severe as partial isolation is prolonged. These maladaptive behaviors include nonnutritional sucking which serves no ordinary purpose, stereotyped circular pacing, fixed and frozen bizarre bodily postures and positions of hand and arm, as well as withdrawal from the environment to the point of complete detachment.

(Harlow & Mears, 1979, p. 244)

This further disproves the theory that human infants don't require affection or that it's dangerous to them. As another well-known psychologist, Erik Erikson, points out, infants' attachment goes much deeper than food or even love but requires trust.

Erikson's Theory of Psychosocial Development: Stage 1—Trust Versus Mistrust

The first stage of Erikson's Theory of Psychosocial Development is trust versus mistrust. This stage occurs during the first year of the child's life. Attachment and an infant's temperament are highly intertwined in this first stage of development.

According to Erikson's theory (1994), the first year of life is a critical period for the development of a sense of trust. The conflict for the infant involves striking a balance between trust and mistrust. This primary psychosocial task of infancy provides a developmental foundation from which later stages of personality development can emerge... Resolution of the trust/mistrust conflict is manifest in a mature personality by behaviors that basically exhibit trust (of oneself and others) but maintain a healthy amount of skepticism.

(Puckett, Black, Wittmer, & Peterson, 2009, p. 159)

Erikson (1963) states that "the first demonstration of social trust in the baby is the ease of his feedings, the depth of his sleep, the relaxation of his bowels" (p. 247).

Infants are totally reliant on their parents and caregivers for every aspect of their needs. If their parents and caregivers are responsive and consistently meet their needs, the infants will then develop a trust in their parents and caregivers. Erikson (1963) explained that the way mothers actually cared for their infants is more important in helping infants develop trust than the "absolute quantities of food or demonstrations of love" (p. 249). Infants require consistency in their care. As infants increase their waking hours, they find that more adventures of the senses give way to feelings of familiarity that coincide with feeling good inside. "Forms of comfort, and people associated with them, become as familiar as the gnawing discomfort of the bowels" (Erikson, 1963, p. 247). It is clear that infants quickly adapt and learn the familiarity of the adults who consistently provide them with the responsive, sensitive care that they require.

The infants will also develop a trust in their ability to successfully elicit a response from their parents and caregivers to get their needs met. This inner trust in oneself is just as important to the infant's well-being as the ability to trust his or her parents and caregivers. As Erikson (1963), page 248, states:

> The general state of trust, furthermore, implies not only that one has learned to rely on the sameness and continuity of the outer providers, but also that one may trust oneself and the capacity of one's own organs to cope with urges; and that one is able to consider oneself trustworthy enough so that the providers will not need to be on guard lest they be nipped.

This ability to trust in oneself lasts a lifetime as does the ability to trust others. This begins at birth for all infants.

On the other hand, mistrust develops if infants are not responded to consistently and in a sensitive way. Infants then begin to have a mistrust in their parents and caregivers as well as in themselves. They just never know if and when someone will respond to them, or if they will be successful in eliciting a response. This can affect them their entire lives and can make it much more difficult to successfully resolve the other conflicts in subsequent stages of this theory of psychosocial development. The development of our deepest and most dangerous defense mechanisms, projection and introjection, occurs in the event of mistrust (Erikson, 1963, p. 248). Erikson (1963), page 248 through 249, goes on to explain:

> In introjection we feel and act as if an outer goodness had become an inner certainty. In projection, we experience inner harm as an outer one: we endow significant people with the evil which actually is in us. These two mechanisms, then, projection and introjection, are assumed to be modeled after whatever goes on in infants when they would like to externalize pain and internalize pleasure, an intent which must yield to the testimony of the maturing senses and ultimately of reason.

In crises of love, trust, and faith, these two mechanisms are often reinstated throughout adulthood, which can be characterized as irrational attitudes toward enemies in a great deal of "mature" adults (Erikson, 1963, p. 249).

Therefore, Erikson showed how infants require respectful and responsive care from their mothers as well as other adults in their lives. Being able to trust that their needs will be consistently met by loving adults is very important for infants to create secure attachments. However, Mary Ainsworth noticed that not all attachments created by infants are secure. Ainsworth looked into what happens with infants when they are given loving, responsive care inconsistently.

Mary Ainsworth and the Strange Situation

Mary Ainsworth worked with John Bowlby for a short time at the beginning of her career because they were interested in how maternal deprivation affected infants. They also believed that it was best to study infants and their mothers and/or primary caregivers in natural environments in order to accurately assess emotional and attachment security. However, Ainsworth was interested in studying the other aspects of the mother-child relationship, such as how everyday behaviors of the mother or primary caregiver affected the quality of attachment. She, as many other psychoanalysts of this time period, still initially believed that infants loved their mothers because of the milk they provided to the infants. Ainsworth traveled to Uganda in order to study the infants and mothers. While in Uganda, she became a part of the women's lives and was an intimate figure of their homes and families. As Ainsworth closely observed the mothers and infants, she quickly noticed that the behaviors toward each other went deeper than just the food that the mothers provided the infants. The following list of behaviors was observed by Ainsworth in the infants during her time in Uganda:

- Crying when the mother leaves
- Following the mother
- Showing concern for the mother's whereabouts
- Scrambling over to the mother
- Burying the face in the mother's lap
- Using the mother as a safe haven when in a strange situation
- Flying to the mother when frightened
- Greeting her through smiling, crowing, clapping, lifting the arms, and general excitement (1967)

(Mooney, 2010, p. 28)

Infants that were securely attached used their mothers as a security base once they became mobile and could explore their environments. These infants could wander away from their mothers to explore the room but could continuously check in or come back to their mothers when needed. Ainsworth observed variations in culture in regards to how some mothers in Uganda cared for their infants as well as the infant's development, and these two things affected the mother-child relationship. Mooney (2010), when speaking of Ainsworth's observations, states, "She noted that many anxious babies seemed to be the offspring of anxious mothers. She noticed that mothers separated from their husbands or families experienced more stress and seemed to pass it on to their infants (1967)" (p. 29). These observations soon led her to label different attachments.

In 1956, Mary Ainsworth and her husband moved back to the United States where she got a position at John Hopkins University. She wanted to try and duplicate her study from Uganda, so she, after much effort, convinced the university to fund her research. She knew that all infants displayed the same attachment behaviors worldwide, but she began to notice that mothers in the U.S. treated their infants differently than mothers in Uganda. For example, infants in the U.S. were used to having their mothers walk out of the room briefly, whereas in Uganda, infants went everywhere with their mothers and would cry uncontrollably if left even briefly by their mothers (Mooney 2010). Therefore, it was clear to Ainsworth that observing the infants and mothers in their homes would not provide an accurate understanding of mother-child attachment behaviors. Ainsworth and her colleagues set up the Strange Situation on the campus of John Hopkins University.

For the Strange Situation study, a room was set up with engaging toys and materials for the infants to explore. The room had a one-way window for observation. There were eight brief episodes in which Ainsworth and her colleagues observed the mother and child's responses and behaviors. The following is the list of episodes in the order that they occurred:

1. Mother, baby, and observer enter the room. The observer introduces mother and baby to experimental room, then leaves.

2. Mother and baby. Mother is nonparticipant while baby explores; if necessary, play is stimulated after two minutes.

3. Stranger, mother, and baby. Stranger enters. First minute: Stranger silent. Second minute: Stranger converses with mother. Third minute: Stranger approaches baby. After three minutes mother leaves unobtrusively.

4. Stranger and baby. First separation episode. Stranger's behavior is geared to that of the baby.

5. Mother and baby. First reunion episode. Mother greets and/or comforts baby, then tries to settle him again in play. Mother then leaves, saying 'bye-bye.'

6. Baby alone. Second separation episode.

7. Stranger and baby. Continuation of second separation. Stranger enters and gears her behavior to that of baby.

8. Mother and baby. Second reunion episode. Mother enters, greets baby, then picks him up. Meanwhile stranger leaves unobtrusively.

(Ainsworth, Blehan, Waters, & Wall, 1978, p. 37)

Throughout the experiment, observers watched the amount of explorations that the infants engaged in, as well as the infants' responses to being left with and without the stranger and the mother returning. Ainsworth categorized three types of attachments based on the observations of the Strange Situation: secure attachment, anxious-ambivalent attachment, and anxious-avoidant attachment (Mooney 2010). The securely attached infant will use his or her mother as a secure base, interact some with the stranger if the mother is close by and shows approval, and gets upset when his or her mother leaves but is happy and easily comforted when his or her mother returns. The anxious-ambivalent, insecurely attached child will show stress and anxiety in unfamiliar places and with strangers, even when the mother is with the child. When the mother leaves the child, he or she becomes extremely anxious but is resistant to reuniting with the mother. "Some psychologists suggest that it is the result of inconsistent parenting styles. Ainsworth suggests that the parent responds to the child on her own schedule rather than that of the infant" (Mooney, 2010, p. 32). The anxious-avoidant, insecurely attached child shows very little interest in interacting with any adults. These infants show no emotion and have given up on trying to elicit a response from the people in their world. They no longer trust in themselves or their mothers much like the infants that Spitz, Pikler, and Bowlby studied in institutions. "It seems very likely to us that maternal behavior plays a large part in influencing the development of qualitative differences in infant-mother attachment" (Ainsworth, Blehan, Waters, & Wall, 1978, p. 137).

Ainsworth observed that if parents' behaviors toward their children at a young age, a one-year-old insecurely attached child, for example, could become a securely attached two-year old. The Strange Situation redefined the term maternal deprivation to include negative behaviors toward infants in addition to the actual loss of maternal care. Ainsworth (1962), page 99, states:

> The term "maternal deprivation" has been used also to cover nearly every undesirable kind of interaction between mother and child-rejection, hostility, cruelty, over-indulgence, repressive control, lack of affection and the like.

As far as the validness of the Strange Situation to current studies of attachment behaviors, Ainsworth, Blehan, Waters, and Wall (1978), page 136, explains:

> It is the patterning of behaviors in the strange situation that 'matches' the patterning of behaviors at home. Consequently, we conclude that the comparison of strange-situation and home behavior provides justification for viewing the strange-situation classificatory system as having continuing usefulness, and not merely as having being useful as an methodological step toward identification of dimensions of behavior that might be assessed independently.

This means that the Strange Situation can continue to be used to study aspects of attachment behaviors.

It is clear that Mary Ainsworth's work provided a deeper insight into attachment types and behaviors. She went deeper than just the loss of maternal care. John Bowlby was also interested in parental behaviors and how they influenced children. He is considered the father of attachment theory.

John Bowlby: The Father of Attachment Theory

John Bowlby had a nanny with whom he was securely attached during the first four years of his life. He had contact with his parents for an hour a day during teatime. At the age of four, his nanny left his family causing Bowlby to become deeply distraught. A few years later his parents sent him away to boarding school, as this was the custom in England during this time period for upper middle-class families. These two separations from maternal care caused Bowlby to become interested in studying the effects of maternal deprivation on children's growth and development. After completing his degree at Cambridge University, he began studying at the British Psychoanalytic Institute to become a child psychiatrist. Bowlby disagreed with the Freudian theories that troubled children were struggling with an internal conflict brought on by their fantasies. Instead, he felt children's troubles could be traced back to what either did or did not happen to them as infants and young children. After Bowlby became a child psychiatrist, he worked with many disturbed children and adolescents where he observed that many of their problems could be linked back to their early childhoods. "Bowlby proposed that often the attitude of a parent toward a child is deeply affected by a result issues from his or her own childhood" (Mooney, 2010, p.19).

Like Spitz and Pikler, Bowlby studied the effects of hospitalism after World War II as many young children were left as orphans due to the war. He also briefly worked with Mary Ainsworth in studying attachment behaviors in mothers and children. He did not accept the theory that infants loved their mothers because of the food they provided them. Harlow and Erikson's work proved that Bowlby was correct in this thinking. In 1950, in a report published by the World Health Organization, Bowlby (1973), page xi, stated:

> "What is believed to be essential for mental health is that the infant and young child should experience a warm, intimate and continuous relationship with his mother (or permanent mother-substitute) in which both find satisfaction and enjoyment" (Bowlby 1951).

It was clear two-year-olds in which he had observed and created a documentary about had serious adjustment and attachment issues after being placed in a hospital away from their parents, then, after months, returning home. They no longer trusted their parents not to leave them (Bowlby 1973).

Bowlby also observed infants' behaviors that promoted attachment if the infants were responded to appropriately. Bowlby (1982), page 204, states:

> Apart from crying, which is never easily ignored, an infant often calls persistently and, when attended to, orients to and smiles at his mother or other companion. Later, he greets and approaches her and seeks her attention in a thousand attractive ways.

He also noticed that infants are keenly aware of their mothers' and/or caregivers' whereabouts. Even if the infant is engrossed in his or her own activity, it isn't long before they notice that their mother or caregiver has left the room and begin to protest. "During his eleventh or twelfth month he becomes able, by noting her behaviour, to anticipate her imminent departure, and starts to protest before she goes" (Bowlby, 1982, p. 204). It is clear that from birth infants' behaviors are designed to create social connections with the people around them in order to try and make secure attachments.

This section has created a detailed overview of the main historical figures and theories of attachment. It is quite interesting that these people who did not buy into the first ideas that infants only love their mothers because of food and that affection could be dangerous to them, all saw the devastating effects maternal deprivation has on infants and children.

> Bowlby, in 1951, introduced his timely review of the research evidence by saying: "The extent to which these

studies, undertaken by people of many nations, varied training and, as often as not, ignorant of each others' conclusions, confirm and support each other is impressive. What each individual piece of work lacks in thoroughness, scientific reliability, or precision is largely made good by the concordance of the whole" (p. 15).

(Ainsworth, 1962, p. 97)

These research findings pave the way for what is considered currently best practices in promoting secure attachments in infants. The next section of this chapter will discuss contemporary attachment figures and theories such as Magda Gerber, Dr. William Sears and Martha Sears, and T. Berry Brazelton.

Contemporary Theories of Attachment
Magda Gerber and the Resources for Infant Educarers (RIE) Approach

The Resources for Infant Educarers (RIE) Approach was founded in the United States in 1977 by Magda Gerber. It originated in Budapest Hungary in 1945 at an orphanage established by pediatrician Dr. Emmi Pikler. Dr. Pikler wanted to try to improve life for infants and toddlers living in orphanages, thus creating this respectful approach. The children in the orphanage were there due to their parents being killed or captured in World War II. Also, some of the infants' mothers died in childbirth. Dr. Pikler wanted a better outcome for these infants and toddlers as they were failing to thrive with many dying despite receiving good medical care. Dr. Pikler observed that when the infants had a few primary caregivers with whom they became securely attached, they were able to actively participate in their daily care with the same caregivers who always gave their full attention to the infants during all daily care routines and were allowed to develop unassisted as well as unrestricted; these infants thrived and were easily transitioned into a family home when adopted at around three years of age. The orphanage is still in Budapest, Hungary, and is directed by Anna Tardos, Dr. Emmi Pikler's daughter. It now also provides care to very young children who have been abused and neglected using the same approach as Dr. Pikler created. This approach was developed further for the U.S. in the 1970s by child development theorists with whom Magda Gerber studied and consulted—Jean Piaget, Erik Erikson, and Dr. Tom Forrest who was a United States pediatrician. Magda Gerber was a student under Dr. Emmi Pikler and studied the interactions of the adults with the infants and toddlers at the orphanage in Budapest. Magda Gerber was surprised at how Dr. Pikler talked directly to her daughter when she was sick and Dr. Pikler visited her to provide medical care. This was the beginning of a lifelong friendship between Magda Gerber and Dr. Emmi Pikler. Magda received her master's degree in early childhood education from the University of Hungary. Then Magda Gerber brought Dr. Emmi Pikler's approach to the U.S., creating the RIE approach from it. Magda coined the word educarer because we care while we educate and educate while we care. Magda Gerber worked with many diverse families and with many children with disabilities.

The practices of RIE help promote secure attachments in infants by providing them a few primary caregivers who can be parents and other adults that consistently respond to the infants' needs. While infants are allowed to cry without being distracted, they are never left to just "cry it out." Infants are always responded to in a positive and supportive way when they cry. Their needs are consistently met, and their feelings are always acknowledged and validated. As Gerber and Johnson (1998) state, "Our goal is to accept and acknowledge a child's feelings, though not always the behavior, and allow her to express them" (p. 87). Having the same people care for them also allows the infants and parents or caregivers to establish a positive rapport with each other. The adults and infants get to know one another deeply and become in tune with each other.

> RIE builds on the foundation of establishing a respectful relationship between the infant and a primary carer, and also with a few other significant adults who form a stable part of a baby's life. Within this relationship, RIE encourages the adult to become acquainted with the non-verbal infant through sensitive observation of the child's cues, and to offer both security and freedom to the infant within the relationship.
>
> (Petrie & Owen, 2005, p. 55)

This clearly does much to aid the formation of securer attachments in infants.

The practices of RIE encourage adults to speak to the infants before doing caregiving routines with them, such as: diapering, feeding, or bathing. They also advocate adults be entirely focused on the infants during these daily care routines. Hammond (2009) states that "When an adult speaks quietly about what is happening and waits for a response, the child does not need to be on alert that a change could be coming at any moment unannounced" (p. 13). The infant can learn to trust his or her environment easier if he or she is never taken off guard by sudden changes.

> In moments of mindful, respectful, sensitively responsive caregiving, babies receive messages and lessons about what it means to be responded to with kindness and compassion, and this is at the heart of learning about empathy (Eisenberg 1992; Noddings 2003).
>
> (McMullen, Addleman, Fulford, Moore, Sisk, & Zachariah, 2009, p. 22)

The RIE practice of talking to the infants and giving them one's total attention during all daily care activities promotes the development of trust, secure attachment, and empathy because the infants will not be constantly in need of attention from the adults in their lives and will begin to understand kindness.

> In Gerber's own words, "If you pay half attention-which nobody does, it's usually much less-but let's say you give half attention all the time, that's never full attention. Babies are always half hungry. But if you pay full attention a little bit of the time, then you go a long way. That's what I would recommend: to be fully with a child, then let her be" (1988).
>
> (Mooney, 2010, p. 40)

These RIE practices strongly provide all infants with the high probability of developing trust in their parents and caregivers, as well as in themselves. They make it more likely that they will develop secure attachments with their parents and caregivers.

Like the practices of RIE, the practices of Attachment Parenting (AP) created by pediatrician William Sears and his wife, registered nurse Martha, advocate sensitive responsiveness to infants and toddlers. They also recommend a technique called Babywearing, which is done in many cultures.

Dr. William and Martha Sears' Attachment Parenting

Christian pediatrician William Sears and his wife Martha created Attachment Parenting (AP) during thirty years of parenting and observing parents and children in their medical practice. It has been observed by many that children who are attachment parented are more compassionate, caring, responsive, and trusting (Sears & Sears, 2001). There are seven facets that comprise Attachment Parenting and are known as the "Baby

Bs." They are birth bonding, belief in baby's cries, breastfeeding, babywearing, bed sharing, balance and boundaries, and beware of baby trainers. As in the RIE approach, AP is about giving sensitive, responsive care to infants starting at birth. "Attachment Parenting is an approach to raising children rather than a strict set of rules" (Sears & Sears, 2001, p. 2).

One of the "Baby Bs" of AP is birth bonding. The birth of an infant is seen as a very intimate occurrence that is to be shared by the family with as little interference by medical personnel as possible. Whenever medically possible, the infant should be given directly to the mother or father after he or she is born. If mother and infant are medically stable, the family should be given privacy for the first hour after birth to help the parents and infant ease into their new relationships. Dr. Sears and the American Academy of Pediatrics suggest that all post-natal tests and exams can be postponed until after the first hour of birth in healthy newborns. While it isn't an absolute must as far as attachment for newborns and parents to spend their first hour together after birth as medical complications may arise, it has been shown that this practice can soothe infants and parents. Sears and Sears (2001) state, "Studies done by Klaus and Kennell and others have shown that a mother's early contact with her baby makes a difference to how she cares for her infant" (p. 36). This applies not only to the birth mother but to whomever the infant will be primarily cared by. Even if the infant cannot be immediately placed with his or her parents, it is very important that the infant is given as much human contact as possible. Holding newborns skin-to-skin has been shown to help soothe and regulate their body temperatures, heart rates, and breathing. This is called Kangaroo Care and is often done with premature infants. However, Dr. Sears highly recommends that it be done with all newborns.

Birth bonding also includes breastfeeding the infant in the first hour after birth, as well as throughout the entire hospital stay. It is also recommended that the infant room in with the parents and that the parents do all of the daily care routines with the infant instead of having the nurses do it. Infants that room in with their parents are responded to quicker than they are in the hospital nursery.

> Rooming-in newborns cry less because they are more likely to receive a quick and nurturing response to their cries. Mother (or Father) helps them calm down before they have a chance to get really wound up and cry uncontrollably. Babies in a large nursery are sometimes soothed by tape recordings of a human heartbeat or of music.
>
> (Sears & Sears, 2001, p. 42)

Responding to an infant's crying is one of the most important aspects of AP.

Belief in infants' crying is another "Baby B" of AP. This means understanding that crying is an infant's way of communicating to the adults in his or her world. Dr. Sears recommends responding in some way every time an infant cries—especially with very young infants as they are learning to trust their parents and caregivers. Sears and Sears (2003), page 6 through 7, state:

> Meeting your baby's needs in the early months means solid communication patterns will develop. With time you can gradually delay your response and gradually your baby will learn to accept waiting a little bit as she learns noncrying language and develops self-help mechanisms.

As with the RIE approach, parents and caregivers are encouraged to observe their infants in order to learn their infants' cues and different cries in order to respond appropriately. For example, Dr. Sears recommends that parents try to respond to very young infants' pre-cries, such as: anxious facial expressions, flailing arms, excited breathing, and quivering lips. This teaches young infants that they don't have to cry full blast to receive a response from their parents and/or caregivers. Dr. Sears, as well as other professionals and parents, have observed that once young infants are crying full blast, it is quite difficult to soothe them. While pre-crying and early crying promotes empathy and responsiveness in adults, as the crying becomes stronger and higher in intensity, it becomes grating on the adult's nerves. This can cause avoidance behaviors in the adult toward the infant.

Early responsiveness has also been shown to decrease infant crying during the second half of the first year.

> In 1974 a group of researchers met to review studies on what makes competent children. In analyzing attachment research, they concluded that the more a mother ignores crying in the first half of the first year, the more likely her baby will cry more frequently in the second half.
>
> (Sears & Sears, 2001, p. 83)

This may be due to the fact that the infant hasn't learned other forms of communication, such as gesturing or babbling, due to the unresponsiveness of the mother. They've been taught to cry long and hard to get a response. As with the RIE approach, allowing infants to "cry it out" is not advocated in AP. It is, however, recognized that infants sometimes need to cry in order to expend extra energy. And as infants get older, they must be allowed to self-soothe and problem solve. But the infant should never be ignored and should always have the adult's support and reassurance.

Leaving infants to cry it out is not a biblically supported practice as I have pointed out in different chapters. Let's look at how God responds to our cries. Does God sleep? According to

Psalm 121:4, God never sleeps and is always ready to respond to us. Infants do not cry to manipulate us; they really need us. How would we feel if God put us in a dark room by ourselves, said, "Nite nite," and shut the door so that He could enjoy a peaceful night? We would feel scared and abandoned. But, thankfully, God is constantly there for us. Psalm 34:17; 55:17; and 145:18 all show that God is ready and responsive whenever we cry out.

> Tune into yourself—you will realize it is comforting to know that God would not have given you a child without the built-in means to raise that child to love and serve the Lord. This would violate the concept of "Creator." God designed within every mother or father the necessary tools to parent their individual child; for example, God would not have given you a child with a temperament that you cannot handle.
>
> (Sears & Sears, 1997, p. 3)

Breastfeeding and bed sharing are also "Baby B's" of Attachment Parenting. The American Academy of Pediatrics recommends that infants are breastfed for the first year of their lives (Gartner & Eidelman, 2005; Sears & Sears, 2003). The many health benefits for infants are improved vision and hearing, improved oral motor development via the suction required while at the breast, and a higher level of immune system function due to antibodies in the mother's milk. Sears and Sears (2001), page 55, state:

> Breastfed babies are protected from many diseases. Breastfeeding is associated with a lower incidence of virtually every kind of infectious disease including bacterial meningitis, urinary tract infection, and infant botulism.

Breastfeeding is also associated with a lower incidence of certain kinds of cancers in women such as breast cancer.

No matter whether infants are breastfed or bottle fed, it is very important that infants are fed when they display signs of hunger instead of sticking to a strict feeding schedule. This goes back to helping infants learn to trust that their needs will always be met by the adults caring for them. By feeding infants on cue, infants also learn to accurately read their bodies' signals for hunger and satiation.

> During the early weeks of breastfeeding, mothers should be encouraged to have 8 to 12 feedings at the breast every 24 hours, offering the breast whenever the infant shows early signs of hunger such as increased alertness, physical activity, mouthing, or rooting. Crying is a late indicator of hunger.
>
> (Gartner & Eidelman, 2005, p. 499)

Feedings should also be a social time for infants and their mothers and/or caregivers. The infant and adult learn to communicate with each other.

While strict schedules are considered to be harmful and even dangerous for infants by many pediatricians and infant specialists, routines help promote attachment in infants and adults. A predictable routine helps the infant to anticipate what will happen next. The infant will also learn the responses certain cues will invoke.

> I would like to replace the rigid idea of a schedule with the more flexible concept of a routine or even with the more flowing experience described by the word "harmony." The more you listen and respond to your baby, the simpler it will be to ease him into a routine that suits both of you. (Sears & Sears, 2003, p. 15)

Routines are based on the infant's and adult's needs, which promotes a healthy, positive adult-child relationship.

Bed sharing is recommended by Dr. Sears in order to make night feedings easier. It has been shown that infants who sleep with their parents sleep better. The infant can be soothed or fed quicker before crying escalates to an uncontrollable level. It is very important that all hazards, such as pillows and blankets, have been removed from the area where the infant will be sleeping. It is also important that parents don't consume alcohol or drugs before sleeping with their infants. The bed should be firmly against the wall. A cosleeper that attaches to the side of the adult's bed can also make bed sharing safer. After all hazards have been removed from the sleeping area, research has shown that bed sharing may decrease the risk of infants dying from Sudden Infant Death Syndrome (Sears & Sears, 2001). This may be because sleeping next to an adult helps young infants get their breathing patterns and sleep cycles in sync with the adult's. However, if bed sharing does not work for the family, it is fine for infants to sleep alone.

Babywearing is another important "Baby B" of Attachment Parenting. Babywearing is practiced in many cultures. Infants are worn on their parents' and/or caregivers' bodies throughout the day. This allows infants to be close to the parent or caregiver much of the day. However, it should be balanced with time for the infant to play on the floor. While the infant is being worn, he/she should be talked to about what the adult is doing to provide plenty of spontaneous learning opportunities for the infant. Infants that are worn get a great deal of natural stimulation. It has been shown that wearing infants helps soothe them because they are warm, cradled, and near their primary caregivers.

Unlike what one may think, babywearing does not cause motor development delays as restrictive devices can. The reason for this is the gentle motions that infants experience stimulates the vestibular system, "and scientists are finding that this stimulation helps babies breathe and grow better, regulates their physiology, and improves motor development" (Sears & Sears, 2001, p. 70). Another reason babywearing does not cause motor development delays is that infants are constantly making adjustments as the adult moves about (Sears & Sears, 2001). Dr. Sears advises against the use of restrictive devices such as infant swings, bouncy seats, walkers, and exersaucers.

The final two "Baby B's" of Attachment Parenting are balance and boundaries and beware of baby trainers. These two go together because anything that is taken to the extreme can create problems in young children. Older infants and toddlers require boundaries and limits. These help young children to feel safe and secure. For example, securely attached infants and toddlers will often look at their parent or caregiver when they encounter something that they are unsure about. If the adult smiles approvingly, the child will usually continue exploring. If the adult frowns, the child will usually stop exploring. Infants and toddlers need discipline and guidance because they lack self-control. Unfortunately, many people think of discipline and punishment as one and the same. This should not be the case whatsoever.

> *Webster's Dictionary* describes discipline as "training that corrects, molds, or perfects." I believe the best and most long-lasting training comes from within. Discipline is first learned externally, based on parental, and then societal expectations.
>
> (Gerber & Johnson, 1998, p. 204)

Positive guidance strategies, such as: modeling, redirection, and natural consequences, work better to truly *teach* children more appropriate ways of behaving. For example, if a toddler gets up from the table, then the natural consequence is that he will be finished eating. This is not punishment; it is cause and effect that directly relates to the toddler's behavior. Baby trainers believe that from the moment infants are born they must be taught that the adult is in charge. Sears and Sears (2001) state that "baby training is based on a misperception of the parent-child relationship. It presumes that newborns enter the world out to control their parents, and that if you don't take control first, baby will seize the reins and drive the carriage" (p. 125).

As the historical and contemporary research cited in this chapter shows, there are negative effects on the attachment process—some quite devastating. Like the proponents of the RIE approach, Dr. Sears and his wife deeply frown upon baby trainers who advocate strict schedules, ignoring infant crying, and the use of physical punishment for infants and toddlers. Dr. Sears implores the importance of understanding the child's perspective in order to appropriately respond and guide the child.

> Authority is vital to discipline, and authority must be based on trust. If an infant can trust his mother to feed him when he's hungry, he will be more likely as a toddler to listen to her for what to do when, for example, he encounters breakable objects on Grandma's coffee table.
>
> (Sears & Sears, 2001, p. 20)

Children raised with respect, responsiveness, and sensitivity of Attachment Parenting are respectful, responsive, and sensitive adults. "This sensitivity carried over into other aspects of life: marriage, job, social relationships, and play. In my experience, sensitivity (in parent and child) is the most outstanding effect of attachment parenting" (Sears & Sears, 2003, p. 17).

Dr. Sears isn't the only pediatrician to observe that infants thrive when provided with sensitive, responsive, and respectful care. Dr. T. Berry Brazelton has researched and worked with infants and their families for well over forty years. The following section will describe his research, observations, and approach to infant care.

T. Berry Brazelton's Touchpoints

Pediatrician T. Berry Brazelton graduated from Columbia University College of Physicians and Surgeons in 1943. He then went to Boston, Massachusetts, in order to complete his residency training at General Hospital. After this, he began his pediatrics training at Children's Hospital. He has worked with many child psychiatrists including Dr. Joshua Sparrow, as Dr. Brazelton was interested in the social-emotional side of medicine. Dr. Brazelton created the Brazelton Touchpoints Center in Boston where he works with infants and their families. With the help of Dr. Sparrow, Brazelton has brought his approach to others around the world. Many hospitals, clinics, and child care centers use the Brazelton Approach. His approach is strengths-based and preventive rather than fixing problems. He came up with three types of infants based on their temperament and personality traits: Average, Active, and Quiet. His idea was to let parents know that one infant isn't better than another due to his or her personality. Every infant is a unique individual.

In 1973 Brazelton created the Neonatal Behavioral Assessment Scale (NBAS). This is used to assess a newborn's visual, audio, and tactile responses to different stimuli. Brazelton begins by meeting with expectant parents to get to know them and discuss their fears and concerns about the impending arrival of their baby. He wants the parents to feel comfortable with him so that when they go through different touchpoints with their infant, they will be more likely to open up to Brazelton and allow him to guide them. Touchpoints are all the milestones children and parents go through. Brazelton believes it is very important to tell parents what to expect next from their child so they can respond sensitively and appropriately.

Once the baby is born, Dr. Brazelton does the NBAS and other newborn assessments with the parents in the room. Not only does he want to get to know the newborn's personality, but he wants the parents to see just how competent their newborn is. Brazelton and Sparrow (2006), page 29, state:

> There is an important mutuality here. Parents seem to have an expectation for the kinds of behavior with which a newborn is equipped. When the baby's skills and ways of communicating are confirmed, parents gain more confidence in their own ability to understand and care for their infant. Our studies have shown that after such a shared assessment, the mother and the father are significantly more sensitive to their own baby's behavioral cues at one month, and they remain more responsive throughout the first year.

This is an important aspect to creating secure attachments in infants. Brazelton and the parents get a glimpse into the newborn's temperament, self-soothing skills, and preferred ways of being handled and soothed. Another thing Brazelton does to help parents connect with their newborns is to hold the infant up and talk into the infant's ear while having the mother talk into the infant's other ear. The infant always turns toward the mother instead of Brazelton in response to her voice. This makes the mother ecstatic as she realizes that her infant already knows and responds to her. He does the same with the father. About 80 percent of the time the infant will turn toward his or her father's voice. On the rare occasion that the infant does not turn toward the father, Brazelton subtly helps the infant do so (Brazelton & Sparrow, 2006).

Dr. Brazelton does not believe that a newborn must be given directly to the mother after birth in order for bonding to occur. Instead, he suggests that the mother be given a choice of being given the infant at birth or after a rest period. The father should be given the same choice. He wants parents to be eager to be with their newborn instead of feeling guilty for wanting to rest after delivering the child.

> When the first greeting must be postponed, parents can still become fully attached to their baby. It is very important that expectant parents and those who assist them in childbirth know not only that each family has its own timetable but also that strong, long-term attachment is the goal.
>
> (Brazelton & Sparrow, 2006, p. 38)

Being ready to respond to their infant's needs such as feeding and soothing is important for creating secure attachments between infants and their parents and/or caregivers.

As the proponents of RIE and AP, Dr. Brazelton believes that infants should be fed on cue and that feedings should be a social time for infants and parents or caregivers. He also highly recommends that infants be breastfed. Brazelton and psychologist Kenneth Kaye did a study on infants sucking patterns during feedings. Brazelton and Sparrow (2006), page 41, state:

> A baby will start out with a short burst of constant sucking. Very quickly, she resorts to a burst-pause pattern. A burst of sucks will be followed by a pause: suck-suck-suck-pause. Psychologist Kenneth Kaye and I studied the pauses to try to understand their significance, for we were aware that babies tended to look around and to listen in these periods... Fifty percent of the pauses are accompanied by a maternal response, and fifty percent go unnoticed... In our study, the baby's pauses when the mother didn't respond were significantly shorter than those when she did. In other words, the baby seemed to prolong her pauses to capture social stimuli. We point to this burst-pause pattern in babies to help emphasize the importance of playing with and talking to a baby at feeding time.

It is clear from this study that infants need feedings to be more than just food. It is another time for learning and communication between the infant and adult. For this reason, Brazelton states that infants should never be propped with a bottle (Brazelton & Sparrow, 2006).

Brazelton reiterates that crying is a late sign of hunger in infants. Parents and caregivers should feed infants who are in an alert state, are rooting and mouthing, and are bobbing their heads as if looking for a breast or bottle (Brazelton & Sparrow, 2006). Parents and caregivers should also observe the infant in order of his or her different cries and cues, so they can respond appropriately to his or her needs. As infants become older, they can go longer periods between feedings, but it is still very important that infants are fed when they are hungry. This helps infants trust that their needs will always be met by the adults in their lives.

Dr. Brazelton recommends that all daily care routines, such as bathing and diapering, be times of social interaction between adults and infants.

> As we talk about the opportunities for play, I like to point out that diapering and bathing can also be important times for communication. Talking to the baby and kissing her stomach are irresistible accompaniments to diapering. Parents can make it a fun time.
>
> (Brazelton & Sparrow, 2006, p. 41)

As the proponents of RIE point out, by talking to infants during daily care activities, a sense of mutuality forms between the infant and adult as they accomplish tasks together. This also allows the adult to learn from the child. Infants will let parents and caregivers know when something is right or wrong. The adults need to be sensitive in order to pick up on what the infant is trying to tell them.

When it comes to nighttime routines for infants, Brazelton recommends having consistent bedtime routines and putting the infant to bed awake but sleepy. He has observed throughout his career that infants tend to sleep lighter and awaken more at night before they are about to achieve major milestones, such as: rolling, sitting, and walking. Therefore, Brazelton warns parents of this before it occurs. He also discusses the pros and cons of cosleeping with parents. He understands that for some families cosleeping is a good choice but not for others.

> In cultures where there is a choice, it is not necessary and does not seem fair to push a child out abruptly later. So, the decision should be made in advance, with full awareness of the changing pros and cons of co-sleeping as the child grows. Parents must examine their own biases and consider the long-term consequences of their decision before they make up their minds.
>
> (Brazelton & Sparrow, 2006, p. 91)

If parents do cosleep with their infant, Brazelton recommends a slow transition for the child such as setting "up a crib next to the parents' bed... Parents can then still roll over to pat the child down when he comes up to light sleep" (Brazelton & Sparrow, 2006, p. 156).

Dr. Brazelton, as the proponents of RIE and AP do, believes that while there are times when infants need to cry a bit to learn to calm themselves, they should never be left to "cry it out." He recommends that parents and caregivers respond in some supportive way to an infant's cries—even at night. The infant may be learning to sleep through the night and may just need his or her parents to let him or her know that they are there. In this, the infant knows that his or her parents haven't neglected him in the night. When care is a necessity during the night, it is important that parents are as low-key as possible with the infant in order to teach him or her that nighttime is not a time to play and socialize. If care is not necessary but the child requires some soothing, Brazelton and Sparrow (2006), page 390, state:

If you have been taking her out of bed to rock her, don't; soothe and stroke her with your hand, but leave her *in bed* (author's italics). She won't like it, but she'll understand. Stand by her crib and tell her that she can and must learn to get herself back to sleep.

This is a much more appropriate way of helping infants learn to sleep through the night without allowing them to "cry it out" as many baby trainers recommend.

Dr. Brazelton highly frowns upon the use of physical punishment with children—especially infants and toddlers. He recognizes that older infants, as well as toddlers, require clear, consistent limits in order to slowly learn self-control. Again, discipline means to teach and to guide children in appropriate behaviors. Spanking does not do this; it controls. "Physical punishment such as hitting or spanking will mean two things to her: one, that you are bigger than she and you can get away with it, and two, that you believe in aggression" (Brazelton & Sparrow, 2006, p. 146). Spanking children causes them to slowly lose their trust in their parents and caregivers. This makes them less likely to listen to parents without the threat of punishment. Discipline, however, has the opposite effect on children.

> Discipline is the second most important thing you do for a child. Love comes first, and discipline second. Discipline means teaching, not punishment. The goal is for the child to incorporate her own limits. Each opportunity for discipline becomes a chance for teaching. Hence, after a brief disciplinary maneuver, sit down to comfort and hold her, saying, "You can't do that. I'll have to stop you until you can learn to stop yourself."
>
> (Brazelton & Sparrow, 2006, p. 147)

Brazelton recommends using time-outs not as punishments but to help the child calm down.

This section has described some of the contemporary attachment figures and theories. It is quite clear that they take the historical attachment research into account because much of the contemporary research is a continuation of how secure attachments are formed in infants. Again, the research of the contemporary attachment figures validates each other even if they have slightly different beliefs. The overall consensus is that infants require sensitive, responsive, consistent, and respectful care in order to thrive and create secure attachments to the adults in their lives. This chapter will conclude by taking a brief look at baby trainers and failure to thrive.

Concluding Remarks

Given the research I have provided throughout this chapter, it is clear that baby training is not only futile but has been proven dangerous and harmful to infants. Books such as *On Becoming Baby Wise* by Gary Ezzo and Robert Bucknam and *To Train Up a Child* by Michael and Debi Pearl, including some books by Dr. James Dobson, recommend putting young infants on strict schedules, parent-directed feedings and sleeping, and using physical punishment with infants and toddlers, which are based on pure opinion, not research nor an experienced background in child care. They are behaviorists like John B. Watson and John Locke, discussed earlier in this chapter, who believed affection was dangerous to young children. While today's behaviorists may not go quite as far as saying affection is dangerous to infants, they have no concrete understanding of infant development or attachment. The American Academy of Pediatrics warns against baby training due to its potentially harmful effects. According to the department of child and family services, it is considered child abuse to hit children under the age of two.

Failure to thrive, disorganized/disoriented attachment, and Reactive Attachment Disorder (RAD) are potential reactions infants may have if they are not provided with sensitive, responsive, respectful, and consistent care from the adults in their lives. These disorders often have long-term effects for children.

> Children who were maltreated in infancy and were scored as having a disorganized attachment at 1 year continue to be disorganized during early childhood (Barnett, Ganiban, & Cicchetti, 1999). Disorganized children are more likely to display evidence of child behavior problems (disobedience, fighting, withdrawal) and adolescent psychopathology, in particular *dissociation* (mental confusion, lack of *subjective self-awareness*, out-of-body experiences, accident proneness) (Carlson, 1998; Lyons-Ruth, Eastbrooks, & Cibelli, 1997).
>
> (Fogel, 2011, p. 327)

In the disorganized/disoriented attachment disorder, infants show severe contradictory behaviors, such as smiling but then turning away from the parent, crawling backward to the parent, and displaying a frozen posture when reunited with the parent. Infants that display this attachment disorder are abused, neglected, and malnourished. "Because parental behavior in this type of attachment relationship is so disturbed, it is not surprising that infants develop severe and disturbed reactions" (Fogel, 2011, p. 320). Reactive Attachment Disorder (RAD) has two types of patterns. The first type of pattern is called inhibitions. "The child is excessively inhibited, hypervigilant, or ambivalent and contradictory" (Fogel, 2011, p. 320). This is much like disorganized/disoriented attachment. The second type of behavioral pattern of RAD is disinhibitions. The child shows no selective attachments and shows over-familiarity to strangers (Fogel, 2011). RAD stems from not having a consistent, stable caregiver, physical and emotional needs gone unmet, and child abuse and neglect.

In fact, one mother found out that had she left her baby to cry it out, it would have literally killed her infant. Here is the touching story of a mother who listened to God and herself and saved her baby's life:

> I gave birth on a February afternoon by repeat caesarean. A pink, squalling bundle was handed to me, and I gazed lovingly into eyes that seemed to recognize me. I whispered sweet words of belonging to this girl child of mine, and comforted her outraged cries. She was the daughter I so desperately wanted.
>
> A week after her birth, a friend dropped off a ring sling. I snuggled my 7 lb bundle into it and went about my way with a mostly content baby. Within two weeks, I was wearing her constantly. Towards afternoon, she'd begin to sob and scream inconsolably. She would arch and thrash, refuse to nurse, refuse a soother, the swing, my arms. The only thing that would quiet her screams was the sling.
>
> Screamy baby began to lose weight. I carried her—day in, day out—in the sling. Repeated trips to the doctor revealed nothing. She was unable to nurse, screaming hysterically within moments of latch on. I was told rudely "Do breast compressions. Breast is best." Breast compressions made her choke and gag...and scream. I began feeding her formula. We went back to the doctor. Reflux. Milk Intolerance. Delayed gastric emptying. Her weight gain was poor, and the screaming increased in volume. Nights were long, filled with arching, thrashing baby. There was many a night that I slept with her in the sling, sitting up on the couch, unwilling to move her from her comfort zone. People told me I was spoiling her. I told them "We're coping. This is all that works." I was told to

let her cry it out, but I had no desire to abandon my child to a dark room to cry out her angst. My responsibility to her did not end when the sun went down. I whispered in her ear that I couldn't stop her crying, but I could hold her while she cried.

I paced the floors with her, snuggled tummy to tummy in the sling. At six months, I begged the doctor to hospitilize her—I knew something was dreadfully wrong. The paediatrician agreed. She was poked, prodded, xrayed, and force fed. The screaming continued.

A day before discharge, my pediatrician's partner waltzed into our room with his holier than thou attitude. He told me I wasn't putting in the effort to feed her, to put her in another room to sleep and let her cry it out. I banned him from treating my child.

I worked part time, baby in sling. I got a mei tai, two more ring slings. I carried her everywhere. In the shower. To the doctor, to the park, on play dates. People nastily asked me how she would learn to walk if I never put her down. I ignored them. Carrying her stopped the screaming.

Just before her first birthday, she developed a high fever and cough. I took her to the ER, still wrapped in my sling. We waited 7 hours. Xrays revealed her heart was enlarged. We were admitted. I carried her nonstop for the next few days – through a terrifying whirlwind of echocardiograms and finally a diagnosis. During one particularly memorable screaming fit, a nurse turned to me in tears, and handed me my sling. My daughter quieted, safe in her sling.

She was in heart failure. A rare and very serious heart defect had been causing massive heart attacks. Fatality rates were 90 percent in the first year. The screaming was her suffering from crushing chest pain. In the hallway, the cardiologist turned to me and quietly told me that it was my parenting—the constant carrying—that had allowed her to survive against all odds.

My daughter never cried alone, left in a room. Had I ever practiced CIO, I would have woken to a lifeless baby. I held her through months of gut wrenching doubt, moments when I cried too. But today, I watch my daughter play and run, and laugh. I carried her through a mom's worst nightmare...and we both survived.

(Kaganovsky, 2009, http://fiercemamas.blogspot.com. au/2009/10/saving-my-baby.html)

This chapter has discussed the historical roots of attachment theory in which Rene Spitz, Harry Harlow, Mary Ainsworth, and John Bowlby showed that infants require more than good physical care and food to thrive. It has shown how contemporary attachment theory is highly based on the historical research. This chapter showed the devastating effects on infants who are left to emotionally fend for themselves. The effects of baby training and physical punishment on infants and toddlers makes it very clear that infants are vulnerable to the world around them. They deserve nothing but kindness, love, and respect.

References

Ainsworth, M. D. (1962). *Deprivation of Maternal Care: A Reassessment of its Effects.* Geneva, Switzerland: World Health Organization.

Ainsworth, M. D., Blehar, M. C., Waters, E., & Wall, S. (1978). *Patterns of Attachment: A Psychological Study of the Strange Situation.* Hillsdale, NJ: Lawrence Erlbaum Associates.

Bowlby, J. (1973). *Attachment and Loss Volume II: Separation Anxiety and Anger.* New York, NY: Basic Books Inc.

Bowlby, J. (1982). *Attachment and Loss Volume I: Attachment.* Second Edition. London, England: The Hogarth Press.

Brazelton, T. B. (1969). *Infants and Mothers*. New York, NY: Dell Publishing Company Inc.

Brazelton, T. B. & Sparrow, J. (2006). *Touchpoints: Birth to Three*. Cambridge, MA: Da Capo Press.

Brazelton, T. B. The Brazelton Institute. http://www.brazelton-institute.com/berrybio.html.

Erikson, E. H. (1963). *Childhood and Society*. New York, NY: W. W. Norton & Company.

Fogel, A. (2011). *Infant Development: A Topical Approach*. Hudson, NY: Sloan Publishing.

Gartner, L. M. & Eidelman, A. I. (February 2005). Breastfeeding and the use of human milk. *Pediatrics, 115*(2), 496-506.

Gerber, M. & Johnson, A. (1998). *Your Self-Confident Baby*. New York, NY: John Wiley & Sons Inc.

Hammond, R. A. (2009). *Respecting babies: A New Look at Magda Gerber's RIE Approach*. Washington, DC: Zero to Three.

Harlow, H. F. & Mears, C. (1979). *The Human Model: Primate Perspectives*. Washington, DC: V. H. Winston & Sons.

Kaganovsky, S. (2009). Saving my baby. http://fiercemamas.blogspot.com.au/2009/10/saving-my-baby.html

Karen, R. (1994). *Becoming Attached: The Unfolding Mysteries of the Mother-Infant Bond*. New York, NY: Warner Books.

McMullen, M. B., Addleman, J. M., Fulford, A. M., Moore, S. L., Mooney, S. J., Sisk, S. S., & Zachariah, J. (July 2009). Learning to Be *Me* While Coming to Understand *We*. Encouraging Prosocial Babies in Group Care Settings. *Young Children, 64*(4), 20-28.

Mooney, C. H. (2010). *Theories of Attachment*. St. Paul, MN: Red Leaf Press.

Sears, W. & Sears, M. (1997). *The Complete Book of Christian Parenting & Child Care.* Nashville, TN: Broadman and Holman Publishers.

Sears, W. & Sears, M. (2001). *The Attachment Parenting Book.* New York, NY: Little, Brown and Company.

Sears, W. & Sears, M. (2003). *The Baby Book.* New York, NY: Little, Brown and Company.

Chapter 17

Authoritative Parenting Is NOT the Same as Permissive Parenting

All of the discipline strategies in this part of the book do exactly that with our children. In this chapter, we will be discussing authoritative parenting versus permissive parenting. We will also discuss how to childproof, model, and introduce God to our children.

Authoritative Versus Permissive Parenting—Not Spanking Does NOT Mean Wild, Rebellious Children

Prospankers often accuse or claim that parents who do not spank or use any type of punishment with their children have wild and rebellious children. This simply is not the case for parents that use the authoritative parenting style. There seems to be much confusion over the three types of parenting styles. We discussed the authoritarian parenting style in great detail in chapter 15. As we begin to focus on how to gently but firmly discipline children, we need to examine the other two parenting styles: authoritative parenting and permissive parenting.

Just as there is a huge difference between authori*tarian* and authori*tative* parenting, there is also a huge difference between authoritative and permissive parenting. Let's look at authoritative parenting (attachment parenting falls under authoritative parenting) as all of the discipline techniques that we will be looking at throughout this part of the book fall under authoritative parenting. And, as we will see, authoritative parenting is biblically supported and accurate as God is authoritative with us.

So, what is authoritative parenting? Santrock (2008), page 76, states:

> Authoritative parenting encourages children to be independent but still places limits and controls on their actions. Extensive verbal give-and-take is allowed and parents are nurturant and supportive. An authoritative parent might put his or her arm on the child's shoulder in a comforting way and say, "You know you should not have done that. Let's talk about how you can handle the situation differently next time." Children whose parents are authoritative often behave in socially competent ways. They tend to be self-reliant, delay gratification, get along with their peers, and show high self-esteem.

Authoritative parents are firm but gentle with their children. They take the time to learn about child development and know at which stage their children are developmentally in order to gain a better understanding of their children's behaviors. Authoritative parents set firm, realistic boundaries and limits for their children based on the developmental stage of their children. While these parents stick to their guns on some things, such as bedtime and not allowing their children to eat cookies before suppertime, they always listen to all of their children's feelings and validate those feelings. In situations where negotiation can occur, such as allowing five more minutes of playtime before having their children clean up, these parents do so. These parents also give their children simple choices when appropriate, but they are not afraid to let their children know when something is not a choice and compliance is absolutely required. When children don't comply, authoritative parents will gently but firmly help their children comply. And these parents use natural and logical consequences with their children instead of punishment.

In sum, authoritative parents give much grace to their children and aim to work *with* their children instead of *against* them. They teach the Word of God to their children instead of using God's Holy Word to justify hurting them. As Robin Grille (2005) states, "Authoritative parenting is more effective, since it is assertive rather than aggressive or manipulative" (p. 214).

Permissive parenting, on the other hand, is the direct opposite of authoritative parenting. Permissive parenting is just as harmful and abusive to children as authoritarian parenting, even though these two parenting styles are on the two polar ends when it comes to parenting styles. Permissive parents do not set limits or boundaries for their children. And when these parents do set limits and boundaries for their children, they often don't consistently enforce them. Some permissive parents allow their children to "walk all over them," to have whatever they want, and rarely do these parents give their children appropriate consequences when necessary. Other permissive parents outright neglect all of their children's needs. They do not even give their children appropriate and necessary care. All of permissive parenting, as I said above, is abusive because either type does not provide children with what they need to thrive. It also exasperates and frustrates children not to have any discipline just like spanking them does. Permissive and authoritarian parents break God's charge for parents not to frustrate or exasperate their children in Ephesians 6:4 and Colossians 3:21. "Permissiveness is disrespectful and does not teach important life skills. True discipline guides, teaches, and invites healthy choices" (Nelsen, Erwin, & Duffy, 2007, p. 8).

For this reason, I would never advocate for permissiveness, just as I would never advocate for authoritarianism. Allowing children to have and do whatever they want is as bad for them as hitting them. And permissiveness simply is *not* biblical.

Now that we have a clear understanding of the three parenting styles, I want us to see why authoritative parenting is what the Bible supports. God is our perfect parent. He treats us with respect, love, grace, and mercy. He wrestles with us and puts up with us when we question and argue with Him. In Genesis 32:22-25, God allowed Jacob to wrestle with Him. He did not punish Jacob, even though Jacob limped away the next day from wrestling with God all night, but instead, God changes Jacob's name to Israel because he wrestled with God and humans and overcame (Genesis 32:28)! Later in Exodus 4:1-17, we see Moses argue with God about going back to Egypt to get Pharaoh to release the Israelites. Yes, God eventually got angry with Moses, but instead of punishing Moses, God makes it easier for Moses to obey. Look at this passage:

> Then the LORD's anger burned against Moses and he said, "What about your brother, Aaron the Levite? I know he can speak well. He is already on his way to meet you, and he will be glad to see you. You shall speak to him and put words in his mouth; I will help both of you speak and will teach you what to do. He will speak to the people for you, and it will be as if he were your mouth and as if you were God to him. But take this staff in your hand so you can perform the signs with it."
>
> Exodus 4:14-17

God lets Moses's brother Aaron go with Moses to help him do God's will. God definitely disciplines us but in a gentle but firm manner.

Jesus often had to discipline and rebuke His disciples. His disciples could be unruly at times, but Jesus only corrected and rebuked them. Never once did Jesus punish His disciples. Luke 9:51-56 is a perfect example of how Jesus rebuked His disciples. Let's take a look at this passage:

> As the time approached for him to be taken up to heaven, Jesus resolutely set out for Jerusalem. And he sent messengers on ahead, who went into a Samaritan village to get things ready for him; but the people there did not welcome him, because he was heading for Jerusalem. When the disciples James and John saw this, they asked, "Lord, do you want us to call fire down from heaven to destroy them?" But Jesus turned and rebuked them. Then he and his disciples went to another village.

James and John wanted to have fire rain down from heaven to destroy the Samaritan town because the town rejected their Savior, but Jesus made it quite clear to James and John that just because they had the power from God to have fire come out of heaven did not mean they could go around destroying towns because they were angry with the people of the town. This is how God disciplines us. And we should follow God's example when we discipline our children. God is authoritative because He is a God of relationships. He wants loving relationships with us, and He wants us to have loving relationships with each other.

> It is clear throughout Scripture that God is very concerned with relationship. He desires relationship with us and we receive much instruction on how to conduct ourselves in our relationships with each other through reading his Word.

> (Lutton, 2001, p. 24-25)

We must always keep this in mind as we seek to discipline our children in a gentle but firm manner.

"Start Off Children on the Way They Should Go"—Discipline by Working with Children's Personalities

Proverbs 22:6 is a very important verse to study as we get into how to discipline our children. But before we get deeper into this verse, I want to once again remind everyone what discipline truly means because—as I've mentioned throughout this book—discipline and punishment are two very *different* things. We must stop equating discipline with punishment and "training." Discipline means to teach and to guide children. As Nelsen, Erwin, and Duffy (2007), pages 4 through 5, state:

> Discipline with very young children is mostly about deciding what *you* will do (and kindly and firmly following through) than with what you expect your *child* to do. And it's never too early to lay a foundation for respectful, effective parenting.

Discipline must begin at birth. Sadly, because so many parents equate discipline with punishment and "training," they either don't mindfully discipline their children until toddlerhood or they begin punishing, and most likely abusing, their infants. Here is a perfect example of why we must stop equating discipline with punishment. Ruth Ann Hammond (2009) states in her book, *Respecting Babies: A New Look at Magda Gerber's RIE approach*, page 70, the following:

> A parent at the orientation for the infant-toddler program at Pacific Oaks once asked, "When should we start disciplining our toddler?" In my head, I thought, "Well,

if you're just now asking, it's already too late," but of course I did not say that. What I did was ask the group, as Magda had regularly done, what the word *discipline* really means. In any group, there is always someone who says, "punishment," and I think the father in this story had this concept in mind when he asked his question. This question was often the jumping off place where Magda would begin to discuss her perspective on discipline, as in "disciple: a follower or pupil of a leader, teacher, philosophy, etc." (*Oxford Illustrated Dictionary*, 1998), wherein a person would want to conform him- or herself to the likeness of an admired other. The father was correct in presuming that punishment is inappropriate with infants; his question, I think, was really about when punishment can be utilized. Magda never advocated punishment as a deterrent; her ideas were much more subtle and presumed that the child's inner agenda included a desire to have the parent's approval.

Now that we have an understanding of what discipline truly means, let's take a closer look at Proverbs 22:6. Most of us know the old version of this verse by heart. "Train a child in the way he should go, and when he is old he will not turn from it." But the updated version is the one I have used for the subtitle of this section, which states, "Start off children in the way that they should go, and even when they are old they will not turn from it" (2011, NIV). I know I have explained this before, but the imagery of this verse is more of a road, and we want our children to follow the road that God has set out for them at conception. However, we can't really train children to follow this road. All we can do is set them down on the road and allow God to help us guide them down this road. However, on whatever version one chooses to concentrate, this is one verse about discipline that is very important to understand in order to correctly apply it to how we are to discipline children.

Proverbs 22:6 is the master verse of Christian discipline…
The Book of Proverbs is noted for short verses with deep
meaning. Dig into this verse and discover what God is
saying to you. God is reminding you of your awe-inspiring
responsibility to discipline your children. What you do
now will affect your child's whole life.

(Sears & Sears, 1997, p. 328)

We must do all we can to accurately apply this verse.

Despite what many Christian prospankers claim, this verse is
not meant to be a promise that if parents diligently spank their
children then the children will grow up to be godly adults. As
we have seen throughout part 3 of this book, "The Effects of
Spanking," this, unfortunately, is not the case, as many that have
grown up in Christian homes where they were spanked, even
"lovingly," have turned from God. Since we know that God *never*
lies, it is obvious that God did not intend this verse to be used as
a promise for spanking. Actually, God intended us to understand
this verse in the direct opposite way that most prospankers do.
God wants us to parent our children in such a way that we *truly*
know our children and can see from their personalities and
temperaments as well as interests which way God is leading them.
We need to work *with* our children and help them to channel
their energies into positive things. For infants, this means gearing
their care and your responses to them in a manner that fits their
temperament. A high-needs infant will need more interaction
and care. A low-needs infant still needs plenty of interaction and
care but may enjoy more down time to him or herself. A high-
needs toddler will require more active gross motor play to expend
his or her energy than a low-needs toddler that may enjoy more
quiet activities. God does *not* want us to battle against who *He*
made our children to be. Yes, we all tend toward sin, but we need
to work with our children to help them learn how to fight the

battle against sin and to know what to do when they sin. After all, we *all* sin every day throughout the day. So instead of fighting a high-needs child to fit into what *we* want/need him or her to be by treating the child harshly or ignoring the child's needs, we need to ask God to help us to figure out ways to work with the child to meet his or her needs while still making time for our own needs.

This verse also means respecting children's interests even if they are much different than your own. For example, if your boy likes dolls, encourage that in him. God may be preparing him to be a teacher or a pediatrician. If your girl enjoys playing with trucks and dinosaurs, encourage her. God may be preparing her to be an archeologist or a missionary that drives trucks full of supplies for poor and needy people.

> Biblical scholars suggest the latter interpretation of this verse [The one we have been discussing]. Each child has an individual bent or "way" and therefore an individual plan. What God is saying to you is to know your child, be tuned in to his individual bent, keep your radar system attuned to the direction he should take, and keep him focused in that direction (which may not necessarily be the direction you want for him). This concept may be hard for parents to understand: "How do we know what direction God has for our child?" If you have parented your child in a way that has helped you to really know him, this question is much less difficult to answer.
>
> (Sears & Sears, 1997, p. 328)

The objective of discipline is not to break children's wills but to help God mold them. We are born broken due to sin, so God wants to mold us into the people He wants us to be. Of course, we'll never be perfect until we reach heaven and there is no more sin. But as long as we live on this broken Earth, God will continue to discipline and mold us according to His plan for us. As Jeremiah 18:4 states, "But the pot he was shaping from the clay was marred in his hands; so the potter formed it into another pot, shaping it as seemed best to him." God knows us better than we know ourselves as He created us in our mother's wombs. Therefore, He works with us to help us overcome sin. We need to do the same with our children. Here are ways we can do this. It begins with the environment.

Setting Up a Child-Friendly Environment

Our first job as disciplinarians is to create a safe and child-friendly environment. This helps getting compliance from children easier. It is up to us to make it as easy as possible for children to comply/obey. For infants and toddlers, our main objective is safety. The environment in which infants and toddlers explore should be completely safe to the point that if we were to accidently get locked out of our house, our infant or toddler would be safe inside. My suggestion is to pick the room in your house where your family spends the most time and completely childproof it. Begin by placing covers on all electrical outlets. Put all electrical wires out of reach from the children. Tie up blind and curtain strings out of children's reach. Secure all televisions, bookshelves, and any other furniture to walls that your child could pull down onto his or herself. Place all breakables out of the children's reach. Use childproof locks on cabinets and drawers that you do not want your children getting into. Keep all objects smaller than a tennis ball out of the children's reach as they are choking hazards to infants and toddlers that naturally use their mouths to explore objects. Furniture with sharp corners should either be removed or have padding installed on the corners to prevent unsteady infants and toddlers from falling and banging their heads on these sharp corners. Childproof doorknobs should be installed on all doors.

And, of course, medications and cleaning chemicals should always be kept out of children's reach.

Do this for every room that your children has access to. As far as other rooms, it is important to use baby gates and/or shut doors in order to keep children out of unsafe rooms when we are not with them. I highly recommend keeping children younger than three years old out of the kitchen while cooking is taking place. Use a baby gate to do this. At any rate, the kitchen should still be childproofed as much as possible. Cover all of the stove's knobs and use childproof locks on all drawers and cabinets. If you choose not to keep your child out of the kitchen, then having one drawer filled with safe things for your child to play with can make children feel special. While cooking, I highly suggest giving your child a special job to do to keep him or her occupied, such as: holding a towel, sorting dish towels, or giving him or her his or her own dishes and pots and pans with which to play.

Safety is so important as infants and toddlers cannot be expected to keep themselves safe. And it isn't fair for us to punish our children for playing with things that we do not want them to break. Some prospankers claim that we should "train" infants and toddlers not to touch things by slapping or swatting their hands, but it is up to parents and caregivers to make the environment safe for them, as well as to supervise them in *all* environments. This is what God does for us. Crystal Lutton (2001), page 66, beautifully states:

> Let's look at how God handles new Christians to see if we can find a model to follow. Maybe you remember when you were a new Christian or when you last talked to one. Didn't it seem like the world was fantastic for them and nothing could go wrong? Maybe they were even struggling with sin issues, but they were still floating. I believe that this is because God is only holding them accountable to the broadest of boundaries. Essentially

these boundaries are the Greatest Commandment given
in Matthew 22:36-40 when Jesus said we are to love God
with all our hearts, minds, souls, and strength, and love our
neighbors as ourselves. What new Christian doesn't love
God, themselves and others? Even Paul, in 1 Corinthians
3:2 explains that he has fed the Christians at Cornith with
milk and not meat because they could not bear it yet.

Therefore, God keeps young Christians away from certain
dangers until they are mature enough to handle them. Even Jesus
did not tell His disciples everything that He could have because
He knew they couldn't handle it all at that time. "I have much
more to say to you, more than you can now bear" (John 16:12).
And 1 Corinthians 10:13 clearly states, "No temptation has
overtaken you except what is common to mankind. And God is
faithful; he will not let you be tempted beyond what you can bear.
But when you are tempted, he will also provide a way out so that
you can endure it." It is important to note that "temptation" and
"tempted" can also mean "testing" and "tempting" in the Greek
translation of this verse.

Now this doesn't mean that we shouldn't begin to teach
children about danger as they become mobile toddlers. We
can do this by telling toddlers about danger, such as: the stove
will hurt if we touch it while it's on. Or holding toddlers by a
road and talking about how fast the cars are going and that if
we run out into the street, the cars will hit us. Toddlers will not
understand this immediately, so we must take every precaution
to keep them out of dangerous situations. However, if a toddler
happens to get away from you and is headed for the street, for
example, you need to say, "Stop!" or "No!" in an urgent, fearful
tone as you run to the toddler and swiftly pick him or her up.
Hitting the toddler will not teach danger, but when toddlers hear
such an urgent, fearful tone of voice from their parents and get
swiftly swooped up by their parents, they learn the seriousness

of the situation. This is particularly true of toddlers being raised using a combination of the Resources for Infant Educarers (RIE) approach and Attachment Parenting because parents usually tell their children from birth before they do anything with them and wait for some type of response from the children before moving on. (See chapter 16 for more information). After the toddler is out of danger, sit the toddler on your lap and look the toddler in the eye and firmly say, "The street is dangerous! You must not go out into the street without me or Daddy!" You may also tell your toddler how frightened you were when he or she tried to run into the street without you, but keep the verbal lecture short and simple so the child doesn't lose the lesson amidst the words. Again, do not spank or punish the child. Do the same for a toddler reaching for a hot stove. Say, "Hot!" "No!" as you swiftly pick up the toddler. If a toddler gets hurt while doing something dangerous, do not rub it in by saying, "That's what happens when you don't obey me." Instead, say, "Yes, the hot stove burned your hand when you touched it and hurt your hand. I'm sorry. Let's make your hand feel better." Comfort the child, validate his or her feelings, and help him or her feel better. After all, this is what God does for us.

Finally, set up the environment so that children have easy access to their books and toys. This will make it easier for them to help us clean up. Low shelves and plastic storage containers work great for children to get and return toys and books. Child-sized furniture can also help children feel more comfortable. Since boredom can cause children to act up, try to rotate some of their books and toys every week, but be sure to leave out a few favorites for them. Also, make sure the home exudes peacefulness because over-stimulated children will also act up more. Parents and caregivers are often surprised at how some behavioral problems disappear by rearranging the environment. This is a very important factor of discipline.

One of your most basic jobs as disciplinarian is to create an environment that does not foster a conflict of wills. Having to fight you constantly will not help your child develop good relationships with authority figures. Having you control him constantly does not allow him to learn or become his own person. Remember that discipline is mainly guidance. If you make your home and your family into a place where it is not too difficult to be a child, the environment will help discipline the child and you will avoid many conflicts.

(Sears & Sears, 1997, p. 338)

Just as making the environment is a crucial part of disciplining children, so is mindful modeling.

Mindfully Modeling Appropriate Behaviors to Children

Mindful modeling is performing behaviors and values in which we want our children to learn and copy from us. Beginning at birth, children are watching and listening to everything we say and do even when it doesn't seem like it. Infants may not understand all that is happening around them, but they are like little sponges and are soaking everything in, which will undoubtedly influence them as they grow and mature.

Every parent wants his or her children to learn to respect him or her as well as others. The primary way that we teach respect is by being respectful to our children from birth onward. We also teach respect to children by being respectful to everyone we encounter. "You can't expect your children to say kind things about people if you're pointing out the faults of others. If you break something that belongs to someone else, you pay for it and say you're sorry" (Kuzma, 2006, p. 657).

It seems like parents seem to forget to model the values that they want their children to learn, such as: prayer, worship, Bible study, and other ethics like not lying or cheating.

> You must live by the same code of ethics you are trying to instill in your children. You can't expect them to resist lying, cheating, or watching questionable movies or television programs if you do any of these things yourself.
>
> (Kuzma, 2006, p. 657)

I have witnessed many devout Christian families not put an importance on saying a quick prayer of thanks to God before eating. If we want children to have a great prayer life, we must model that to them by regularly praying throughout the day and before eating even a snack. Prayer, worship, and Bible study needs to be introduced to our children at birth. This means doing these things throughout the day by ourselves and with our children. We must make a commitment to live Christian-disciplined lives.

> Make a commitment that Christian discipline is a top priority in your life as well as in your relationship with your children. We stress this term *commitment* because it forms the basis of all parenting. You are well on your way to effective Christian discipline of your child if you love and fear your God and walk in His ways.
>
> (Sears & Sears, 1997, p. 329)

I'm not saying that parents should not spend quiet time alone with God every day. Alone time with God is very important. But our children need to see and hear us doing this as well. Children are never too young to be introduced to our loving Lord and Savior! Christ must be at the center of our family so that our children will want to pursue a relationship with Him as they grow.

It is much easier to bring God into discipline at this stage if God is already at the center of your life, your marriage, and your family. If you have already made this commitment, you are well on your way to helping your child experience God's presence in his life.

(Sears & Sears, 1997, p. 332)

Start simple by praying short, fun prayers with the new baby during daily care routines. My sister-in-law would pray with her son when he was a baby. She'd hold his little hands and pray happily, "God, thank you for this day and for Wyatt!" Wyatt would smile, coo, and giggle every time she prayed with him. Infants love praying. They also love being involved in family worship and singing. Dr. William Sears (1997), page 333, shares the following story of his infant daughter enjoying worship and even reminding them to pray before meals:

Initially, Erin would simply watch this family praise. Eventually, she began raising her hands when we did. By fifteen months, as soon as the mealtime grace was finished, in anticipation of the praise song to follow she would raise her hands right on cue (sometime reminding us to sing). Praising the Lord was being imprinted upon her heart even before she could grasp intellectually the meaning of what was being sung. As we all joined hands, bowed our heads, and became quiet for prayer, she did the same. At seventeen months she was able to remind us to say the blessing by reaching for Dad's hand on one side and Mom's hand on the other side.

It is very important to tailor prayer time, worship time, and Bible time to your children's ages and developmental stages. These times should be upbeat, fun, and short in duration for infants, toddlers, and preschoolers. Children this age can only handle ten to fifteen minutes. And they should be acting out songs and even some stories through flannel boards where they can attach characters and animals in the story to a board. As children grow, they will be able to handle more and more, but these times should still be fun and geared to their interests. Plus, they must see us truly enjoying ourselves when we spend time with God. It is totally unrealistic to expect young children to sit quietly for an hour at church. And be sure to plan these times of prayer, worship, and Bible study at times when children are happy and well rested. God does not want us to force our children to worship Him, otherwise it will become a negative, legalistic experience for them and us. God wants true worship, not forced worship. If your toddler or preschooler refuses to pray or join in family worship, do not make a big deal about it, just begin praying or singing and your child will more than likely join in with you, as most young children hate to be left out of things. How we help our children form their first impressions of God will impact them for the rest of their lives. Teresa Whitehurst (2003), page 145, states:

> Children form impressions of God based on what they observe in and experience with their parents. For good or for bad, children tend to view God as they see their parents, including their habits, attitudes, even hair color! Through our words and symbolic conduct, we send the message that God is a harsh judge, who is always looking for reasons to criticize, correct, and punish, or that he is a loving parent who is always looking for opportunities to listen, forgive, and guide.

Many parents forget how important play is for children. Play is the primary way that young children learn, so play is also a great tool to use to model appropriate behaviors and social skills to their children. As Dr. Kay Kuzma (2006), page 426, states:

> Play also increases social skills. When parents play with their children, the parent-child bond is strengthened, but

it also tends to improve children's behavior. A study from Oxford University found that the more time children spent playing with Mom at age three, the better their behavior by age four. Apparently, by getting down on a child's level to play, you not only show interest and commitment to your child, but you teach cooperation and social skills much more effectively by modeling this behavior than you can teach through telling.

Along these same lines, as with worship and prayer, I don't believe in forcing toddlers and preschoolers to say, "Please," "Thank you," or "I'm sorry," when they don't mean it. When we force this on them at a very young age, we teach them to say things when they don't mean it. We need to be constantly modeling how to say these things to others because if children hear us saying "please," "thank you," and "I'm sorry" to them and others, then they are much more likely to follow suit.

Jennifer McGrail uses modeling as one of her discipline strategies with her children and has had positive results from it. Here is what she says about modeling:

> One thing that I think a lot of people are confused about is how children can learn things like manners, respect, and the like without it being somehow drilled into them. My answer is this: I model the behavior that's important to me. I say please and thank you. I say excuse me. I'm polite to waiters and bank tellers and cashiers. I'm true to myself. I respect other people's things. I respect other people's feelings. I don't lash out at strangers on the Internet because they do things differently than me. I say I'm sorry when I make a mistake. I treat my kids—and other people—*the way I'd like to be treated.* My children have learned it because they have lived it.
>
> (McGrail, 2011, http://www.jennifermcgrail.com/2011/04/gentle-discipline-so-what-do-you-do/)

Now, of course, no one besides God is perfect. And it is actually good for children to see their parents occasionally make mistakes. This is especially true if their children also get to see their parents right their wrong. It is so important that we turn our own mistakes into learning opportunities for our children. I really like how Dr. Sears (1997) explains this on page 367:

> When we blow it—and we have—we correct it, so that the impression our child gets is "Yes, adults make mistakes, but the right thing to do is correct them." In fact, we have come to understand that there are no mistakes, only lessons. It's up to you to make sure the lesson is constructive rather than destructive. This is hard to do because it is a new way of being for many of us. Remember Romans 8:1, "Therefore, there is now no condemnation for those who are in Christ Jesus, because through Christ Jesus the law of the Spirit of life set me free from the law of sin and death." God never condemns us as believers—He convicts us. What a difference that makes for us! We need to be sure our children experience conviction from us, never condemnation. From this they learn a valuable discipline lesson: a person takes responsibility for their actions.

So, is modeling biblical? As a matter of fact, it is indeed. Jesus's entire life was a model for us to follow in dealing with others. We need to model to our children what God models to us.

> He got down on our level, was born a man, and taught us while He modeled for us how to behave. He loved us and sacrificed himself for us. He became a servant for us. He warned us about natural consequences and, when they are not too dangerous, allows us to experience them. Ultimately, He died so that we don't have to.
>
> (Lutton, 2001, p. 26)

One specific example of Jesus modeling how to be with each other is when He washed His disciples' feet in John 13:1-17. Jesus wanted to model an attitude of servitude because His disciples often argued among themselves about who would be the greatest. But Jesus wanted them to learn how to be humble and serve each other because He knew His time with them was quickly coming to an end. Therefore, He modeled this very important lesson to them, and to us. We must do the same for our children and others.

> To teach a child to love God and have Jesus as a friend and a role model in the way He treated people is to give a child a wholly different approach to morality. The child will still value the Commandments, but will now aspire to ideal far beyond the mere minimal requirements of the Commandments.
>
> (Whitehurst, 2003, p. 24)

Let us be sure that we are consistently modeling God's love, mercy, grace, and forgiveness to our children starting at birth.

Conclusion

We have seen the difference between authoritative and permissive parenting, and that authoritative parenting is God's parenting style. We have discussed Proverbs 22:8 and how God wants us to work with our children as we strive to discipline them. God creates us, so even though we all have a sinful nature, He created us to become who He wants us to be in Him. But we must stop equating discipline with punishment as they are completely different. Finally, God wants us to make it as easy as possible for children to obey us. We must model God's goodness to our children. It is my hope that you will see that, when done consistently, all of these discipline strategies work as well as help lead children *to* God instead of away from Him! "Trust in the LORD with all your heart and lean not on your own understanding; in all your ways submit to him, and he will make your paths straight" (Proverbs 3:5-6).

References

Grille, R. (2005). *Parenting for a Peaceful World.* New South Wales, Australia: Longueville Media.

Hammond, R. A. (2009). *Respecting Babies: A New Look at Magda Gerber's RIE Approach.* Washington, DC: Zero to Three.

Kuzma, K. (2006). *The First 7 Years.* West Frankfort, IL: Three Angels Broadcasting Network.

Lutton, C. (2001). *Biblical Parenting.* Salt Lake City, UT: Millennial Mind Publishing.

McGrail, J. (2011). Gentle Discipline: So What Do You Do? http://www.jennifermcgrail.com/2011/04/gentle-discipline-so-what-do-you-do/

Nelsen, J., Erwin, C., & Duffy, R. A. (2007). *Positive Discipline: The First Three Years.* New York, NY: Three Rivers Press.

Santrock, J. (2008). *Educational Psychology (Illinois Version).* Boston, MA: The McGraw-Hill Companies.

Sears, W. & Sears, M. (1997). *The Complete Book of Christian Parenting and Child Care.* Nashville, TN: Broadman & Holman Publishers.

Whitehurst, T. (2003). *How Would Jesus Raise Your Child?* Grand Rapids, MI: Fleming H. Rewell.

Chapter 18

Validation of Feelings and "Time-In" Not "Out"

In the last chapter, we looked at how Proverbs 22:6 means to discipline children in a way that works with them instead of against them. God is not an adversarial parent to us; therefore, we should not be adversarial parents with our children as we are also sinners and actually sin more than our children do. The purpose of this part of the book is to learn how to discipline our children in a manner that will lead them to God instead of away from Him. We must provide gentle yet firm discipline to our children. In this chapter, we will look at how to validate feelings, deal with temper tantrums, and why we shouldn't use time-out as punishment but instead use something known as "time-IN" to help children calm down in a helpful way.

Validating Feelings— "It's My Party and I'll Cry if I Want To!"

Many people fail to realize just how much of an emotional life infants have right from birth. The young infant feels happy, sad, angry, and scared. But because crying is the only way of communicating their feelings, many infants do not get the validation that they require. Tragically, some infants are ignored and/or punished for crying. It is very important to understand infants' emotions are also their *needs*, and those needs must *always* be responded to in a sensitive and respectful manner.

> It seems wise for caregivers to make the assumption that infants of all ages have feelings, since it helps us to understand their needs. The interventions we make that are consonant with our interpretations of infant emotions often seem to have the intended effect. We pick up a crying baby to soothe what we believe to be the child's pain or discomfort as much as to stop the crying, and the subsequent relaxation of the infant confirms our belief about his or her feelings.
>
> (Fogel, 2011, p. 280)

While crying is the main way that newborns express their feelings, if we observe them closely, we will see that they also use their bodies to communicate with us. Fogel (2011), page 278, states:

> Crying generally occurs in situations in which one presumes the newborn might feel some distress or pain. In addition to facial expressions, newborns can convey emotion with other parts of their bodies. During distress, for example, there may be reddening of the entire body, kicking and thrashing, contorted arm movements, and stiffening of the body. These whole body responses reflect the activation of the sympathetic nervous system and hormonal secretions that activate changes in behavior and physiology and that are consistent with emotional responses.

By two months of age, infants' emotions become more defined and elaborated. They can make the facial expression for the emotion that they are feeling. Some Christians claim that an infant's crying is manipulation and their sinful nature coming out. As I explained in other parts of this book, this is not true. Also, an infant twelve months and under is totally developmentally incapable of manipulating anyone. Lutton (2001), page 46, explains:

> It's what God designed them to be able to do at that time. This is especially important when dealing with infants. It is normal for infants to cry and their wants are their needs. This is normal. This is the way God created infants to be. When dealing with normative, we are dealing with cultural preferences. The Bible was not written about people living in nineteenth-century Victorian England, although when many Christians talk about getting back to "traditional family values," this is the historical time to which they are referring. The Biblical cultures (for there were several) had different normative practices for parenting. However, the idea of formula feeding, separate rooms for children, and scheduling are unique to the Western Culture within the last hundred years. No one should feel pressured to abide by any of these practices under the belief that they are God's ideal.

Because God created infants to cry in order to communicate their needs and emotions, crying should *never* be viewed as sinful or manipulative. While, as I point out in chapter 16, there are times when infants need to cry, they must always be supported and validated as they cry and should *never* be left alone to cry for more than five minutes *if that long*. The reason I say this is sometimes parents need a short break from an infant that will not stop crying in order to prevent themselves from hurting the infant or saying something that they will regret. Shaken baby syndrome often occurs when an infant won't stop crying and the parent loses control and shakes the infant. *Never* shake an infant as they lack head and neck control, and the shaking causes the infant's brain to slam against the skull often causing brain damage and even death to the child. A five-minute break from the child is always better than harming the child, but the child should not be left alone for very long.

> Soothing a child literally builds the wiring in the brain for the child to internalize that comfort and those responses and begin to soothe himself!
>
> My husband didn't learn to self-soothe either. While I plunge into depression he reacts with anger. It sure doesn't do much for intimacy when you both are looking to the other to get the comfort that you need. We've discovered that first hand and now here we are, ten years into marriage, finally learning how to deal with our own emotions and soothe ourselves.
>
> (Freeman, 2012, http://realchilddevelopment.com/ inspiration/did-you-ever-learn-to-self-soothe)

Talking to infants about how they are feeling is very important. Many well-meaning people shush infants and/or say, "You're okay." As I pointed out in chapter 11, this teaches even the youngest infant to start to repress their feelings. We need to validate the infant's feelings by saying, for example, "I know you're hungry. I will feed you now." After saying this, offer your breast, or, if necessary, a bottle to your infant. This validates the infant's need and lets the infant know what we will do to help him or her to feel better. Young infants may not understand every word that we say to them, but they do quickly pick up on the general meaning of what is being said. So giving them words for their feelings is very helpful and important. If the infant is crying and we cannot figure out what he or she needs then we ought to say, for example, "You're so upset, and I'm trying to figure out what you need, but I'm having trouble. I will hold you while you cry." This lets the infant know that we are trying to help them and will continue to be there for them until it is resolved. "Even if you can't fix the problem, it is a much healthier lesson that you are teaching your child if you hold them until they feel better. This will teach them that life is safe and mommy and daddy can be trusted" (Lutton, 2001, p. 48). Our aim as parents is not to always stop the crying at all costs. Our aim is to meet the child's needs as best we can while *always* validating his or her needs.

> Crying must be responded to. But *how* is a more complicated issue. To follow the advice, "Do not let your baby cry," is practically impossible. At times the harder a mother or father tries to stop the baby's crying, the more anxious everyone becomes.
>
> (Gerber, 2002, p. 40)

Infants are highly sensitive to their parents' emotions, so the more upset and anxious we are, the more the infant will feel the same way and cry all the more.

Communicating with our infants from birth will help our infants and us develop a unique communication style. As we learn our infants' cues and cries, they will learn to anticipate our responses to them. The more this happens, the more accurate their cues and cries will become as they learn to depend on us. Even when we are having a hard time figuring out what they need, speaking to them can help us eventually figure it out. As Gerber (2002), page 41, states:

> Remember, crying is a baby's language—it is a way to express pain, anger, and sadness. Acknowledge the emotions your baby is expressing. Let him know he has communicated. For example, you might tell him, "I see you're uncomfortable. And hearing you cry really upsets me. I want to find out what you need. Tell me. I will try

to understand your cues and, in time, you will learn to give them to me." Or, "I see you are unhappy. I wish I knew what is making you unhappy." Then think out loud. "Could it be that your diaper is wet? I don't think you are hungry, because you just ate. Maybe I've been holding you long enough and maybe you want to be on your back for a while." This is the start of lifelong, honest communication.

The more we talk to and validate infants, the likelier it will become easier to understand them. Sadly, many well-meaning parents will immediately offer the infant the breast or bottle when the infant begins crying. While it is usually true for young infants that they are hungry, and, if that is the case, then please feed them. However, crying is not the first sign of hunger. Rooting and sucking are cues that the infant is hungry. Crying should not automatically be responded to with an offering of food. While this may quiet the infant temporarily, we are missing the actual need. And we do not want to condition the infant to accept food if that is not his or her need. The infant may be wet or need to be adjusted more comfortably in the sling, or something may be pinching him or her, or he or she may want a toy, or to be held differently, or put down, or to see something again that looked interesting and wants to look at it again. Infants have so many different needs that must be met. And infants also have a right to cry and feel how they feel.

> It will take your baby some time to function more smoothly, to relax, to anticipate and respond to your care. Do not just try to stop the crying. Respect the child's right to express his feelings, or moods... Try to find and eliminate discomfort.
>
> (Gerber, 2002, p. 41)

The same notion applies to the use of pacifiers. Newborns should not be given a pacifier if the mother is trying to breastfeed because this could cause nipple confusion. Nipple confusion makes latching onto the breast difficult for the newborn. Sadly, I have seen parents shove a pacifier into a crying infant's mouth and hold it there as the infant cries harder and struggles. This is not sensitive or respectful at all. This teaches infants that their parents do not care why they are crying and are willing to do just about anything to get the child to "shut up."

> The pacifier is a plug. It does stop a child from crying, but the question is, does an infant have a right to cry? Should an infant be allowed to express her feelings and communicate them? Plugging her mouth gives the message, "Don't do what comes naturally. Do what pleases me, your parent. I am in control of how you should feel and how you should show your feelings." (Gerber, 2002, p. 50-51)

This is *not* a healthy message to send to infants!

Now, there may be times when an infant needs to suck on something to soothe themselves; a pacifier or teething ring may be offered to the child as he or she gets older, but allow the child to choose whether or not to use it. Many parents discourage thumb sucking because they are afraid their children will take too long to outgrow it. The majority of children will wean themselves off sucking their thumbs just as they wean themselves off of the breast. The thumb is a natural self-soother. Even babies in utero suck their thumbs, and, therefore, should be allowed to do so after they are born. This is completely natural, just as at times only the breast will suffice. The important thing is for us to allow our children to have their needs met and for us to help them and validate them.

The thumb belongs to the infant. She has to discover it and learn how to use it as part of her own body. It is always available. It doesn't fall on the floor and get dirty or get lost when needed. The infant can put it in her mouth and pull it out according to her own needs and desires. In the process, she learns how to soothe herself and how to become self-reliant. When there are no misgivings about it, she will use it when and for as long as she really needs it.

(Gerber, 2002, p. 50)

Help your child coregulate by validating him or her and providing for his or her needs.

After all, this is what God does with us. He validates our feelings and our hearts. For example, in Matthew 9:2, Jesus first tells the paralytic to "Take heart, my son, your sins are forgiven." See, being disabled in New Testament times was quite a hardship emotionally as well as physically because people treated people with disabilities as beggars. They were outcasts. Some even believed that they were disabled due to sin, which John 9 shows isn't the case. Jesus is more concerned with our hearts than our physical beings.

Jesus was validating the paralytic's heart! He called him "son." To me this is almost like when I called a young girl I was ministering to last week, "Sweetheart." It was tender. It was non-religious. It was validating... Jesus was more concerned with validating the paralytic's heart than he was with healing him physically. He was healing him emotionally. Think of how much pain and discouragement the paralytic must have had throughout the years! Think of the judgment and condemnation he had endured from the religious crowd who said he was paralyzed because of sin.

(Lawrence, 2012, http://sermonseedbed.com/
the-grace-that-validates-devotional/)

We see another example of Jesus validating someone's feelings and heart in Luke 8:48 where He comforted and reassured the woman that had been bleeding for twelve years after she touched His cloak and was healed. Again, Jesus knew how much she had suffered emotionally due to her condition because, under Jewish Law, women who had their periods or were bleeding for any other reason were considered "unclean." They were shunned just like people with disabilities. Yet, Jesus comforted her once she came forward and admitted that it was her that had touched His cloak.

> Jesus again said, "Cheer up, daughter." Why would Jesus say, "Cheer up" to a woman whom had just gotten healed after 12 years of sickness? I wonder if somehow he was as concerned about her "heart" as he was her "body." And again, look at how he spoke to her, "Daughter." It was endearing, tender, compassionate. I am so grieved as I think of how parts of the "Church" have used God's Word to hurt God's children. We have told them that if they have enough faith they can be healed – so the implication is that if you are not healed, it is your fault. We have told them that others can have enough faith for them to be healed, which implies their lack of healing is our fault. Must make God want to curse! Okay, not really, don't throw anything at me. It must make God very angry! How about that?
>
> (Lawrence, 2012, http://sermonseedbed.com/
> the-grace-that-validates-devotional/)

Due to the fact that Jesus was 100 percent human just as He was 100 percent God, He experienced every human emotion there is. Our God is able to fully relate to us in our emotions. And He validates and comforts us if we ask Him. God is not against us having negative emotions; He just doesn't want us to use those negative emotions to sin against Him or to have them be our main focus. He also does not want us to punish our children for having negative emotions.

> The 100 percent humanness of Jesus causes people to connect their hearts with God's. The misunderstanding of his 100 percent Godness keeps people away. They wouldn't stay away if they could see God's heart, but our fears of God in His holiness and power cause us to stay at arm's length. But when we see Jesus in his 100 percent humanness and 100 percent Godness, it makes a bridge in our hearts to cross over from our hearts to God's.
>
> (Lawrence, 2012, http://sermonseedbed.com/ the-grace-that-validates-devotional/)

And look at what Isaiah 40:1 states, "Comfort, comfort my people, says your God." I love how God comforts and validates us when we need him to do so. As infants get older and begin to get angry or frustrated when their bodies won't yet allow them to do what they want or when we set simple limits for them, we need to keep in mind how God validates us when we get upset. Allowing some frustration in older infants is important so that they learn how to appropriately cope with frustration. It also helps drive them to meet developmental milestones, such as crawling or walking. I am a big proponent of allowing infants to develop unassisted without us manipulating their bodies to do things that the infant is not ready to do. God created infants to develop naturally and research shows that infants that are allowed to develop naturally have more graceful movements and are more competent human beings. "When development unfolds naturally without adult intervention, physical security increases and skill development is remarkable" (Gonzales-Mena, 2004, p. 3). However, too much frustration can cause the opposite effect in children. It is important for us to observe our infants in order to see when they are getting too frustrated so that we can step in and help. An outright angry cry usually indicates that the infant has had enough. Sometimes infants will start crying before they have reached their limit but a simple word of encouragement will help them to continue trying. But if the word of encouragement does not help, then it is time to step in and offer the minimal amount of assistance necessary to help them achieve their goal. For example, if the infant is playing with a ball and the ball rolls out of his or her reach, first, let him or her try to retrieve it. If the infant cannot get the ball, then say, for example, "I see you're frustrated because you can't reach the ball. I will get it for you." Then put the ball within the child's reach. This validates the child's frustration.

This is also important to do when the infant doesn't want to do something that the daily care routine requires, or a limit has been set. I'll give an example of my own. I worked with a high-needs infant that screamed whenever she was angry. One day she was playing outside. She was between ten and twelve months old at the time. While she was playing outside, she needed to come in and have her diaper changed. She was respectfully told that it was time to come in and have her diaper changed and then she could come back outside afterward. Well, this did not make her happy and she began to scream her head off. When she came in, I began to calmly talk to her. I did not get angry and scold her. I also did not just say, "You're okay." Instead I said, "I know you're angry because I have to change your diaper. I need your help with changing your diaper and then you may go back outside." She did not immediately stop crying, and I didn't expect her to either, but I validated her feelings and told her what had to happen as well as what I expected from her. I remained calm but firm with her. After a few minutes, she did start to help me. I made it as fun as possible and she calmed down. Before we both knew it, she was changed and was back outside playing. Even if she would have fought me, I would have still validated her feelings, set limits, and completed the diaper change. I also would have given a meaningful consequence, such as having her help me clean up diapers that she threw if that had happened, but I would not have punished her in any way.

When setting limits (which I will describe in-depth in the next chapter), such as "cups are for drinking only," infants and toddlers will get angry when we enforce the limit by taking away the cup after the third time they've thrown the cup. This usually means they are finished anyway. Still, it is important to say, for example, "You're angry because I won't let you throw your cup. Let me put you down and you can throw the ball (or whatever is appropriate for your child to throw)." Many times children will comply easier if we will validate their feelings. Dr. Kay Kuzma (2006), page 359 through 360, provides an excellent example of this:

> It was a busy time at the Wilsons' family reunion as preparations were being made for a picnic. Four-year-old Jacob was running through Grandma's kitchen with his cousin, David, when he bumped into the table. The watermelon crashed to the floor. It split open and made a mess. Mom, realizing it was an accident, calmly asked Jacob to help her clean it up. "No," he shouted he ran out the back door, "you can't make me." There were dozens of relatives milling around, and immediately two older cousins bent down and started cleaning up the mess. It would have been easy to just let Jacob go. But Mom was too smart for that. She said, "Leave a couple pieces on the floor so Jacob can help. I'll be back with him shortly." Mom casually walked outside, visited with some grown-ups, and then found Jacob kicking a ball with his cousins. She watched their play for a few minutes. She even kicked a ball back to the group when it came toward her. She didn't push immediately to right the wrong. She knew Jacob needed time to calm down. Then she spoke to the

cousins. "Would you please excuse Jacob for a minute? As soon as we've finished, Jacob will come back out to play." It was Jacob's turn to be surprised. His defenses were down. Mom further disarmed him by showing she was on his side by quietly saying to him, "I know you didn't mean to knock the watermelon off the table." She reached into his heart for the emotion that caused his behavior. "You were embarrassed that your mistake made such a big mess, weren't you? Then in front of the relatives when I asked you to clean it up, it made you angry that I would embarrass you even more. All you wanted to do was get out of there. But, Jacob, it's always important to do the right thing, no matter how we feel. So let's go back and help pick up that watermelon. It makes Jesus happy when you do the right thing." After talking for a few minutes, Jacob relaxed. He felt sorry for what he had done. Jacob admitted that running through the kitchen was not a smart thing to do. To right the wrong, he agreed to apologize to Grandma and then help pick up whatever was left. Together, they walked back to the kitchen. Mom could have acted quickly. In two minutes, she could have collared Jacob and marched him back into the house to make things right. But she didn't. Instead, she listened to his emotions and recognized his hurt. When he felt understood, he willingly obeyed her request. Here's the lesson for parents: Guard your child's feelings of personal value. If Jacob had been pushed in front of an audience to apologize when he was embarrassed, he would have resisted. By waiting until negative feelings cooled, Jacob had a chance to make things right himself and save face.

I really like the above story because many parents would have taken Jacob's response as defiance and would have forced him to apologize right away and help clean up. Some parents would have physically punished him as well or punished him by making him go sit by himself. All of this would have made him feel even worse and would have bred resentment and anger in his heart. We always want to help children save face. We need to look beyond the behavior to the emotion that may be causing it. And the child was not manipulated into feeling guilty for running away before cleaning up. If children feel right, then they will act right. Sadly, many parents seem to be more concerned about their children's behavior rather than the feelings behind the behavior.

I would like to revisit teaching children manners because this is an area in which many parents embarrass their children by forcing them to say, "I'm sorry," to another person. I have had a great deal of parents force their young children to apologize to me. It actually makes me more upset when parents do this than what their children did because their children were just being typical young children. I didn't want or need an apology, and I could see how embarrassed the child was as he or she would look down and quietly say it as I would anxiously pray that the parent wouldn't make the child say it louder. Then I always say, "I forgive you," to the child to help everyone move on. As I said in chapter 17, there's nothing wrong with gently teaching young children manners by constantly modeling politeness, but when we force young children to be polite, it makes them feel embarrassed and have a sense of shame.

> But many children squirm and look downward as they utter their politeness, probably because when you are pressured to be polite, it also can stimulate a sense of shame that you didn't come to it on your own. And shame is not fun for a child, or an adult, for that matter.
>
> (Bialik, 2012, p. 156)

Dr. Bialik has also had the experience of a parent forcing her child to apologize to Dr. Bialik. Dr. Bialik (2012), page 155 through 156, states:

I was once at the park with my sons, and a three-year-old boy whom we did not know was using one of our sand toys, a small plastic block shaped like a castle. (One of my rules for our boys is that whatever we take to the park is for all the kids there to play with; if it's too special to let others play with it, leave it at home!) When it was time for this boy to go home, his mother reminded him to give back the castle, which he did by tossing it at me from a good three feet away. It landed gently at my feet and I giggled at his obedience and sweet lack of finesse that only a three-year-old can demonstrate, while inwardly noting that his mother probably didn't have that method of delivery in mind. I was right, she looked very disappointed and said to him sternly, "Say you're sorry." He mumbled a lackluster "Sorry" as I tried to open my mouth to say, "It's okay!" She didn't think he said it loud enough, so she told him to say it again and to speak louder. This made the situation even more awkward because: 1) I had heard him the first time, and 2) I did not need an apology! If he had deliberately tried to hurt me with malicious intent, I could see having a meaningful exchange about the value of empathy, but this was not the case. This was a plastic castle being returned as she had asked, just not as politely as she desired.

Since young children are just learning how to be polite, it is always better not to embarrass them by forcing them to say things they don't completely understand. Instead, say it on behalf of them and soon they will follow suit. This will also help to say these phrases when they truly mean them.

Finally, when validating children's feelings, it is important to do so when children have accidents and falls instead of rushing over and saying, "You're okay." The child may seem "okay" to us, but if he or she is crying, obviously, he or she does not feel okay. Instead, ask the child if he or she is okay. Allow the child to tell you how he or she is feeling even if the fall just frightened him or her. If the child was just frightened by the accident, then say, for example, "It scared you when you tripped. Do you need a hug?" If the child is hurt, then say, for example, "It must have hurt when you fell. Are you okay? I will get you a Band-aid (or) an ice pack to help you feel better." Do whatever your child needs you to do to help him or her feel better. Do your best to remain as calm as possible as overreacting can make children unnecessarily upset. Comforting boys and girls appropriately does *not* create wimpy children. Boys and girls have the same right to cry. As Dr. Bialik (2012), page 144, states:

> Shushing in order to stop a child from crying, and phrases like "You're okay," "Stop crying," "Big boys/girls don't cry," and "There's nothing to cry about" send a message that getting hurt and expressing your pain makes people uncomfortable. Sure, we objectively may think or even know that they are okay, but a child who falls or gets hurt is sometimes scared and startled, and she is, in her opinion, *not* okay! Crying or wanting to be held and cuddled is appropriate for both sexes. Boys and girls alike should be encouraged to express pain and discomfort without us telling them how to feel or react; it won't make them weak or "sissies." Don't we want our children to understand and care for others? Let's start with letting them express their hurt without judgment or unnecessary redirection.

Another great response to a child that has fallen is to simply ask, "Hurt? Scared? Both?" A toddler can easily answer this. Small children have big feelings. Many times toddlers do not know how to handle these big feelings and will have temper tantrums because they feel out of control. In the next section of this chapter, we will discuss how to help our children get through these meltdowns.

Small Children, Big Feelings! Dealing with Meltdowns

Toddlerhood is full of intense emotions and transitions over which they have no control. They are discovering their independence, while, at the same time, still requiring much dependence on their parents. Striking a balance between dependence and independence can be difficult for them. Plus, they still lack the vocabulary to tell us how they feel or what they want. On top of all of this, as they can finally walk, climb, and run in order to explore their world more fully, there are limits added that weren't there before, and sometimes they may not always get what they want. Yes, toddlerhood is not an easy time for toddlers. Developmentally, they cannot control their impulses. They test everything out of curiosity, *not* maliciousness. And they are egocentric, which, as I pointed out in part 3 of this book, is completely normal for this age. Yes, they are sinners, but they do *not* mean to be.

> Sometimes toddlers completely lose control. This kind of behavior is often called a tantrum. There are lots of possible reasons: over-tiredness, too much excitement; being rushed when we're in a hurry; frustration over wanting to do more than they really can.
>
> (Van der Zande, 2011, p. 71)

Sadly, on top of all I have just described that toddlers are going through, this is the age that they get spanked the most. They get punished for having big, negative emotions as they try to figure everything out. As we all know, this is the age for temper tantrums. I prefer to call them "meltdowns" as I believe "meltdown" is a more accurate description of what is happening. Guess what? Adults have meltdowns too! God does not punish us when we have meltdowns; therefore, we should not punish our children for having meltdowns either. Sometimes we may be able to prevent our children from having a full-blown meltdown by validating their feelings and giving them appropriate ways of releasing negative emotions such as punching a pillow or biting a teething ring.

> Children need rules for behavior, but their emotional responses to the limits we set (or to anything else for that matter) should be allowed, even encouraged. Toddlerhood can be a time of intense, conflicting feelings. Children may need to express anger, frustration, confusion, exhaustion and disappointment, especially if they don't get what they want because we've set a limit. A child needs the freedom to safely express his feelings without our judgment. He may need a pillow to punch—give him one.
>
> (Lansbury, 2010,
> http://www.janetlansbury.com/2010/04/no-bad-kids-
> toddler-discipline-without-shame-9-guidelines/)

Allowing simple choices, such as what color cup they'd like or if they'd like to hop, skip, or walk to the bathroom, can also help prevent meltdowns as they feel like they have more control over the situation. It is also important to tell toddlers what is expected of them. For example, if we are going to the grocery store, we need to tell our toddler what we will and will not be buying at the store. This will help them not be so disappointed when we remind them that candy wasn't on the list when we are at the store. A well-fed, well-rested, and well-loved toddler is less likely to have a meltdown. But despite everything that we may do in order to prevent toddlers from having meltdowns, there are always going to be times in which a limit has been set or a "no" has been given to something the toddler really wants and the toddler is going to get very upset and have a meltdown. As upsetting and tiring it is for us, this is a normal stage of child development for young children and is just as upsetting and tiring for them.

When a toddler is having a meltdown, it is important for us to remain as calm as possible and help the child get through the meltdown. Do not scold or punish the child because this will make the child even more upset and, in the long run, keep meltdowns going because negative attention is better than no attention. And, as we saw in chapter 12, angry and resentful children tend to act out more. "A parent screaming at a screaming child will only make matters worse" (Van der Zande, 2011, p. 74). Of course, it is just as important *not* to give in to the child having the meltdown.

> It can be tempting to give in to whatever the child wants, just to avoid a scene. Although we've all done this, it's a big mistake in the long run. If a toddler finds out that having a tantrum is a way around our limits, the child may start throwing tantrums all the time.
>
> (Van der Zande, 2011, p. 72)

Our job as parents is to allow the child to safely have the meltdown and try to help the child get through the meltdown. As Sears and Sears (1997), page 350, states:

> Our job as parents is to take a young toddler from the stage of being at the complete mercy of his emotions to a time, later in childhood, when he can manage his anger. Being angry is not the problem—Jesus had anger. So many adults never learn to control anger, so when we see it in our children it can trigger anger in us, make us very anxious and unable to help our child. The goal of Christian parents is in Ephesians 4:26, "In your anger, do not sin." Remember, the goal is to help your toddler get through a tantrum.

To help our toddlers get through meltdowns, whether we are home or in public, it is essential that we remain *calm*. This can be difficult, especially when a crowd is staring at us in a store. If you feel that you and your toddler can get through the meltdown in the store, then ignore the stares and rude comments and focus on helping your child get through the meltdown. If it helps your child to go out to the car to get through a meltdown, then go out to the car. We need to do whatever it takes to allow the meltdown to pass. During meltdowns, speak calmly and quietly to the child. Say, for example, "You're very upset right now. I will remain close by until you calm down. After you calm down, it will be lunch time." Some children need to be held during meltdowns; others need space. Respect these needs. However, do not allow the toddler to hurt him/herself, others, or materials during the meltdown. Say, for example, "I won't let you hit." But try not to say too much during the meltdown as it may agitate them even more.

> In this situation, we can give the toddler space to kick and cry, while making it clear that we won't let anybody get hurt. "You can lie on the pillows and kick, but I won't let you kick me." And we can let the child know what will happen when the upset behavior is stopped. "When you're finished screaming, we'll get some dry pants and you can go play."
>
> (Van der Zande, 2011, p. 72)

A professor of mine loved to tell the story of a teenage girl that would babysit a toddler. One day the teen took the toddler to the park. When it was time for them to go home so that they could eat lunch, the toddler had a meltdown because she didn't want to go home. The teen remained calm and simply told the toddler that as soon as she finished having her fit that they would go home and have lunch. The toddler calmed down and they went home and ate lunch.

Another example of a parent remaining calm during a meltdown was when my professor took her four-year-old daughter to the mall and her daughter wanted my professor to buy her a toy. My professor told her daughter no. Of course, her daughter got upset and said, "If you don't buy me that toy, I'll scream!" My professor calmly said, "Well, I'm still not going to buy you the toy." So, her daughter began screaming. My professor ignored her and kept going about her business. Seeing that screaming was getting her absolutely nowhere, the four-year-old soon stopped screaming and never pulled that stunt again. As I said, even negative attention will often keep meltdowns going in the long run. Being firm but gentle will help children outgrow having constant meltdowns as we teach them more appropriate ways of dealing with and expressing emotions.

> Young children grow out of becoming so upset that they lose control of their bodies. As they get older, they learn to use words to express feelings. They become able to do more for themselves and to find choices that work for them.
>
> (Van der Zande, 2011, p. 74)

We must being willing to allow our children to show us their big negative feelings without us judging them. "Global critical comments create anxiety because they make the child believe he or she is intrinsically bad. 'You are bad'; 'Dummy'; 'You are so stubborn;' 'You never listen' are common examples" (Lieberman, 1993, p. 139).

At the end of a meltdown, it is okay to talk to the child about more appropriate ways of dealing with their anger. If they made a mess during the meltdown, have them help you clean it up. This should *not* be a punishment. Make it fun. Also, right after the meltdown, pray with your toddler to help him or her feel God's peace within him or her.

> You can end the scene on a spiritual note, with an offer to pray with your child. Our little ones welcome prayers

as a way to regroup, as though sensing God's blessing and forgiveness—a sense of having a fresh start.

(Sears & Sears, 1997, p. 351)

I also recommend singing a favorite Christian song after the meltdown. Children must learn that God loves them *no matter what*, and we do too!

Time-IN Not Out!

Many parents use "Time-Out" to punish their children, especially parents that do not want to spank but feel that they must punish or "discipline" their children somehow. While I would much rather have parents that are bent on punishment use time-out over spanking, time-out is still harmful to young children when it is used as punishment. As with spanking, time-out is most often used with very young children. The youngest child that I have witnessed with whom a time-out was being used was eighteen months old. Like being slapped, eighteen-month-olds do not understand why they are being forced to sit alone for one minute. And like spanking, it very temporarily stopped the behavior, which means multiple time-outs for toddlers that lack impulse control. This is not good and sends the wrong message to children.

Time-outs require that children sit alone, sometimes facing the wall, quietly for the amount of minutes corresponding with their age. For example, if the child is one, they sit for one minute; for a two-year-old, it's two minutes; for a three-year-old, it's three minutes, and so on. What's even worse is if the child gets up, talks, or even cries during the time-out, then their time starts completely over until he or she "successfully" completes the time-out. This can mean a five-minute or more time-out for a toddler that cannot fulfill the requirements of a time-out. As with physical punishment, I'm afraid that whoever came up with the time-out and its associated rules did not understand child development, nor did they understand our loving God. Christ never banished anyone. So why should we banish our children when we can't deal with their behaviors? Young children cannot sit still and quietly with nothing to do for very long. And they are not sitting there pondering why what they did was wrong. Time-outs are totally developmentally inappropriate for young children and sets them up for failure. As Dr. Bialik (2012), page 182 through 183, states:

> However, this teaches the child nothing about *why* the behavior was unwelcome, nor does it give motivation to internalize why to stop. Now, I know that parents do tend to tell children why they are being put in a time-out, and I also know that 'You're going to get a time-out!' is heard as often at our local park as 'Mommy, I need to pee.' But the use of a threat of being alone and crying is not the motivation we want for our children to behave well, or to follow the rules and expectations we have of them. We want them to behave in a certain way because it feels right, makes sense to them, and makes for positive interactions with everyone around them.

As with spanking, time-outs teach children that they are "bad" and deserve to be in isolation. Being in isolation is very scary and difficult for young children that desperately need our support and guidance.

> You confirm what she suspected—she is a bad person. Not only does this lower self-esteem, it creates bad behavior, because people who feel bad about themselves behave badly. As Otto Weininger, Ph.D. author of *Time-In Parenting* says: *"Sending children away to get control of their anger perpetuates the feeling of 'badness' inside them...Chances are they were already feeling not very good about themselves*

before the outburst and the isolation just serves to confirm in
their own minds that they were right."

(Markham, 2012, http://www.ahaparenting.com/
parenting-tools/positive-discipline/timeouts)

Another thing time-out does is to set up an adversarial
parent-child relationship. As with physical punishment, the goal
of a time-out is to teach the child who's boss.

They set up a relationship that pits you and your authority
against the child. It's true that as long as the parent is
bigger than the child, the parent wins this power struggle,
but no one ever really wins in a parent-child power
struggle. The child loses face and has plenty of time to sit
around fantasizing revenge. (Did you really think she was
resolving to be a better kid?)

(Markham, 2012, http://www.ahaparenting.com/
parenting-tools/positive-discipline/timeouts)

I also believe that using any type of punishment with our
children not only erodes their empathy, but also our empathy for
them. I find it very difficult to listen to a crying child and not
offer any comfort to that child. Dr. Bialik (2012), page 182, has
had this same experience as she states:

I can often identify a child who is having a time-out first
by the sound of screaming. When I identify the locus of
the screaming, I typically have observed a child in a chair
in the corner of a restaurant or at the park or in a car seat,
alone and sobbing and usually facing a wall. The parent is
often close by, looking appropriately concerned and often
murmuring reminders that this is because the child did
so-and-so, and she can come back when the time is up or
when she stops crying. By this point in my observations,
I often tend to start crying as well. The sight and sound

of a crying child being forced to be alone in his sadness is something that really bugs me and makes me feel very bad for both the child and the parents who think this is the way to get their child to behave in a certain way. I cannot leave small children alone with emotions they don't yet know how to handle, no matter how uncomfortable I am with the emotions it brings up for me.

We want to teach young children how to handle their big emotions in a healthy, helpful way. We also want to teach young children how to behave appropriately. As we have seen throughout this book, punishment most often leads our children into more sin and does not help them internalize the lessons that we want them to learn. Dara found this out with her children as she and her husband made the change from using punishment to actually disciplining their children. On May 14, 2012, Dara conveyed the following to me in an electronic message:

> The main social event for my family of eight kids was Tuesday and Thursday nights at the youth center playing soccer. Three of my older kids liked going, and then there were two of the younger ones—ages eight and six—who also liked going.
>
> So, one Tuesday night neighbor kids were all showing up to go along as usual and my house was all abuzz with everyone getting ready to go. Something happened and my eight-year-old, Josh, got mad at his younger sister, Evelyn, and hit her.
>
> My husband took over, dealing with the situation, and the way I am is that if he gets to it first I try to not "interfere" so there is just one person talking to whoever is getting talked to. I figure that's less intimidating and less confusing for the child. So, I sat nearby and was just "observing."
>
> We had just made the change that year from spanking to not spanking and I had been doing a lot of reading

about punishment and it's ineffectiveness, but you can't just read something and change one day to the next so we were "in process" at this point.

As I watched the situation happening, I was watching my eight-year-old son's eyes. Dad was talking to him about what he'd just done and why it's wrong to hit your little sister. Then, my husband said something that changed the whole situation. He told him he was being punished, "And so, you're not going along to the youth center tonight." It was then that all the stuff I'd been reading on paper came into focus right before me in real life.

As I watched, Josh's eyes changed. His whole countenance changed. His posture and his movements changed. He went from looking calm and remorseful for hitting his sister and disappointing his dad to utter panic. I could see that every cell in his body was focused on one thing: "I am not allowed to go to the youth center!"

Now, I don't like arguing in front of the kids about "discipline" but I also don't think that for them to see us working through things and changing our minds together is bad so I said, "Dad, wait! Wait! Stop! You need to tell him that he can still go tonight because you lost him. He's not hearing a word you are saying anymore." Trusting me, my husband told him he took it back and he was still allowed to go, and I kept watching Josh and I could see him change back again. As the seconds passed it was as though the stress and panic was visibly draining from him and his eyes and his countenance and his movements all returned to calm and he again focused on my husband. Then, he was hearing what my husband was saying again and told his sister he was sorry all on his own.

A lot of parents would have scolded us for "letting him get away with something" by taking the punishment back after he started to react to it. They would have seen that as rebellion. But, our goal was not to "hurt" our child, but for him to understand that hitting his sister was not acceptable. And, punishment is pain. The pain of the punishment, like all pain in any situation, rose to the top of my son's focal attention. No matter how much he wanted to listen to his dad and no matter how much he agreed that hitting his sister was bad, he was distracted by the pain of the punishment and that became his sole focus. It is the nature of pain because pain is supposed to get our attention and punishment hurts, therefore, it wins. It gets the attention because it requires it. So, adding "pain" to the situation when Josh hit Evelyn only served to take Josh's mind and focus it squarely on his pain and off of what we really wanted to teach him. And, now I not only have read this on paper, I have seen this happening in my own children with my own two eyes.

Instead of punishment, children need discipline and guidance. This is where "Time-*In*" can be very useful. Time-in, unlike time-out, is *not* punishment. To use time-in with young children, set up a "comfy corner" in the most lived in room of your house. The "comfy corner" should contain soft pillows and chairs, blankets, stuffed animals, and a few favorite books. The "comfy corner" should be away from the main action of the room but not isolated in any manner. When your toddler is having a hard time with his or her feelings and complying, the "comfy corner" can allow your child (and you) to decompress. It should be a safe, welcoming place to express big feelings, while receiving comfort. Toddlers are *not forced* to go to their "comfy corners" and may choose whether or not they want their parents to accompany them. While in the "comfy corner" pillows can be punched and/or kicked and/or hugged, stuffed animals can be held tightly, books can be read, songs can be sung, and prayers can be prayed. The purpose is to calm down. Even if the child chooses to go to his/her "comfy corner" alone, the parent is still nearby and can offer support to the child.

When you realize your child is getting to that dangerous over-wrought place, suggest that the two of you take a

"Time *In*." This signals to your child that you understand she's got some big emotions going on and you're right there with her. If she's just a bit wound-up and wants to snuggle or even read a book, fine. If she's ready for a meltdown, you're there to help. Just let her know you're there and she's safe.

(Markham, 2012, http://www.ahaparenting.com/
parenting-tools/positive-discipline/timeouts)

If we use time-in consistently without forcing the toddler to go to his or her "comfy corner," the toddler may begin to ask to go there when he or she senses his or her big feelings welling up. Toddlers learn that their feelings matter to their parents and to God. This is such an important step for teaching young children self-management skills because their feelings are validated and respected, and they are given appropriate choices for dealing with their feelings.

Now, for parents, as with infants, there are times when toddlers are having a particularly tough day and are having their fifth meltdown of the day. A parent "time-out" is very appropriate for these types of situations so that you don't lose it with your child. This is *not* punishment for either the parent or the child. All parents need a break from their children.

If you have older children, you can simply say you are having a hard time and need a moment to gather yourself. Some people add that they feel out of control and do not want to do or say something that would hurt their child, but that should be done only with a child who can comprehend this kind of discussion. You then need to either physically take a moment or hone the skill of taking a time-out in the child's presence, using breathing techniques or some sort of mantra or short meditation.

(Bialik, 2012, p. 191)

Praying truly is a must during a parent "time-out." Allow God to fill you with His peace that surpasses all understanding (Philippians 4:7).

For a toddler, we can simply say to them, "I need a break. I am going to the bathroom, and then I will hold you again." If you can, leave your child with your spouse so the toddler isn't being left alone. If this is not possible, you will have to go to the bathroom as your toddler follows you, most likely crying. Gently close your bathroom door as you reassure your toddler that you will be right out. Turn the water on in the sink and breathe deeply. Pray to God for help, strength, and peace. Pray for your child, who is right outside the door screaming, that God will fill him or her with peace. After you pray, say aloud to yourself, "My child will grow out of this." And while you're in the bathroom alone, take this opportunity to use the toilet. All of this should take less than five minutes and should only be done when absolutely necessary. When you open the bathroom door, smile at your child so he or she knows this wasn't his or her fault and that you're now ready to help him or her again. Now, if someone is able to take over with your child, I suggest getting out of the house for a bit. Being a good parent means taking care of yourself as much as possible. Our goal is to teach our children that God is the God of comfort, and that He will comfort us in order that we may comfort each other—"who comforts us in all our troubles, so that we can comfort those in any trouble with the comfort we ourselves receive from God" (2 Corinthians 1:4).

Conclusion

We have seen how important it is to validate children's feelings from birth onward. This, after all, is what God does for us. We have also seen that toddlers have big feelings that they cannot control. They need us to provide support and comfort when they are having meltdowns instead of scolding and punishment. They also need us not to give in when they are having meltdowns. Time-ins are a wonderful way to help young children calm down when they are out of control. Finally, I need to mention how important not labeling young children is based on typical toddler and preschooler behavior. "Terrible twos" is a common label for toddlers. "Little sinners" is common among Christians. These labels are quite harmful to children and can last a lifetime. They often become self-fulfilling prophesies for a great deal of children.

> What I've learned, from my son, my siblings, and various kids that I've cared for over the years is that *children listen to authority figures.* It may not always seem like it, but they do. Your words are imprinted on their psyche. And try as you might, a two year old is not going to grasp the doctrine of total depravity. So telling him that he has been a "bad, bad boy" (actual quote I recently overheard at kiddie class) is absurd, perplexing, and psychologically detrimental. Telling a little one that they are bad won't stem unwanted behavior. It will, however, create tiny fissures in a whole spirit. These fault lines, with added pressure, slowly come together as a child's naturally positive self-perception— and your relationship with him—crumbles.
>
> (Rach, 2012, http://theincorrigiblegingers.blogspot. com/2012/04/my-toddler-is-not-bad.html)

We need to love our children as God loves us. "See what great love the Father has lavished on us, that we should be called children of God! And that is what we are!" (1 John 3:1a).

References

Bialik, M. (2012). *Beyond the Sling.* New York, NY: Touchstone.

Fogel, A. (2011). *Infant Development: A Topical Approach.* Hudson, NY: Sloan Publishing.

Freeman, L. (2012). Did You Ever Learn to Self-Soothe? http://realchilddevelopment.com/inspiration/did-you-ever-learn-to-self-soothe

Gerber, M. & Weaver, J. (2002). *Dear Parent: Caring for Infants with Respect.* (Expanded ed.). Los Angeles, CA: RIE.

Gonzales-Mena, J. (September 2004). What Can an Orphanage Teach Us? Lessons from Budapest. *Beyond the Journal Young Children on the Web.* http://www.naeyc.org/yc/pastissues/2004/september

Kuzma, K. (2006). *The First 7 Years.* West Frankfort, IL: Three Angels Broadcasting Network.

Lansbury, J. (2010). No Bad Kids: Toddler Discipline Without Shame 9 Guidelines http://www.janetlansbury.com/2010/04/no-bad-kids-toddler-discipline-without-shame-9-guidelines/

Lawrence, M. (2012). The Grace that Validates. http://sermonseedbed.com/the-grace-that- validates-devotional/

Lieberman, A. F. (1993). *The Emotional Life of the Toddler.* New York, NY: The Free Press.

Lutton, C. (2001). *Biblical Parenting.* Salt Lake City, UT: Millennial Mind Publishing.

Markham, L. (2012). What's Wrong with Time Out? http://www.ahaparenting.com/parenting-tools/positive-discipline/timeouts Rach. (2012). My Toddler is Not Bad. http://theincorrigiblegingers.blogspot.com/2012/04/my-toddler-is-not-bad.html

Sears, W. & Sears, M. (1997). *The Complete Book of Christian Parenting and Child Care.* Nashville, TN: Broadman & Holman Publishers.

Van der Zande, I. (2011). *1, 2, 3… The Toddler Years.* Santa Cruz, CA: Santa Cruz Toddler Center.

Chapter 19

Limits, Encouragement, and Consequences

Throughout this part of the book, we are discussing ways of disciplining children that are more in line with what God had in mind. All of the discipline strategies in this part are very effective when used consistently and in conjunction with each other. They are all biblically supported and sound. And none of these methods, when used properly and respectfully, will ever cause any harm to children. In this chapter, we will look at how to set appropriate limits and boundaries for our children by which they can abide. We will see that allowing children simple choices and giving appropriate alternatives for inappropriate behaviors also help children comply with our limits and boundaries. Next, we will see why using encouragement with our children is better than using rewards and praise. Finally, we will discuss using natural and logical consequences with children. Consequences are not the same as punishment. And discipline should *not* be equated with punishment.

Setting Limits and Boundaries—
"Three Basic Rules for Life"

We all need limits and boundaries in our lives for without them life would be very chaotic. This is especially true for children as this world is too overwhelming for them to handle on their own. Children feel most secure when they know what the limits and boundaries are. In fact, young children will test limits and boundaries to make sure that the adults in their lives will enforce them.

> Children need secure, loving boundaries in order to feel safe, just as adults need a house with strong walls and a roof to feel protected from the weather. Still, any self-respecting child will feel obliged to cruise up to the boundaries you've set and test them occasionally, just to make sure they're firmly in place. He's not deliberately trying to drive you insane; he's either exploring at his age-appropriate level or learning about consistency and whether or not adults mean what they say (another version of trust).
>
> (Nielsen, Erwin, & Duffy, 2007, p. 44)

Toddlers are extremely good at testing limits and boundaries. Despite what many Christian "experts" may claim, toddlers are not being "evil" or "sinful" by testing limits. This is developmentally appropriate for young children to do. They are learning about their world by exploring limits and boundaries. "Toddlers test limits to find out about themselves and other people. By stopping children in a firm but respectful way when they push our limits, we're helping them to figure out their world and to feel safe" (Van der Zande, 2011, p. 18).

Sadly, many Christians see toddlers pushing and testing limits as sinful. They feel their toddlers' wills must be broken or else there is no hope for them to grow up to be godly adults.

As I have pointed out throughout this book, children do not intentionally sin as adults do. Yes, an eighteen-month-old will smile as he or she is reaching for a forbidden object, but this is how God created toddlers to behave during this particular developmental stage. They are making sure that we will hold firm to the limits and boundaries in a playful way. It is important that we Christians understand that while sin affects every part of our lives, that sin can also make us misunderstand our children's intentions. As Nielsen, Erwin, and Duffy (2007), page 45, state:

> Adults mistakenly read motives—that is, intent—into children's behavior that reflect adult thinking rather than childish thinking. Some act as though their child lies awake at night plotting ways to drive them crazy. Martha's repeated warnings to her son not to touch things aren't terribly effective; kind, firm action would be more helpful. Toddlers are highly impulsive little people, and the warnings are simply overpowered by the desire to touch, hold, and explore. A toddler straining over the edge of his stroller to touch a shiny cup on the store shelf does not intend to disobey. The fact that this cup is at the bottom of a highly breakable pyramid of cups has no special meaning for him. The colors on the cup attract his attention; he reaches for it and wants to examine it. He is a mad scientist using his hands, mouth, and imperfect coordination to determine the properties of the marvelous world around him. Your real tasks as a parent are prevention, vigilance—and very quick reflexes.

I love what one of my good friends always says. She points out that limits and boundaries should be firm yet stretchy so that when children run up against them, they give a little and are comfortable, but do not allow children to break through them nor do they cause pain for them.

When it comes to setting limits and boundaries for young children, there are three basic rules on which all boundaries and limits should be based. The first rule is respect for others. The second rule is respect for ourselves. The third rule is respect for property. And if we think about it, these three rules encompass much of what Christ said in His Sermon on the Mount. If you wish to add a fourth basic rule, we could say reverence of God. The reason why we should only have three or four basic rules on which to base limits and boundaries is that giving children too many rules to follow, especially at a young age, will only frustrate and overwhelm them. These basic rules are easy to understand and will make sense to children, though young children will require much guidance and reminders to help them comply with these.

It is important that while boundaries and limits are a bit flexible that they are consistent and hold firm. Some parents may set boundaries and limits based on the three or four basic rules, but then they allow their children to break right through them.

> As children grow, many parents fail them by not knowing how to maintain a consistent, reliable environment. During the toddler years, children ask, "How much of the world is mine to control? Where are my boundaries?" Children find it frightening when parents fail to establish limits or are inconsistent in their enforcement and allow children too much control. Unconsciously, children reason, "If I'm the strongest person in my world, who's going to watch out for me? Who's going to protect me?" So, insecurity sets in. And knowing that their skills are limited, children try to control their environment by acting out.
>
> (Kuzma, 2006, p. 157)

Therefore, when we set a limit or boundary for our children, we must be able to enforce it consistently.

Tine, a mother of two young children, conveyed to me in an electronic message on June 14, 2012, how she found out firsthand that young children desire boundaries. She writes concerning her daughter:

> I took her out on a hot day, to the fruit shop. She wanted an icypole, a fair enough request, so we went to the milkbar first. Then the icypole had to be eaten at the park across the road, and no amount of talking, telling her it was dangerous to cross the road there, not safe to sit in front of the milkbar refusing to get in the car, had any effect. I lost patience, and in the end gave up, got "T" back out of the car, put him in the Ergo and walked them across the road to the park.
>
> She played. For hours. It got late and the fruit shop would soon close. I gave her some lead-ins, "One more play on the castle then we are going to the fruit shop," "The fruit shop is going to close so we have to go now..." Eventually she came. And walked at a snail's pace, examining every flower and stone.
>
> Then she started down a slope toward a steep drop to the golf course. "Stop," I said, "that's dangerous!" "Time to go to the fruit shop you can walk or I can carry you." She looked at me, a clear challenge, and took off to the drop. That was my limit. With "T" in the ergo on my front, I picked her up with her screeching, wailing, and kicking violently. Sweat running down my face, I carried her under my arm, "T" quite amused, "F" practicing her possessed banshee impersonation.
>
> I walked the half-kilometer or so to the fruit shop like this, stopping to unpeel her fingers from a fence we passed. At the fruit shop I offered her a plant, but the protests continued. I gave her a basket and asked her to help, but the tantrum shifted to the corner of the shop. I started collecting fruit. Suddenly she stopped. A little voice, "Shall we get some lemons, Mummy?" YES! Get a thousand

lemons! The relief! We shopped in quiet co-operation, and I never felt the need to say a word more about it.

Her relationship with me shifted then, vastly for the better. I had to carry her off with me on two other occasions, but the protesting was mild and very token. I think the trick is simply to know your child. She was pushing me to set a boundary for her and when I did, in a way that was utterly free of blame or castigation and that was a natural consequence of the situation, she seemed to feel relieved and could relax. Our relationship rebuilt after that, and she has no more intense or frequent tantrums now that most three-year-olds do.

Another thing that we must remember when setting limits and boundaries with our children is to make sure the limits and boundaries are logical and reasonable. If the limit does not make any sense to the child, he or she is more likely to fight the limit. Most children will comply with limits and boundaries if they know there is a good reason for them. Many parents feel that they don't have to give a reason for a limit. And we have all heard the "Because I said so" line from either our own parents or others' parents. I remember getting so angry as a child whenever my parents said, "Because I said so" to me. It didn't make me want to comply with them at all. Most children feel this way. They truly want to know the reason for the limit that is being imposed on them. I believe mutual respect dictates that we supply even the youngest child with a simple reason for a limit. An example would be "Please walk in the house so you don't trip and fall." Dr. Kuzma (2006), page 372, explains:

> Whether or not children keep the rules has a lot to do with how reasonable they are and whether or not the rules can be remembered. Reasonable rules are almost always principle-based. Although young children may not always understand why rules are important, it's important to tell

them. For example, "It's important to keep your room clean because being organized and having everything in its place is a valuable lesson to help you be successful in whatever you do." Or, "When you put your toys back where they belong, you can always find them."

Not only do providing simple, logical reasons make it more likely that children will comply with our limits and boundaries, but so does telling them what *to do* instead of telling them what not to do. For example, saying, "Be gentle with your baby brother," is often more effective than saying, "Don't hit." Another example is saying, "Walking feet," instead of saying, "Don't run." Parents say "No" and "Don't" and "Stop" so often to their young children that the children begin to tune their parents out. Tine has two young children and has found this to be very true. On June 14, 2012, Tine conveyed the following to me in an electronic message:

> I noticed at one point when she was about two that I was saying no, no, no, no all day, and as soon as I made an effort to change that she responded by being more easy to be around. The other day I was at the playground with the kids and chatted to a grandmother who was there with her two grandkids, a girl of two and a boy the same age as "F." She was a kind woman and clearly adored her grandchildren, but I noticed that everything was "no" or "don't." "F" and the little boy ran off to the cricket nets, now closed off for winter. Grandma shouted, "No, 'A,' no! Don't go in there! No!" "A" continued on his merry way through a gap in the fence and straight into the nets. I called out, "Stop 'F'!" and she did immediately (because I only used "stop" when it's important), then I walked over to her and explained that there's broken glass in there so it's not safe to go in. She didn't. If I have to say "no" or "don't," I try to always say what I do want her to do instead. On that occasion I said, "Let's go back to the playground" and all of us did.

Obviously, Tine's daughter knew to listen to her mom because she doesn't constantly hear "No," "Don't," and "Stop" all the time. Even if we have no choice but to phrase something negatively, it is very important to follow it with something positive that they *can* do. For example, say, "You may not draw on the wall, but you may draw on this piece of paper." This sets an appropriate limit while telling the child what he or she can do. It is frustrating for children if all they hear is what they can't do without ever hearing what they can do. Adults tend to assume that young children will know what is appropriate after being told what is inappropriate, but this just isn't the case as they are only beginning to learn how to navigate their world. As I discussed in chapter 18, just as they need appropriate ways to act out their negative feelings, they also need appropriate behaviors to replace the inappropriate ones.

Some Christian "experts" often teach parents that first time obedience should always be expected from children beginning at young ages. First time obedience is when children obey the first time a command is given. While this may sound like a wonderful thing, it is completely developmentally inappropriate to expect children to be obedient the first time. What these Christians do not understand is that young children's brains take longer to process things, especially when children are engrossed in an activity—which is a *good* thing. For example, it can take infants and toddlers up to twenty-five seconds to process new stimuli—including verbalizations (Greenwald, 2008). This is called Tarry Time. It is important to give children time to process what we are saying to them. And, often, it is necessary to repeat what we have said to them. This is perfectly normal and okay. Dr. Kuzma (2006), page 357, gives the perfect example of using what she calls "The Broken Record Strategy" with her two-year-old grandson:

> I used a modified broken record strategy with my two-year-old grandchild and was surprised how successful it

was. He wasn't trying to divert my attention with questions; he was ignoring my requests. Here's what happened. Levi had found a lollipop that I thought was hidden. He was sucking on it by the time I noticed. I knew if I took it away too quickly I was facing a possible tantrum. Instead, I waited a few minutes until it was nap time and I could offer a good reason to give it up. I held him on my lap with a plastic cup in one hand. "Levi," I said cheerfully. "It's time for a nap. Please put your lollipop in the cup." He sat there as if he didn't hear me. "Levi, it's nap time. Please put the lollipop in the cup so you don't get the blanket sticky." He sat there. "Levi, put the lollipop in the cup. I'll put the cup right here beside the bed. It will be here when you wake up." And without a protest, he took the lollipop out of his mouth and put it in the cup. If only it were always that easy.

She allowed her grandson time to process her request, gave him a good reason for the limit, and reassured him that the lollipop would still be there when he woke up. This allowed him to eventually willingly comply with her. "Parents of young children need to remember not to push for compliance too quickly, or they may end up getting increased resistance unnecessarily" (Kuzma, 2006, p. 357). People who say that they have children who obey the first time are not aware of the harm that must be done in order to force children to obey the first time all the time. As scientific research has shown, children are incapable of this without brain damage being done to them in order to get them to always obey the first time. Now, I understand that there are times when we need our children to comply with us immediately. When this is necessary, we should simply tell our children that this is something we must do right now. Older children will usually know from our tone of voice that they need to comply right away. But, for a younger child, be prepared to help them comply. They don't mean to disobey; it is just very difficult for most young children to make transitions quickly. Also, giving children lead times will help make it easier for them to comply. Say, for example, "In five minutes it will be time to clean up and get ready for bed." Be sure to get on the child's level and say this. In fact, getting on children's level whenever a limit or boundary is being set will help the child feel respected, making compliance and cooperation more likely.

Giving simple choices when setting limits and boundaries when possible aids in getting young children to comply. "Of course, it's important to set limits. At the same time, offering choices wherever possible within these limits gives even very young children the feeling that they have control" (Van der Zande, 2011, p. 4-5). I used this with what most Christians would call a "strong-willed" toddler with which I once worked. She was happily playing in the sensory table with sand when she began throwing sand out of the table. I told her to keep the sand in the table so no one would trip on it. She threw more sand out of the table, and once again I told her she needed to keep the sand in the table. This time she looked me in the eye, testing me. She threw a small amount of sand out of the table a third time. "E," I said, "you know better. Either you keep the sand in the table or you will need to choose another activity." She stared at me for a moment and then she chose to go play somewhere else. She wanted to make sure I would stand firm in the limit that I was giving her, and allowing her to choose between complying or playing somewhere else ultimately helped her to control her behavior. It worked many times after that as well.

While giving simple choices when possible is always a good thing, sometimes parents give limits in question form, thus, giving the child the impression that the limit or boundary is a choice when it really is not. An example of this is asking the child, "Do you want to get ready for bed now?" The child is likely to answer, "No!" Since getting ready for bed is not a choice, it is better to say, "It's time to get ready for bed. Do you want to walk or hop to the bathroom?"

Van der Zande (2011), page 6, states:

> To toddlers, these polite "fake" questions can be confusing and upsetting. If we ask a happily playing toddler, "Are you ready to take your nap now?" she's sure to yell, "No!" If we're not sure a child will cooperate, we sometimes soften our statements by adding, "Okay?" as in "I'm going to leave now. Okay?" By making this a question, we give the child a choice we really didn't mean to offer. It's possible to say something clearly and still give a choice; for example, "It's time for you to take a nap now. Do you want to bring the book with you or leave it here?"

When we do give a simple choice, we need to remember, as with compliance with a request, to allow children time to process and decide.

> Just like adults, young children may need a moment to make up their minds. It's important, when offering a choice, to give a child a chance to think. If the child has trouble making a decision, we can repeat the choices. "Do you want to wear your sweater or your jacket?" If the child can't decide after a reasonable period of time, it's time to take charge: "I'll help you choose so we can leave. Here's your jacket."

(Van der Zande, 2011, p. 6-7)

God gives us limits which we can obey that keep us safe and healthy. But none of His limits are arbitrary or difficult to follow thanks to what Christ did for us on the cross. And God will always help us obey Him when we ask. Look at what Jesus says in Matthew 11:30: "For my yoke is easy and my burden is light." Also, 1 Corinthians 10:13 states, "No temptation has overtaken you except what is common to mankind. And God is faithful; he will not let you be tempted beyond what you can bear. But when you are tempted, he will also provide a way out so that you can endure it." These verses from Matthew and 1 Corinthians mean that God never places unnecessary limits and boundaries on us. He is our perfect Father and does not want to frustrate us. He, in fact, will help carry some of our loads if we allow Him to do so. This is how we ought to be with our children when setting limits and boundaries for them. As Dr. Kuzma (2006), page 331, states:

> Your goal as a strong, gentle parent is to have your children obey you because they love you, not because they fear you. You can't have limits without love or love without limits! God set the standard: "For whom the LORD loves He corrects, just as a father the son in whom he delights" (Proverbs 3:12, NKJV).

Finally, when it comes to setting limits and boundaries with children, it is important to allow children to appropriately voice their objections even if we can't negotiate on a limit or boundary. As I wrote in chapter 18, we must hear children's negative feelings and validate them. God does this for us. He listens to us and validates us even though He may not change His mind. He wants us to test the spirits to make sure it is really Him speaking to us (1 John 4:1-3). We need to follow God's example and do the same for our children. "Thoughtful, respectful, cooperative— Yes, absolutely. Kids grow up that way when we listen to their thoughts, treat them with respect, and invite cooperation by working together on solutions" (Markham, 2012, http://us2. campaign-archive.com/?u=775b94b440ad73397931a9ad7&id=e aa90025f5).

How do we respond when our children comply with us? In the next section we will see why encouragement and affirmations are better than praise and rewards.

Encouragement Vs. Praises—
"Do Not Love the Praises of Men"

Many Christian "experts" in child rearing teach parents to use praise and rewards with their children for "good" behavior, but using praise and rewards with children constantly for "good" behavior actually gives children the wrong message. While the Bible does say that believers that do their best to do God's will on Earth will receive a reward in heaven, the Bible also says not to love the praises of men (John 12:43). When it comes to life on Earth, God's Word says we are not to do things out of needing people's approval. We are to be humble in all that we do as Galatians 1:10 states: "Am I now trying to win the approval of human beings, or of God? Or am I trying to please people? If I were still trying to please people, I would not be a servant of Christ." The Apostle Paul clearly understood that in order to truly serve Christ, he could no longer be concerned with pleasing other people.

Now, it is completely natural for children to want to please their parents, and this is a good thing. However, we often hear very well-meaning parents say to their children, "Good girl or boy!" Or, "Good job!" The problem with these types of statements is that they are actually degrading to children as they are not animals, but little people. It sends the message to children that they are only "good" when they are pleasing their parents. But what about when children are having a bad day or aren't happy? Are they still "good" then? I believe children are always "good" even if they are doing something "bad." Also, many people commonly ask new parents if they have a "good" baby. Aren't *all* babies "good?" Yes, some children are easy while others are difficult, but all children are good. God gives us His love, grace, and mercy unconditionally even though we sin against Him all the time. He does not wait for us to perform before He blesses us. Therefore, we should not tell our children that they are "good" only when they please us. And since God is the only one worthy of praise, we should not get in the habit of praising our children for every little thing that they do. For example, I know a person who was given a lot of praise growing up, and this person still struggles with the need to have constant praise for everything. Therefore, encouragement and affirmation is better so that children don't feel the need to hear praise for doing well. They should know that they are loved and good in our eyes no matter what, just as God does with us. Lutton (2001), page 37, states:

> If we withhold our love when our children do something that doesn't please us, they will see God as withholding His love and they will fear losing their salvation. If you have either of these views of God yourself I encourage you to read His Word and see that He is a God who loves us sacrificially and unconditionally and "when we are faithless, He remains faithful; for He cannot deny Himself" (2 Timothy 2:13).

Another thing that we do when we provide children with a lot of praises and rewards when they perform how we want them to is that we teach them to do things just to get the praises and rewards. Since God is concerned with our hearts and motives for why we do things, He does not want us to obey Him just to get a reward. He also does not want us to obey Him out of fear. We need to teach our children to do things because it's right, not out of fear or the desire for praise and reward. Look at what Jesus says about the Pharisees in John 12:42-43:

> Yet at the same time many even among the leaders believed in him. But because of the Pharisees they would not openly acknowledge their faith for fear they would be put out of the synagogue; for they loved human praise more than praise from God.

They wanted human approval more than they wanted God's approval. Also, God does not want us to compare ourselves with others (Galatians 6:4), and I believe too much praise and reward in childhood can lead people to compare themselves and what they have with others. Giving children a lot of praise and reward is not biblical.

So, if we are not supposed to praise each other, but instead, encourage one another, you may be asking, "Why do so many Christian 'experts' on child rearing teach parents to give children praise and rewards?" It goes back to them using behaviorism, which I explained in great detail in chapter 9. Behaviorism uses positive and negative reinforcements to control children's behavior. If we give a child or an animal positive reinforcement through the use of praise and reward, then it is more likely that the child or animal will continue doing a desired behavior. Therefore, these Christian "experts" of child rearing have somehow turned an outdated branch of psychology into something they claim as biblically supported child rearing.

Now that we know why we shouldn't use much praise and reward with our children, let's discuss using encouragement and affirmations with them.

Encouragement and affirmations focus on the child's actions rather than using global comments and labels about the child. For example, if your child picks up the blocks, instead of saying, "Good boy/girl," or "Good job," say, "Thank you for picking up your blocks! That was very helpful!" Another example is if your child draws a picture, say, for example, "Wow! You used a lot of bright colors!" By focusing on the actions of children, we are encouraging and affirming them. Praise does not do this, but instead, focuses mainly on *who* the child is, rather than on *what* they have accomplished. Tine does this with her daughter. In an electronic message dated June 14, 2012, Tine writes:

> I have always been always concerned about the effect of language on children, and naming what she's doing rather than saying "good girl" (she's not a dog!) seems to really

have been effective. She's great at picking up on things she does well now, and lately in others too. This evening she wanted to hop in the bath with "T," so I said, "Could you please put your clothes in the laundry basket?" She said, "You asked really nicely, Mum" and put them in the basket! She also says things like "T's doing some really good jumping" which I find very encouraging!

Research has proven that the use of encouragement and affirmations is better for children than praise. Carol Dweck from Stanford University has been studying children's coping and resilience mechanisms for forty years. The last fourteen years she has focused on her suspicions as to what may be causing children to become less resilient in recent years. She believes that praise is the culprit. Her latest research study entitled "Parent Praise" is a longitudinal study where researchers observed and coded parental praise of children between the ages of fourteen to thirty-eight months. They checked back in with the children when they were seven to eight years old to see how the praise had affected them. This study found that what Dweck calls "process praise" is much better for children than person based praise.

> "The parents who gave more process-praise had children who believe their intelligence and social qualities could be developed and they were more eager for challenges," Dr. Dweck told me.
>
> In her previous research, she's showed that praising children for their intelligence or abilities often undermines motivation and hurts performance. Kids who are told they are smart care more about performance goals and less about learning. Kids praised for their efforts believe that trying hard, not being smart, matters. These kids are "resilient" and take more risks.
>
> (Anderson, 2011,
> http://parenting.blogs.nytimes.com/2011/10/27/
> too-much-praise-is-no-good-for-toddlers/)

Obviously, we need to be encouraging and affirming our children from birth onward. But does this mean we can never celebrate their milestones and accomplishments? Of course, it doesn't. The Bible encourages rejoicing with each other. Rejoicing is different than praise. For example, your baby has begun to crawl or walk for the first time. It is perfectly okay to say, "Yay! You're walking!" Or, if your toddler uses the toilet, to say, "Yay! You went potty!" And by all means, feel free to do the "Potty Dance" with your child. Life with children is full of happy, joyful moments, so celebrate each and every one of them with your children. Just remember to praise God for them instead of your children. And, in those quiet or difficult moments, remember to tell your children how much you love them and that you are proud that they are your children. "Try to use more affirmative words in talking with your toddler and fewer negative words" (Sears & Sears, 1997, p. 345).

Finally, as I previously said, God doesn't wait for us to perform in a way that pleases Him before He blesses us. Look at what Lamentations 3:22-23 says, "Because of the LORD's great love we are not consumed, for his compassions never fail. They are new every morning; great is your faithfulness." His mercies and blessings are new every morning before we even do anything. Give your children blessings when they are least expecting it because you love them. If your child has been wanting a new book, surprise him or her with it just because you love him or her. Don't make special outings and gifts hinged on their behavior. This is a great way to show our children that we love them and enjoy doing things for them on occasion just because. On a side note, as children get older and are able to take on the responsibility of doing chores and yard work, it is perfectly acceptable to give them an allowance. This teaches older children about responsibility and about being good stewards of their money.

There are consequences for everything we do. Children must learn this through natural and logical consequences.

Using Natural and Logical Consequences— "Every Behavior Has a Consequence"

All behavior has consequences. Some are positive and others are negative. Most of these consequences happen naturally and are never meant as punishment. As with discipline, many people equate consequences with punishments, but consequences are meant to teach us and help us grow instead of just merely stopping behaviors as with punishment. Punishment involves intentionally inflicting pain on the child. Consequences do not involve intentionally inflicting pain on children. And consequences are directly related to the child's behavior whereas punishment is not. Gerber (1998), page 212, states:

> Try to provide natural consequences, which relate to what the child did, rather than punitive ones, which are either unrelated or too harsh. An example is saying calmly to your toddler, "You didn't get ready to go to the park. You didn't come when I called you, so today we're not going."

After all, God disciplines us by allowing natural consequences to happen to us to guide us back to the narrow road. Many people believe God punishes His people, but when we look at the Bible as a whole, we see that what people see as punishment is really God using natural consequences. And some of this has to do with God's ultimate plan for us. Take Moses for example. In Numbers 20:8, God instructs Moses to speak to a rock in order to make water spring forth from it. But Moses was fed up with all the grumblings from the people and, in fact, did not fully trust God at this point, so Moses hit the rock twice to make water spring forth from the rock (Numbers 20:11). This was in direct disobedience to God. So, God gave Moses a natural consequence. "But the LORD said to Moses and Aaron, 'Because you did not trust in me enough to honor me as holy in the sight of the Israelites, you will not bring this community into the land I give them'" (Numbers 20:12). Now, most people would say that God *punished* Moses, especially since the English Bible does use the word *punish*, but as with the rod verses, I do not believe the word *punish* meant to the Old Testament writers the same as it does for us. But when we look at what Deuteronomy 34:1-5 says, we see that Moses was allowed to climb a beautiful mountain that overlooked the promised land and see it. He died on that mountain after 120 years of life. And the second that Moses died, he went to heaven. I would not call that punishment. Yes, I'm sure Moses was very disappointed that he wasn't allowed to enter the promised land after everything he had been through, but he did not lose access to the *ultimate* promised land—heaven. Heaven is more glorious than any of us can imagine. Much more so than the Earthly promised land.

And going back to some consequences being a part of God's ultimate plan for His people, as we continue on with the story after Moses died, we see that God intended for Joshua and Caleb to be the ones strong enough to win the victories that allowed God's people to enter the promised land. We see throughout the Bible that every good person that God used for His plan, except for Jesus (who is God), sinned and had natural consequences occur due to their sin. David lost his child after sleeping with Bathsheba and having her husband killed in battle (2 Samuel 12:1-24). David fasted and pleaded with God while the infant was sick and dying, but as soon as his son died, David got up, consecrated himself, and praised the Lord. Why? Because David knew his son was in heaven and he would see him again someday (2 Samuel 12:23). Then God allowed David and Bathsheba to have Solomon. Therefore, using natural consequences with children that do not sin as much as adults do is biblically supported discipline.

As I said, natural consequences happen naturally as an effect of a behavior. For example, if a child spills something, it must be cleaned up. Or, if a child won't wear shoes outside, his or her feet will get cold and/or wet. If children hit someone, the person reacts in pain. If a child doesn't speak nicely, he or she won't get what he or she wants. If the child cleans up, he or she will have more time to listen to his or her favorite bedtime story. This is everyday life and learning about cause and effect.

> By using cause/consequence your child learns to be in charge of the consequences of his actions. His confidence is enhanced as he begins to take responsibility. During and after the consequence, let your child know that you are still on his side and still love him. Then forget about it. Don't remind your child of what he did.
>
> (Gerber, 1998, p. 212)

Magda Gerber tells a story of how a mother used natural consequences with her toddler in *Your Self-Confident Baby.* Gerber (1998), page 212, states:

> A mother told me her son went through a stage where he enjoyed ripping apart any book she gave him, even the heavy cardboard variety. The mother told her son that because he ripped up his books (the cause), she was taking them away from him (the consequence). She gave her son magazines to rip apart. Toddlers love pulling things apart, and especially the sound of paper tearing. After this, the mother told me, her child stopped ripping up his books because he wanted them back.

This is a great example because not only was he given a natural consequence, but his mom also gave him an appropriate alternative to fulfill his need for ripping things. Helping children learn is the whole point of using all of these positive discipline, or grace-based discipline, techniques that this part of the book describes. As Lutton (2001) states on page 64 through 65 (GBD stands for grace-based discipline):

> Unless there is imminent danger involved, the GBD parent does not feel threatened by allowing their child to suffer natural consequences. This is different from imposing punishment (the response inflicted by an authoritarian parent who is disobeyed). If a child dawdles and is late for a birthday party and misses the cake, they miss the cake. If a child wants to see a movie but spends the money on a toy, they do not get to see the movie. The child may not like the consequences, but the GBD parent knows that the child must understand there are consequences to actions.

Now, I need to point out again that infants and toddlers learn through repetition. So, even though we may set a limit, validate their feelings, model appropriate behavior, give consequences, and provide appropriate alternatives, sometimes a young toddler will get something in their heads that they really want to do because it is very interesting to them, such as: play with an electric cord that cannot be fully out of their reach. Sadly, this is when most hand slapping occurs as parents become frustrated that their very young child keeps going back to the forbidden object. But, we know from part 2 of this book about the effects of spanking that all hitting and punishment is harmful and infants and toddlers cannot understand being slapped or swatted. When your child is determined to do something that he or she shouldn't, remember that the child is *not* disobeying you on purpose. The forbidden object may be so interesting to the child that he or she cannot help but be drawn to it. This is a brain problem, not a defiance problem. You need to help your child redirect his or her brain on to something that is acceptable. First, if you can block the forbidden object off from your child, do so. If not, calmly state, "The cord isn't for you. It's dangerous. You may play with your blocks instead." As you are saying this, you need to be moving your child away from the forbidden object to the appropriate activity. Get your child engaged in the activity. If he or she starts to look or head toward the forbidden object again, calmly but firmly remind him or her that the object is not for him or her and redirect again. You may have to do this several times, but eventually the child will learn that the object is not for him or her. If the child gets upset, validate his or her feelings. And use time-in to help soothe the child. (See chapter 18 for more info on time-in). Whatever you do, do not slap or yell at your child. It will only scare him or her. Pray for patience as you keep calmly redirecting your child. We must constantly guide children on to the correct path just as God does with us.

> Life is a big field and non-believers are free to play anywhere in the field that they choose. God's children, believers, are instructed to stick to the path and continue moving forward. What is the path? Jesus said, "I am the Way, the Truth, and the Life." Moving forward on the path is becoming more Christ-like. The path has definite boundaries within which there is much freedom.
>
> (Lutton, 2001, p. 65-66)

I like how Lutton goes on to explain how God helps us grow and remain on the right path toward Him. Lutton (2001) explains on pages 67 through 68:

> Paul discusses the development of believers as compared to the development of an infant maturing to adulthood (1 Peter 2. 1-3). When a person becomes a new believer he is a baby in Christ. They are allowed to walk anywhere on

the path and be safe. They are the ones who are giddy at recently having found God and He is gentle in teaching them the perimeters of the path. Often, even when they wander off the path, God blocks the consequences and quickly restores them to the path. This is where believers identify the unsafe practices of their life before Christ and deal with getting on the path. As the believer matures there will be times where they must follow a certain portion of the path to be safe. At those times, the Holy Spirit walks beside them to help them maneuver that portion of the path. Sometimes the believer will stop to rest in the grass. There may be consequences for this if they stay too long, but God will allow them to make this choice. There is freedom on the path. God is also a good God and will encourage the believer to not stay sitting too long because there is a place they are going and they need to get there. It is as the believer matures that God teaches them a more structured walk.

God understands us developmentally and knows that if He pushes us before we are ready that it will only discourage us. We must keep this in mind as we guide our children. This is why using natural consequences with children, especially young children, is best. However, as children become school age and older, we may need to use logical consequences in addition to the natural ones. Logical consequences work similarly to natural consequences in that they relate to children's behaviors and are not meant to be punitive. For example, if the child refuses to turn off the TV to do his or her homework, he or she won't finish his or her homework on time and will get a lower grade. And since TV is interfering with homework, he or she may not be able to watch as much TV for a while. If a child lies about where he or she went with his or her friends, then he or she won't be able to go out with friends alone until he or she wins back our trust. "The beauty of using natural and logical consequences is that children seldom shout,

'Unfair!' They begin to learn that the consequence fits the act, and they must suffer the results" (Kuzma, 2006, p. 392). One thing I must caution with using logical consequences with children is that it is very easy to use them to punish children. Again, the idea behind logical consequences is *not* to punish our children. They are to continue helping our children take responsibility for their actions, to help produce godly sorrow in them instead of worldly sorrow. (See chapters 11 and 12 for more information about godly sorrow versus worldly sorrow). As I have already pointed out, consequences should never be equated with punishments. Kuzma (2006), page 392, states:

> Some parents say, "I use consequences all the time. If my child breaks a window, I spank him. If he gets into a fight, I spank him. If he spills his milk, I spank him." These are parent-imposed consequences, but they are *not* logical consequences related to a child's specific behavior. Remember, the closer the consequence fits the "crime," the more effective it will be.

Punishment, especially physical punishment, is *never* logical or natural for children at any age. A good way to check to see if you are using a consequence against your child is to ask yourself, *"Am I trying to intentionally inflict pain on my child or help him?"* Yes, a consequence may not be pleasant, but if it's intended to hurt, then it is punishment and should *not* be used. As I pointed out in chapter 18, when explaining to children why what they did was wrong or inappropriate, never label them as "bad" or say what they did was "bad" because, as with praise, we do not want children believing that they are "bad" every time they make mistakes. Discipline should make children ultimately come away feeling refreshed and positive, not sad, angry, or fearful.

Finally, if you tell your child a natural or logical consequence will happen if he or she does something and your child comes to you to tell you the truth about what he or she did, be sure to thank your child for being honest. And while you will still need to apply the consequence, make sure you always do so in a way that encourages the child to continue telling the truth. We must always let children know that we will never punish or judge them for coming to us when they make mistakes. We are here to help and to guide them.

Conclusion

We have discussed setting and enforcing appropriate limits in this chapter. When children have appropriate boundaries, they feel safe and secure. Natural and logical consequences, when consistently used, also help make children feel secure and empower them to start taking responsibility for their actions. Affirmations and encouragement teach children that they are valuable as humans. Praise and rewards actually teach children that they are only "good" when others are pleased with them. It is important to remember that God disciplines us using similar techniques as shown in this part of the book..

> Jesus had to actively shepherd his disciples through good times and bad. He was there for them, whether they were tired, angry, frightened, or sad. We who seek to raise our children as Jesus would must be there for them, whether they're making our day or breaking our heart. When we meet our children's many needs—even when some parents would back away or call it quits—we are, Jesus taught, caring for God as well.
>
> (Whitehurst, 2003, p. 185)

Wise words by which we all should live.

References

Anderson, J. (2011). Too Much Praise is No Good for Toddlers. http://parenting.blogs.nytimes.com/2011/10/27/too-much-praise-is-no-good-for-toddlers/

Gerber, M. & Johnson, A. (1998). *Your Self-Confident Baby*. New York, NY: John Wiley & Sons Inc.

Greenwald, D. (Spring 2008). Using (Tarry) Time Wisely. *Educaring, 18*(3), 2, 9.

Kuzma, K. (2006). *The First 7 Years*. West Frankfort, IL: Three Angels Broadcasting Network.

Lutton, C. (2001). *Biblical Parenting*. Salt Lake City, UT: Millennial Mind Publishing.

Markham, L. (2012). Do You Want to Raise an Obedient Child? http://us2.campaign-archive.com/?u=775b94b440ad733979 31a9ad7&id=eaa90025f5

Nelsen, J., Erwin, C., & Duffy, R. A. (2007). *Positive Discipline: The First Three Years*. New York, NY: Three Rivers Press.

Sears, W. & Sears, M. (1997). *The Complete Book of Christian Parenting and Child Care*. Nashville, TN: Broadman & Holman Publishers.

Van der Zande, I. (2011). *1, 2, 3... The Toddler Years*. Santa Cruz, CA: Santa Cruz Toddler Center.

Whitehurst, T. (2003). *How Would Jesus Raise Your Child?* Grand Rapids, MI: Fleming H. Rewell.

Chapter 20

The "Strong-Willed" Child

I want to take a look at using all of these positive discipline strategies that I have discussed throughout this part of the book with "strong-willed children." All of the strategies from mindful modeling, setting up the environment, setting limits, and using natural and logical consequences, etc., all work with all children. Some children may require a bit of creativity, but since all of these strategies are biblically based, they will work even with a "strong-willed" child. In this brief conclusion to this part of the book, I want to focus on using positive, grace-filled, firm discipline with "strong-willed" children.

"Strong-Willed" Children—"Positive Discipline Doesn't Work for My Children!"

As we know from chapter 5, breaking children's wills has been a theme throughout history of Christian prospankers even though there is no biblical support for parents to break their children's wills. Yet, even today, most Christian prospankers advocate the need to break children's wills and having a "strong-willed" child is seen as negative because that child's parents must work even harder to break his or her will. What these Christian prospankers fail to understand is that using physical punishment with "strong-willed" children actually makes these children even more angry and defiant. Sadly, as we've seen throughout this book, some of these children have died because the multiple spankings broke their bodies before their wills.

I believe that there is no difference between our wills and our spirits. They are one and the same just as the Holy Spirit, Jesus, and God are one and the same. God creates us with a will. If God creates wills, then why would He want us to break the wills of children when they are discovering who they are and who God is? For adults, we talk about willpower as a good thing and we often pray for the will to live for sick people or severely depressed people. Therefore, we'd think that having a "strong-willed" child as a good thing instead of a negative thing. After all, it is usually strong-willed people who have the most determination and do things to further God's kingdom, thereby changing the world for the good.

In the Bible, God used many strong-willed people to do His will. The most strong-willed person in the Bible that God used to do so much good for the kingdom of God, I believe, is the Apostle Paul. We see in Acts 9:1-2, and even in the previous chapter, that we meet Paul first as Saul, a devout Hellenistic Jew and a Pharisee that enjoyed persecuting Christians. He approved of the stoning of Stephen in Acts 8:1. Needless to say, this Saul guy was one bad dude. And yet, God had a radical plan for Saul. In Acts 9, we see that as Saul was on his way to Damascus to persecute even more Christians, Jesus got Saul's attention in a big but non-painful way. Saul went blind. Jesus asked Saul why he was persecuting Him in Acts 9:4. Jesus told Saul to meet a man in Damascus who would tell him what to do. Saul, blind, obeyed God and look what happened:

Then Ananias went to the house and entered it. Placing his hands on Saul, he said, "Brother Saul, the Lord—Jesus, who appeared to you on the road as you were coming here—has sent me so that you may see again and be filled with the Holy Spirit." Immediately, something like scales fell from Saul's eyes, and he could see again. He got up and was baptized, and after taking some food, he regained his strength.

Acts 9:17-19

From this moment on, Saul, who became Paul, lived his life for God, fearlessly proclaiming the gospel to all surrounding nations despite numerous beatings, imprisonments, and shipwrecks. Through the Holy Spirit, Paul wrote between thirteen and fourteen books of the New Testament—this is over half of the New Testament. And anyone who is very familiar with the New Testament knows that Paul tells it like it is. He didn't sugarcoat anything that God inspired him to write. He encouraged his fellow believers but also rebuked and corrected them in his letters. Through Paul, God gained many believers into His kingdom.

God did not break Paul's will. God molded Paul's will into doing good instead of persecuting Christians. Had God broken Paul's will, do you believe Paul would have clung to God through all the suffering he went through to share salvation through Jesus Christ? Broken, compliant people are usually not strong people in that they find it very difficult to press against the tide. Strong-willed people have an easier time of questioning authority. They also have an easier time of pressing on when persecution occurs. Look at what Paul writes in 2 Corinthians 4:8-9 concerning all the persecution he and the other apostles were enduring for Jesus Christ's sake: "We are hard pressed on every side, but not crushed; perplexed, but not in despair; persecuted, but not abandoned; struck down, but not destroyed."

God uses strong-willed people so much. Yes, having a "strong-willed" child can be extremely difficult at times, but these children *can* be disciplined through all of the strategies in this part of the book. These children need a bit more consistency than "easier" children. Some of these strategies may need to be adapted for your particular child, but if we listen to these children and allow them to tell us what works best for them, God can use these children for big things. Our job as parents is to teach and guide all children into making good, biblical decisions instead of constantly trying to win "the battle of the wills."

> *When your child is stubbornly sticking to their guns about something...it is because they believe they are right.* They believe in their cause. They believe they should be allowed to have that toy! They believe they should be allowed to eat that cookie right now because it looks good and they are hungry! From *their* perspective, their reasons are right! They are not trying to "push your buttons" or make you mad. *The last thing any of us want, even as adults, is for our parents to be mad at us!* So, if your child is insisting on having their own way...the problem is not their "will"... the child's "problem" is immaturity and lack of reasoning skills which has led them to a wrong conclusion that they are right.
>
> *And, so how do we encourage maturity and proper reasoning skills?* Can a person learn to become more mature by being "controlled"? Can a person learn to become more mature by being "punished"?
>
> *In order to learn to reason...they must be reasoned with.* They must learn the process of comparing two choices and looking at the potential effects of each...and they can't do that on their own. You have to show them how to do it.
>
> *Does it take more time to do this than to give them a whack on the hiney and tell them to "not do that again or else"?* Sure. Controlling someone is always the quickest way for someone to get a behavior to stop. But, stopping your child

from making *certain* bad choices (like the things which you forbid and punish for) doesn't teach them the broader picture of what is a good choice and what is a bad choice and how to decide between the two.

(Stoltzfus, 2011, http://everythingisknowable.blogspot.com/2011/10/strength-of-your-childs-will.html)

Conclusion

All children deserve respect and love from conception on. These discipline strategies point children toward God instead of away from Him. God never intended for us to spank or hurt children. Even "strong-willed" children will respond to respect better than punishment. And just because parents don't punish their children does not mean they are permissive parents. I hope this will help you raise your children in a Christlike manner.

Reference

Stoltzfus, D. (2011). Strength of Your Child's Will. http://everythingisknowable.blogspot.com/2011/10/strength-of-your-childs-will.html

Conclusion

All throughout this book we have seen that spanking children is *not* from God and that spanking causes much harm to children. The rod verses were never meant to be taken literally, otherwise, we would have to beat our precious children with a huge, deadly weapon in anger and all the time according to Proverbs 22:15, which states, "Folly is bound up in the heart of a child, but the rod of discipline will drive it far away." Sadly, some Christians do follow this verse to a "t" and spank their children for being children. Knowing what we now know after going through this journey together, God created children to think and behave the way that they do. To constantly hit them for being "unwise" by adult standards is neither biblical nor fair. And you can't beat foolishness out of children any more than you can beat the devil out of them. We have seen throughout this book that Jesus has raised children's status and has called us to be like little children in order to enter the kingdom of heaven. We are to drive out folly by teaching, guiding, protecting, and comforting our children as I talked about throughout the last section of this book. To do anything other than that, especially to take the above verse literally, would be to teach children that no matter what they do, they will never be able to measure up. Does this sound like the way to raise children up in the Lord?

I pray this book will help you to truly raise your children up in the Lord. I leave you with the following stories. May God bless you and your family.

—∾—

Linda conveyed the following to me about her sons on January 9, 2013, via an electronic message:

> My sons are 20 and 22. They were raised with Attachment Parenting ideals and were not spanked. We have a great relationship with them and they are now both United States Marines. They are not perfect, but they are both Christians and fine young men who have never been in trouble with the law.

Dara conveyed the following to me in an electronic message dated November 15, 2012, about her four-year-old daughter Tori:

> My four-year-old said this to me, "When we be bad, you need to forgive us, Mom, or we will be sad."
>
> I've never punished or hit her, and so this is how she sees the process of being bad and what she finds to be the "worst thing" that can happen from being bad and that is that if I don't forgive her then that will make her sad. My forgiveness is what matters to her...not worrying about being punished. I think that's a pretty cool positive effect.
>
> This was being said while we were driving...she and her sister (7) were sitting in the back seat talking about spilling ice cream I think...and my four-year-old also then added, "And, you need to say 'I forgive you' right away or we will run away!" And, I wondered where she came up with the "running away" business but we always stop and look at the "missing children" and we do always all talk about how we suspect the teens who are missing are probably most of the time runaways from abusive homes. And, so, in my four-year-old's mind apparently the worst she can imagine life being is to live with me not forgiving

her for something...and that's what makes her think a kid would run away...

And, I believe this is going to be how she applies her actions someday to her relationship with God...She's going to want to obey Him not because she fears "punishment" or because it's become a habit over the years because she's always been "forced" to obey. She'll obey Him 'cause the idea of Him being unhappy with her will make her sad and when she does something wrong she'll ask forgiveness... right away.

After a lifetime of doing so many wrong things with my kids I feel like that said to me today that I did something *right!*

And, this is something the Pearl's ways...and the ways of so many others...will never achieve!

The final story is about a nine-year-old girl. She was riding her bike home from school and a sixteen-year-old guy was watering flowers in his yard. When he saw the girl coming, he decided to spray her with the hose. The girl got soaked. She stopped and was very upset. But she wasn't upset because of being sprayed. You see, her parents were very strict but not abusive in society's eyes, and she knew that if she came home in wet clothes, no matter how she tried to explain, her parents would punish her. So, instead of continuing on home, this girl went in the house with the sixteen-year-old. The guy got her out of her clothes, tied her up, did horrible things to her, and kept her hidden under his bed for two days until she died.

Of these three true stories, what children and their parents are in line for God's plan for godly families?

Dear loving, heavenly Father, we humbly ask that through Your Holy Spirit we constantly strive to keep our hearts open to Your will, and that our actions toward our children reflect the grace and patience You have so abundantly bestowed upon us. May we be willing to dive into Your Word so that we never become stuck in human traditions that You did not intend for us, and may we always give our children and the world an accurate view of who You truly are. Thank You, Jesus, that by Your stripes You have brought us peace that we may bask in Your mercy, grace, and forgiveness. In Your name we pray, Amen.

Appendix A

How Did You Come to Understand
Spanking Is Harmful and Not
Biblically Supported?

I asked this question to a variety of people. Here are their responses. Only first names are being used to protect personal privacy.

Ricky: The way I see it, spanking is really a violent act. When a child is confronted with violence, he or she will respond to violence and use violence. As far as Christians, fear should never be a tool, and when you hit a child it brings fear.

Meghan: I could never see Jesus hitting a child. If a child was struggling to control himself or having a hard time, I could only see Him getting on his level and pouring love on him.

Heather: I knew because as a child, the only things I "learned" from it were rage, humiliation, lying is better than being hit, to hit other people, might is right, power is achieved through violence, etc. When I was fifteen, I had a choice—I could walk the path of violence and destroy everyone around me, as I'd always been told I'd do, or choose pacifism. Pacifism starts at home. "I object to violence because when it appears to do good, the good is only temporary; the evil it does is permanent."

Debra: My head listened to the prospanking crowd because theirs were the only voices I heard, but my heart was never at peace with hitting children. I also learned about attachment parenting and normal child development. I also learned how to dig deeper into the original languages of the Bible and the culture in which those words were written and how horrid some of the translations are. One thought really did it for me: Jesus died for our sins and trusting in Him is the only thing we need to do to be forgiven; why would the standard be higher for children?

Carolyn: The article on your blog about the meaning of the verses in proverbs.

Wade: Jesus Christ is the gentle savior, the prince of peace. He would never lift His hand to a child.

Amber: I knew it was wrong when it happened to me and my sister as children. I knew it was wrong as a child, which confuses me how most adults think it is okay.

Becky: I was raised non-violently and it was just natural for me! I was only spanked once or twice, not because my parents believed in it, but because my mom lost her temper and made a mistake. It did not hurt physically, but I still remember how humiliating it was. And I also believe that God is full of love and mercy and would never want us to use violence, especially against smaller beings!

Anne: I believed spanking was the Way because of course if you didn't spank, your kids were going to end up brats. Then I realized you know what? I hated being spanked...it was demeaning and humiliating. So I decided I was against spanking mostly: that it should be just for those really rare occasions. It wasn't until I found out more about alternative parenting methods that I became 100 percent against spanking. It made me really happy when I found out people didn't have to spank to have great kids, and that it wasn't weird that I thought spanking was humiliating and demeaning.

Rose: For me, it took awhile. I did spank my older kids occasionally. Then I noticed—through maturity, I think—that when I spanked, their behavior got worse. I tried every typical parenting trick, spanking, time outs, etc. None of it really seemed to make a difference. I got the idea to hug them and show them lots of love when they misbehaved, and it worked!! Everyone's behavior became so much better! Now, when we're in public or around extended family, people compliment me on my children's behavior. This is no small feat, because I have five children, ages 11, 7, 4, 3, and 2. I was thinking about it one day and thought, well, if I was so upset that I had to resort to throwing things, would I want my husband to hit me, or hug me? I can't imagine it would be any different with the kids. It was only after these revelations that I found natural parenting.

Susan: I seemed to know from as far back as I can remember that hitting is wrong period. And as for biblically—I suppose I was lucky in that in the UK, I was part of the church of England and it seldom addresses parents on how to parent— just how to love do right–which–for me encompasses it all. If God is *love*, everything, *everything* falls into place. Hitting is not love.

Laurie: I never forgot what it felt like to be a child. I knew it was wrong as a child to be hit, and I knew I would never subject any child in my future to such abuse.

Paola: I spanked three out of my four children. I spanked but never really thought about *why* I was spanking, it was something that I just did because it was done to me. When I looked at spanking deeper, I realized that there was *no* reason why I should hit my child. See we call it spanking and we disconnect the hitting part because we call it spanking, but if you were to say I "hit" my children, that brings another association to the word. When I looked at it as *hitting* because that's what it is, it just seemed wrong. That is how I started to open my heart to change and, of course, then reading the studies etc.—totally opened my eyes to the fact that we are teaching our children that violence is the solution. We are hypocrites if we say to children, 'You don't hit,' but then we hit them. What helped me see that God doesn't want us to hit is the entire point of God main message, which is to love one another. Hitting is *not* part of loving."

Dara: For me it was a friend asking a question. When I went to answer her I stumbled upon a short post about the ancient "shepherd's rod," and it was a stick with a ball and spikes on the end, and it said the shepherd's rod was for hitting predators. I immediately called a "cease fire" in the house with spanking until I could investigate it further…and of course…the more I looked into it, it was obvious and we never went back.

Ryanne: When I was about 7, I saw a show featuring a woman who decided not to spank her child. I thought it was great, because I didn't like being spanked, and tried to tell the grownups that they didn't have to. Of course, I was laughed at, and in time I forgot about it. Fast forward to college where I had way too much free time that I used to surf the net in school library. I stumbled upon a book that was against it, and it piqued my curiosity, so I started surfing the net about alternatives to spanking. And I'm glad I did.

Tasha: Spanking is wrong and it doesn't work! I hate when Christians quote Scripture about "the rod." Jesus would never raise a hand to anyone. He loved children! He encouraged adults to be *more like* children! I get very upset when people twist Scripture and use religion as a way to justify their behavior. I am a born-again Christian and I love my God. We should be firm but loving. Children need discipline… not punishment.

Amanda: Maybe due to my infertility struggles it took me over a year to get pregnant, then being pregnant for nine months. It was a big build up to meeting my daughter. Once I had her, I didn't want to put her down. I just wanted go stare at her and love her. Breastfeeding was torture and left scars. But I knew it was the best and since I loved her so much I didn't care. I couldn't imagine letting her cry it out. So I obviously headed down the Attachment Parenting road. I couldn't imagine spanking her. Yet I was concerned about the Bible telling me that I had to spank her. Until I read Crystal Lutton's book, then I was at ease. My faith is *very* important to me, and I wanted to be sure my parenting was biblical. I believe this really helped me in my walk with the Lord. I can't look at the Holy Scriptures on a surface level. I need to dig deep, understand the original language, and understand the culture. And, of course, showing love and grace to my children help me understand, to a remote degree, how much God loves me.

Linda: The white man called Native Americans savages, but they never hit their children. They thought the white man was crazy for beating their children and their animals.

Index

A

B

C

Child Development 1, 16, 113, 133, 181, 334, 374, 400, 438, 443, 490

Compliance 218, 273, 401, 408, 461, 462, 463

Consequences 36, 42, 45, 48, 54, 73, 93, 106, 144, 150, 179, 206, 212, 214, 216, 250, 255, 259, 266, 280, 281, 289, 313, 331, 338, 339, 352, 353, 357, 383, 389, 401, 417, 453, 470, 471, 472, 473, 475, 476, 477, 479

Cooperation 416, 462, 464

Co-sleeping 389

Crying 32, 292, 366, 381, 422, 425, 426, 436

Cry It Out 374, 379, 389, 390, 393, 394, 493

D

Dependence 48, 211, 437

Depression 120, 191, 203, 225, 295, 302, 303, 304, 306, 307, 308, 309, 310, 315, 318, 321, 323, 324, 327, 346, 347, 424

Developmentally Appropriate 81, 113, 114, 171, 198, 211, 254, 258, 297, 319, 358, 454

Discipline 1, 2, 17, 26, 29, 32, 35, 36, 37, 45, 59, 73, 74, 75, 93, 100, 125, 130, 151, 163, 168, 176, 177, 181, 182, 197, 203, 212, 215, 223, 224, 234, 236, 242, 245, 248, 254, 258, 264, 265, 269, 272, 278, 279, 280, 285, 288, 290, 293, 300, 305, 308, 312, 328, 329, 343, 352, 353, 357, 383, 384, 390, 399, 400, 401, 403, 404, 405, 406, 407, 408, 411, 412, 413, 414, 416, 417, 418, 419, 421, 438, 442, 444, 446, 447, 448, 451, 453, 470, 472, 473, 479, 483, 485, 493

CPSIA information can be obtained at www.ICGtesting.com
Printed in the USA
LVOW01s1528080115

422027LV00018B/871/P